BY THE SAME AUTHOR
Women Of the Celts
King Arthur King Of Kings

Celtic Civilization

J. Markale

Gordon & Cremonesi

© Payot, Paris 1976
© Translation Gordon & Cremonesi Ltd 1978
First published as Les Celtes et la Civilisation Celtique by Payot, Paris 1976

Designed by Heather Gordon
Set in 10 on 11pt Baskerville
by Input Typesetting Ltd., London,
and printed in Great Britain
by The Pitman Press Bath

British Library Cataloguing in Publication Data
Markale, Jean
  Celtic civilization
    1. Civilization, Celtic — History
    1. Title   II. Hauch, Christine
940'.04'·916   CB206   78-40395

LCCN: 78-040395
ISBN: 0-86033-045-1

Gordon & Cremonesi Publishers
London and New York
New River House
34 Seymour Road
London N8 0BE

In memory of my grandmother

Jeanne Le Luec

Contents

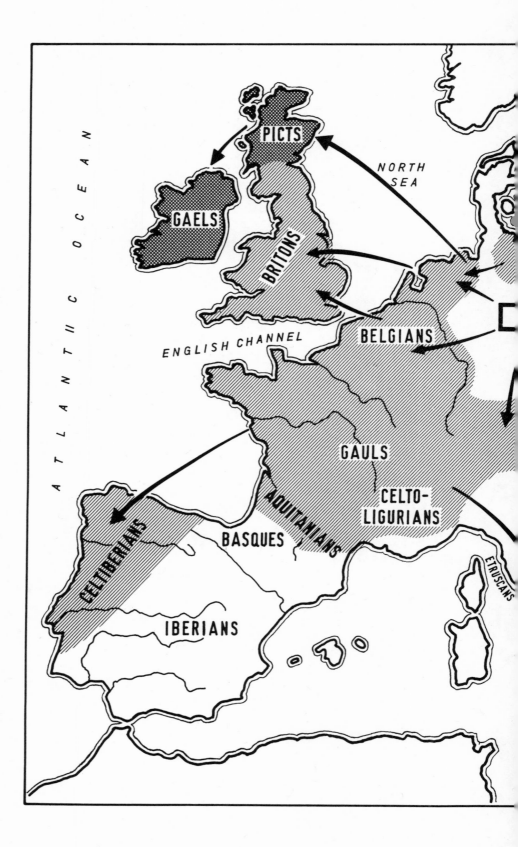

Movement of the Celts after the Hallstatt period

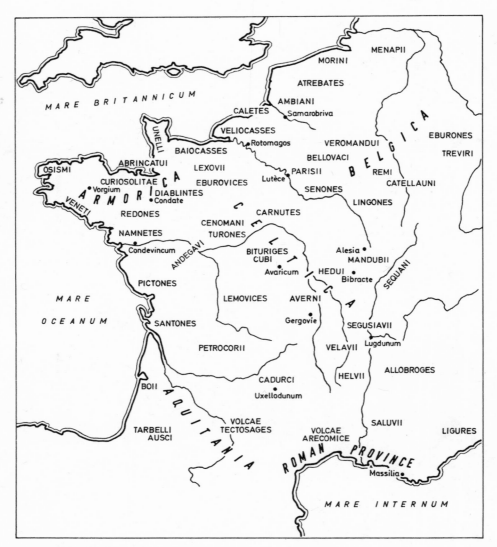

Gaul in the first centuries B.C.

The British Isles in Roman times

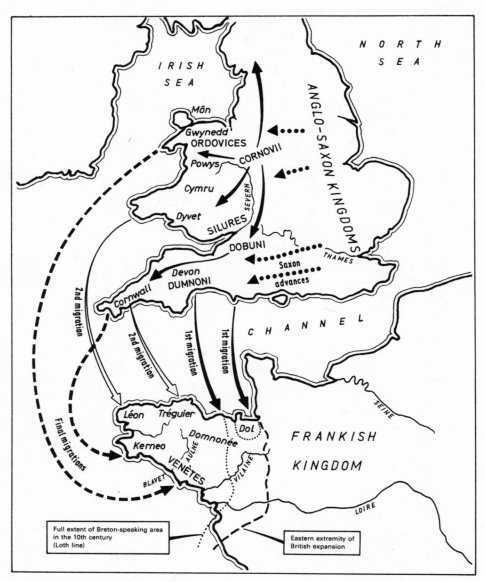

British emigration to Armorica

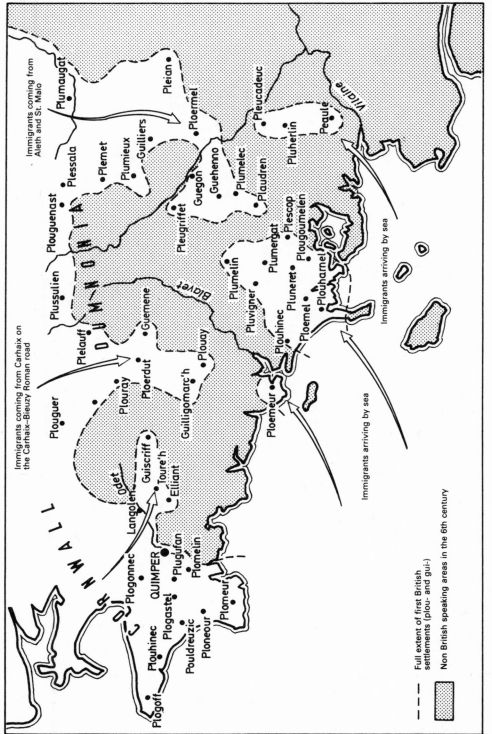

British immigration between the Odet and the Vilaine

Myth and History

NY student of Celtic history is continually confronted by the all-pervading features of myth which impose their own singular colours on the entire field to make it the most impressive example of harmonious synthesis between the imaginary and the purely real. Having risen, apparently from nowhere, in around the 5th or 6th century BC to conquer the whole of Western Europe before being beaten back into obscurity by the combined pressure of Romans, Germans and Christians, the Celts offer us a most strange and perplexing subject for investigation.

It appears that the Celtic peoples and everything about them has vanished and yet they have made a unique and profound contribution to later events, even though their influence has rarely been visible in the mainstream of European thought. For the Celts were dreamers who built their castles in the air and the audacious and often misunderstood orientation they gave to Western Europe is sometimes difficult to discern through the successive layers of culture and civilization which came to the fore after their political collapse.

The great strength of the Celts was, and still is, myth. But what is this myth?

We should start by defining its meaning. Originally the word myth meant a sacred story, appertaining to the divine. Since the time of the ancient Greeks however and more especially since Xenophon wrote in the 5th century BC, myth has popularly come to mean anything which cannot exist in reality; any fiction or narration which cannot be defined as *logos* in the Greek or *historia* in the Latin.

Since *logos* can mean "reason" as well as "word", the world of myth becomes the world of the irrational. And since history purports to be a logically and cohesively arranged succession of events, it automatically precludes anything irrational. So myth is left as an isolated, disconnected phenomenon, which cannot be placed in a chronology. It is illogical or even a-logical.

The later Greek interpretation of myth was subsequently taken up and modified by Christianity. If the Holy Scriptures were to be the absolute expression of truth, then any other tradition had to be regarded as fabulous or mythical; and myth came to be seen as false and illusory because it had not been justified or validated by the Bible.

An obvious answer to this argument is that the Scriptures themselves have never been validated. But our problem lies not so much in justifying myth as in determining what people today understand by it. In his *Aspects du Mythe*, Mircéa Eliade defines it as "sacred tradition, primordial revelation, exemplary model". There is no need to establish whether myth is true or false, real or unreal, since its very existence suggests that there is a reality and the different aspects under which this reality appears can only be evaluated in their own context. It is shallow-minded to view the complex cultural reality of myth as something simple.

Eliade's further assertion that myth is "a true story because it is always related to reality" gives myth an importance rarely, if ever, accorded it by the scientist, but the statement remains open to discussion nonetheless. A myth can after all be a false story about real facts. Indeed if we support the notion of myth as an idealization of the real, and accept Freud's suggestion that it is the expression of profound human tendencies, then myth can quite easily be false. For logical distinctions between truth and falsehood can only be made by comparing the material point of departure and its final idealization in myth. If truth and reality belong to separate spheres of examination, the claim that myth is a true story has little value. What matters is that the myth is real, that it has a real existence. It might be better to define myth as a reality in itself or a concept, disregarding for the moment the question of whether it is born of experience or constructed like an abstract theorem. Since every myth is a statement, it must have its own indisputable and basic reality, its truth or falsehood being observable only in practice. To take an example, when General Boulanger attempted to seize power he was obeying a myth, the Napoleonic myth of the leader. This myth existed, neither true nor false. If Boulanger had succeeded, the myth would have become true inasmuch as the idea had converged with external reality. Since he failed, however, the myth became false because no such convergence had been achieved. Again, the death of Jesus was deliberately made to coincide with the Christ myth, or rather with one specific Christ myth. And this Christ myth, which was real in itself, thereby became real for others, acquiring the value of truth for the believer, while being condemned as false by the Jews who chose not to recognize the myth in practice.

The definition of myth as a reality assumes that there is some axiomatic principle from which everything can be argued mathematically. In fact, the myth itself is the axiom, the first thesis of a Hegelian dialectic. Given this axiom, all further argument can proceed quite logically, for since the advances on logistics and the formulation of a relativity theory we have learnt to distrust the over-coherent solution.

We would do better to look upon myth not as a simple-minded act of human fable-making, but as an operational technique of the same epistemological value as mathematics. It is possible that we may then be able to understand the lessons of history more fully, for history is crammed full of lurking myths like fatherland, freedom and right. We will also gain a better understanding of the Celts and their intellectual processes.

But if myth is to be regarded as an operational technique, we must determine to what end this technique is employed. And it is here that the basic problem lies.

Mircéa Eliade says that myth "narrates an event which took place in the earliest times, the fabulous times of our beginnings". But this eminent mythologist has confused his terminology. Myth narrates nothing. It is legend which tells the story of our beginnings, and it does so by placing myth in the cultural context inherent in a specific civilization. To split hairs even further, we should perhaps replace the word "beginnings" by the word "initiations", although initiation has become so debased a term that it is either virtually meaningless or tainted with a whiff of esotericism and magic totally alien to the present discussion. In any case, by confining his definition of myth to our beginnings, Eliade neglects the myths of Tristan, the Grail, Arthur, Orpheus, Oedipus, or any which refer to consequent rather than initial situations. It is as if he has looked only at the myths of some "primitive" societies and deliberately overlooked the myths which have been created, and are still being produced, in "civilized" societies. It would be interesting, for example, to study the present day myth of the car.

Eliade also regards customs and behaviour as expressions of myth. Obviously when no other explanation can be found, we must look to the sacred as the source of tradition. As myths describe the intrusion of the sacred into daily life, it becomes clear that it is "this intrusion of the sacred which creates the world". Eliade continues very pertinently, "Myths narrate . . . the primordial events after which man became what he is today, a mortal, sexual being organized into societies and obliged to work to live and to do that work according to certain rules".

We follow these rules virtually blindly, without understanding either their origins or their early significance. Now that it has become fashionable to explain the world and not to accept anything unquestioningly, we are suffering from the constraints imposed by the past in a symbolic, developed form adpated to our own rhythm of life. Mircéa Eliade seems to have put his finger on one of the basic elements of the story of mankind, but without exploiting all that can be inferred from it.

For Eliade argues, "A primitive man might say: I am as I am today because a series of events took place before me. Only he must then immediately add: events which took place in mythical times and consequently form a sacred history, for the characters in the drama are not human but supernatural. Moreover, while modern man feels in no way constrained to know the whole history of the universe, even though he regards himself as the result of the course it has taken, a man belonging to an ancient society was obliged not merely to remember the mythical history of his tribe but also, on occasion, to re-enact large parts of it."

This arbitrary differentiation between "modern" man and "ancient" man smacks of Levy Bruhl's over-restrictive and artificial ideas on the "prelogical" mentality of "primitive peoples", ideas which even he abandoned in the end. Eliade also overlooks what Freud and Jung have been able to demonstrate about the rôle of myths in our daily behaviour. Clearly there are fundamental archetypes in the collective subconscious of peoples, and the events in which these archetypes can be seen have as much effect on "modern" man as on "primitive" man. It is even possible that the more complicated and evolved a civilization becomes, the more the most ancient myths tend to reassert themselves, to be psychologically liberated. Surely the myth of the superstar comes from the myth of the hero or heroine, that righter of wrongs, spiritual medium, scapegoat, in whom all the unconscious longings of the public are personified. Surely the similarities between the violent and apparently incoherent demonstrations of young pop-fans round their idols, and the ritual rapture and frenzy of their ancient forebears suggests that both forms of behaviour originate in the same myth of affliction, the same incantatory rites. And surely the avid interest of sincerely democratic and republican peoples in the activities of royal families is a distortedly romantic reflection of the myth of the king as a sacred and inviolable figure, who is both fearful and attractive.

Freud has demonstrated quite adequately that myths which have become unconscious have more effect than conscious myths. It is therefore quite conceivable that "modern" man is more affected by myths than "primitive" man who, being fully conscious of them, could suit his actions to them under the restrictive threat of punishment. Sandor Ferenczi has shown that the human foetus passes through all the successive mutations of the species in the womb. If genetics provides evidence of the influence of previous acts on the biological present, there is little difficulty in demonstrating the link between one psychological condition and another as a continuous repetition of some original act, a process of re-enactment.

To re-enact is to make the past coincide with the present. Any discussion of memory and habit, any suggestion that re-enactment is in some sense re-use and thus a new use is irrelevant. Where the influence of the unconscious is at work, it makes no difference whether we posit the past as past, or experience it as the present. The end result is the same.

Ancient myths can only be re-used in this way if they have acquired some kind of structure over the ages. Having lost the conscious significance of myths, man is moved to think and act by their symbolic form, whether it be an image, a cliché, or a group of words. It is in this respect that semantics comes to the aid of the mythologist, the philosopher and the historian. The history of mankind could be rewritten from the history of words, just as modulations of thought could be traced through the syntactical changes in any one language.

Eliade claims that ancient man was obliged to remember the mythical history of his tribe, but that modern man feels no compulsion to know the whole history of that great human tribe, the world. This is a mistaken argument, for what Freud calls the *id* in us is based on all the experiences of mankind, which each man is constantly recognizing in himself as he adapts to life, and which he is perpetually comparing with the external present. Having recognized this much, traditional Marxists would go one stage further and say that man must not only know history but interpret it and attempt to project it into the future, adapting it as necessary. In this sense, Marxism is possibly the only doctrine which has given myths their true value.

However, we have still to determine what we understand by myth, and whether it is possible to define it in relation to history, or vice-versa. And this is an epistemological question.

Plato regarded myth solely as moral allegory, which means that we have to use his writings with a great deal of caution. For Max Muller, myths were transcriptions of solar phenomena. This view led to a whole school of solar myth, but it has done little to elucidate the problem, except perhaps by offering some curious comments on the Napoleonic myth. Saintyves thought myths must be the traces of ancient seasonal ceremonies, an argument that gave rise to all kinds of wild speculation, from a rash of interpretative comment to ridiculous novels about the lives of the ancient initiates. Edouard Schuré's ideas are the direct result of this kind of fantasizing. As far as a solar interpretation is concerned, Muller's ideas are more interesting, being based on an opposition between sun and shade which can be observed quite easily in reality and which is reflected in the work of such Manichean writers as Victor Hugo. It was as an extension of these arguments that Frazer, who was much used by Freud, came to see myth as a spiritualization of nature in continual relation with totemism. The present day Soviet philosophers, who are still basically rationalistic in their approach, explain away myth as just another poetic or literary creation, a view already propounded by Joseph Bédier in connexion with the *Chansons de geste*. For Freud, naturally enough, myth could only be a liberation of the unconscious in its efforts to regain man's primitive condition. The psychologist Wundt sees myth as a translation of the dream or hallucinatory state which, considering the fact that dreams and hallucinations are actually the product of myth, does not tell us very much. In its concern to apply Freud's discoveries in a therapeutic way, the psychoanalytical school follows Loeffler-Delachaux in emphasizing the cathartic effects of myth on the mind.

But none of this really explains how myths came into being. Freud may be right in his supposition that myths are a translation of repressed desires, but he is careful not to expand on this proposal. For the materialist in him would have rejected the next step in the argument, which is that these repressed desires correspond to some previous reality, a claim which we have no hesitation in making. Myth precedes history, not only because of its indisputable influence on the development of human history, but also because it was fundamentally the only reality. What has happened since those early days is encapsulated by Rabelais. "What has become of the art of evoking thunder and celestial fire from the heavens, that art invented so long ago by the wise Prometheus? You have obviously lost it; it has left your hemisphere and is now used here, under the earth." (Chapter XLVIII.)

In fact, the only precise and unambiguous connexion between myth and history was established by Euhemerus, who argued that myths were distortions of historic events, and that the gods were heroes made divine. In this case the opposition between myth and history is resolved in a chain of argument which runs: history becomes developed becomes myth.

But Marxism has shown that the line of argument can be reversed. And if we turn this chain on its head we find: myth becomes developed becomes history, a perfectly acceptable formula when we remember that myth has undoubtedly influenced history. In any case, if we accept that practical, individualistic technique has produced the impartial understanding of the world we call science, then we can equally claim that the technique of myth has produced the science of history.

For myth is simply the everyday behaviour of early mankind. History is the understanding of that series of myths which are experienced through constant re-enactment. If the Christ myth had not preceded Jesus, no one would remember him and he would not have acted (nor be recorded as having acted) in the way he did. The Christ myth is developed throughout the Old Testament, but it first appears in Genesis after Adam and Eve are expelled from their earthly paradise, or, from the psychoanalyst's viewpoint, at the time when the first man on earth was born. So, according to the very ancient Hebraic tradition, the first myth known to man was the myth of redemption. And this myth is part of human nature, not a later acquisition but an innate, inner reality. The question of where this reality came from has already been discussed by Descartes in connexion with his proofs of the existence of god and need not concern us here.

What matters is that significant myths have existed since the birth of man, and as such they must be related to characters and deeds of the very earliest times. Whether they are a memory of paradise lost, a yearning for some future paradise or a wish for present happiness is not important when the task in hand is to gain a clear understanding of history and to examine it in critical fashion. For whether myth precedes history or history myth, a new look at both the incomprehensible and the apparently unequivocal can still reveal surprises. In 1793 Scelling wrote that the kernel of myth contained the truth in historic form, a supposition close to Plutarch's argument in his treatise *On the Far Side of the Moon*, that the great divine truths and the great cosmic metamorphoses are divulged to common mortals in the form of fables. The truth is there to be found behind every fable; and since the fable is simply one adaptation of the myth it is by grasping the essence of that myth that we shall discover the truth.

If we assume, as the authors of antiquity suggest, that the whole Celtic field is ambiguous and pervaded by legend, then we must recognize that the history of the Celts has come down to us in symbolic form. And though these symbols must be interpreted, they may ultimately make the subject easier to understand.

We must proceed by psychoanalysing the myth, the legend, and at the same time the purely historic, or what is believed to be historic. This does not mean that a Freudian interpretation must be accepted to the exclusion of all others. Neither does it mean that only psychoanalysis can help us understand the Celts. It should merely be regarded as one of the chief methods of investigation, not as the sole discipline.

As we discover the myths which are generally recognized as Celtic, we should remember that they are not in fact specifically Celtic, but merely one aspect of a mythical fund common to all mankind. The particular interests of the Celts, however, have made some myths more important for them. So, although the myth of the Submerged Town, for example, exists elsewhere, it found its most frequent utterance in the Celtic world.

Other myths may be grafted on to the original myth adding their own shade of meaning, exploring new areas but the original myth tends to emerge as the most conspicuous and effective and finally becomes a repository for all the others. The Arthurian myth, for example, provides us with an admirable summary of the way the Celtic mind works. It must be interpreted in several ways. For Arthur is the myth of supreme kingship, the myth of the predestined envoy, the myth of the sleeping man who will wake to save the world, the myth of the cuckold king who must share his sovereignty with his people in the shape of the queen's lover. And then, of course, there is the historic Arthur who led the struggle against the Saxons, as the personification of yet another myth, the Celtic fatherland.

We must therefore guard against the definitive answer and the single one-sided interpretation. The problematic tangle of the Celts is too complex for anyone to wholly unravel it. But it may be helpful to look at the problems afresh and to re-examine some of those accepted facts which are either too facile or too uncritically believed.

The Celts have been saddled with so many foolish and unjust images that it is right to try and redress the balance. Fettered by the clichés of our schooldays, by statements like "The Gauls lived in huts" we tend to believe that the Romans brought civilization to Western Europe when all they ever did was to adapt the civilizations of others to their own needs. Just as Rome owed an immense debt to Greek civilization, so the Roman Empire took from the Gauls. The comments of Greek and Latin historians who have always been used against the Celts can actually help us to set the record straight. Centuries of official culture based on an unthinking and arbitrary belief in "Greco-Roman" models have blinded us to the basic fact that Western Europe is the legacy of the Celts.

It is by uncovering this heritage that we shall rediscover the Celts in the present-day manifestations of their myths. We should also be able to draw on the lessons of the past to build some vision of a future, a culture, a civilization.

For the answer to the present search for a new ideal and a new humanism among Western man lies in re-enactment. This work is intended not only to bring understanding of the Celts, but also, in Marx's words, to try to change. Archaeology, mythology and historical studies should not be acts of exhumation and mummification but works of construction. "To do that," says André Breton, "we have had to attack everything in Western man which conspired to shamefully repress his past, for this has been the lasting effect of the tenet 'might is right' imposed by the Roman legions nineteen hundred years ago. Historically, there is no doubt that this assault was facilitated by the increasingly general awareness that the thinking of a past era was blatantly ill-equipped to define the conditions of life in the nuclear age. From that point we were led by an atavistic leap in the mind to inquire about the possible aspirations of the men who lived in our land before the Greco-Latin yoke descended so heavily upon them."[1]

CHAPTER ONE

The Submerged Town or The Celtic Myth of Origins

N Plato's *Timeus* the priests of Sais answer Solon's questions about the ancient times with the sybilline words, "There have been a thousand holocausts, which have occurred in a thousand ways and will recur, both by fire and by water and by many other means." It is what follows, however, which should interest anyone seeking to know more about man's origins, particularly as regards the quasi-mythical history of the Celts. For the priests go on to say, "You have a tale that one Phaeton, the son of Helios, having unharnessed his father's chariot but being unable to drive it, burnt everything on earth and was himself killed by a thunder bolt. In this form, the story is clearly a fable; but what is true is that there were great revolutions in the space around the earth and in the heavens, and that at long intervals huge conflagrations wreaked havoc on the surface of the globe."

The myth of Phaeton here narrated relates to the specific reality of destruction by fire and has its necessary counterpart in the myth of the flood. As the priests of Sais continue, "When the gods flooded the earth to purify it with water, the cowherds and priests on the mountains escaped the calamity, but the inhabitants of your cities were swept into the sea."

It is not clear whether the function attributed to the flood has been accorded it by the priests or by Plato, but either way it would seem to be a misinterpretation. For the great purifier is surely fire, as the Indian *Maharabhaia* has personified it in the shape of Agni (Latin *ignis*). The Judeo-Christian tradition then elaborated on this theme in the *agnus dei*, the Lamb of God slain for the sins of the world who purifies by taking upon himself the evils committed by mankind as a scapegoat burdened with the sins of others.

Water on the other hand, is primarily fertile. It is the generative moisture of the mother, of our mother Eve. Far from being an expiatory catastrophe, the flood is a return to the original mother. Our sense of sin and of punishment by flood is so deep-rooted that we find such ideas hard to grasp. But baptism is not a washing away of sin; it is the beginning of a new life through water. The myth has been clouded by the later, edifying interpretations of events found in the Bible.

Clearly there has been a reversal of the actual state of things, a reversal which Sandor Ferenczi describes as by no means unusual according to the teachings of psychoanalysis. "The first great threat to animal life, which was originally aquatic, was not the flood but drought. So, contrary to what the Bible says, the emergence of Mount Ararat from the waters represents not only safety but also the original catastrophe, the narrower concept possibly being developed at a later time by the inhabitants of *terra firma*. The psychoanalyst has no difficulty in identifying the basic, symbolic equation between Noah's ark and Ararat, or earth, and in recognizing both these as representations of the maternal body, from which all higher animals are born." (*Thalassa*, Payot, Paris, p. 86.)

However our argument does not concern the circumstances surrounding the Biblical story of the flood, even though the myth recurs in both European and non-European traditions and is therefore related to the Celts. What matters is that we examine the theme of opposition between Fire and Water, *mors* and *vita*, inasmuch as it concerns the Celts.

One of the best known and probably least understood of the Breton legends is the tale of the town of Ys. But to appreciate its true meaning we have first to cut away much of the artificial romanticism now surrounding the story. Those legends which form part of a traditional, oral folk-lore undergo continual modification to suit the fashion, attitudes and morality of the time in which they are being told. Once written down they become fixed and static. The best known version of the story of Ys has undergone just such a process, acquiring all the airy-fairy trappings of the Romantic era. It has been further adulterated by the development of a provincial folk-lore designed specifically for the tourist market. We do, however, have access to a more traditional, medieval version of the tale through the 12th century lay of *Graelent-Meur* attributed to Marie de France, and a 16th century manuscript of the Breton drama the *Mystère de Saint-Gwennolé*, as well as the *Vie des Saints Bretons* by the 17th century monk, Father Albert le Grand. Even these versions, however, are very Christian in orientation, a fact which should not be overlooked.

> King Gradlon of Cornwall returns from a war in the North with a magically beautiful woman, a kind of Nordic fairy. In the ship bringing them home a little girl is born out of the sea and the fairy dies in labour. This girl is Dahut or Ahès, and Gradlon treats her with great tenderness and affection, blindly allowing her to follow her every whim. Although Gradlon falls under the influence of Korentin, bishop of Quimper, young Ahès rejects Christianity. And partly for this reason,

partly from a desire to return to her birthplace in the sea, she manages
to persuade her father to build her a new city on low-lying ground,
protected from the waves by a huge dyke and gates of bronze. Ys or
Keris (the Low City or City of Below) as it was called was situated,
according to Albert le Grand "on the edge of the sea between the cap de
Fontenay and the pointe de Crozon where the gulf or bay of Douarnenez now stands". Our pious hagiographer goes on to describe the
activities of Saint Gwennolé. "He often went to see King Grallon in the
superb city of Ys and preached aloud against the abominations practised in that great town, which was wholly and unrepentantly taken up
with pleasure, debauchery and vanity. God revealed to Saint Gwennolé
the just punishment he intended to inflict on the town. When Saint
Gwennolé went to see the king, as he frequently did to converse with
him, God revealed to him that the time had come to make an example
of the inhabitants of that town. The saint . . . said to the king: Ah, sire,
let us leave this place as quickly as we can, for it will soon be overtaken
by the wrath of God. The king immediately gathered together his most
prized possessions and taking them, his officers and servants, he rode
out of the town, spurring on his mount. As soon as he had passed
through the gates, a violent storm arose and the wind blew so fiercely
that the now unconfined sea dashed furiously down on that wretched
city, instantly covering it and drowning several thousand people.
Chiefly responsible for the disaster was Princess Dahut, the shameless
daughter of the good king whom she had tried to ruin. She perished in
that abyss, in a place which has since been known as Toul Dahut or
Toul Alc'huez, that is the fall of Dahut or the fall of the key,[1] since
according to the story, she had taken from her father the key which he
wore hanging from his neck as a symbol of his kingship."

If we strip away the more edifying overtones from this tale, we are left with
various basic elements: Dahut-Ahès's Nordic origins; her birth from the sea and
the death of her mother (the baby replacing the woman); her attraction for the sea
and her drowning in the waters. Also worth considering are the fact that Ys or
Kaer-Is means the Citadel of Below and the relationship between the name Ahes
and the key, *alc'huez*. But before any discussion of these points it would be as well to
attempt to restore the legend of Ys to its Celtic framework and to look at the
traditional Welsh and Irish versions of the tale.

The Welsh legend most closely related to that of Ys is the tale of Gwyddno
Garanhir, which appears in a poem attributed to Gwyddno Garanhir, mythical
king of Caernarvonshire, contained in the 12th century *Black Book of Carmarthen*. It
is also mentioned in one of the *Triads* of Britain. "Three drunken men in the island
of Britain. The third was Seithynin Veddw [the Drunkard], son of Seithyn Saidi,
king of Dyved, who in his drunkenness unleashed the sea on Cantre'r Gwaelod [the
Lowlying Land]; all the land and houses there were lost. The sixteen strongholds
previously standing there were the most important in Cymru [Wales] apart from
Carlion on Wysg. Cantre'r Gwaelod was part of the land of Gwyddno Garanhir,
king of Caeredigiawn. This event occurred in the days of Emrys Wletig [king
Ambrosius]. The men who escaped the waves settled in Ardudwy in the land of
Arfon, the Mountains of Eryri and other previously uninhabited places."[2]

Note the similarity between the name Kaer Is and the name Cantre'r Gwaelod, both of which mean low-lying ground. The fact that the flood is unleashed by a drunkard is interesting in itself, for the drunkard is thirsty and parched, he longs for the wet and the flood. The underlying mythical theme here can be compared to the theme of sacred intoxication. In Indo-European languages the word for drunkenness (Celtic *meddu*, Sanskrit *mada*, with which compare English *mead*) is closely related to the word for middle (Celtic *medio*, Latin *medium*, Greek μεδος). So the drunkard, like the medium, is half way between the world of the living and that mysterious Other World of the dead which haunted the Celtic imagination.

The character of Ahès does not appear in the *Triad* quoted above, but in the poem attributed to Gwyddno:

> Seithenhin, arise, go from here and see
> the green battle-line of the waves.
> The sea has covered the land of Gwyddno again.
> Cursed be the girl,
> guardian of the spring, who sighed
> before freeing the fearful sea.
> Cursed be the girl,
> guardian of the spring, who struggled
> before freeing the ravaging sea . . .[3]

It is clear that the flood has been produced by a spring overflowing. This spring is guarded by a girl whom King Seithenhin has raped in his drunkenness, and while she is distracted the catastrophe has occurred. Such is certainly the logical explanation of the Irish legend found in the *Leabhar na hUidre*.[4]

In this case, also, the negligence of the woman set to guard it results in a magic spring in Ulster overflowing and drowning King Ecca and his land. The king's daughter, Libane, escapes the disaster and lives for a year in a room under lake Neagh before being changed into a salmon. Three hundred years later she comes back to life in human form and is baptized as Muirgen or "Born of the Sea".

The overflowing spring is obviously a sexual symbol of fertility. The woman guarding it is identified with the spring, just as the vagina is symbolized by the well. The fact that once raped she becomes fertile is sufficient an argument to suggest that the myth of the flood is not always a myth of punishment and destruction. There is a similar legend attached to the spring of Barenton, in the Paimpont-Broceliande forest, which remained the objective of local processions even into the 17th century, since it was believed that the act of pouring water onto the stone steps around it would unleash a storm of rain. According to Chrétien de Troyes in *Yvain or Le Chevalier au Lion* Yvain, son of Uryen, who successfully underwent the trial of the spring, had to marry the widow of the knight he had killed there. This woman was herself the real guardian of the spring and in some way identified with it. The same story occurs in the Welsh tale of *Owein or the Lady of the Fountain*.

This same theme embraces the innumerable sacred springs venerated under Christian names in France and in originally Celtic countries (the spring of Saint Mathurin which cures madness, of Saint Nicodemus which cures horses, etc.) and the wells often found in sanctuaries consecrated to the Virgin as at Chartres or Puy. It is interesting as a literary curiosity to note that Hersart de la Villemarque adopted the theme of the spring in his poem about the Submersion of the Town of

Ys in *Barsaz-Breiz* and that he assigned to Gwyddno the role of the girl who unleashed the sea:

> The key will be taken,
> the well will be opened . . .
> (*Barsaz-Breiz*, pp. 39–46)

Of course every legend has some historical backing, just as every symbol has a basis in a material object. The submersion of the town of Ys fits closely with the historical and geological evidence. The Latin writer Ammianus Marcellinus quoting a lost work by Timagenes clearly states, "According to ancient druidic teachings, the population of Gaul is only partly indigenous, and expanded at various times to include foreign islanders from across the sea, and people from beyond the Rhine who had to leave their homes either because of the hardships of war, a constant problem in those countries, or because of the invasion of the fiery element which roars on their coasts." (Ammianus Marcellinus, XV, 9.)

It has, in fact, been proved that there were major physical upheavals in Northern Europe towards the end of the Bronze Age, which resulted in whole scale migrations of peoples. The Celts left their early homeland in the Harz Mountains to spread throughout Northern and Western Germany, along the Baltic and North Sea coasts. Before long they had established trade relations with their neighbours around the Elbe and in the British Isles, particularly in Ireland, which would tend to suggest that there was a first Celtic migration of Gaels into Ireland while the mass of the Britons remained faithful to their former territories.

Geographical and geological evidence shows that in the middle Bronze Age, around 1200 BC, the water level of lakes and marches fell, indicating that a warm, dry period had followed a cold, wet period. This climatic change may well have sparked off the shrinking of the Turco-Siberian Sea, which has now been reduced to the bounds of the Caspian and Aral Seas. All the buildings which can be roughly assigned to this period are at some distance from the former shore lines, near some source of water. The great forests of Central and Western Europe became less dense. And the peat bogs of Northern Germany and Sweden as the Swedish geologist Sernander has observed contain evidence of a stratum of dry land corresponding to this era.

This would appear to have been the time when the civilization of the Scandinavian Straits was at its height; when the Dorians arrived in Greece and when the Urnfield civilization flourished in Western and Central Europe together with the British Battle-Axe civilization.

At the end of the Bronze Age, after the first Halstatt period, i.e. around 530 BC, the lake villages were hastily abandoned by their occupants. Western Europe became suddenly cold and wet again. The Scandinavian bogs indicate that new formations of peat followed a period of comparative drought. The North Sea and Baltic coastlines became areas of inundated marshland. Archaeological evidence indicates vast southward migrations of people escaping the flooded regions. The first and most important migration of Britons to Great Britain can be dated from this period and these movements were echoed in the strange Welsh traditions which followed at a much later date.

First, there is the legend of Hu Gadarn which tells of a kind of flood caused by an *afang*, a monstrous beaver which according to one of the *Triads* broke the dyke of the pool of Llion [the Waves]. Hu Gadarn and his horned steers dragged the *afang* to dry land "after which the pool never broke its banks again" (Triad 150, *Mab* II, 323).

Then there is the legend of the men of Galedin. "The third invasion [of Britain] was that of the men of Galedin who sailed on ships without masts or rigging to the isle of Gweith [Isle of Wight] when their country was flooded. They obtained land from the nation of the Cymry. Though they had no right in Britain, they were granted land and protection on certain conditions: not until the ninth generation would they be entitled to the privileges of the true and original race of Cymry." (Triad 109, *Mab* II, 297.)

This Triad and the age-old tradition it mirrors would appear to suggest that the Celts driven from the continent by the waters were not the first arrivals in Britain, since the existing inhabitants are called "the original race of Cymry". But there is no reason why both groups should not have belonged to the same race. The fact that the newcomers were not to be assimilated until the ninth generation may reflect concern on the part of the Cymry about the large numbers of immigrants. Galedin itself is situated between Devon and Somerset (The Land of Summer, or Kingdom of the Dead, in Welsh tradition); but since the men of Galedin clearly came from the continent it is possible that the name was merely given to an area highly populated by the new arrivals. The first half of the word Galedin appears to be derived from the same root as the words Gaul and Galatia, the second half, *din*, meaning fortress. It is hard to tell therefore whether these men of Galedin represented the purest strain of the Gallic race or whether they were emigrants from Belgica, like those who arrived in Britain in the La Tène III period.

Not all the Celts living by the Baltic and North Sea made for Britain, however. Others journeyed to the Rhineland and from there to what later became Gaul, either assimilating or driving back before them the proto-Celtic indigenous peoples of the Bronze and Megalithic civilizations.

This mass migration obviously created considerable disturbances, echoes of which can be seen in the legends concerning Atlantis, so obligingly passed on by Plato. As nothing has yet emerged to suggest that Atlantis was anything more than a myth cobbled together by Plato to support his arguments on cycles of civilization, we do not propose to add anything to existing debate on the subject. But the fragment of *Timeus* concerned does raise some interesting questions.

Plato reports the story as having come from the Egyptian priests of Sais, a convenient device for shrugging off any responsibility for it. "Our [Egyptian] books tell how 9000 years before Solon, Athens destroyed a powerful army which had come from the Atlantic Ocean and was insolently invading Europe and Asia. For at that time it was possible to cross that ocean. There was in fact an island facing the straits you call the 'Pillars of Hercules'. This island was larger than Lybia and Asia put together."

Asia here refers only to Asia Minor, and the supposed date of the event is clearly invented. 9000 years before Solon, neither Athens nor the Greeks existed. It is merely a symbolic figure. The island beyond the Pillars of Hercules could refer either to Britain or to Scandinavia. Early accounts of voyages and maps demonstrate considerable confusion over the geography of Western Europe. The *Timeus* continues, "This vast empire gathered all its forces together and undertook to subdue our land and yours and all the people this side of the straits . . . Now, as time went on, there were great earthquakes and floods. And in the space of one day and one fatal night, all your warriors together sank into the earth, and the isle of Atlantis vanished under the sea."

It is hard to tell from this whether the isle of Atlantis is meant to be a vast landmass on its own or part of Western Europe. It is equally difficult to decide who was responsible for the invasion of the Mediterranean basin which coincided with these natural disasters. Perhaps it was a movement of megalithic peoples at the end of the neolithic era, i.e. around 2000 BC. Perhaps the Celts were driven southwards into the warm, welcoming Mediterranean regions by the returning cold and wet in the North caused by a series of earthquakes. It might even have been a group of Italic peoples separated from the main Italo-Celtic group. We may never know.

And yet there is a possible clue in the fragment of *Timeus*. "That is why even today one can neither explore nor journey across that sea; for it is impossible to sail over the insurmountable deposits of silt left by the subsiding island." In his *Critias*, Plato mentions this phenomenon again, "In its place there is only a silt bed which blocks the sailors' path and makes the sea impassable."

Further traces of this impassable sea are to be found not solely in the Mediterranean tradition. The twelfth canto of the Scandinavian poem, the *Kudrun*, describes a mountain in the far West, in the middle of a motionless sea. This theme is also taken up by Tacitus, whose relationship with Agricola (his father-in-law) makes him a generally credible authority on the British Isles. "This sea, the size of Scotland, is motionless and resists the efforts of the oarsmen. Even the winds cannot raise waves there, doubtless because there is so little of the land and so few of the mountains where storms are first formed, and because this bottomless and limitless sea takes longer to set in motion." (*Agricola*, X.) Tacitus also claims that in the Baltic, "Beyond the Suiones, there stretches another sleeping and almost motionless sea, which one would suppose surrounded and enclosed the universe since the last rays of the setting sun continue to shine until it rises again so bright that the stars pale beside it. The superstitious also believe that god can be heard rising from the waves and that divine forms and a head surrounded by rays of light can be seen there" (*Germania*, XLV). The extremely cautious Greek historian Polybius criticizes the navigator Pytheas for his words on this subject. "Pytheas has misled the public . . . about Thule and the neighbouring lands by saying that there is neither earth, sea nor air in those places, but a mixture of all three elements like a marine lung lying under the earth, air and sea, which links them together in such a way that it is impossible either to sail or walk over this matter." (Polybius, XXXIV, 5.)

Pliny the Elder pinpoints the spot more precisely. He speaks of an island; "where amber is thrown up by the waves in the spring. It is where the Western Ocean, which Hecate calls the Amalchean Sea, bathes the land of Scythia, this name meaning 'frozen' in the language of those people. Philemon claims that the Cimbri call it *morimaruse*, which means dead sea" (*Hist. Nat.* IV, 27). The etymology of the Celtic word *morimaruse* is correct, and the mention of amber means that this sea can only be the Baltic.

All these various comments suggest that the Celts living on the Northern coasts of Europe must have suffered some natural disaster and that their memory of it was transformed into a myth, a common enough practice among Celtic peoples who looked on history merely as an auxiliary to religious thought.

But the unusual ways in which this memory lived on were frequently misunderstood by the Mediterranean peoples. Strabo the geographer took everything he heard about the Cimbri, whom like many authors he confused with the Celts, to be pure fable. "How are we to suppose," he wrote, "that the Cimbri were driven from their original homeland by a high tide in the ocean when we can see them today living in those same places? ... Is it not absurd to suppose that a whole people could be driven from their homes by resentment against a natural and continual phenomenon which recurs twice a day? In any case, this extraordinary tide appears wholly fictitious, since variations in the level of ocean tides are quite regular and seasonal." (Strabo, VII, 2.) Some of these questions are easy enough to answer. The Cimbri driven from their homeland were actually Celts, while the Cimbri of Strabo's day were the true Cimbri. Strabo is also unfamiliar with the whims of the Atlantic ocean, but that is understandable enough when one considers that the Mediterranean is tideless. It is the further doubt and scepticism he expresses, however, which is interesting.

"Neither do I believe, as this historian had told us, that the Cimbri [Celts] brandish their weapons at the mounting waves to drive them back, nor, as Ephorus says of the Celts or Gauls, that they train themselves to fear nothing by calmly watching the sea destroy their homes, which they later rebuild, and that the floods have claimed more victims among them than war." (Strabo, VII, 2.)

Strabo is wrong to reject these fables, for they are evidence that the Celts performed some kind of water ritual. Aristotle mentions it both in his *Nicomachean Ethics*, "When one goes to the extent of fearing neither earthquake nor the rising waves, as the Celts claim to do . . ." (VIII, 7) and his *Eudemian Ethics*, "The Celts who take up arms to march against the waves . . ." (III, 1, 26). It is clear, however, that Aristotle has no more understanding of the rite than Strabo, and that this apparent naivety on the part of the "Barbarian" Celts made them the laughing stock of the rational Greek writers.

Further proof that a water ritual did exist can be found in a poem attributed to the bard Taliesin.

> When Amaethon came from the land of Gwyddyon,
> from Segon with the powerful gate,
> the storm raged for four nights at the height of the fine season.
> Men fell, even the woods no longer sheltered against the wind of the deep.
> Math and Hyvedd, the masters of the magic wand, had unleashed the elements.
> Then Gwyddyon and Amaethon held counsel.
> They made a shield so strong
> that the sea could not engulf the best of the troops.[6]

It is difficult to know whether this shield was merely a protective device. Arthur's shield Prytwen [white shape] is also his boat. But we can be sure that if Math and Hyvedd were responsible for the disaster, it was a supernatural phenomenon. Apart from the mention of the magic wand (Math being the best magician in Britain according to the *Triads*), there is also the fact that Math is a wounded king who can only live in peacetime if his feet are in a virgin's lap. And this disability identifies him with the Fisher King, Pelles, who is guardian of the Grail and thus a person from the Other World.

The Celts' terror of the unbridled sea ravaging their former lands remained a constant theme in Celtic tradition. In a poem attributed to the bard Myrddin (Merlin), the *Chant of the Piglets*, the mad poet says:

> Since the battle of Arderyd I have become dead to
> everything,
> even were the sky to fall and the sea to overflow.[7]

Looking for a metaphor for King Uryen's formidable presence in battle, Taliesin compares him with a marine disaster:

> Ho, that sound, is it the earth quaking?
> Is it the sea overflowing
> from its usual banks
> to reach the feet of men?[8]

Indeed, in his enigmatic poem the *Cad Goddeu* Taliesin declares that he had witnessed the disaster himself and was one of the emigrants:

> I was in the boat
> with Dylan, son of the Wave,
> on a bed in the middle
> between the knees of the kings
> when the water like unexpected spears
> fell from the sky
> to the depths of the abyss.[9]

Further echoes of the disaster are to be found in the poetry and epic writing not only of the British tradition in Wales, but also of the Gaelic tradition in Ireland. In the tale of the *Feast of Briciu*, the heroes Loegaire Conall and Cú Chulainn have to undergo various trials during their night watch at the fortress of Curoi mac Daere. "That evening, the monster of the lake nearby threatened to swallow up the fortress together with all the men and animals inside it. Cú Chulainn heard the waters of the lake rising and the loud sound of the sea whipped up by the storm. Although very tired, he wanted to know what was causing that terrible din. He saw a monster more than thirty cubits high appearing on the surface of the water. The monster leapt rearing towards the fortress and opened a mouth wide enough to swallow it whole."

The monster is evidently a symbol of a tidal wave. The fact that it is said to come from a lake rather than from the sea does not necessarily argue against this, since the word for lake could be used to denote a lagoon, a swamp or an inland creek like the Welsh and Breton *ebyr* or *aber* and the Scottish lochs around which so many legends have arisen. (Remember the Loch Ness monster.) Like Gwyddyon and Maethon in the Welsh poem, Cú Chulainn manages to ward off the disaster and save the fortress by slaying the monster, earning himself well-deserved praise for the deed.

In another Irish tale, Cú Chulainn abandons his role as the protector and becomes the man responsible for the flood. The vast epic from which this tale is taken has unfortunately come down to us in a rather fragmentary, confused and adulterated form, but the main ingredients are unmistakable. This time the victim is Curoi, lord of the fortress mentioned in the story above. His name means Dog King, or the Dog of the King, while Cú Chulainn is the Dog of the smith Culainn. Curoi is a kind of Cerberus guarding the other world, though he is never included among the numbers of the godlike Tuatha de Danann who live there.

Some time before the episode concerned, Curoi had stolen Blathnait, now his wife, from Cú Chulainn and she now listens sympathetically to Cú Chulainn's suggestions that she should betray Curoi. On the appointed day she washes Curoi's head in a stream in order to distract him, and pours milk into the water as a signal for Cú Chulainn. Since that time the river has been called Finglais [white milk]. At the point in the story when Cú Chulainn and his men arrive in the neighbourhood, together with King Conchobar, the prose narrative of the *Death of Curoi* breaks off to include the following quatrain, doubtless a fragment from an older poem, which was used as a model for the whole tale:

> Curoi mac Daere came upon them.
> He killed a hundred men, that powerful fighter.
> He would have battled with Conchobar
> had the sea monster not drowned him.

This verse is inexplicit, to say the least, though the compiler of the tale does think it right to enlighten the reader.

"Here is the explanation: at the moment when Curoi was going to fight Conchobar, he saw his fortress in flames north of the sea. So he went towards the sea to save it. But the water was deep and he drowned."

At first sight this explanation is scarcely any more satisfactory than the quatrain itself. However, it does leave room for the hypothetical interpretation that Curoi, realizing his situation was hopeless, took refuge in the sea deliberately leaving the surface for the submarine world. The theme of submersion and of disappearance under the water recurs in a Welsh poem entitled the *Lament for Corroy*, which is attributed to Taliesin:

> Your vast spring, the wave has filled it,
> it comes and goes, it dashes and races.
> The Lament for Corroy disturbs it . . .
> Your vast spring, the waters filled it,
> the arrows cross the strand, unhesitant, unabated . . .
> Once it had entered the walls of the cities
> the pure stream soon whitened
> while the morning conqueror continued his slaughter.[12]

Another instance of disappearance under the water being designed to protect a person or a stronghold occurs in the medieval *Elucidation*, written as an alleged preface to Chrétien de Troyes' *Perceval*. Here the story concerns the Castle of the Grail, where young women once welcomed travellers with cups full of a refreshing beverage. But then King Amangon assaulted one of the girls and stole her cup, whereupon the kingdom was laid waste, the waters rose from all around and the Fisher King's palace, once so fine and so richly decorated, was submerged. The springs overflowed and totally flooded the castle. Irish folk-lore has preserved the same tradition in connexion with Lough Erne. Erne, guardian of the queen's cups is supposed to have disappeared into the lake with her followers when some travellers tried to assault them.

It becomes increasingly and unmistakably evident that all these legends referring to submersion can be interpreted both as acts of concealment, in which certain secrets or traditions are sheltered away from the world, and as acts of enrichment from the fertile waters of the flood. It is these themes which run through all the many versions of that submerged city, the town of Ys. What we now have to do is to define that symbolic object which is being hidden away or made fertile.

Taliesin tells us in the *Mysteries of the World* that:

> There are three springs
> under the mountain of gifts.
> There is a citadel under
> under the wave of the ocean.[13]

and this theme is elaborated in another of his poems, the *Seven Cities*:

> A pleasant town lies on the surface of the ocean.
> May great feasting gladden the heart of its king
> at the time when the sea grows greatly daring
> may the bards' crowns be above the cups of mead.
> A wave will come swiftly to cover it
> unfurling towards the green pastures of the land of the
> Picts . . .
> A pleasant city lies on a large lake
> an impregnable fortress encircled by the sea.
> (*Book of Taliesin*, poem 21)

It is clear that these verses are expressing the Ys theme. They also reveal that symbolic identity between lake and ocean seen in the Irish tale and suggest that the submerged town has the appearance of a fortress. In some versions of the myth it is both the town and all the surrounding countryside which lie under water, but never do they present a scene of desolation to those fortunate enough to see them.

"Before long they made their way into a cloud-like sea which they did not imagine could support the weight of their boat. Then they looked under the sea. There were the roofs of fortresses and a lovely land . . ." (*Imramm Mailduin*, XXIII.)

In the *Story of Taliesin*, the town is merely a house. "At that time there lived in Penllyn [Head of the Lake], a man of high birth named Tegid Voel [the Bald]. His house was in the middle of Lake Tegid." In the 14th century *Reductorum Morale* by Pierre Bercheur, Gawain discovers a magnificent palace under the waters of a lake, where a feast is prepared. In Chrétien de Troyes' *Lancelot*, Gawain crosses a bridge under the water to reach the fortress of Meleagant. This under-water palace is very much of the Other World, a kind of Grail Castle with its own Maiden of the Grail. The Welsh legend of Lake Tegid makes her Keridwen, a sorceress-cum-goddess who owns the cauldron of knowledge, and who casts her son Taliesin on the waves in a leather bag after his birth.

It now becomes possible to interpret the symbolism much more specifically. For the submerged town is the definitive image of the maternal womb. As Sandor Ferenczi rightly remarks, "Some aspects of the symbols present in dreams and in neuroses suggest a profound symbolic analogy between the maternal body and the nurturing sea or earth." (*Thalassa*, p. 84.)

By investigating this analogy we may be able to find explanations not only for certain facets of human behaviour, but also for all the myths concerning water.

The first woman and mother of mankind was, after all, called Eva or "Water". If we accept the biblical picture of the spirit of God moving upon the face of the original waters and the confirmatory scientific evidence that life started in the sea, then it follows quite naturally that the attraction towards water is an attempt to halt the evolutionary process and achieve a journey of retrogression. Mankind has probably dreamt of such an achievement since its earliest days. Many world religions view death as a necessary return to our original condition, a point of departure towards a new life. But because death is mysterious and forbidding, man tends to try to avoid it by returning to the less frightening mysteries of the maternal womb, to the sense of comfort and security which hidden memory preserves in all sentient beings. The return beyond birth, the desire to nullify the effects of birth must therefore motivate certain forms of human behaviour, in particular the sexual act. "If we accept," writes Ferenczi, "that the fish in water represents the child in the maternal womb, as so many magic fertility ceremonies indicate, and that many dreams can only be interpreted by regarding the child as a symbol of the penis, then it becomes clear why the fish is used as a sign for the penis and the penis for the fish. Leading on from there, we can also understand the notion that the penis in coitus represents not only that form of human existence which preceded and coincided with birth, but also the tribulations suffered by that animal ancestor which experienced the great cataclysm of drought." (*Thalassa*, p. 87.)

For the cataclysm is drought, or sterility. In the 17th century Father Christophe de Vega wrote the following commentary on the story of Saint Anne: "In the beginning God created the heaven and the earth (Joachim and Anne). And the earth was without form and void (Anne was barren). And darkness (affliction and confusion) was upon the face of the deep (on the face of Anne), and the Spirit of God moved upon the face of the waters (the waters of Anne's tears to console her). And God said, Let there be light (Let there be Mary) . . . and the gathering together of the waters (the gathering of the graces) he called *maria* (seas or Mary)." It seems amazing that such a clear definition of the myth of the waters and of the dry land should have been achieved in the days before psychoanalysis. We shall return later to the myth of Saint Anne, the Celtic myth of the mother of waters. Suffice it to say for the moment that Anne is a symbol of sterile divinity, made barren by the universal conflagration.

It is in accordance with this theme that Curoi drowns himself trying to save his burning fortress, that Ahès drowns herself after burning her city in the flames of pleasure and herself in the fires of love. The kingdom of the Grail is a waste and barren land, too dry for anything to grow there, and it is only when Perceval or Galahad fulfil the Grail ritual that its earlier life-giving moisture is restored. The symbolic thread underlying all these tales is based on the historic pattern of droughts and subsequent flooding which affected the Baltic and North Sea coasts at the end of the Bronze Age. But the fact that this symbolic thread was used for metaphysical purposes meant that the ideas it was transmitting lost all but the most tenuous links with real events.

"It is very probable that this motivation is equivalent to the endeavour to re-establish the lost way of life, in a damp and sustaining environment, i.e. the aquatic existence within the damp and nourishing interior of the mother." (Thalassa, p. 92.)

Anyone doubting the equation of birth and drought has only to look at language. *Agni* and *ignis*, the Sanskrit and Latin words respectively for fire belong to the same root as the Latin *gigno*, I bear a child. And with unrelenting logic, the idea of birth

(Latin *nascor*, I am born) leads on to the idea of knowledge (*Cognosco*, I know), the prefix *co-* indicating contact with the surrounding world. Thus, by some age-old process of analogy, fire, birth and knowledge become essentially the same, all of them seen in opposition to the unconscious but blessed life in the womb preserved somewhere in our memory. It is this analogy which explains the myth of paradise lost. For it was their desire to acquire knowledge which forced Adam and Eve out of the Garden of Eden, and once the earth had become dry and barren, redemption could only take the mythical form of the son, whose mother, as symbol of moisture and water, offered the only possible counteraction to the flames enveloping the earth. "By reversing the symbolism, as has proved necessary on occasion, we find that it is the mother who symbolizes the ocean or takes its place, rather than the reverse" (*Thalassa*, p. 92.)

The divinity is essentially feminine. As E. Saillens writes in *Nos Vierges Noires*, "Throughout man's perpetual musings on the universe and on himself, he had been haunted by two symbols, from the earliest times and in many different places: the symbol of the virgin and the symbol of darkness."

In the face of the mysteries and darkness around him, man gradually conceived the notion of some higher divinity, the mistress of heaven and earth. And this divinity was inevitably seen as the *Nature naturans* symbolized by woman. For woman is synonymous with fertility. It was generally believed amongst early man, as it still is by some Australian aborigines today, that the wind rather than man makes woman conceive. That is surely why the oldest representations of the divinity are female figurines like the Aegean idols and the Venus of Lespugue which emphasize woman's fecundity . It was not until the male realized that he, too, was fertile that the female divinity was given a consort. And once the myths concerning male gods had been created, certain races, the Hebrew among them, came to accord these later myths the chief place in a kind of retaliatory gesture.

The earliest societies gave special importance to the mother and thus to woman in general. The Hebraic tradition, in which woman's status was diminished and god became a solitary male warrior or shepherd, and the Islamic religion which it inspired, were both conceived by nomads used to the dryness of the desert. And the female divinity undoubtedly sank to her lowest position during the period when Rome forced its empire to accept both its patriarchal regime and its amazingly sterile religious formalism, part of which survived in early Christianity. Even within the Christian era, however, it was not long before the influence of Eastern cults like that of the Syrian mother-goddess, Isis, Cybele and Demeter, and the effect of druidic cults, which gave women a highly important role, combined to produce the concept of the Virgin Mary. The fact that the cult of the Virgin is now reaching similar proportions to the cult of Jesus, is surely a sign of the times; and a sign not unconnected with the waning power of the idea of the fatherland. For the age-old concept of motherland lives on, if only in the present day attempts to bring those of a common tradition within some supra-national unity. In the face of drought men turn towards the mother. And in many languages the mother is also Mary who is herself marine.

Whether one looks at it from a religious, a psychological or a political point of view, the return to the mother must surely be linked with the sexual act. It seems probable that coitus represents both man's attempt to resume his place in the woman's womb, and woman's attempt to take back her lost child (an unconscious desire on the part of the childless woman). Having established that sexual bimorphism developed only in terrestrial species, and thus among creatures past the drought stage, Sandor Ferenczi offers the following pertinent comment, "After the drought, the first attempts at copulation among fish were efforts to regain their former, moist and nourishing home, the sea. A similar, but even older disaster may have induced the unicellular creatures to devour each other. But as neither one of these two enemies managed to annihilate the other, it became possible to achieve a union based on compromise, a kind of symbiosis which, after a period of co-existence, always reverts to the original form because of the fertilized cells' produc-tion of primitive cells and their separation." (*Thalassa*, p. 103.)

It is a point worth remembering that sexual symbolism makes conscious use of marine objects like fish and shells. The link between women and the sea is appar-ent not only in the 28-day cycle which governs both menstruation and the influence of the moon on the tides, but also in the fact that erotic stimulation of women gives rise to the secretion of a vaginal fluid containing the same chemical substance as is found in rotting fish.

"In the act of coitus and the closely connected act of fertilization, the individual disaster of birth, the most recent disaster suffered by the species and every disaster undergone since the appearance of life, are all fused into one entity. Orgasm is therefore the expression not only of intra-uterine calm and the kind of peaceful existence ensured by a more welcoming environment, but also of the calm which preceded the appearance of life, the dead calm of inorganic existence." (*Thalassa*, p. 104.)

Freud contributes to this argument in his *das Ich und das Es*, where he suggests that ejaculation can be likened to the separation of the *germen* from the *soma*. That is why sexual satisfaction is like death, orgasm a death rattle. It is a poetical or mystical sublimation of this physiological relationship between love and death which lies at the basis of all the great myths from Oedipus to Tristan and the Grail.

For love becomes the semblance of death. In the legend of the town of Ys, Ahès the sacred courtesan is drowned with the city, but lives on in another world. When fisherman lean over the site of the submerged town they can see the church belfry and hear the bells. To some of them Ahès appears in her divine beauty, seeking to draw them down under the waves. She is a siren looking for the male to bring fertility to her town. But, fearing a trap, suspicious man refuses to follow her, just as Ulysses has himself bound to the mast so that he cannot respond to the call of the Other World in the song of the sirens.

However, the Other World is not merely mysterious, it is also forbidden, and so totally that access is barred by the prohibitive force of anathema. Woe to the man who tries to enter the submerged city, for, "If the sacred myths were divulged they would become profane and lose their mystic value" (Levy Bruhl, *La Mythologie Primitive*, 1935). It is this desire to protect the secret which underlies all the litera-ture dealing with taboo, all the dreadful, diabolical descriptions of the Other World, and all the sexual prohibitions which cannot otherwise be explained by modesty or biological necessity.

Another aspect of the myth of Ys comes to light in a Breton tale entitled the *Night of Pentecost*, which forms part of a collection by Emile Souvestre. A dare-devil named Perik Skouarn is walking on the sand dunes of Saint Efflam (Côtes-du-Nord) when he remembers the words of an old beggar. "Where the dune of Saint Efflam now lies there was once a powerful town . . . It was governed by a king whose sceptre was a hazel wand with which he could transform anything he wished. But the town and the king were damned for their sins, so that one day, on God's command, the sandbanks rose like the waves of a troubled sea and submerged the city. Just once a year, on the night of Pentecost, at the first stroke of midnight, the hill opens to reveal a passage through to the king's palace . . . But you must hurry, for as soon as the last stroke of midnight has died away, the passage way closes again and will not open until the following Pentecost." Intent on acquiring the hazel wand for himself, Perik Skouarn goes into the city, enters the palace and walks through rooms full of gold and precious stones to where the wand is kept. But there he finds "a hundred girls beautiful enough to damn the souls of saints; each of them holds a crown of oak in one hand and a cup of fiery wine in the other". Having resisted the attractions of the gold and jewels, Skouarn succumbs to the charms of the girls. He lets the twelfth stroke of midnight pass and disappears with the town into the darkness.

The traditional elements of this tale are easy enough to recognize. Though sand has replaced water as the medium of submersion, a simile brings the two together. The magic hazel wand was used by the ancient druids of Ireland, and the girls, whom Christian ethic makes a symbol of sin, can be identified by their crowns and their cups as images of fertility. But despite his fate, Perik Skouarn is not damned, for he has passed the trial of initiation into the Other World so that it may accomplish another year's cycle.

Further light is shed on the subject by a Swedish legend told in the romance writer Selma Lagerloff's work *Nils Holgersson*. "There was once a town called Vineta here by the shore. It was so wealthy and so fortunate that it outranked all other cities in its splendour; unfortunately, though, its people were proud and intemperate. As a punishment the town of Vineta is said to have been submerged by a fierce tide and swallowed up by the sea . . . But its inhabitants cannot die, nor does their town completely vanish. Once every hundred years it rises from the waves in all its glory and remains on the surface for one hour . . . But when the hour has passed, the town sinks into the sea again, unless one of the merchants of Vineta has sold something to a living man." (*Nils Holgersson*, chapter XIII.)

No living man, however, is ever able to buy something from the merchants of Vineta. When Nils Holgersson makes his way into the town, the merchants wordlessly entreat him to buy, but he has no money. The town returns to its apparent gloom for another hundred years.

What is interesting about this Swedish legend is that it refers to a place on the Baltic not far from where the Celtic lands were submerged at the end of the Bronze Age. Surprisingly, the name Vineta seems to be derived from the same root as the names Veneti, Guened, Vannes and Gwynedd. One wonders how it is that the name of the Veneti should be attached to a legend about a submerged town in the Baltic. Vineta almost certainly means "the white town", a term still used in Brittany to denote the sites of ruined or vanished cities.

It is also significant that this town does not really disappear, and that its inhabitants cannot die. Like the people of Ys they live on in the Other World, in a kind of immortality. The submersion of their town has given them the semblance of death. They have returned to the original mother, with whom they have become identified. And since the living are also the sons of the mother, they too will try to enter her, as do Perik Skouarn and all the heroes of Celtic epic. The submerged citizens who need the living are bound to help them.

The only thing missing is any real communication between the two worlds, any religion in the original sense of the word, from *religare*, to rebind. Of course it is possible to cross the threshold. The *sidh*, or mounds of Ireland open once a year on the night of Samain; Vineta appears once every hundred years; the town of the dune of Saint Efflam becomes accessible on the night of Pentecost; the town of Ys is visible under the waves. But the inhabitants of the Other World do not speak the same language, they are dumb like the *silentes* of the classical poets and cannot tell the living what ritual must be fulfilled. In the Grail Castle Perceval is witness to a mysterious ceremony which no one can explain to him until he asks them to do so; but this he does not know.

It is as if the Other World were waiting impatiently for the living man to fulfil the rite which will enable it to continue its work. The Other World is the original mother, symbolized here by the submerged town. God's need of man to do his work is reflected in many traditions, including the Celtic. Saint Paul in his Epistle to the Romans, writes "For the created universe waits with eager expectation for God's sons to be revealed . . . the universe itself is to be freed . . . Up to the present, we know, the whole created universe groans in all its parts, as if in the pangs of childbirth." (Epistle to the Romans, VIII, *N.E.B.*)

The act of creation is the divinity giving birth to the created universe. It is the mother, the woman who cannot give birth until her sons have returned to her and made her fertile through an incestuous union between the two worlds. However horrified the Roman Catholic flock might be to hear it, this sacred incest underlies the basic Christian equation between God the father and God the son, in which the son automatically becomes the mother's consort. For though the symbolic values of the Christian religion have been totally forgotten they, too, mirror the concepts inherent in our age-old traditions. After the disaster of drought, the sons of the submerged town have scattered over the face of the earth. They must therefore return, as the knights of the Grail legend must return to the Grail Castle, to bring fertility to their home that the creative process may continue.

It is this message which is transmitted through the myth of the submerged town. Once we have stripped away the distortions imposed on it by more recent customs and attitudes and more especially by the introduction of an Eastern and sin-based Christianity into a Western culture where the only sin was to come to a standstill, this myth founded as it is on historical fact forms the last barrier to our understanding of the whole mystique of the Celts.

CHAPTER TWO

Who Were The Cimbri?

HE Cimbri make their first appearance in recorded history around the year 113 BC. For it was then, according to Greek and Roman historians, that a disastrous tidal wave forced them to leave their home in Cimbrica Chersonesus (the Jutland peninsula) and hasten southwards with their women and children to make new settlements.

They went first towards the Danube where they encountered the Boii who had settled in Bohemia. "The Boii, who once commanded the Hercynian forest, were attacked by the Cimbri but drove them back." (Strabo, VII, 2, 2.) Thrown back on the Volcae who promptly drove them into the land of the Taurisci, they travelled on into Pannonia "and the land of the Scordisci, a tribe of Galatian or Gallic origin and then to the land of the Tauristi or Taurisci, another Gallic tribe." (*ibid.*) Encountering fierce opposition in that area, the Cimbri were forced back into Noricum and made their way as far as Noreia.

As allies of the Taurisci, the Romans demanded that the Cimbri leave the region, whereupon the Cimbri opened negotiations with the consul Papirius Carbo and asked to be granted land. These talks were rudely interrupted by the Romans whose demand the Cimbri ignored. The Cimbri then continued their way westward and finally settled in the region of the Main where they were joined by the

Teutones, the tribe with which their name has been coupled ever since.

Between 113 and 109, the Cimbri and the Teutones appear to have taken a rest from their wanderings. But they had not lost their taste for adventure, and in 109 they went on the march again, leaving various settlements on the Main, notably at Greinberg, near Miltenberg in Franconia. They then formed a huge confederation with the Helvetii who originally lived in the area between the Hercynian forest and the Rhine (Tacitus, *Germania*, XXVIII). An army of Teutones and Helvetians crossed the Rhine and marched to a position near the Rhone where they were met by a Roman army commanded by the consul Silenus. Meanwhile, the Cimbri, who appear to have been controlling operations, sent an envoy to Rome to renew their request for land, which was again refused. The Cimbri then rejoined the Teutones and the Helvetii and all three tribes united to attack Silenus who was forced to flee.

Over the next two years all trace of the Cimbri's activities has disappeared. But the mystery surrounding their origins, their astonishing speed of action and the terror they inspired among all the peoples they encountered had all contributed to their legend. Before long, both the Gauls and the Romans were beginning to tremble at the very mention of their name.

In 107 BC, the Tigurians, one of the four Helvetian tribes, which was led by the Diviacus whom Caesar knew (*De Bello Gallico*, I, 12), marched south towards Provence which had just become a *provincia romana*. They crossed the Rhone and went to the aid of the Volcae Tectosages of Toulouse who had risen against the Romans and were laying siege to the Roman garrison. The consul Cassius Longinus set off in pursuit, but he was killed near Agen in the land of the Nitobriges, and his army sent under the yoke (*ibid*. I, 7 and 12).

The other consul, Servilius Cepio, managed to defend the garrison at Toulouse and demanded that the Tectosages should hand over the treasure of 200,000 pounds of gold, reputed to be the cursed gold of Delphi brought back by the survivors of Brennus' expedition (Appian, *Illyrica*, IV). This treasure was sent to Marseilles but never arrived, probably because Cepio had appropriated it for his own use.

The Tigurian expedition, however, was only a minor affair. In 105 BC, the Helvetii, Cimbri and Teutones joined forces again, and together with a crack force of Ambrones, marched down the Rhone, leaving a trail of ruin and devastation in their wake. They defeated Servilius Cepio, now proconsul, and the consul Mallius Maximus at Orange.

For some inexplicable reason the allies then divided forces again. The Cimbri pushed on over the Pyrenees and vanished into Spain, while the Teutones continued southwards across Gaul, destroying anything which stood in their way. The only effective opposition to them came from the Belgi, though even they could not prevent the invaders from settling some 6000 men on the banks of the river Sambre near Namur. It was this colony of Teutones which founded the tribe of Atuatuci so troublesome to Caesar during his conquest of Gaul.

The Helvetii journeyed back up the Rhone to settle beyond Lake Geneva in what is now Switzerland, only to be driven from the region later by the Suevi under Ariovistus.

Then, in 103 BC, the Cimbri crossed back over the Pyrenees and advanced along the South coast of France, clearly intent on pushing into Italy. Following what must have been a pre-arranged plan, the Teutones joined them there.

That this advance was the result of carefully considered tactics clearly emerges from what followed. For, instead of following the Ligurian coast, which was well defended by the Romans, the invaders tried to emulate Hannibal's crossing of the Alps and take the Romans from the rear. The Teutones made for the north-western passes over the Alps, following the river Durance, while the Cimbri went back up to Lake Geneva where they could count on support from the Helvetii. There they persuaded the Tiguri to advance towards Noricum, while they themselves went south over the Brenner Pass into the Po valley.

It was at this point that Rome recalled Marius from Africa to lead an army against the invaders. With their past record of total failure against the Cimbrian-Teuton coalition, the Romans were all too aware of their impending danger. Marius set up a fortified camp near Arles and with the help of the Massiliots rapidly dug a long trench, the *fossae Mariannae*, from Arles to the sea at Fos. Having thus ensured that there would be a continual line of communication along which to send for reinforcements and supplies from Massilia, Marius settled down patiently to wait for the attack.

Escorted by the Ambrones, the Teutones arrived within sight of this camp and tried unsuccessfully to storm it. They then marched round the camp for six days jeering at the Romans and taunting them with offers to deliver messages to their wives back in Italy. They then turned eastwards towards the Southern Alps.

Marius realized that he had been outwitted. With admirable quick-thinking, he struck camp and followed the Ambrones and Teutones almost as far as Aix, where he drew up his forces in the high ground overlooking the Arc near Pourrières. When his soldiers complained that there was no water in their camp, and that they were growing thirsty, Marius pointed to the enemy forces around the Arc and said, "There is your water, but we shall have to pay for it with blood." (Plutarch, *Marius*.)

The terrible battle which then ensued resulted in large scale slaughter not only among the two armies, but also among the Ambronian and Teuton women and children who followed their men everywhere. In the end Marius won the day and took 300,000 prisoners, a debatable but not improbable figure considering that entire tribes were involved. The Teuton chief Teutoboduus managed to escape, but was shortly afterwards captured by the Sequani who handed him over to Marius.

The battle at Pourrières was long remembered by the Romans, who had seen the Teuton threat coming too close for comfort. A pyramid was erected to Marius' glory in the centre of the battlefield and a temple to Victory built on the highest point in the area. It was obviously this pagan temple, subsequently turned into a chapel dedicated to Saint-Victoire which gave its name to the mountain overlooking Aix-en-Provence.

Meanwhile the Cimbri were continuing their march through the Northern Alps. Having routed the consul Catulus, at Adige, the road to Rome lay open before them. But they then committed the same mistake as Hannibal had done. Instead of making straight for a defenceless Rome, they dispersed to look for plunder and to wait for the Teutones, unaware that their allies had been defeated.

In the event, it was Marius who came to meet them. The anxious Cimbri sent him messengers to restate the old request for land both for themselves and their brothers the Teutones. Marius replied that he had already given the Teutones land for ever. Baffled by this reply, the Cimbri threatened the Romans with terrible things when the Teutones arrived in Italy. "They are already there," said the consul, and he brought out Teutoboduus and the Teuton chiefs in chains. When the Cimbri realized what had happened their chief Boiorix came with great ceremony to ask Marius where he wished the final encounter to take place. The consul indicated a plain near Verceil. Two days later, on July 3, 101 BC, the two sides met in a battle which proved to be just as terrible a massacre as Pourrières. And once again, Marius emerged the victor, although only after heavy losses. The Cimbrian threat had been removed once and for all.

The prisoners taken by the Romans provided the Republic with more slaves than they really needed. This surfeit was one of the causes of troubles in later years, including the slave war led by the remarkable figure of Spartacus.

When the Tiguri heard that the Cimbri and the Teutones had been overwhelmed they went back to Switzerland and resumed their old life among the Helvetian tribes.

So ended the adventures of that remarkably disciplined and well organized mass of people, the Cimbri. Behind them they left memories of terror in Gaul and Italy and evidence of the most spectacular migration undertaken by men and women in search of a new home.

Who Were the Cimbri and the Teutones?

They appear to have been Germanic peoples, but for various reasons they were assumed by contemporary historians to be Celtic.[1] For one thing they were associated with the Helvetii, and more especially with the indisputably Celtic Tiguri. For another they all have Celtic names as do the Ambrones.

The word "Teuton" itself is Celtic in form, being derived from a root word *toot* or *teut*, which also occurs in the Irish *tuatha*, meaning people or race, and the Breton *ty*, a house. This root word was used to mean tribe, race or people and is common to the Celtic, Germanic and Italic languages. The word Cimbri may be related to *Cymry*, the name by which the Welsh called themselves at the time of the Saxon invasions (from which *Cymru*, Wales and *Cymraeg*, the Welsh language). But *Cymry* suggests that there was an old Celtic word *combrog*, meaning people of the same country, *bro* meaning country in Breton, and that the Irish used this for their *combraic*, meaning Welsh. Cimbri, on the other hand, seems more closely related to Old Irish *cimb*, a tribute or ransome, and *cimbid*, a prisoner. This would also fit in with the etymology suggested by Festus "*Cimbri lingua gallica latrones dicuntur* (the Cimbri are called the Brigands in the Gallic language)" (*Epitome*, XLIII.) The Cimbri would certainly have enjoyed that kind of reputation in a Gaul devastated by their troops, though the word must have existed before their arrival.

Festus also says of the Ambrones that they were a Gallic tribe (*gens gallica*). Their name is indeed typically Celtic and is related to Ambra, a name given to several rivers in the ancient Celtic world, including the Emmer, an upper tributary of the Weser. There was also a Celto-Ligurian tribe from near Genoa with the same name who served as auxiliary forces in Marius' army.

The Cimbrian and Teuton chiefs also had Celtic names. Teutoboduus, for example, contains the root *teut*, and the word *budd*, victory or *bodu*, crow; Gaesorix is the king of the lance, from *gaesa*, lance; Lugius is a theonym from the god Lug; Boiorix means king of the Boii.

All the evidence suggests that they spoke a Celtic language, too, The Cimbri called the Baltic *morimaruse*, "dead sea" (Pliny, *Hist. Nat.* IV, 27), which clearly contains the two Breton words *mor*, sea and *maro*, dead. Moreover, Marius' spies, who were commanded by Sertorius and could understand the Gauls' language, were able to find out all they needed to know about the Cimbri and the Teutones.

Their weapons were Gallic in style (Isidorus Hispalensis, *Origines*, XVIII, 77). Tacitus may have been speaking of one of their tribes when he described the Estonians on the Baltic: "Their customs and habits are Suevian, but their language is closer to British. They worship the mother of gods and the emblem of this religion is the boar" (*Germania*, XLV). Tacitus knew a great deal about both the Germans and the Britons and was unlikely to have confused their two languages. In any case, the boar is an essentially Celtic symbol, found on many Gallic coins and on the Gundestrup Cauldron which was discovered in the homeland of the Cimbri.

When they left the Baltic shoreline to wander through Germania and Gaul, some of the Cimbri remained in their original settlements in Jutland and it was there that an expedition sent by Augustus met them in the peninsula known as Cimbrica Chersonesus.[2] They even sent a deputation to Augustus, offering him "their most precious possession, namely their sacred cauldron" (Strabo, VII, 2). Given that sacred cauldrons were typically Celtic objects and that the Gundestrup Cauldron found in their homelands is a carved monument to the druidic religion, it is safe to assume that, if not Celtic, the Cimbri were certainly very celticized.

The Cimbrian prophetesses were also very like the Celtic priestesses, particularly the fairies and goddesses of Irish mythology. Strabo says in this connexion that, "It was customary among the Cimbri for their women, who took part in all their expeditions, to be accompanied by priestesses or prophetesses . . . When prisoners were brought into their camp, these priestesses approached them sword in hand and, after wreathing them in flowers, led them to a great copper bowl large enough to contain twenty amphora, against which a kind of ladder had been erected . . . One of them climbed up until she stood over the bowl, pulled each prisoner up to the edge and cut his throat." (Strabo, VII, 2.)

These priestesses-cum-prophetesses are closely related to the warrior furies represented on some Gallic coinage and to the Mórrígan who spurred on Irish warriors in battle. The rite of the bowl appears to be linked both to the sacred cauldron and to the sacrificial rites in honour of Teutates during which a man would be plunged head down into a basin.

The Teutones, who were of the same race as the Cimbri, must have inhabited the Danish islands known to ancient geographers as the Sinus Codanus. They controlled the market in amber, "a favourite topic for ethnographic confusion. The ancient geographers took the easy way out by calling the Teutones and the tribes that marketed amber between Estonia and the mouth of the Elbe Celto-Scythians" (H. Hubert, *Les Celtes*, I, 193). Almost all the expeditions mounted by the Teutones and Cimbri follow the amber trade route from the North Sea to the Alps and the Pyrenees.

They obtained this amber from the people of the celtically named island of Abalum (Oesel) in the eastern Baltic which has strange links with the isle of Avalon. Abalum is the island of apple trees and there is a village there named Aboul. *Abal* is identical with the British *aval*, an apple. If we look at the symbolic significance of the apple and some of the special properties of amber, we may be able to draw some interesting conclusions about the Cimbri.

Yellow amber had been an important source of trade between the Baltic shore dwellers and South West Europe since very early days. The oldest evidence of its use has been traced in the Auresan cave (Hautes Pyrénées). There were small deposits of amber in France itself and it can still be found on some parts of the

Seine-Maritime coast,[4] but it was chiefly found on the Baltic coasts of North Germany, Sweden and Denmark.

The Estonians, who spoke a language like the British, were also described by Tacitus as mining the sea and "they were the only people to collect the resin they called *gless* . . . from the shallows and the shore. It might be the sap of a tree since it is possible to look through it and discern crawling or winged insects which were caught in the substance when it was liquid and remained inside when it hardened. I would imagine . . . that the Western islands and plains are covered with lush forests and that when the sun came near the sap from these forests was expressed and flowed into the sea to be thrown up on the opposing shores in stormy weather. If you place the yellow amber near a flame to test its properties, it catches fire like a torch and burns a greasy and fragrant flame before hardening like pitch and resin" (*Germania*, XLV). The word *gless* used to denote a kind of distilled, dew-like sap, can be compared with the Breton *gliz*, meaning dew, and must therefore have been of Celtic origin. Tacitus describes the sea in which it was found as "dormant and almost motionless", a place from which divine figures are popularly supposed to emerge, in particular a "head crowned with rays of light" (*ibid.*) surely the image of the sun god. *Gless* also has long-established electrical properties. It catches fire easily; it is the burning stone. It can be used decoratively, obviously, but also as a prophylactic. Indeed amber necklaces are still made to protect young children from illness to this day.[5]

The fact that the word *gless* is so closely associated with the Breton *gilz* underlines the divine origins of yellow amber. In his *Argonautica*, Apollonius Rhodius calls amber beads "tears of Appollo" and "tears of the Heliads". Diodorus Siculus makes them "the tears of the sisters of Phaeton". Lucian of Samosata describes the Gallic god Ogmios being attached to men by chains of gold and amber. It is easy to discern a similarity between dew and the tears of Apollo. Moreover, amber is yellow, a solar colour, and as Tacitus says, the sap is drawn out by the action of the sun.

The Gauls had an equivalent for Apollo, the Greeks' solar god, in Belenos, the Shining One, who became Abellio in Aquitaine and Beli in Welsh mythology. The Irish fire festival of Beltaine was held in his honour on May 1. Both Apollo and Belenos derive their names from the same root as the German *apfel*, Breton and Welsh *aval* and English apple. So, too, do Avallach, Avalon and Emain Ablach, the names given by the Celts to their blessed island where Arthur was taken by his sister Morgan la Fée after being wounded at the battle of Camlann.

And then, of course, there is the isle of Abalum. If we can find links between amber and the sun, then we have only to look at the ancient myths concerning golden apples, like that of the Garden of the Hesperides, to find equally valid connexions between the apple and the sun.

And the apple is a symbolic fruit, not only because it represents the sun, but because it is the quintessential fruit, the fruit of the "knowledge of good and of evil". The apple tree of the Garden of Eden stands in an earthly paradise like that Other World of Celtic legend which finds its purest expression in the Isle of Avalon. So, disconcerting as it may seem to find the Cimbri and the Teutones involved in a story more mythical than real, their isle of Abalum is surely as much of the Other World as is Avalon.

Obviously the myth here has a basis in reality, but even so, the Cimbri were traditionally regarded as fabulous people. "Not all of what history tells us about the Cimbri is true," writes Strabo, "and apart from some facts of which we can be absolutely certain, there are many lies." (Strabo, VII, 2.) To a certain extent this scepticism is justified, although even Strabo's positivist tendencies did not prevent him passing on some highly improbable information. But we can use this state-ment to examine those parts of the story of the Cimbri which are purely mythical.

For apart from being confused with the Celts and labelled Celto-Scythians, the Cimbri were also shrouded in an almost deliberate veil of mystery throughout antiquity and were frequently identified with the Cimmerii. It is obviously tempt-ing to link the word Cimbri with the word Cimmerii. (19th century Celtic scholars showed no hesitation in regarding the Cimmerii, the Cimbri and the Cymry as one and the same.) However, the rules of phonetics would demand that the Cimbri precede the Cimmerii, the *mb* of the former becoming an *mm* in the latter. And since records of the Cimmerii predate any mention of the Cimbri, the ancient historians must have based their connexion between the two on strictly non-linguistic argu-ments.

Strabo offers one explanation for the association: "Posidonius . . . believes that the Cimbri, natural looters and vagabonds, must have reached as far as the Palus Maeotis and that it is because of them that the Bosphorus was called Cimmerian (for Cimbrian), the Greeks having apparently changed the name Cimbri to Cim-merii." (Strabo, VII, 2.) Posidonius and Strabo had presumably noted the im-possibility of *mm* developing into *mb* already and therefore believed that the Cimbri existed before the Cimmerii.

Plutarch, however, makes indiscriminate use of both names. Indeed, his *Life of Marius* confuses the Cimbri with both the Celts and the Cimmerii. But then Plutarch's historical works were influenced by his priestly duties at Delphi; his treatise on the *E of Delphi* even mentions wise men, or priests, who tell of abstruse realities in the form of mythological tales. This is what Plutarch writes about the Cimbri:

> As these barbarians inhabited very distant lands, we did not know to which nations they belonged and from which lands they had come to thunder like a storm cloud on the Gauls and on Italy. Their great height, their black eyes and their name, Cimbri, which the Germans use for brigands, led us merely to suppose that they were one of those races of Germania who lived on the shores of the Western Ocean. Others say that the huge expanse of Celtica stretches from the outer sea and the western regions to the Palus Maeotis and borders on Asian Scythia; that these two neighbouring nations joined forces and left their land . . . And although each people had a different name, their army was collectively called Celto-Scythian. According to others, some of the Cimmerii, who were the first to be known to the ancient Greeks . . . took flight and were driven from their land by the Scythians. The others lived at the ends of the earth, near the Hyperborean Ocean, in a land covered in woods and dense shade where the sun rarely penetrates forests so huge that they spread into the Hercynian forest. They were situated under the part of the heavens where the slope of parallel circles makes the pole so high that it is virtually the zenith of these peoples, and the year is divided exactly in half by days which are always the same length as the nights, whether at their shortest or their longest. This is what gave Homer the idea for his fable about Hell. That is where those barbarians first called the Cimmerii came from before they

went to Italy, whence presumably the name Cimbri. (*Life of Marius*, ch. XI.)

One of Plutarch's sources for this passage was Herodotus who obviously knew nothing whatever about the Cimbri. "It is said that the land now inhabited by the Scythians once belonged to the Cimmerii." When the latter had fled, "The Scythians entered and found it deserted. The enclosures and walls which the Cimmerii built for their towns can still be found there. Certainly there is a country named Cimmeria and a Cimmerian Bosphorus." (Herodotus, IV, 11.) Diodorus Siculus says that these men bore the name Cimmerii and that "shortly afterwards they came to be known as Cimbri by corruption of their name" (Diodorus, V, 32).

Further echoes of this confusion occur in the *Triads of Britain*. "Three usurping tribes came to Britain and never left . . . The second was that of the Pictish Gaels who came to Alban [Scotland] across the sea of Llychlyn." (Triad 110.) Since Llychlyn meant Scandinavia, the sea of Llychlyn must have been the Baltic, though according to the 8th century priest and chronicler, the Venerable Bede, the word Llychlyn could also mean the land of the Scythians. Triad 107 adds to the confusion still further: "Hu Gadarn was the first to come to Britain with the race of the Cymry: they came from the Land of Summer which is called Defrobani, where Constantinople stands. They crossed the Tawch sea [Misty] and came to Britain and to Armorica where they stayed." It seems hardly credible that a people should have journeyed from the Black Sea to Britain by way of the Misty or North Sea, and therefore via the Baltic. But then all the geographical information in this particular Triad seems somewhat fantastical. Defrobani may well be a corruption of Tabrophane, or Sri Lanka, and although the Land of Summer has been identified with Somerset, it is primarily a mythical denotation for the kingdom of the dead, such as the fabulous and distant land referred to by the Scythians.

The Black Sea Cimmerians have also been rather curiously identified with the descendants of Gomer, eldest son of the biblical Japhet (Genesis X, 2–3). A people named the Gimerri are actually mentioned in 7th century BC cuneiform texts from Assyria (notably those of Assurbanabal), in which they appear as the enemies of the Assyrians and conquerors of Gyges, the fabulous king of Lydia. It has even been claimed that the Cimmeri gave their name to Tauris which then became the Crimea, and Staroï-Krim has been identified as one of the Cimmerian settlements mentioned by Herodotus.

The first Greek author to speak of the Cimmerii was Homer. "Thus she brought us to the deep-flowing River of Ocean and the frontiers of the world, where the fog-bound Cimmerians live in the City of Perpetual Mist. When the bright Sun climbs the sky and puts the stars to flight, no ray from him can penetrate to them, nor can he see them as he drops from heaven and sinks once more to the earth. For dreadful night has spread her mantle over the heads of that unhappy folk." (*Odyssey*, XI, v 14 ff.) It was there that Ulysses was to evoke the spirits of the dead in an Other World clothed in a suitably mysterious twilight.

While the Greeks placed their Cimmerii at the ends of the earth, however, the Romans claimed to have encountered them in Italy itself. The ancient inhabitants of the land near Lake Arverno were called Cimmerii because they lived by looting and dwelt in dark caves. Pliny also mentions that there was a large town there (*Hist. Nat.* III, 9). Ovid describes this land of darkness in some detail: "In the land of the Cimmerii, there is a deep cave hollowed out of the side of the mountain; it is the unknown home of sleep. At no time do the rays of Phoebus reach this place, whether he be rising in the East, travelling the middle of his journey or diving into the waves. The land round about breathes out dull mists and the only light comes from the murky glimmer of a perpetual twilight. Never there has the wakeful bird with its crests of purple summoned Aurora with its song; never yet have the faithful dog, nor the more faithful bird of the Capitol disturbed the silence with their voices . . . It is the empire of silent repose. Only at the bottom of the cave a stream full of the water of Lethe flows over the pebbles, echoing with a murmur of drowsy gentleness. At the entrance there grows a crop of poppies and soporific herbs." (*Metamorphoses*, XI, 8.)

Lake Averno, which lies between Pouzzole and Baia in Campania, is the crater of an extinct volcano, parts of which reach a depth of 60 metres. It is surrounded by thick forests and the putrid vapours given off by the waters of the lake used to kill the birdlife there, which is why the Greeks called it Aornos, or "birdless". Virgil used the place as a location for Aeneas' descent into the Underworld, led by the sybil of Cumae, to evoke the ghost of his father Anchises.

Even Cicero speaks of the Cimmerii "who are robbed of the sight of the sun, either by some god, by nature or by the position of the place in which they live, but nevertheless have fires which they are allowed to use as light" (*Academica*, II, 19). Strabo quotes Ephorus as saying that the Cimmerii dug out underground dwellings which they called *argel*, a statement reminiscent of Pliny's description of the Hyperboreans "hiding themselves in caves at night" (*Hist. Nat.* IV, 26).

Indeed, the classical authors altogether appear to have attributed the same peculiarities to the Cimmerii and to the Hyperboreans; and there is any amount of literature describing the latter. The name Hyperborean, however, is used sometimes to denote the Northern and British Celts and sometimes to refer to a fabulous race connected with the mysterious island of Thule.

Much of the Hyperboreans' reputation in the ancient world sprang from Herodotus' complex descriptions of Northern Europe. But it is difficult to deduce very much from his improbable jumble and Pliny, who was frequently inspired by Herodotus, tried to make some sense of the subject.

> Beyond the North Wind, if the stories are to be believed, there is a joyful nation called the Hyperboreans, among whom men live to a great age; fabulous marvels are told about them. It is said that the hinges of the world are there and that the stars reach the ends of their orbit there . . . There is only one sunrise a year at the summer solstice, and one sunset at the winter solstice. The land is very open, balmy in climate and free from harmful breezes. The inhabitants live in forests and sacred woods; worship of the gods is conducted by some special men and by the people as a whole. Discord is unknown, so too are all diseases. There men die only when they have had enough of life; after a meal, after the pleasures of the last hours of old age, they jump into the sea from a particular rock. They see that as the most pleasant form of burial . . . We must assume that this nation does exist since so many writers have described their custom of sending the first harvests to the isle of Delos for Apollo, whom they especially revered. These offerings were brought by virgins who received respect and hospitality from the interjacent nations for some years. But then these messengers were assaulted and the Hyperboreans decided to leave their offerings on their borders with neighbouring peoples." (*Hist. Nat.* IV, 26.)

For the purposes of the present discussion, this passage holds a great deal of interest. The discrepancy between the warm climate and the position of the country beyond the Arctic Circle, together with the immortality enjoyed by the inhabitants confirm that the whole story is mythical. It inevitably calls to mind the Tuatha de Danann of Irish mythology "who lived in islands at the North of the world, learning magic, druidism, sorcery and wisdom . . ." (*The Battle of Mag Tured*).

The Tuatha de Danann, whose islands at the north of the world seem to be the same place as the land of the Hyperboreans, were the ancient inhabitants of Ireland. Conquered and enslaved by the Gaels, they were relegated to the barren lands which imagination transformed into the *sidh*, or fairy mounds formed by dolmens and tumuli. This made them the inhabitants of the dark world, like the Cimmerii. Others of the Tuatha de Danann were supposed to be found in the mysterious islands, like the isle of Emain Ablach (Avalon) where Manannan, son of Lir is king. There

> Pain and treachery are unknown,
> so, too, are grief, mourning and death,
> disease and infirmity,
> that is the sign of Emain . . .[6]
> What a marvellous land is this!
> The young do not grow old at all . . .[7]

The maidens bringing their offerings to Apollo at Delos must surely have been fairies of the kind who appear in so many Celtic tales. They are messengers from the Other World, who come with magical fruit, usually apples, to tempt the living to their realms.

> Here is a bough from the apple tree of Emain
> that I bring you like the others;
> it has twigs of white silver
> and brows of crystal with flowers.[8]

The Grail Castle has similar maidens who welcome travellers with refreshing drinks. The Latin chronicle of Gervais of Tilbury mentions a mound in the county of Gloucestershire where huntsmen could halt and ask for something to drink. A hand would then rise from the mound proffering a cup full of nectar. The Irish hero Conle the Red is described as taking an apple offered him by a fairy and being obliged to follow her.

But the days when the fairies were prepared to reveal themselves to mortals have passed, or so Pliny seems to be saying. For men have assaulted them and they have become invisible. In this, Pliny's account of the Hyperborean maidens is remarkably like the medieval *Elucidation*, in which the welcoming fairies of the Grail Castle disappear along with the castle itself when King Amangon rapes one of their number.

Apart from Pliny's fairy tale the classical authors are unanimous in suggesting that there is something sacred about the Hyperboreans. Apuleius speaks of the "Hyperboreans griffons engendered by another world". Atheneius tells of a legend which describes the crane as turning from bird to man in the Hyperborean islands. Diodorus Sicilus includes Britain among the Hyperborean islands and says that the soil produces two harvests a year there. He also describes it as the birth place of Leto, which explains why the islanders particularly revere Apollo, her son, and mentions a huge, round temple, presumably Stonehenge. "Most of the inhabitants play the lute and accompany their continual hymns to god in the temple on their instruments." Apollo is also, "said to descend to this island every nineteen years" (Diodorus Sicilus, II, 47). Pomponius Mela mentions the six-month-long days and nights and adds, ". . . a sacred land, their country is open to the sun and extremely fertile. As scrupulous respecters of justice, they lead longer and happier lives than any other people in the world. Living always surrounded by peace and pleasure, they have never experienced war or conflict. They perform sacrifices in honour of their gods, especially Apollo . . . They spend their lives in sacred woods and forests." (*Mela*, III, 5.)

This whole hotch-potch of legends, however confusing, does suggest that the Cimmerii were identified both with the Hyperboreans and the Cimbri. Then, of course, there is the further confusion between the Cimbri and the Celts, and their relationship with the Scythians, whose land is a place of mystery. We seem to be going round in circles. The mythical aspect of the problem, however, provides a possible explanation.

For all these peoples, whether Hyperborean, Cimmerian, Cimbrian or even Tuatha de Danann are represented as belonging to a race of mysterious origins which lives at the ends of the earth and was supposedly driven from its original home. In mythological terms they are all Tuatha de Danann.

As we have already said, the Tuatha de Dannan were the ancient inhabitants of Ireland who were forced to give way to the Gaels and to become the gods of Celtic imagination, the lords of the subterranean world. There is no doubt that the name Tuatha de Danann was given to the pre-Celtic inhabitants of Ireland and that it must have been they who built the megaliths. Their uncertain origins combined with their curious stone constructions to give them a cloak of mystery. It is equally certain that the historians and writers of antiquity saw the fabulous Hyperboreans and the mythical Cimmerians as being essentially of the same nature, as the fairy-tale-like quality of their descriptions demonstrates. Given that the origins of the Cimbri were equally mysterious, it was found easy enough to make a connexion between the two.

It is possible, however to identify the Cimbri even more specifically. If the Celts drove out the megalithic peoples of Ireland, there is no reason why the same thing should not have happened on the continent, where much of the region occupied by the Celts still bears traces of megalithic monuments.

Since the Celts were always in a minority and did not, strictly speaking, constitute a single Celtic race, the Celtic world was primarily a conglomeration of different nations under a Celtic élite, the indigenous peoples being first enslaved and then fused together by a common Celtic language, civilization and religion. But no invading force in history has ever been able to totally assimilate the native inhabitants; and some of the megalithic peoples of Western Europe must surely have been driven back into the less productive and less strategically important areas.

The myth of the Tuatha de Danann and the druidic religion prove that the Celts were contaminated by megalithic tradition just as Rome was contaminated by the culture and religion of a conquered Greece. And since the Hyperboreans supposedly initiated the solar cults at Stonehenge and Delphi, both Greeks and Celts must have owed aspects of their civilization to their predecessors. But this in no way detracts from the argument that some remnants of the aboriginal race, less influenced by Celticization, took up residence in the more desolate regions of Western Europe. There is no reason why the Cimbri and the Teutones should not have been descendants of just such a group of people, driven into the wastes of Jutland, an area abandoned by the Celts at the end of the Bronze Age because of the havoc wrought by the sea.

Until now the general concensus has been that the Cimbri and the Teutones were either Germanic or Celtic peoples. The suggestion that they were Germanic rests solely on the fact that they came from Germania which considering that there is no other evidence of their Germanicism seems very insubstantial proof. There is much more evidence to suggest that they were Celts, since they spoke the Celtic language and had adopted a good number of Gallic customs. It is also true that some Germanic tribes were influenced by the Celts. Yet it is hard to believe them Celts, for despite their alliance with the Helvetians, they seem so much a separate body of people.

In fact the Cimbri and the closely related Teutones were neither Celtic nor Germanic, but non Indo-European megalthic peoples, whose lands had been usurped by the Celts and who were attempting to wrest back their homes from the invader.

This identification brings new light to a particularly vexed question which cannot be solved in a purely historical framework. The confusing cloud of mystery surrounding the Cimbri and the Teutones is itself mythical in nature and one which they had every interest in maintaining. But an analysis of the myth which they created, or which was created in their name, reveals quite clearly that they were the last descendants of the dolmen-builders who showered Western Europe with their strange monuments around the year 2000 BC, before disappearing into the mystical dreamworld of the Celts where they became heroes and gods.

CHAPTER THREE

Rome and Celtic Epic[1]

IVY is generally regarded as a great writer but a mediocre historian, whose passion for the Roman fatherland frequently led him astray. There has been no serious critique of his facts. According to René Pichon, "He muddles praetors and consuls, quotes the same fact twice and jumbles dates and names" (*Histoire de la Littérature Latine*, p. 314). His *Ab Urbe Condita* is really a kind of companion work to Virgil's *Aeneid*, which was written at about the same time, both authors being concerned to paint an epic fresco dedicated to the glory of Rome. Even Livy's style is epic in nature. With his feeling for the magical and his evocative sense of the past, however, it matters little that he relies on suspect sources or that he uses mythological colours to cover his canvas. The early books concerning the origins of Rome are hardly worth commenting upon. Such legendary accounts of Romulus and the Etruscan kings, whether written by Livy or any other well-intentioned historian, cannot possibly be taken literally. But there is one aspect of the *Ab Urbe Condita* which deserves special attention because few commentators have perceived its exact meaning or significance; and that is the passages concerning the Gallic wars. These include the capture of Rome in Book V and the various episodes of confrontation between Gauls and Romans which are scattered haphazardly throughout the work, even in the sections on the Punic wars when the Gauls are known to have supported the Carthaginians with considerable enthusiasm.

"The history of the Gallic wars," writes Henri Hubert, "has its own particular fabulous and very epic nature" (*Les Celtes*, II, p. 37). The capture of Rome by the Gauls in 387 BC remained a major event for the Romans, partly because the very word Gaul continued to inspire terror in their hearts and partly because their armies had been totally and apparently inexplicably defeated by bands of Gallic marauders looking for plunder and for new lands to settle. In his *Histoire de la Gaule*, Camille Jullian expands on this: "As Livy clearly states, the defeat of the Romans was due to the magic (*miraculum*) terror inspired in them by the warcry of the Celts. It has always seemed to me that the lively, detailed and precise accounts of the war written by Livy, Appian and Plutarch, full as they are of religious fervour and apparent sympathy with the Celts . . . must have been inspired, at least in part, by some Gallic epic brought to their notice by the Insubrian Cornelius Nepos. Polybius' and Diodorus' accounts, which are more sober, more pro-Roman and shorter, represent a different tradition." (*Histoire de le Gaule*, I, p. 294.)

Needless to say, there was no authentic, documented evidence concerning the Gallic invasions for Livy to draw on. Being obliged to use whatever sources he could find, he may well have based his work on those Celtic epics which still lingered among the originally Gallic, if long since romanized, families of Cisalpine Gaul. Livy, himself a native of Patavium (Padua) came from such a family. As Henri Hubert says, "This story in which we believe the two sides collaborated, is more epic and heroic than historic." (*Les Celtes*, II, p. 11.) It is true that no Gallic writings have been discovered, even less epics. But the reason for this is clearly explained by Caesar: "The druids believe that their religion forbids them to commit their teachings to writing . . . because they did not want their doctrine to become public property and in order to prevent their pupils from relying on the written word and neglecting to train their memories." (*De Bello Gallico* VI, 14.) In other words, there never was any Gallic writing. But that does not mean that there was no literature. Once romanization had been urged on the Gauls and the druids and bards were officially banned, the literary works which had been handed on from master to pupil and from father to son began to disappear, along with the Gallic language. Celtic literature survived in the Gaelic and British languages, because Ireland and Wales were never exposed to the aggressive push of Latin. But although the British and Gallic languages were closely related, extant Welsh works were actually written down in the Middle Ages and can therefore only be taken as a very distant echo of Gallic literature.

However, the existence of a literature in Gaul is attested by a number of Greek and Latin writers. Strabo says, "The poets are bards, that is sacred cantors." (IV, 4.) Diodorus Siculus states, "Before engaging in battle . . . they chant the exploits of their ancestors and boast of their own virtues, while insulting their enemies." (V, 31.) "They express themselves in riddles . . . They use hyperbole a great deal . . . Their speeches are threatening, arrogant and tend to the tragic . . . Friends and enemies obey the chants of the bards. Often when two armies are drawn up for battle . . . the bards launch themselves into the thick of the fighting and calm the soldiers." (V, 31.) Pomponius Mela comments, "These people have an eloquence all of their own." (III, 2.) In his *Pharsalia* (I, v. 50), Lucian addresses the Gallic poets: "You, whose chants of glory bring back the memory of strong men lost in battle for the distant future, O bards, you fearlessly pour out your fertile vein." Valerius Flaccus says that, "These people disdain to march to battle to the sound of trumpets; they chant the exploits of their former warriors." (VI, 93.) Finally, Polybius, that most cautious of historians, says of the peoples of Cisalpine Gaul that, "The authors of dramatic stories tell many magical legends about them." (II, 17.)

This last statement encapsulates the whole position. Whenever the historians of antiquity mention the Gauls, there is always some reference to magical legends. Obviously the Gauls were regarded as an exceptional race, gifted with super-human powers; and to survive them, the Romans and the Greeks of Delphi had to be equally outstanding in their courage. Caesar played on this idea in his *De Bello Gallico*. If the Gauls could be made to seem a terrible threat to Rome, then he, Caius Julius Caesar, could lay claim to being the saviour of the Latin capital. In his account of the Second Punic War, Silius Italicus introduces a Gaul named Crixus, "proud of his forebears . . . Etched on the madman's shield was a picture of the Tarpeian Rock and the Gauls weighing their gold at the foot of the sacred hill" (V, v. 150). Clearly the traditional attitude was still at work.[2]

Given that the Gauls did indeed have their own epics of war, therefore, it seems more than likely that Livy was familiar with them. Romanized though he was, he may well have remained sensitive to the instincts of his Gallic forefathers. And if this was the case, then he may equally well have passed on fragments of some Celtic epic in his Latin work, providing us with a rare and precious trace of our ancestral literature.

We can usefully start by looking at the work of the Greek historian Polybius, an impartial recorder of events taking place in Italy. "Eighteen years after the battle of Aegos-Potamos," he writes (I, 6), "and sixteen years before the battle of Leuctra . . . the Gauls fought their way into Rome and occupied the whole city except for the Capitol. The Romans signed a treaty with the conquering army, on the latter's terms." This admirably concise account of events exposes two untruths in Livy's work. The first is Livy's picture of an open and undefended Rome; the second his invented account of the return of Camillus to chase the Gauls out of Rome before the humiliating treaty was concluded. This second flight of fancy is repeated by Florus and Plutarch, though in all fairness Plutarch did have his doubts about the whole story of the capture of Rome. "If we can believe that an accurate picture of those ancient times has been preserved, considering the confusion which existed then . . . Herclidus Pontus, who lived very close to that time, says in his *Treaty of the Soul* that an army from the Hyperborean lands took a Greek town named Rome in the West near the great ocean." (Plutarch, *Camillus*, 27.) Obviously the Hyper-boreans seen by the Greeks have enabled the Gauls to leave one legend and enter another.

The fabulous aspect of Livy's work is already present in his picture of Transalpine Gaul at the beginning of the Second Iron Age, the first La Tène period, though where his information comes from he does not say and we do not know. He writes of Celtica, the area more or less bounded by the Seine and the Garonne, which became Lugdunensis under the Roman occupation. This anachronistic application of a much later name for the area to a time around 400 BC appears somewhat arbitrary. But the most interesting thing is his description of a confeder-ation of the tribes of Celtica under the supreme king, Ambigatus, a Biturigan. The fact that the name Bituriges means "kings of the world" and that they lived around Bourges, the centre of Celtica and of present day France, suggests a connexion with the Celtic cosmogonic concept of the *omphallos*, or navel of the world. Ireland was also ruled by a high king, who lived at Tara, the supposed centre of the island.

According to Caesar, the druids held their assemblies in the land of the Carnutes, the centre of Gaul. Similar considerations had influenced the Greeks in their choice of Delphi as a sacred place, an *omphallos* where the rays of the sun converged. And this sun was worshipped as Pythian Apollo, whose cult may well have been Hyperborean in origin.

The immediate reasons for the Gallic invasion of Italy are quite logical, nonetheless. As Gaul was overpopulated, a number of people decided to go and conquer new lands, mounting two expeditions, one into Greece and the other into Italy. The romanized Gaul, Trogus Pompeius, likens this movement of Gauls to the *ver sacrum*, or sacred spring (Justinus, XXIV, 4), a customary expedition of young people among the Italic tribes who originally formed a single ethnic Indo-European group with the Celts. There are traces of this march towards the Alps in Irish literature. The second part of the epic entitled *Tain Bo Fraech* (the Raid on Fraech's Cattle) has the hero returning home to be greeted by his mother saying, "Your cattle have been stolen, so too have your three sons and your wife; and they are in the mountains of the Alps," a rather curious place for rustlers to take their cattle one would have thought. But Fraech and his friend Conall Cernach "cross the sea, the North of England and the sea of Wight and reach North Lombardy and the mountains of the Alps." They have then to overcome a dragon and loot a fortress before rescuing Fraech's wife, sons and cattle and returning home. For while the *ver sacrum* is a perfectly adequate explanation for the Gallic advance, which conforms with what we know of Celtic sociology, we should also consider the idea that it was one of those expeditions into strange lands, possibly even into the Other World, which form the subject of so many remarkable tales among the Celts. Livy clearly hints as much when he describes the religious fear of the Gauls as they wondered whether they should cross the alps to reach a "different world". Pliny the Elder also mentions a tradition connected with the Celtic expeditions to the Other World when he suggests that the Gauls decided to go to Italy "because Helicon, a Helvetian citizen, who had worked in Rome for some time as a smith, had brought back figs, grapes, oil and fine wine" (*Hist. Nat.* XII, 1). In epic tradition, the smith is a person from the Other World, whether he be one of the Cyclops of the *Odyssey* or one of the smiths encountered on an island by the Irish hero Maelduin during the course of his meandering voyages (*Immram Mailduin*, XXI). The Hephaistos-Vulcan figure of Mediterranean religion has a Welsh equivalent in the magic smith Govannon, son of Don, who is mentioned by the bard Taliesin[3] and becomes involved in the exploits of the magician Manawyddan ab Llyr.[4] Govannon also appears to be modelled on the Irish Gobniu, the smith of the Tuatha de Danann. In the Gaelic tale of the *Battle of Mag-Tured* he appears as the divine keeper of wondrous secrets and is most celebrated for the "feast of Gobniu", a kind of banquet of immortality at which the Tuatha de Danann can eat for ever in their gloomy haunts.[5] The fruit Pliny's Helicon uses to tempt the Gauls is evidently infernal, like the pomegranate eaten by Proserpine and the apple which the people of the Celtic Other World offer to men they wish to follow them. Dionysius of Harlicarnassus emphasizes the way in which these fruits are offered to the Gauls, in a kind of ceremony which is followed by ritual questions about the vast and fertile land "on the other side" (XIII).

Livy and Plutarch, however, suggest an apparently much more down-to-earth reason for the Gauls' invasion of Italy. According to them an inhabitant of Clusium named Aruns went to the Gauls and asked them to help him avenge his betrayal by his wife and adopted son. This story may be based on another character named Aruns who was murdered in 508 BC by Tarquinius Superbus who wanted Aruns' wife (Dionysius of Harlicarnassus, IV, 15). Indeed the general theme of wifely betrayal is a much used device in Celtic literature, and in epic altogether. It is Helen's betrayal, after all, which sparks off the Trojan War. The twelve chief tales which the medieval Irish *filid*, or bards, were required to know included the Abductions of Women (*aithid*), while the emigrations (*tochomlada*) and military expeditions (*sluaigida*) were classified as of secondary importance. The abduction of Etaine, wife of the High King Eochaid Airaein, by the god Mider started a war. King Arthur, the medieval equivalent of Eochaid, had to fight against Meleagant (the Christian version of Mider), against Lancelot du Lac and against Medrawt (Mider again), all of whom had successively stolen his wife, Guienevere. Finn, the king of the Fenians, mounted an expedition to find his wife who had run away with Diarmaid. In all these cases, the theme of vengeance is linked with the idea of mysterious expeditions to an unknown world.

The Gauls, then, advanced southwards, led by a man whom Livy and Plutarch both call Brennus. At one time it was believed that this name was merely a title, a Gallic translation of the Latin *regulus* (little king), since the Welsh *brenin* (from *brenn*, height) means "king of a tribe". Today, however, it is generally, and more justifiably held that Brennus is the Latin form of Brannos in old Celtic which, without the last syllable becomes Bran, the Breton, Welsh and Irish word for crow. The classical historians also mention another Brennus, the Gallic chief who was reputed to have taken and sacked Delphi in 278, nearly one hundred years after the fall of Rome. But of the similarities and differences between the two we shall have more to say in the next chapter.

We now reach the decisive encounter between the Gauls and the Romans. The Roman troops took up their position on the banks of the river Allia, prepared to confront the more dispersed bands of Gauls who uttered wild chantings and strange shouts (Livy, V, 37). What followed is difficult to determine. Livy has nothing to say about the battle proper, but merely describes the Romans' headlong flight, without giving any clear reason for it. Florus says of the event that, "No defeat was more horrible." (I, 13.) According to Livy there had been some mysterious announcement of this defeat beforehand, since after the Gauls had left Rome an act of atonement was made "in honour of that nocturnal voice which had, unheeded, predicted the disasters suffered by Rome, and it was decided to erect a temple to Aius Locutus, the god who had spoken" (V, 50). But this type of forewarning is a universal theme of folklore and was much in use among the Celts. The prophecies of Merlin, of the druids and of the Irish Devins must surely be the most poetic utterances of this type.

The rout at the Allia seems to suggest that the Romans took fright in a way totally at odds with their reputation for courage. Livy argues negligence on the part of the officers, but he seems unconvinced; and the fact that there was no real battle makes this suggestion unsatisfactory. Evidently the Romans were gripped by some kind of religious terror, a purely magical phenomenon. The battle of the Allia is a mythological battle, which may never have actually taken place. The Romans suffer the same panic when faced with what must be the magic clamour of the Gauls described by Polybius in connexion with the Punic Wars (II, 29). "They were frozen with fear by the appearance of the Gallic army and their tumult. The Gauls had innumerable horns and trumpets; and at the same time the whole army set up such a shouting that not only the instruments and the warriors but the hills around seemed to be raising their voices in echo." This realistic description gives us a very clear and impressive idea of what the Romans on the banks of the Allia must have felt. A very similar account of Celtic behaviour in battle occurs in one of the earliest Irish epic tales, the *Tain Bo Cualnge*, although the magical aura here is unmistakable. "Cú Chulainn seized his two spears, his shield and his sword, and loosened the hero's shout from his throat; the pale-faced, goat-shaped demons, the fairies of the valleys answered him, frightened as they were by that powerful cry to such an extent that . . . Bodb, goddess of war, sowed disorder among the ranks of the army. The warriors of four of the five great provinces of Ireland made such a clamour with the points of their spears and their weapons that a hundred men among them died of fright that evening, killed by a deadly pain in the heart . . ." Later, "he bellowed as loud as a hundred warriors. This one cry continued, apparently echoed by every nook and cranny . . ." Near the end of the tale, the four armies flee trembling from the solitary figure of Cú Chulainn, but for reasons of magic. For Cú Chulainn's former master, Fergus, now allied with his enemies, had undertaken by virtue of a taboo to retreat from his pupil when Cú Chulainn asked him to do so. There is no battle, merely a rout like the Roman defeat at the Allia.

The Gauls were now free to march into Rome, but according to Livy they hesitated, in case their surprising victory was a trap. Meanwhile, the Roman citizens, still prey to their supernatural terror, abandoned the city, leaving the gates wide open; and a few brave men took up positions in the Capitol. Anyone familiar with the Roman mentality would find all this very improbable. The seeds of the story must first have developed among the Gauls, for, to their honour rather than their shame, the Celts have always had a wild imagination and preferred imaginary wars and victories to real battles. It was thus that they conquered the whole world in their strange Arthurian dream, a combination of flamboyant fantasy, boundless megalomania and resolute searching for the World Beyond. There seems little doubt that the Gauls did indeed take Rome; the event had too marked an effect on the Romans to be pure fantasy. But Livy's account cannot be strictly accurate. The description of Rome as "an open city" has much in common with the spell-bound cities of Celtic epic. It is the mysterious town of the mabinogi of *Manawyddan*; the "gaste Cité" entered by the anonymous knightly hero of the 13th century French work, *Le Bel Inconnu*, written by Renaud de Beaujeu. "The Bel Inconnu made the sign of the cross, passed through the gate and entered the deserted town. He went along the main street, looking at the stretches of tumbledown walls, pillars and marble windows fallen to the ground." It is the Dead City; the Grail Castle seen by Perceval; the desolate land of premature winter where nobody lives any longer and nothing grows. Most of all, it is the Irish *sidh*, or fairy mound, the mysterious home of the Tuatha de Danann. These apparently empty and defenceless dolmens under their tumuli were the dwelling places of the dead which men came to plunder because of their vast wealth. Irish epic literature abounds in expeditions of this kind, attacks on the *sidh*, descents into the Other World. In *Echtra Nerai*, the Adventures of Nera, the hero wanders into a *sidh* and marries a woman there. After a while the woman says to him, "Go back to your own people and tell them to be on their guard on the day of Samain [1 November, the day of the dead and the Celtic New Year] and to destroy the *sidh*. For it has been said that the *sidh* must be destroyed by Ailill and by Mebdh and the Brown Bull of Briun must be taken by them . . . May they come on the day of the dead, for the *sidh* are always open on that day."

It is from the *Adventures of Nera* that we may gain an explanation of Livy's work. First, there is a specific date chosen for the capture of Rome, as there is for the capture of the *sidh*. Plutarch, who uses the same sources as Livy, says that the battle of the Allia took place "towards the summer solstice and under a full moon" (Camillus, XXII). This was an inauspicious day for the Romans, for it was supposedly the day on which three hundred and six Fabii had been defeated and killed by the Veians in 479, with only one survivor. Aulus Gellius, copying a fragment of a lost work by Verrius Flaccus, tells how, the evening before the battle of the Allia, the tribune Quintus Sulpicius offered a sacrifice to the gods, although every sacrifice made the day after the calends, nones or the ides, had always resulted in the ensuing battle being a disaster (Aulus Gellius, V, 18). However, the Gauls did not enter Rome straight away. They hesitated for a day or more, we do not know exactly how long; and whatever obscure reasons prompted this delay, they were almost certainly connected with a desire to wait for the solstice. Plutarch's mention of the full moon suggests that his sources may have been influenced by the Gauls, since unlike the Romans the Celts based their calendar on the lunar month. Be that as it may, if the Gauls were to have their day of triumph, they could scarcely pick a better date for it than the summer solstice, the zenith of the year.

Second, the *Adventures of Nera* tells us that the *sidh* stood open on the day of the dead. If Rome was to be likened to a city of the Other World, the Gauls would have to wait until the sacred day when the gates were opened. Livy's description of the Gauls entering through the open Colline Gate (V, 41) must be more than mere coincidence.

Finally, there is the fact that the people of the *sidh* in the *Adventures of Nera* are betrayed by one of their own number who destroys her own home for love of Nera. Obviously any comparison between this facet of the story and the capture of Rome must be treated with some caution but it does give rise to interesting speculations.

The basic theme of a woman's being responsible for the evils of mankind is common to virtually every religious tradition in the world, including Celtic mythology. It is the story of Eve, of Pandora and of Delilah. But in the case of Nera this theme is directly linked with the idea of forbidden secrets being wrongfully communicated between the world of the dead and the world of the living. Nera's wife tells him the secrets of the *sidh*. In another Irish tale, the *Murder of Curoi*, Cú Chulainn is helped by Curoi's wife, Blathnait, to kill Curoi, the king of the Underworld, and take his lands. A poem recounting Cú Chulainn's expedition into the Other World to find a magic cauldron, which is the source of life and inspiration, says,

> This cauldron was given us
> by the king's daughter.[6]

Similar women make frequent appearances in the Romances of the Round Table in the shape of maidens who lead the heroes into the Other World. Even the Grail cannot be found without the help of women. The same role is surely performed by the prophetess, the Pythia of Delphi, the Sybil of Cumae, or for that matter by the witches of European folk-lore who, by revealing the future to men, are betraying the gods for the sake of mortals. We might compare them with the druidesses of the Isle of Sein described by Pomponius Mela as keeping "their remedies and their predictions for those who have journeyed over land and sea with the sole purpose of consulting them" (III, 6).

Such is the confusion surrounding the early centuries of Roman history that the classical authors of a later era, Livy among them, tend to jumble the facts relating to the different wars against Sabines, Samnites and Gauls. If we look at the legend of the Tarpeian Rock, we find an apparently straightforward story. During the war between the Sabines and the Romans, a young Roman woman, Tarpeia, betrayed her country for the love of the Sabine King Tatius and promised to surrender the citadel to him. The Sabine conquerors later crushed her under their shields. However, "It is further said," writes Livy, "that the Sabines used to wear heavy gold bracelets on their left arms and rings set with precious stones" (I, 11), a description which ties in almost exactly with what Strabo, Polybius, Pomponius Mela, Pausanias, Diodorus Sicilus and Justinus have to say of the Gauls. And then the Sabine king has a Latinized Celtic name, Tat-ius from *tat* or *tad*, father. A different reason for Tarpeia's treachery is suggested by Florus, who merely abridges the work of other historians in an uncritical way. He explains that she was motivated by "a vanity natural to her years" (Florus, I, 1). The confusion between Sabines and Gauls is further emphasized in *De Strategematibus veterum ac recentium Gallorum*, a curious work written entirely in appalling Latin by a Frenchman signing himself Polyaenus Gallicus. This book first appeared in 1658 and contains a strange link between the legend of Tarpeia and that of the second Brennus who plundered Delphi. "First chapter: the feminine world. A young Ephesian who surrendered her country was buried under the gold and precious stones of the Gauls. The reward which the young Tarpeia received from the Sabine Tatius for having delivered Rome, this young Ephesian received from Brennus, chief of the Gauls, for having betrayed her fatherland." Even more decisive evidence of the confusion comes from Plutarch, "As far as the poet Simylos is concerned, we must assume that he was dreaming when he said that it was not to the Sabines that she [Tarpeia] surrendered the fortress, but to the Gauls for whose king she had developed an ardent passion. This is what he wrote:

> Near to that place came Tarpeia
> who lived on the Capitoline Hill
> and who destroyed ancient Rome.
> Mad with love for a Gaul
> she forgot family and fatherland.
> In her insanity she surrendered to the enemy
> That Rome which had mastered all the kings in the world."
> (*Romulus*, 21).

The fact that the Tarpeian Rock was etched on the shield of the Gaul Crixus as described by Silius Italicus (IV, 150) shows that the kind of Gallic victory suggested by Simylos was part of the fabric of Latin legend. For, although the Gauls had cause to remember the Tarpeian Rock as the site of their disastrous assault of the Capitol, Crixus is unlikely to have worn the scene of a past defeat as part of his battle regalia.

Obviously one can argue that the Gallic-Sabine equation is chronologically invalid, but then chronology has little to do with a web of legends assembled some centuries later, without the benefit of written documentation. In any case, Livy's system of dating is recognized as being "erroneous and unreliable; he muddles and confuses the facts, and jumbles their dates".[7] Events are remembered, but the background to them changes and imagination sometimes alters their importance.

(Overleaf left) The Witham Shield, found in the River Witham near Lincoln (England) and believed to date from the third century B.C. (Overleaf right) The Battersea Shield found in the River Thames in London and believed to date from the first century B.C. Both these shields typify high Celtic art and advanced workmanship in bronze. They are now both at the British Museum.

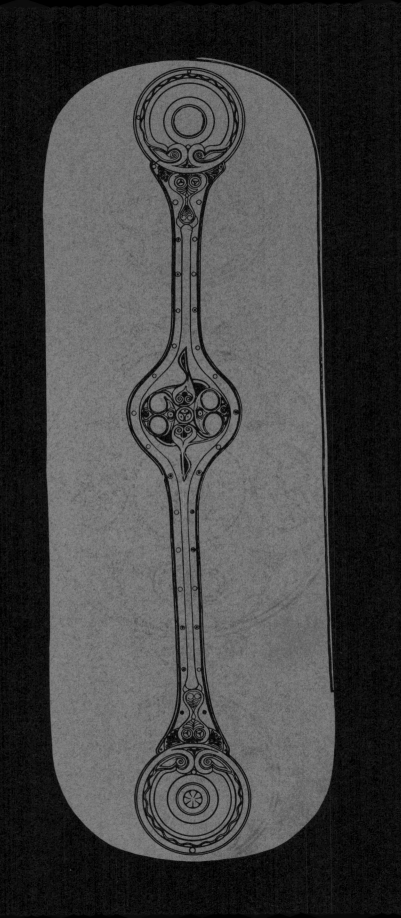

Once the Gauls had entered Rome, they were gripped by a new fear. That this was the natural astonishment of Barbarians confronted by the splendours of the Eternal City seems very unlikely. Rome was then merely a brick-built fortress, the marble monuments not being erected until the age of Augustus. It appears more likely that their reactions were the natural consequence of their hesitation in entering the gates. Having now breached the Other World, everything looked mysterious, even the Roman senators sitting motionless in their official seats. But when one of the fascinated warriors pulled the beard of Marcus Papirius, the Roman struck the Gaul and this sacrilege was the signal for massacre and looting.

This episode is as improbable as all the others, at least in the way Livy tells it. It is incredible that warriors drunk with victory and impatient to start looting should have stood for so long looking at those living statues. But what Livy describes as "a kind of reverence" is linked to the Gauls' respect for the dead and for the inhabitants of the Other World. The Roman senators really were mysterious figures, they were living dead. Minor objections that the dead cannot be killed are easily countered by the fullness of the Celtic imagination. For all the Celtic epics tell of battles against the inhabitants of the *sidh*, who are as vulnerable to mortal wounds as the living.

The occupation of Rome lasted seven months, a fact which Florus (I, 13) finds almost unbelievable, as indeed it is. Only the Capitol held out. Some of the Gauls plundered the surrounding countryside and gorged themselves on food and drink, a well known failing among the Celts. According to Diodorus Sicilus, "With their excessive love of wine, they drink so greedily of it that when drunk they fall into a deep sleep or into fits of temper." (V, 26.) And it is always then that they start fighting amongst themselves. The Welsh bard Aneurin's poem the *Gododin* is the tale of a battle lost after too much drinking, as the various refrains indicate: "They were foolhardy, our warriors, after becoming drunk . . . Only one man returned from the over-congenial feast . . . With Mynyddawg, the libations were disastrous." Livy gives this love of drink as the reason for the ease with which the exiled dictator Camillus, who had led a small army from Ardea, cut the throats of the sodden Gauls as if they were sheep.

In Rome, meanwhile, the siege of the stronghold continued. And it was then that the celebrated incident of the Capitoline geese occurred, an episode which betrays all the hallmarks of legend. For the protective role of birds is a constant theme in Celtic epic, whereas this is the only incident of its kind in Roman literature apart from the tale of Marcus Valerius' fight against a giant Gaul which Livy and various other writers record as a much later event. This Gaul appears to belong to the same tradition as Cú Chulainn. Quoting from the *Historiae* of Claudius Quadrigatus, Aulus Gellius describes him as "naked without any other armour of weapons than a shield and two swords". The Gaul, "cries out in a fearful voice, challenging anyone who wishes to confront him to stand forward. The huge size and dreadful face of the Barbarian inspire so much terror that no one dares reply. Then the Gaul starts to laugh and to stick out his tongue at the Romans." This description, which is more detailed than Livy's (VII, 26) but was obviously drawn from the same source, is exactly like the account in the Irish *Tain Bo Cualnge* of Cú Chulainn, armed with two spears and a shield, magically contorting his body to frighten his enemies. "Then the first contorsion occurred in Cú Chulainn; it was terrible, marvellous, multiple, incredible . . . He deformed his features, his face . . . His mouth was monstrously twisted . . . His hair stuck out in spikes around his head." When the Roman Marcus Valerius dares to fight the Gaul, a crow appears by some miracle to protect him and help him overcome his enemy, thereby earning him his nickname Corvinus.

Both Valerius' crow and Juno's sacred Capitoline geese belong to a very wide-spread mythical theme among the Celts. They are part of the theme of the heroic man, a kind of god, who is kept safe from danger by celestial powers manifesting themselves as birds, since the bird flies in the sky and itself belongs to the Other World.[8] One of the foremost of these is the Irish war goddess, the Mórrígan [demon of the night], the daughter of Buan [the eternal] or of Ernmas [murder]. The Mórrígan is also known as Bodb [the crow or raven] since she appears in the form of a bird. D'Arbois de Jubainville has identified her and her sisters as the three cranes with a bull carved on the *Tarvos Trigarannos*, a Gallo-Roman altar stone found in the foundations of Notre Dame and now in the Cluny Museum. The bull is the objective of *The Cattle Raid of Cooley*. The Mórrígan, as a crane, "landed on the raised stone . . . She tried to warn the Brown Bull of Cooley of the danger." She roused the warriors by chanting, "Crows gnaw men's necks. The blood of the warriors spurts out." Another passage in the *Tain Bo Cualnge* describes crows hovering around the two fighting heroes. "These birds descended onto the bodies of the two warriors and carried drops of blood, pieces of flesh from their wounds and scars into the air and right up to the clouds." A good warrior is one who knows "the way of the black ravens". The French romance *Didot-Perceval* tells of a fight between Perceval and Urbain, a medieval counterpart to the Welsh hero Uryen, son of Kynvarch, in which a flock of birds "blacker than anything he had ever seen" comes to defend Urbain. Perceval kills one of the birds which changes into the corpse of a girl, and it transpires that the birds are the sisters of Urbain's wife Modron, the Welsh goddess. Modron is easy enough to identify with the Gallic goddess Matrona who gave her name to the Marne, with the Irish Mórrígan, or even the Morgan la Fée of the Arthurian cycle. A virtually identical adventure occurs in the *Quête du Saint-Graal*, and bird-women appear in a number of epics, notably the *Conception of Cú Chulainn*. In his comments on the Welsh romance of *Culhwch and Olwen*[10], Joseph Loth mentions a legend from the *Iolo Manuscripts* which tells how Drutwas ab Tryffin had acquired some birds which obeyed his every command. Having issued a challenge to Arthur, Drutwas then sent his birds to the appointed place with an order to kill the first man who appeared. But Arthur was delayed and Drutwas, caught in his own trap, was torn to pieces by his birds. In his *Geographica*, (IV, 6), Strabo passes on a tradition recorded by Artemidorus. In an ocean port, when two people quarrelled over something "they would place a plank of wood in a high place, and set two cakes on this plank, one for each side". Crows, with white right wings, then flew down onto the cakes. "Whichever side saw his cake knocked off the plank had won." Of all the legends about protective birds, however, the strangest is undoubtedly contained in the Welsh *Dream of Rhonabwy*. Here Arthur and Owein, son of Uryen are playing chess. On two occasions messengers come to tell Owein that Arthur's men are chasing away his ravens. And twice Owein asks Arthur to stop them, but Arthur pretends not to have heard. The third time, Owein orders that the standard be raised, and his ravens fall on Arthur's men and slaughter them. Twice Owein refuses to stop his ravens. The third time he has the standard lowered and calm is restored. We are not told who these ravens are, nor what role they are playing. The end of the legend of *Owein* merely states that he "went to his own land with the three hundred swords of Kynverchin and his flight of ravens and they were victorious wherever they went".

There is doubtless some remnant of totemism in these epics, as there is in the epic of the Gallic Wars. But while traces of totemism were a familiar part of Celtic life, they appear to have been unknown amongst the Romans and Etruscans.[11]

Whatever the mythical aspects of Juno's geese, we do know that the Gauls' attack on the Capitol failed. A furious soldier named Manlius threw them bodily from the top of the Tarpeian Rock, earning himself the nickname Capitolinus. The history of the Gallic Wars actually contains two people called Manlius, though they may be one and the same. The second appears in Livy's Book VII in an episode which starts in a very similar way to the Corvinus incident with the giant Gaul. But then a new element creeps into the story in the shape of a bridge separating the Gauls from the Romans. This would appear to be nothing extraordinary, were it not that Livy describes it as a "bridge which no army would destroy so as to avoid showing their fear". Such an explanation must surely be mistaken. If the Romans were under attack, they could presumably have defended themselves quite easily by cutting the bridge as Horatius Cocles and his courageous companions had done during an Etruscan attack on Rome at the Pontus Sublicius. In the end, however, Manlius takes up the challenge of the giant Gaul and kills him. "The only outrage he committed on the prostrate corpse was to remove its necklace which he placed, still bloodstained, around his own neck," thereby winning himself the nickname Torquatus (from torc, the Gallic necklace).

The idea of the indestructible bridge is another common theme in Celtic epic literature. The bridge, and its equivalent the ford, form an untouchable boundary or point of contact between the worlds of the living and of the beyond. This concept is typified by the Ford of Souls in the Welsh romance of *Peredur*. "On one bank there was a flock of white sheep, and on the other a flock of black sheep. When a white sheep bleated a black sheep would cross the water and turn white, and when a black sheep bleated a white sheep would cross the water and turn black." The poetical vision of *Peredur* illustrates the druidic doctrine of the transmigration of souls, as expressed by Lucian in his *Pharsalia* (I, v, 60). "The same breath animates our bodies in another world, and death, if we understand your songs aright, is only the middle of a long life." The Irish *Voyage of Maelduin*, tells of a glass bridge leading to a magic fortress, while the medieval *Sone de Nansai* describes the island governed by Meleagant, an Other World character, as being linked to earth by a bridge of swords. In Chrétien de Troyes' *Chevalier à la Charette*, Lancelot du Lac crosses the "bridge under the water". The Irish heroes Fiachna and Loegaire also cross a "bridge under the water" to reach the castle of an underworld divinity. The crossing of such bridges or fords is subject to a number of taboos and any fights taking place there are inevitably magical. In the *Tain Bo Cualnge*, we read of many such taboos. In an attempt to stop the men of Ireland advancing, Cú Chulainn says, "It is forbidden to the men of Ireland to cross this ford before one of them has with one hand drawn out this fork which was buried with one hand". Indeed all those battles in which Cú Chulainn alone stands against the four armies take place on a ford, the ideal nomansland since spirits cannot cross the water.

When Fraech advances towards the ford where Cú Chulainn is bathing, Cú Chulainn says, "Do not come near me, if you do you will die . . ."; "Certainly I will come," replies Fraech, "I will come so far that we can meet in the water and your game with me will be equally hazardous for us both."

If Fraech's fight with Cú Chulainn is a game, then so too is the battle between Manlius Torquatus and the giant Gaul. The dead man is the victim of a ritual sacrifice in which the two combatants have exchanged roles. The Gaul is the guardian of the treasures of the Other World symbolized in his torc, a mark in Celtic art of the wearer's strength and divinity. The raising of the torc is a religious gesture represented on many coins, sculptures like the altar of Treves and on the Gundestrup Cauldron.[12] When Manlius sets foot on the other bank, seizes the torc (his sole preoccupation according to Livy) and puts it round his own neck he is, mythologically speaking, replacing the Gaul as guardian of the treasures. The legend of sacrifice recurs in the *De Prodigiis* of Julius Obsequens (LXX, frg. 19). "When the Salasses [or Salluvii] defeated the Romans [in 143] the decemvirs declared that they had read in the sybilline books that anyone wishing to make war on the Gauls had first to sacrifice on their frontiers."

The magical nature of the Gallic Wars extends not only to Manlius Torquatus, but also to Manlius Capitolinus, who defended the divine treasures of the Capitoline temples and barred the path to an imaginary bridge by throwing the Gauls off the Tarpeian Rock. Some years later, according to Aulus Gellius (XVII, 21), Manlius Capitolinus "was accused of having tried to seize the throne and condemned to death; and according the Varro he was thrown from the top of the Tarpeian Rock". If the story is true, the hero met an ironic end, though it may of course have been a legend put about by the vindictive Gauls.

Having failed to take the Capitol, the Gauls fell ill and were prepared to leave. Although this attack of disease can be quite naturally attributed to the unhealthy atmosphere of Rome, to which the Gauls were unaccustomed, it is worth noting that illness is frequently used in epic legend as a reason for an army's failure to capitalize on an advantage. The Greeks outside Troy fell sick after Apollo had vented his anger on them. Obviously the Gauls' collapse had to be explained away somehow, and the epidemic may have been invented by the Gauls themselves to excuse Brennus' army. The Romans would hardly have wasted an opportunity to take the credit for the downfall of their enemies, as some of them actually did. It therefore looks as though some magical affliction spread over the Gallic army, like the disease which struck down the Ulstermen in the *Tain Bo Cualnge* as a result of the curse of the goddess Macha.

The besieged Romans had also sunk so low as to start negotiations with the Gauls, in which the treasures, the good faith of the tribune Suplicius and the arrogance of Brennus were all weighed in the balance. This episode is the only really authentic passage in Livy's account of the Gallic War. Their ignominious offer of ransom inflicted a lasting wound on Roman pride and on what could then be described as their avaricious meanness. They afterwards called on their allies to help them pay the ransom, as if they were some chosen race. Justinus records how the people of Marseilles clubbed together to help Rome (XLIII), and a good many other cities must have followed this example.

In any case, the Gauls left Rome peacefully with their ransom, undisturbed by any attack from Camillus, for the Roman victory was a later invention intended to soothe the wounded pride of Rome. Indeed the Gauls appear to have won considerable support from the Romans who, according to Frontinus "went so far as to carry them to the other side of the Tiber and send them supplies" (II, 6). Polyaenus adds that "the Romans treated them like friends, sent them wine . . . They drank too much of it and became intoxicated. The Romans, finding them asleep, killed them all. And so that it would look as if they were respecting their agreement [they were to leave one of the gates of Rome permanently open], they erected a gate on an inaccessible outcrop and left that open" (VIII, 25). As we can see, there are any number of legends connected with the Gauls and Rome.

Theoretically, the vast Celtic epic which inspired Livy ends at this point. But as the wars against the Gauls continued intermittently until Caesar's time, we may justifiably expect to find elements of legend scattered at various points throughout Livy's work and the work of other Greek and Latin authors.

At the beginning of Livy's Book XXXIX, there is a very curious description of Liguria as a wasteland full of traps, very like the perilous, deserted moorlands dotted with enchanted castles in which the knights of the Round Table live out their magical adventures. The druidic forest described by Lucian in his *Pharsalia* (III, v. 399) is also, unless we are much mistaken, very similar to the forest of Broceliande.

Polybius's account of the battle between the Boii and the Transalpine Gauls who had actually come to their aid (II, 21) could easily be one of the many events based on mistaken identity which occur in the Arthurian romances. The battle of the Salluvian Gauls against Marseilles, recounted by Justinus (XLIII) comes to a strange end and can be examined according to similar criteria. The death of the Gallic chief Crixus during the Second Punic War, as described in remarkable epic style by Silius Italicus (IV, v. 180), the startling appearance of the Gauls described by Polybius (LL, 29) and Livy's unexpected panegyric of the Gauls' unnatural courage (XXXVIII, 21) all belong to the tradition which later gave birth to the Irish epic and the Welsh legends. The battles are no longer between men but between godlike and demoniacal heroes.

Then there is Livy's strange account of the battle of Clusium in his Book X, 26. At first sight it looks exactly like the disaster at the Allia, but in this case Livy adds what he had learnt of the Gauls' custom of decapitating their enemies and keeping the heads. According to Livy they bore these severed heads "on the breasts of their horses". This custom is not a legend, though it did give rise to legendary stories. The remains of the Provençal cities of Glanum, Saint-Blaise and Entremont, and the Borély Museum in Marseilles all contain pillars from which such heads were hung and which still bear the nails used as hooks. The Borély Museum, the Aix Museum and the Clavet Museum at Avignon also have Gallic sculpture representing severed heads.[13] And then there are the Gallic coins of the Osismi, a number of which show heads which look very like trophies of war.[14] Diodorus Siculus (V, 29) and Strabo (IV, 4) are in virtual agreement on this subject. "They cut the heads from fallen enemies and attach them to their horses' necks. They give blood-stained spoils to their servants to carry and sing the chant of death and the hymn of victory. They nail these trophies to the doors of their houses . . . The heads of their most famous enemies, they embalm in cedar oil and preserve like relics." Compare that with the legendary accounts and we can see the similarities clearly.

"Cú Chulainn cut off the heads and put one on each of the four points of the fork. He unleashed the horses before the Irish army . . . It seemed to Cú Chulainn that to take the clothes, horses and weapons of the men he had killed would have been an ignoble act." (*Tain Bo Cualnge*) "A bronze palisade surrounds the castle and a man's head is fixed on each stake . . . The young man overcame Coinchend Cenfada [Dog-head, Long-head], he cut off his head and went and placed it on an empty stake." (*Eachtra Airt Meic Cuind*). "Goreu seized Yspaddaden Penkawr [Big-head] by the hair, cut off his [Bran's] head and made to cross the sea with it." (*Branwen*) "Two girls entered bearing a large platter with a man's head covered in blood on it." (*Peredur*) "I carry at my side the head of Uryen, the generous chief of the army[15]." "I have an axe, let one of you take it and cut off my head today; tomorrow I will cut off his." (*Feast of Briciu*) "I know that you will not go without my head; so I give you my head as well as yours." "The head of Lugaid was placed on a stone . . . and, wondrous to relate, the head had melted the stone and passed through it." "Every time the Ulstermen killed a hero, they drew his brains from his head, mixed the brains with earth and made a hard ball."[16]

Livy himself expatiates quite calmly on the fate that befell the head of the consul Postumius, killed by the Boii, which was decorated with gold and used as a ritual drinking vessel (XXIII, 24). This would appear to corroborate certain suggestions, made specifically in connexion with the hero Bran, that the sacred use of severed heads has links with the myth of the Grail.

The death of Postumius, however, raises various other problems. To start with, there is some confusion between the many Postumii who acted as consuls at various different times. Livy places the event in 216 BC during the Second Punic War, but he is very rarely reliable about dates. When it comes to mentioning another consul Postumius who was defeated by the Gauls in his Book X, he even states that there is some disagreement about the events of that year.

One of the best known of the Postumii was the consul who found himself and his army enclosed in the ravine of Fourches Caudines by the Samnites in 321, and who was later captured. And then there was the early Postumius who was beaten in battle in a forest, supposedly by the Sabines. Julius Obsequens (LXXXVI) tells of yet another consul Postumius who in 154 "before leaving to take up office, had made a sacrifice. In several of the sacrifical victims, the upper part of the liver was found to be missing. But he went nevertheless and nine days later he was taken back to Rome ill, to die there." In that year, adds Julius, the Gauls inflicted heavy defeats on the Romans. Obviously the name Postumius brings bad luck. It is used as a kind of generic term for the ill-starred hero, amalgamating several characters now forgotten into one symbolic figure.

Apart from the legendary ritual implicit in the use of Postumius' head, we can also discern a strange epic theme underlying the apparently historical events which led up to the consul's death. Frontinus' account of this episode is very like Livy's, except that he does not mention Postumius at all and merely relates a tale to which he attributes no date, almost as if it were part of folk-lore. "The Boii hid themselves on the edge of a forest on their route. They sawed through the trees until the trunks were held on their stumps by a single thread; then, when the troops passed through, they pushed down the nearest trees which fell, one on top of another, to crush the majority of the army." (Frontinus, I. 6.) The supposed effects of this ruse differ from author to author. Livy states, "Everything was crushed, men, weapons and horses: scarcely ten soldiers escaped," which seems an extraordinary achievement for a few falling trees when we remember that a whole legion was involved, or, as Dio Cassius puts it, about 25,000 men. It is hard to take the story literally. There may have been a battle, but it was probably a minor skirmish between a few Roman soldiers and a band of Gauls lying in ambush. Two possible explanations for the tale suggest themselves. Either Livy, and those who followed his version, were camouflaging a Roman defeat behind a mythological mishmash, which is quite plausible considering they had done so before; or else the tale was drawn from a fable of Gallic origin which was still common currency in the Cisalpine countryside.[17] For Livy's tale is actually an account of a battle between men and trees, exactly like that in the Welsh *Kat Goddeu* or Battle of the Bushes, a poem attributed to the bard Taliesin. The *Kat Goddeu* is a confusing and complex work, but the bare outlines of the story emerge clearly enough. During the course of a war, the Britons found themselves hard pressed by the enemy. Fortunately they had with them the powerful magician, Gwyddyon, son of Don, who cast a spell over his men:

> Take the form of trees
> and stand in battle line.
> Then they were magically changed into trees . . .[18]

An improbable, though poetical, battle then takes place, together with much further comment of an esoteric and metaphysical nature. The bard describes the heroism of the various trees, the oaks, pears, hazels, birches, elms, cherries and so on. And in the end, this ruse helps the Britons to win the day.

It is no coincidence that the same legendary tradition appears both in the Welsh poem and in the mythical, epic account of the Gallic expeditions against the South.

Whether these expeditions achieved anything, and whether the Gauls themselves considered them successful are more debatable points. The rout at the Allia was a magical phenomenon. The capture of Rome was only half a victory. The Gauls may have annihilated many Roman armies, but they too were slaughtered in great numbers and, perhaps more seriously, ultimately became assimilated. But the Celts would not have measured success in such terms. They appear to have delighted in stories with what we would call unhappy endings, in expeditions which brought no earthly rewards but spiritual enrichment. The Quest for the Grail ends in death for Galahad and Perceval who find it; only Bohort survives. The Round Table story also ends in total disaster, with Arthur and all his knights, except Bohort, being killed. Bran's stormy expedition to Ireland is so catastrophic that "there was no victory save for the escape of seven men" (*Branwen*). The Welsh bard Aneurin finishes his poem *Gododin* with the words "Of three score generals who hastened to Kattraeth, only one man returned home . . .[19]" In a poem describing Arthur's expedition to the Other World, Taliesin uses the following line as a refrain:

> Except for seven, no one returned from Kaer
> Sidhi . . .[20]

Even the great *Raid of Cooley* proves vain, for the bull over which the two sides fight eventually dies and there is neither winner nor loser. Celtic legend is the legend of blood and of death. "Not a single enemy escaped to bear the news," writes Livy (V, 49). Yet this is how the Celts entered history, as every race has done, through legend. And as the Celts left no written legends of their own, we must look for them in the fragmentary, romanized, but fascinating versions left us by Livy. For there is much to be learnt about the Celts from this great writer, provided that we remember that he was a Roman and an ardent patriot whose Gallic origins drew him towards the magical and imaginary tales of a race which refused to die.

CHAPTER FOUR

Delphi and Celtic Adventure[1]

CCOUNTS of the Celtic expeditions out of Gaul in the 4th and 3rd centuries BC have a legendary quality which makes it hard to take the historians of antiquity at face value. We have already seen the vast Celtic mythological epic shining through Livy's work on the capture of Rome and the Gallic wars. But the less well-known Gallic expedition into Greece and thence to Delphi is similarly strange and disquieting, both because of the epic nature of certain episodes and because of the ambiguity in the writings of historians like Pausanias and Diodorus Sicilus. The one certainty is that there was a Gallic invasion of the Balkan countries and of Asia Minor which culminated in the foundation of the kingdom of Galatia. However, the recorded evidence is so confused that even the central element of the whole adventure, the capture of Delphi, remains unsure. Without denying that the events took place, we must realize that what we are reading is yet another synthesis in which history merges into one of the fanciful dreams born of the exalted and creative imagination of the Celts, who saw everything on an ideographical plane.

This particular expedition originated in the great *ver sacrum* or sacred spring when young people migrated towards new lands which Livy dates as taking place at the time when Tarquinius Priscus was reigning in Rome. The Bituriges were then the largest and most influential tribe in Gaul and their king, Ambigatus, sent his nephews to attempt the great adventure. The one, Bellovesus turned towards Italy with an army composed of various tribes from Celtica, while the other, Segovesus went towards the Hercynian forest beyond the Rhine.[2]

There is no further historical evidence of Bellovesus' and Segovesus' activities, though we can presume that the conquest of Cisalpine Gaul and the capture of Rome were an extension of the Italian contingent's migration. Whether this means that Segovesus went on to conquer the Balkan area is more difficult to determine. In his summary of a lost work by the Gaul Trogus Pompeius, the Latin historian Justinus corroborates Livy's account of the expeditions without naming the leaders. According to Justinus, three hundred thousand men left Gaul, some going to Italy, others "guided by the flight of birds" crossing Illyria and settling in Pannonia (XXIV, 4).

It was possible to reach Illyria and Pannonia both by way of the Black Forest and the Danube and by way of the Po Valley. The Gauls who settled in Pannonia may therefore have originally been members of the Italian expedition. But in that case they would have had to cross the Adriatic coastal area occupied by the Venetians who had settled there some time before and formed a fairly cohesive force.

It seems more likely that the Gauls followed the Danube and then headed South, across the Eastern Alps, drawn by the mild climate and the hope of finding wealthy and mysterious new lands. It was then that they came up against the Illyrian peoples.[3] The Illyrian Wars appear very complicated and belong as much to the realm of fable as of politics. In about 393 BC, the most powerful of the Illyrian tribes, the Antariates, who were in constant conflict with the Macedonians, removed Philip's father, Amyntos II, from the throne. When Philip became king, he used the Gauls to establish a second front behind the Antariates. Indeed there is evidence that Alexander followed his father's example for Arrian tells in his *Anabasis* (I, 4) how the Gauls made a treaty of friendship with the conqueror of the world, proudly declaring themselves afraid of nothing except that the sky would fall on their heads, a statement which did not fail to impress their audience.

The Gauls probably demanded that the Macedonian king pay them handsomely for their help, for considerable numbers of golden "Philip" staters have been found in the lands occupied by the Danubian Celts. The fact that no such coins have been found in the home of the Cisalpine Gauls would suggest that the Gauls in Greece had indeed arrived by way of the Black Forest and the Danube, the Gauls in Italy being kept there by the wall of Venetians.

In 310 BC the Gauls launched a large-scale offensive which panicked the Antariates into mass flight. The true reasons for this exodus are rather difficult to discern. Appian (*Illyrica* IV) claims that Illyria was invaded by swarms of frogs and that these animals emitted such a stench that there was an outbreak of plague which decimated the Antariates. The survivors fled, but were forced by the neighbouring tribes, who feared infection, to settle in waste and marshy areas. Appian claims to be basing his tale on an eye-witness account by Ptolemy, son of Lagos, although he tends to list his events at random without any regard to chronology. And it appears much more likely that he had picked up some legendary tale of a mythological battle fought by supernatural powers. Atheneus views events in a more rational, if frivolous way (X, 60). In his version, the Gauls were supposed to have exploited the Illyrians' deplorable habit of indulging in unbridled orgies and tricked them into attending an extraordinary drinking bout, at which they had mixed the wine and food with a herb "which relaxes the stomach". One can just picture the Antariates being felled by colic rather than blows.

Whatever the reason, however, the Antariates were indeed overcome and the Gauls settled in their homelands. Appian adds to existing confusion on the subject by saying that the Antariates called the Gauls "Cimbri", but we can be certain that there really were Gauls in Illyria around 290 BC. Two centuries had elapsed since the departure of Segovesus. The Illyrian Wars lasted about fifty years.

It was probably then that cultural exchanges took place between the Asian Scythians and the Western Gauls. The Gauls saw Bohemia, Pannonia and Illyria as areas of strategic importance, offering contact with the Eastern Mediterranean. The Danubian Celts may well have been responsible for coinage appearing in Gaul. They acquired Macedonian coins as part of the large settlements they received from the Balkan kings, either to refrain from fighting or to attack common enemies. And these coins circulated back through the interjacent Celtic peoples until they reached Belgica, where they were copied by the Ambiani and the Venelli. As native Gallic coinage developed, it gradually altered to fit the artistic and religious aspirations of the different tribes. The advent of coinage was an event of prime importance in the history of Gaul and of Celtic civilization. For, apart from the development of monetary trade as opposed to barter in kind, the coins offered an outlet for religious and philosophical expression among a people whom Ammianus Marcellinus describes as "taking pleasure in commenting on the sublime secrets of nature, their minds ever straining towards the most abstract and difficult of questions" (XV, 9). It is hardly surprising, therefore, that Gallic coinage should have been continually changing, continually directed towards the most symbolic and abstract forms of representation.[4]

However, the Gauls in Illyria were becoming restless. As believers in an all-governing dynamism, they were anxious to be on the move again. The Celts looked upon the present as a mere function of the future, as a continual process of evolution.

The legends of Brittany, Wales and Ireland all serve to illustrate this theme. The mark made by the Celts on the ancient historians is no more than a manifestation of their anti-historic desire to deny the present and create the future, if only in the imagination. This singular attitude is inherent both in the capture of Rome and the expedition to Delphi; and was later responsible for the 12th century Round Table Romances of Christian Europe, a cycle of magical adventures to match the aspirations of a fallen race which refused to accept that it had died.

The Gauls' choice of Macedonia as their initial area of expansion was probably dictated by two considerations. First, they knew that Alexander's expeditions had left the Macedonian leadership in some disarray; and second, the capture of Macedonia would enable them to isolate the rest of Greece and push on towards Asia. The Gauls therefore split into three groups, one of which marched into Macedonia under the command of Bolgios, possibly a Belgian, and crushed the army of Ptolemy Keraunos. The king of Macedonia was killed and his head borne aloft on a spear. Bolgios ordered a human sacrifice, but there things rested.[5]

The March on Delphi

It was then that Brennus made his first appearance, the second Brennus as he is sometimes called to distinguish him from the Senonian chief who captured Rome. But while the Roman Brennus was little more than a minor military leader with luck on his side, the second Brennus had a profound influence on the events that followed. If there is a Celtic epic in Greece, then he is its hero. As commander with Kichorios[6] of the third section of the Gallic army, he was angry that Bolgios had been content to rest on his laurels. A figure of great daring and temerity, he immediately raised a powerful army by means of flagrant propaganda not only among the Gauls but also among the indigenous peoples. Even the Gauls' former enemies, the Antariates of Illyria probably sent a strong contingent of men into Greece under Brennus' command (Appian, *Illyrica*, IV). Brennus painted a glowing picture of the Greek treasures and had no scruples in suggesting that Greek resistance would be weak by drawing unfavourable comparisons between the short Greeks he had taken prisoner and the strong and well-built Gauls (Polyaenus, VII, 35). Having thus assembled over 150,000 foot soldiers and 2000 horsemen, Brennus set off to conquer Greece.

Pausanias the geographer relates this conquest in some detail in his Book X. Brennus succeeded in crossing his whole army over the river Sperchios, although the bridges had been cut. He then laid siege to the town of Heraclea and, having driven out the garrison there, marched on to Thermopylae where he defeated an army raised by a confederation of Greek cities. The Greeks were afforded a temporary respite when Brennus decided to cross Mount Oeta by way of various secret passages known to him only to find that these pathways were guarded by a contingent of Etolians. But despite Gallic doubts about the potential success of their manoeuvres, Brennus successfully tricked the Etolians into abandoning their positions by sending two of his lieutenants to devastate the Etolian homelands. When the Greek soldiers hastened home to defend their families, Brennus left Kichorios with the bulk of the army and took 40,000 men to cross Mount Oeta, guided by his new allies from Heraclea. It so happened that the mountain was shrouded in a dense mist that day and the Phoceans posted on the pass were taken totally by surprise..

Brennus then advanced across Greece, looting everything he could find. Dissatisfied with such paltry rewards, however, he decided to go on to Delphi which was reputed to be the treasure house of Greece. The historians naturally accuse Brennus of sacrilege, a criticism to which he would have retorted , "the gods do not need treasures since they shower them so liberally upon men" (Justinus, XXIV, 6). This line of argument is perfectly in accordance with the way he laughed aloud on entering a temple to see that the Greeks represented their gods in human form.[7]

Without waiting for Kichorios, Brennus and his army of 40,000 set off to attack the temple of Apollo, the ultimate goal of his expedition. But the Gauls dispersed to plunder and drank too much wine. While Brennus was wasting valuable time regrouping his men and urging them on with promises of fabulous spoils, the Greeks took the opportunity to consolidate their defences at Delphi. Finally, however, the reassembled Greek army charged headlong into battle.

At this point Pausanias, who is otherwise very close to Diodorus Sicilus, Justinus and even Cicero[8] as far as the main events of the story are concerned, enters fully into the realm of legend with earthquakes, thunderbolts which reduce the soldiers to ashes, snow storms, showers of great stones and "ancient heroes appearing in the heavens". It appears that after a long battle the Gauls were forced to retreat before they could reach the Delphic treasurers. And yet there is a tradition which obstinately maintains that they did indeed sack the temple. This tradition is mentioned by Strabo (IV, 1) in connexion with the hoard of gold in Toulouse reputed to have come from Delphi. Diodorus Sicilus even says in a different context (V, 32)

that the Gauls ransacked the temple and there were a number of legends current
about the Cursed Gold of Delphi to which Atheneus alludes (IV, 4) with reference
to the tribe of Scordisci.

A curse seems to have fallen on the Gauls. The following night they were seized
by some inexplicable panic and in the confusion began to kill one another. When
they finally regained their camp at Heraclea, after some difficulty, Brennus who
had been wounded three times became drunk, presumably during some festivities,
handed the command to Kichorios and "poisoned himself, since he felt responsible
for all the ill luck which had befallen the Gauls and feared resentment from his
fellow citizens" (Pausanias, X, 32). Justinus' version of Brennus' death is that
"being unable to bear his pain, he put an end to his days with a blow from a
dagger" (XXIV, 8), while Diodorus Sicilus, who adds more detail, says that
Brennus advised the Gauls to kill him but eventually "killed himself with a dagger" (fragment XXII).

The Gallic epic in Delphi and in Greece virtually ends with the death of its hero.
His successor Kichorios buried him, killed the wounded and marched back with
what remained of the expeditionary force. The Gallic army was gradually whittled
away in ambushes and Justinus and Diodorus both claim that not a single Gaul
returned home. It is worth pointing out, however, that these same two writers,
Polybius (IV, 45) and Livy (XXXVIII, 16), all refer to the remnants of Brennus'
army as being the Gauls who moved on to Byzantium and thence into Asia Minor
where they founded Galatia. Appian even goes so far as to say that some of the
Gauls returned to the Pyrenees, which would explain how the Tectosages of
Toulouse came to acquire the Delphic gold (*Illyrica*, IV).

The Gold of Delphi

The Gallic expedition to Delphi had failed just as the Gauls in Italy had failed,
though, as we have already noted, the Celts found spiritual victory in material
defeat. No matter how serious the intentions of the Greek and Latin historians, the
constant interplay of magic and realism in their accounts casts considerable doubt
on their historical accuracy. The unreal, irrational atmosphere colouring the whole
story of the Celts at this time exactly matches their own anti-historical attitude.
For the Celts entered history through legend at a time when the Greeks and the
Romans already had a written history. The Latin historian Ammianus Marcellinus, writing in the 4th century AD, even admits that "lacking precise evidence,
the ancient authors have passed on to us only rather incomplete ideas about the
Gauls and their origins" (XV, 9).

The very way in which the Gauls were defeated at Delphi, by the elements
unleashed by an angry god, rather than at the hands of man, is lifted almost word
for word from Herodotus' account of the Median Wars. "When the Persians
approached the sanctuary of Pallas Pronoas . . . a thunderbolt fell from the
heavens upon them and two huge chunks of rock broken from Parnassus came
crashing down upon them with a terrible din, crushing large numbers. Finally a
voice and a warcry were heard emerging from the temple of Pallas. In the face of so
many simultaneous marvels, the Barbarians were seized with terror." (Herodotus,
VIII, 36.) There is no doubt that Pausanias, Diodorus, Justinus and even Cicero
all plagiarized from Herodotus for their accounts of the events at Delphi. It is
possible that the Greeks and the Romans deliberately embroidered on Herodotus'
theme to mask what may well have been a disaster of considerable proportions for

the Greeks. When we remember that Livy was quite prepared to invent a retaliatory counter-offensive by Camillus against the Gauls who took Rome, it seems
quite feasible that the Gauls did indeed succeed in sacking the temple of Apollo,
despite his divine protection.

Apart from the fragments of Diodorus Siculus who lived in the first century AD,
the most important source for a possible Gallic epic here is the *World History* by
Justinus which is an abridged version of a much longer, and unfortunately lost
work by the Augustan historian Trogus Pompeius. Trogus was a Vocontian Gaul
and must have been familiar with some of the Gallic traditions concerning the
expedition to Delphi. Since he pre-dated Pausanias and Appian, we can assume
that they drew much of their material from him, and thus from the Gallic version.
Diodorus has clearly shown in his Book V that he knew of a number of Celtic
customs and traditions.

Considering how much of the classical writings on these events was influenced
by Celtic fables, it is also conceivable that the Gold of Delphi, the Cursed Gold,
was a fictitious myth like the Grail, and thus the object of a fabulous expedition.
This argument would appear to be supported by various facts. First, there is no
real confirmation that Delphi was looted; second, there is the choice of Delphi as
goal of the expedition; and finally, there is the whole mythological background to
the story.

As Strabo correctly states, the Treasures had already been looted by the Phoceans during Philip's time, a fact of which Brennus who appears to have known so
much else about Greece was surely aware. His determined march on Delphi is
more likely, therefore, to have been prompted by religious motives. Delphi was the
most revered of the sacred sanctuaries to Apollo, the sun-god; and the notion of a
sun-god with all its attendant symbolism and metaphysical implications was an
Indo-European import into the West espoused by the early Celts, Acheans and
Latins alike. According to Diodorus Siculus, who borrowed the basis of his account
from the Phocean navigator Pytheas, island Britain was the birthplace of Leto,
Apollo's mother, "which explains why the islanders worship Apollo in particular.
They are all, so to speak, priests of that god . . . One can also see in that island a
huge enclosure dedicated to Apollo, and a magnificent round temple and a number
of offerings". This temple is obviously the megalithic monument of Stonehenge.
Diodorus continues, "Apollo is said to descend to this island every nineteen years"
and the inhabitants "are kindly disposed towards the Greeks and Delians, and
these feelings go back to very distant times." (Diodorus II, 47.)

The idea of Apollo's being Hyperborean is part of obscure and ancient Indo-
European traditions. The links between the inhabitants of Britain and the Greeks
have their origins in that fund of legends told by Herodotus and Pliny the Elder
about the Hyperboreans and Apollo's birth at Delos.[9] Cicero actually distinguishes
between four different Apollos, the third of whom "left the Hyperborean regions
for Delphi and was the son of the third Jupiter and of Leto." (*De Natura Deorum*,
III, 23.)

In his list of the gods worshipped by the Gauls, which includes Apollo, Jupiter,
Minerva and Mars, Caesar lays special emphasis on the cult of Mercury, though
perhaps without realizing the full implications of this worship. For the Gallic
Mercury has been identified with Lug, the divinity recorded in a number of towns
including Lyon, Laon and Leyde, which were all Lugdunum (the stronghold of
Lug). Apart from being the hero of a number of Irish epics, Lug is known to have
been one of the gods of the ancient Celtic world, and his roles as artistic innovator,

initiator and *psychopompus* (like the Greek Hermes) all affirm the Mercurial aspect of his character. What tends to be overlooked, however, is the Apollonian aspect. For Lug's name means whiteness or brightness and the Irish epics make him a shining, solar hero who, like the setting sun, never really dies. Both he and Apollo have their sacred animal in the crow, which happens to be one of the meanings of his name. Finally, Lug reigns over the Tuatha de Danann, the mythical people of the Irish mounds and of the Other World, who can be identified with the equally mythical Cimmerians and Hyperboreans. It would therefore appear that the Gauls' worship of Mercury was very much connected with the cult of an heroic, solar god. Apollo himself is also represented on Gallo-Roman inscriptions by the name Maponius. And the Gallic Maponios is comparable to the Welsh mythological figure of Mabon, son of Modron, who enters Arthurian legend on various occasions as a prisoner.[10] In this respect he is surely reminiscent of that Hyperborean Apollo who, as the sun, remains in his prison for six months, but never dies.

Apollo was also known among the Gallo-Romans as Belenus, the shining one. But, tempting as it may be to draw comparisons between Apollo-Belenus and Lug, the bright one, especially as one of the Greek epithets for Apollo was *Lukios*, Belenos derives his name from the Indo-European root word for apple, as does Apollo. We have already discussed the connexions between Belenos, Apollo, the apple and amber in the chapter on the Cimbri; but further clues as to the solar nature of Belenos can also be found in the place names he gave to Gaul.

There are places called Saint-Bonnet (Mons Belenos) in the Massif Central, the fountain of Barenton (once Belenton) in the forest of Paimpont-Brocéliande, and many places named Bel-Air throughout France. But perhaps the most significant of all is the mountain of Bel-Air in Côtes-du-Nord, which is also known as the *Signal de Bel Orient* (Rising Sun). In this case Bel is obviously no adjective, but an abbreviation of the name of the solar god.

These considerations have brought us to the nub of the whole problem concerning the Gauls' expedition to Delphi. For surely the gold they had come to seek was not a precious metal, but the sanctuary of the Hyperborean Apollo. Atheneus speaks of the Gauls "who went armed under Brennus' command to consult the oracle at Delphi" (VI, 4). Seen from this perspective, the Gallic leader's outburst of laughter in the temple becomes an expression of his contempt for the idols and of his desire to restore the solar cult to its erstwhile glory, to the exalted position still accorded it by druidism. For greedy and sacrilegious as the Greek authors claimed him to be, the fact that Brennus did not even look at the gold and silver offerings there (Diodorus, fragment XXII) proves that he was interested in more than material riches.

Then there is the significance of Delphi as the centre of the world or *omphallos*. There was even a stone before the temple of Apollo which marked this central point. The name $\Delta\varepsilon\lambda\varphi o\iota$ came from $\Delta\varepsilon\lambda\varphi\iota\varsigma$, the symbol of the inhabitants of the water and thus, according to the zodiac, the symbol of the creator. It was only later that it was dedicated to Pythian Apollo after his victory over the serpent Python. This victory, which can be equated with the Christian story of Saint Michael, represents the dynamic aspect of the divinity, symbolized in the zodiac by the scorpion. As a result, Delphi became the place from which this divinity radiated its energy, just as the sun spreads its rays round its fiery orb.

While the sun is the most perfect image of the divinity, it is symbolically represented by gold. The gold of Delphi is therefore the image of god, and a perfectly valid image for the Celt who rejected anthropomorphism. Brennus is drawn towards Delphi as the goal of an expedition into sacred ground, just as the Celts were obsessed by the idea of quests into the Other World. And once he had reached his objective, Brennus could only die, as the Galahad of legend had to die.

Moreover, the concept of *omphallos* is very much part of Celtic tradition. Just as there was a stone before Apollo's temple at Delphi, so at Tara, the centre of Ireland and the seat of the High King, there was a magic coronation stone called the *Lia Fail*, Stone of Fal. Even today, the isle of Dumet in the Guérande peninsula, which is the geodetic centre of the emergent lands, has all kinds of strange traditions and superstitions attached to it, including tales of a lost treasure.

Why Delphi should have been chosen as the site of the *omphallos* we do not know, although Plutarch does mention the following legend in his treatise on the *Disappearance of the Oracles*. "According to a mythological tradition, some eagles or swans, having left the ends of the earth to reach the centre, met at Pytho, near what is called the *omphallos*. As time passed Epimenides of Phaestos is said to have asked a god whether this tale was true, and obtaining only an obscure and ambiguous pronouncement, he said 'On earth or on sea, no central navel except that known to the gods alone, not men'." Even so, ancient eye-witnesses describe the stone of the *omphallos* as being decorated with two eagles.

Finally, Delphi was a place of prophecy. The Pythian oracle was famous the world over. The Celts, too, had their oracles. The nine Gallic priestesses of the Isle of Sein were attributed with "the extraordinary ability to unleash the winds and storms, of knowing and predicting the future; but they kept their remedies and predictions for those who have journeyed over land and sea with the sole purpose of consulting them." (Pomponius Mela, III, 6.) If the Gauls were accustomed to consulting oracles of this kind during the course of their journeyings over land and sea, it is unlikely that they committed the sin of looting the sanctuary at Delphi simply out of greed. They must have been motivated by some more important reason.

This something was the search for the Blessed Land inhabited by strange women; the land of the Fairies, the Tirna-nOg (Mound of the Sons of Ogme), Avallon or Emain Ablach. In the Irish tale of the *Voyage of Bran son of Febal*, the hero Bran becomes spellbound by the song of a mysterious woman who sings the praises of the land of the fairies. She offers him a silver branch with white flowers on it and invites him to come with her, but vanishes before he can take it. Bran sets sail[11], discovers Emain and stays there. For Emain is the country whence no man returns. And Emain is the land of prophetesses, of women who possess knowledge of the future, just as Delphi is the land of the oracle and the Pythia.

Brennus the Blessed

The character who breathes life through this epic tale is Brennus, its hero, and it must be he who holds the key to the riddle.

Who was Brennus? Strabo believes him to have been a Prausian, though he tells us nothing more about that ancient tribe and merely proffers the comment in connexion with the Tectosages of Toulouse who took part in the Greek expedition and reputedly acquired the Delphic gold (Strabo, IV, 1.) Certainly, the Tectosages made their way to Asia Minor where they founded the kingdom of Galatia, together with the Trocmeians and the Tolisto-Boii. But Brennus' armies must have been composed of groups of warriors from all over Gaul, and even from Britain, if we are to believe the Triads. "Help went with Yrp Lluyddawc [the chief of the army] to Llychlyn . . . With these warriors he won victories wherever he went. He settled in two islands on the shores of the sea of Greece: Clas and Avena[12]." Although Llychlyn is usually used to denote Scandinavia, the Venerable Bede identifies it as Scythia and we know that the Eastern Celts had contact with the Scythians. Joseph Loth has suggested that Clas is a corruption of Gals or Galatia, and as Yrp Lluyddawc is clearly a cognomen, it is always possible that the character referred to is Brennus. In his *Historia Regum Britanniae* (XXXV-XXXVII), Geoffrey of Monmouth tells of two brothers named Belinus and Brennius who quarrelled over the kingdom of Britain, were reconciled and left together for the continent. In Geoffrey's account, Brennius went on to capture Rome, which brings us back to the first Brennus who led the Gauls at the Allia.

Historically a century separates the two Brennuses, but, in view of the mythology which grew up around them, they can only be one person. The heroes of legend never really die, and a hundred years was neither here nor there for the Celts. Their champions remained unfettered by logic and could even be reborn through the transmigration of souls.[13]

It has been argued that Brennus was the Latin form (and Brennos the Greek form) of Brenn, a petty king as in the Welsh *brenin*, a tribal king, derived from the root *bren* meaning height. But Brennus seems to be used much more as a proper name than as a title and a far more satisfactory explanation is that the name comes from the old Celtic word *brannos*, which gave rise to the word *bran*, the Irish, Welsh and Breton word for crow or raven.[14] It so happens that a character named Bran plays an important part both in the mythologies of Ireland and Wales and in the Arthurian tradition.

He first appears in Ireland as Bron, son of Ler, i.e. of the Waves, and brother of Manannan, chief of the Tuatha de Danann, who gave his name to the Isle of Man.[15] Of other epic characters called Bran or Fiach, another word for crow, it is worth singling out Bran mac Faibal, the hero of a strange voyage to the land of the fairies which, together with the Voyage of Maelduin, was used as a model for the *Voyage of Saint Brendan in search of Paradise*.[16] The imposition of Christian ethic on legendary material made the pagan hero into a saint.

Bron also appears in the *Didot-Percevel* by Robert de Boron as the Fisher King who guards the Grail[17], though as J. Vendryes says, "It was quite natural that the Welsh should have changed the Bron whom Irish legend had given them as brother of Manannan, into Bran, that they might beatify him." (*Manannan mac Lir*, Études Celtiques, VI, p. 253.) For in Welsh tradition he became Bran the Blessed or Bendigeit Vran who, according to the Triads "first brought the Christian faith to the nation of the Cymry from Rome where he had spent seven years as a hostage," and who founded one of the three saintly lines of the island. There is nothing in the legend of Bran, however, to suggest that he was a Christian or that he should be placed in such a pseudo-Christian context as the Round Table romances. For the legends are druidic in origin, if considerably adulterated. Even so, there is evidence from the rather confused picture of events in the Triads that the name Bran was closely linked with the idea of an expedition to the continent. "Bran, son of Dyvinwal, and Kustenin, son of Elen, had been emperors in Rome," though the Bran here is obviously the Brennius son of Dunvallo mentioned by Geoffrey of Monmouth.

The full significance of the legend of Bran, however, becomes clear in the Welsh mabinogi of *Branwen*, and it is this version which is most closely related to the story of Brennus. Bran has given his sister Branwen [White Crow] in marriage to

Matholwch, king of Iwerddon [Ireland]. But Matholwch is insulted by the Welsh and begins to treat Branwen like a common servant. Branwen manages to send a message to Bran, who organizes an expedition to Ireland partly to avenge his sister and partly to recover a magical cauldron which brings the dead back to life and which had been given to Matholwch as a gift. Bran crosses the sea, carrying his men on his back, and himself acts as a bridge over a river. Before long the expedition proves a failure. The cauldron of rebirth is broken, Bran is wounded and asks the seven survivors, who include his brother Manawyddan and the bard Taliesin, to cut off his head, carry it back to Britain and bury it in the White Hill at London. The seven survivors then spend seven years in the happy oblivion provided by the "hospitality of the head" before carrying out Bran the Blessed's last wishes.

Having once established that the complexities of mythology, however confusing, accord Bran and Brennus the same identity, the curious similarities between the Welsh legend and the pseudo-historical accounts by Pausanias, Diodorus and Justinus of events at Delphi are all too apparent.

Like Bran, Brennus sets off in search of treasure, but it is an ambivalent quest. For, just as the alchemist is attempting to manufacture a material substance and to construct a spiritual structure, so the Celt is motivated by the hope of acquiring both base, worldly riches and the fabulous treasures of the Other World. This theme recurs continually throughout Celtic epic, and is manifest in the Quest for the Grail, if not in its definitive fashion, then at least in a version comprehensible to the Western mind of today.

To start with, like every mythical adventure of this kind, Brennus' expedition is brought to an abrupt halt by water. Of course, there is nothing strange about the Gallic army's being confronted by the river Sperchios or having difficulty in crossing it, but legend has obviously influenced accounts of the event so powerfully that the boundaries between image and reality have become blurred. Water forms a natural frontier between man and man, between weapon and weapon, and between spirit and spirit, and effectively marks the threshold of the kingdom of the dead. But since the kingdom of the dead is forbidden to the living and vice versa, any crossing of the water is always attached to the idea of mythical trials and tests of endurance. Epic literature abounds in such episodes, from the *Odyssey* to the *Quête du Saint-Graal*. The voyage on the ferry of Charon, the ferryman in *Peredur*, the glass bridge of Maelduin, the Bridge of the Sword and the Bridge Under Water in Chrétien de Troyes' *Lancelot*, Manlius Torquatus' combat with a Gaul on a bridge in Livy's work, the fights on the fords in the Irish *Tain Bo Cualnge*, all these are typical examples of water's being regarded as a sacred boundary.

The "cunning and resourceful" Brennus, as Pausanias describes him, manages to cross his army over the Sperchios by arranging for some to swim across, some to use their shields as boats and some to wade over, the Gauls being tall enough to do so.

There is another reference to the use of shield as boat in the *Spoils of the Abyss*, an obscure and complex mythological poem attributed to the bard Taliesin. Here King Arthur and his companions are engaged in an expedition to the Other World to bring back a magic cauldron of knowledge and rebirth, but the story seems to be the same as Bran's.

> With three times the load of the boat Prytwen we went.
> But for seven, no one returned from Kaer Sidhi, the

> town of the Fairies . . .
> With three times the load of the boat Prytwen we went
> over the sea,
> But for seven, no one returned from Kaer Rigor. . .
> With three times the load of the boat Prytwen we left
> with Arthur,
> But for seven no one returned from Kaer Kould, the
> dark citadel
> (J.M. 83-85)

According to Geoffrey of Monmouth (IX, 4), the 'boat Prytwen" (white face, white shape) is Arthur's shield. In another poem attributed to Taliesin, the *Lament for Aeddon*, Gwyddyon and Aeddon "made a shield so strong that the sea could not engulf their best troops." (J.M. p. 93.) The idea of the tall men being able to wade across the Sperchios provokes the following comment from Pausanias: "It was an advantage which Brennus could easily identify among his troops, the Celts being taller than all other peoples." (IX, 4.) This height had acquired legendary and almost frightening proportions for the Romans and the Greeks, especially as the Gauls always placed their tallest and strongest-looking men in the frontline to impress the enemy.[19]

Celtic gigantism was nowhere more evident than in the legends of Cú Chulainn and Bran. In a Gaelic poem inserted into the tale of the *Murder of Curoi*, which seems to be the Irish version of the *Spoils of the Abyss*, the hero Cú Chulainn tells of his exploits during an expedition to a mysterious fortress from which he has brought back a cauldron:

> We took three cows
> They swam on the sea. . .
> When we set sail on the ocean,
> . . . the men of my boat were drowned. . .
> Then I bore. . .
> nine men on each of my hands,
> three on my head,
> and eight on my two thighs
> hanging onto my body[20]

The same theme recurs in the mabinogi of *Branwen*, this time with Bran as the hero. "Since the sea was not deep, he waded through . . . Bran took all the string musicians on his back and made for Ireland." Those who saw it were amazed. "What is the forest that was seen on the sea?' 'The masts and yardarms of the ships.' 'Alas! What is the mountain that was seen alongside the ships?' 'That was my brother Bran wading to shore.'" Having reached Ireland Bran is temporarily halted by a river. "His men said to him, 'Lord, you know the property of the river: no one can cross it nor is there any bridge. What do you propose for a bridge?' 'Simply this,' said Bran, 'Let him who is a chief be a bridge. . .' Bran then lay down across the river and hurdles were placed upon him, and so the host crossed over, on top of him." (*Branwen*) Brennus and his giants wading across the Sperchios belong to the same tradition. The mythical battle of the crossing of the waters has come to an end. Once on the other side Brennus "Turned his eyes towards the temples of the gods, as if he disdained the spoils offered him by the land" (Justinus,

XXIV, 6). For he was in another world, a kind of sacred land, the magical realm of the fairies.

The King of the Alder-Trees

Indeed, the fairies do appear in the shape of white virgins. Cicero immediately identifies them as snowflakes, while Diodorus Siculus thinks they were two goddesses, Pallas and Artemis, whose ancient chapels stood within the temple boundaries. The historians may have been thinking of the three Moerae, or Fates, who were particularly revered at Delphi. But the accounts we have of this part of the story seem very incomplete, and the white virgins appear to be guardians of the sanctuary, part of the mythological trappings essential to any sacred spot. Like the Pythia, they are Vestals, whose job it is to look after the sacred flame. And like the symbolic Roman fire which Plutarch describes as being obtained "by drawing a pure and unadulterated flame from the sun" (*Numa*, XIII), the fire of Delphi is clearly spiritual and intangible. The sun, and therefore Apollo, is obviously connected with the temple of the Vestals. Indeed, Numa Pompilius who started the institution may well have brought Celtic ideas and traditions with him to Rome.[21] The white virgins, the Pythia and the Vestals would seem to have much in common with the Sorceresses of the isle of Sein or the Namnetian women who Strabo describes as assembling "on an island opposite the mouth of the Loire and being possessed by Bacchanalian frenzy" (IV, 4).

We can also compare then with the strange maidens who guard the Grail Castle in the *Elucidation* and with the whole theme of guardian women already explored in the chapter on the Submerged Town. For any attack on a sanctuary guarded by women is bound to spark off disaster. At Delphi, the appearance of the white virgins coincides with snowfalls and a violent earthquake. The gods have come to play their part in what can be called "the ritual of rape". In the Irish tale of the *Battle of Mag Tured*, the appearance of the Mórrígan is the signal for terrible slaughter and for strange magical battles in the *Tain Bo Cualnge*. In her stand against the Roman legions, the Briton Queen Boudicca becomes a bloodthirsty fury and starts a chain of horrors which bring death to the Romans.[22] Indeed, the atrocities perpetrated by Boudicca take place in a sacred wood dedicated to Andarta, goddes of Victory, who was compared by the Romans to Bellona (from *bellum*, war, or Belenos, the Celtic god) or to Pallas-Minerva, one of the white virgins of Delphi.

The theme of the sacred wood is closely linked to the theme of guardian or warrior women. The *Myvyrian Archaeology of Wales*, a collection of ancient Welsh texts, claims that the battle of Goddeu celebrated by Taliesin[23], where the combatants were magically transformed into trees, was attended by "a man who could not be saluted unless his name were known, and on the other side a woman called Achren [trees] whose army could not be saluted unless her name were known". Taliesin himself does not name her, but describes her as "controlling the wild tumult at the head of the army". The fact that she has the qualities of "a shameless cow" suggests that she went naked into battle.

The battle of trees undoubtedly belongs to some very ancient and very complicated myth. Apart from Livy's use of the legend in his account of the death of Postumius, there is a further echo of the tradition in Strabo's description of the land of the Morini, Atrebatians and Eburones where the inhabitants form their defences by weaving together the branches of thorn trees and planting huge stakes in the ground (IV, 3). The theme recurs in a 13th century *chanson de geste*, the *Prise de Cordes* and in the *Chronique du Faux Turpin* (VIII-X) where the Franks who are laying siege to the town of Cordes, stick their spears into the ground where the shafts begin to sprout green leaves. It is possible that memories of this same tradition prompted Shakespeare to move Burnham Wood in Macbeth and Pliny the Elder to mention a forest felled by the Gauls during the expedition to Delphi (*Hist. Nat.* XXX, 1).

The *Myvyrian Archaeology of Wales*, however, has more to tell us about the battle of Goddeu. For it is to the warrior whose name must be known that Gwyddyon the magician who turned the Britons into trees cries out, "The high branches of the alder-tree are on your shield. Your name is Bran of the dazzling branches . . . The high branches of the alder-tree are in your hand; Bran you are by the branches you bear." This identification of Bran with the alder-tree is supported by Taliesin's lines, "The alder-trees at the head of the troop form the advance guard", which would also suggest that the chief of Britons in the battle was Bran. In the *Hostile Conjuration*, another poem by Taliesin, the bard writes, "I know why the alder-tree is purple in colour", presumably implying that the regal aspect of purple is associated with the alder and by implication with Bran. Aneurin also takes up the image in his *Incantations for Tutvwlch*, "The spear of alder wood is king. Around him are the horns and the bent swords". In the mabinogi of *Branwen*, Bran's sister gives birth to a son named Gwern, "alder-tree", who is tragically burnt in a fire like a piece of wood.

It is possible that the same myth is also expressed in Goethe's ballad, the *King of the Alders* (1781) which was inspired by the *Danish Popular Songs* translated by Herder. Here the king of the alders appears as the god of the Other World who sings the praises of his marvellous kingdom. Some critics have assumed that Herder misread king of the alders for king of the elves, there being no legendary alder king. Since elves are very much of the Other World, the sense of the ballad would be virtually unchanged by this interpretation. But there is no way of proving that Herder made any such mistake, and the symbolic nature of the alder-tree as it appears in Celtic mythology suggests that Goethe was right to use "King of the Alders".

What is beginning to emerge from this discussion is the special quality of the system of symbols used by the Celts, a system based on analogy and on the ternary significance of the object. In fact, *Gwern* could mean either alder-tree, mast or marsh according to context. Having identified Bran as the alder-tree, we can use this principle of analogy to make him mast and marsh also. Indeed he is linked with both these ideas in the mabinogi of *Branwen*, first as the mast of a boat when he transports his army to Ireland, and second as a marsh when he wades over the sea, less deep in those days according to *Branwen*. The name Bran itself (together with its variants Bron and Bren) has three different meanings: raven or crow, womb and height. He is a raven because he is a black god, the hero of the Other World. He is the womb because he owned the cauldron of abundance and rebirth. He is height because he was too tall to stand either in a house or a ship and was described in *Branwen* as "the mountain that was seen alongside the ships".

Once we have understood this process of analogy, the whole of Celtic mythology opens out in a new way before our eyes. For the identification of Bran with the alder-tree is only one link in an age-old chain of interwoven ideas. Suppose that we start our chain with the Bran = raven equation. We have already mentioned that the concept of raven can also be represented by Lug, the Celtic Mercury or Apollo.

But apart from raven, Lug could also mean light (from the same Indo-European root as the Latin *lux*) and whiteness (like the Greek *leukos*). So raven gives us a whole series of analogous concepts, which runs raven-alder-mast-marsh-womb-height-light-whiteness. The raven is whiteness, the marsh is height. These startling leaps inherent in the Celts' extraordinary way of thinking are equally important in the study of present day poetical expression.

The ternary significance of the name Bran is part of the Celts' concept of the triad, which is graphically represented by the triskele, a solar symbol of Eastern origin derived from the wheel. The triskele contains both the two-directional spiral of the Chinese *yin* and *yang*, or me and non-me, and a third spiral which alchemists called the Secret Fire, itself a three part concept and the archetype of cohesive force (Hermes Trismegistus = thrice great Hermes = 3 times 3). Hegel expresses this same triad as thesis, antithesis and synthesis. And it finds definitive expression throughout the world as the divine trinity, whether in the form of Father-Son-Holy Spirit, Mithra-Ormazd-Ahriman, Rama-Vishnu-Siva, Sin-Shamash-Ishtar, Amon-Ra-Ptah, Osiris-Isis-Horus or Teutates-Esus-Taranis. There are several examples of tricephalic gods in Gallic art[24], all of which appear to resolve the inherent contradictions of the triad by uniting three interpretations of a single figure through the rationally untenable proposition that 3 = 1. It is for this reason that Celtic mythology remains virtually indecipherable. When ternary analogy can make the same hero appear three times running in the same adventure with different features and a different name, the kind of irrational confusion created is hardly conducive to enlightenment.[25]

It was in this way that the mysterious notion of correspondences grew up among the Celts, a notion which has continued to haunt poets, artists and alchemists for whom the Grand-Oeuvre was based on the doctrine of correspondences in every sphere.[26]

The chain of analogy we have attempted to reconstruct makes Bran the same person as Lug, an equation scarcely borne out by the respective attributes of the two characters. But seen against the fight between Brennius and Belinus related by Geoffrey of Monmouth, this equation may shed some light on the *Battle of Goddeu* and on the expedition to Delphi. It is in fact likely that the legend contained in the battle of Goddeu is the same as that in Geoffrey's *Historia*: the two warring brothers are Belinus, or Belenos-Apollo, and Brennius, or Brennus, Bran or Lug. There is a dispute over rank in the divine hierarchy, a form of rivalry common to all Indo-European mythologies.

The Apollonian cult at Delphi was not Greek in origin, but Hyperborean. In Celtic mythology, the mythical Hyperboreans in whom the ghosts of the megalith-builders may well reside, become the subterranean race of the Tuatha de Danann, one of whose leaders is Lug. Before settling in Ireland, the Tuatha de Danann had to fight the equally mythical Fomoré, whose leader the giant Balor was killed at the battle of Mag Tured by Lug, himself half Tuatha, half Fomoré. The fact that the early Irish calendar, like the Gallic calender of Coligny, sets the feast of Beltaine (the fires of Belenos) on May 1, while the feast of Lugnasad (the triumph of Lug) is on August 1 suggests that some memory of Lug's accession to power survived through the legendary tangle passed on by the Irish Christians and even by the Mediterranean peoples who did little to foster Celtic customs and concepts.

The Greek traditions concerning the Delphic cult are extremely vague.[27] According to them, the Hyperborean Olenus founded the oracle of Apollo and

invented the hexameter. The sacred objects venerated at Delos were also supposedly Hyperborean in origin, and the arrow with which Apollo killed the Cyclops is said to have been hidden by him in his great round temple in the land of the
Hyperboreans. A Hyperborean named Abasis is then said to have travelled all over
the world on this arrow before it flew to heaven to form the constellation of
Sagittarius. The two ancient heroes who appeared to the Gauls during the attack
on Delphi are supposed to have been two Hyperboreans named Hyperchos and
Laodcos.

Needless to say, none of this has very much to do with reality, but there does
seem to be an established link between Delphi and the circular temple of the
Hyperboreans (Stonehenge). The Greeks did not found Delphi any more than the
Celts built Stonehenge, but they both took up the megalithic inheritance attached
to these sanctuaries. It is therefore possible that the expedition to Delphi, which
has never been acceptably substantiated by fact, was a web of legends haphazardly
reworked by Greek and Latin authors who did not really understand them, from a
Celtic source based on events at the circular temple of Stonehenge. And it may be
this source which has given us the *Battle of Goddeu* and Geoffrey of Monmouth's
account of the Brennius-Belinus episode in the *Historia Regum Britonniae*.

The Sacrifice of the Hero

The ritual accomplished by Brennus at Delphi is not yet complete, however. After
the Gauls' miraculous defeat (perhaps revenge for the battle of the Allia) they took
refuge for the night in some insecure spot, and there fell prey to a kind of hysterical
fright, presumably yet another magical phenomenon. The Gauls began to fight
amongst themselves, as so often happens in Celtic epic, and the survivors were left
to gauge the success or otherwise of the whole enterprise. Naturally enough, like
every Celtic expedition, the Delphic adventure had been a disastrous failure.

It is at this point that the Greek writer Diodorus and the Welsh mabinogi of
Branwen come closest. For Diodorus tells how Brennus, being wounded three times
and having lost several thousand men, gathers the survivors, gives his final orders,
drinks himself into a stupor and stabs himself (fragment XXII). The Welsh version has Bran being wounded in a terrible defeat for the Britons and ordering the
seven survivors to cut off his head and take it to the Gwynn Vryn in Llundein,
where it is to be buried with the face turned towards France.

The hero's death is virtually identical. Brennus and Bran, both of them
wounded but not dying, deliberately choose to die in an unreal act of self-sacrifice.
Pausanias tries to explain Brennus' act as the behaviour of a man who feels
responsible for his army's defeat and fears resentment from his fellow countrymen.
Justinus claims that Brennus found his pain unbearable. In yet another version
Valerus Maximus says, "No sooner had Brennus entered the temple of Apollo at
Delphi than by the will of that god he turned his weapons upon himself" (Valerus
Maximus, I, 1). None of these authors seems to have understood what really
happened, although Valerus Maximus comes some way towards the truth in his
suggestion of divine intervention. For Brennus' suicide is of a sacred kind.

One explanation for the gesture, or at least some inkling of its significance can be
gleaned from Posidonius, as quoted by Atheneus. "Sometimes, while feasting, the
Celts engage each other in single combat, since when armed and aroused they will
come to blows. On occasion they will even inflict wounds, and excited by this will
go so far as to take each other's lives. . . . Others, after receiving gold and a specific

number of jugs of wine, will bear solemn witness to the gift, divide and distribute it among their family and friends and lie supine on their shields, where one of those present will cut their throats with a sword." (Atheneus, IV, 37.) The following comment on this account comes from Marcel Mauss's *Essai sur le Don*. "The hero challenges his dining companions, who may not be aware of what is to follow but must obey for fear of forfeiting their rank, to give him what they cannot refuse. These gifts are presented in all solemnity . . . The spectators guarantee the lasting nature of the gift. Then the hero, who would otherwise be expected to return these gifts with interest, pays for what he has just received with his life. He distributes the gifts to his family, whom he is enriching through his sacrifice and by dying sidesteps any counterclaim or the dishonour he would suffer were he to subsequently refuse to return the gifts he had accepted. Indeed, he dies the death of the brave man on his shield. He sacrifices himself to his own glory and to the benefit of his family." (*Année Sociologique*, 1923–1924, pp. 30–186.)

In Brennus' case, the gifts are the mysterious treasures of Delphi, the object of the whole expedition. Having distributed them to his own men and his lieutenant Kichorios, he pays for them solemnly with his death, just as Bran pays with his head for the safety and happiness of the seven Welsh survivors. In the romance of *Culhwch and Olwen*, the giant Yspaddaden Penkawr stakes his head against Culhwch's being able to bring back from the Other World the objects necessary to win the hand of Olwen, and loses his head when Culhwch succeeds.

The theme of self-sacrifice however, is part of the even more universal idea of sacrifice being symbolically represented by a severed head. We have already discussed the significance of the severed head among the Celts. All the legends about head-carrying saints (Saint Denis, St Mitre, Saint John, etc.) are of the same kind. Bran's head is magic since it enables the seven survivors to spend seven years outside time in a kind of feast of immortality. It is also, according to the primary meaning of Bran's name, the head of the raven or crow, and the crow's head was a symbol commonly used by the alchemist to denote one of the basic phases on the road to creating the Philosopher's Stone. "Our mercury," wrote the alchemist Albertus Magnus, "will remain at the bottom . . . change into a black mud which is called the Head of the Crow." (*The Composite of Composites*.) Raymond Lully ends his description of various delicate operations with, "You will then have the Head of the Crow which the Philosophers have sought for so long, and without which the Magister cannot exist." (*The Clavicle*, VIII.)

Further comments on the Head of the Crow are to be found in Nicolas Flamel's *Book of Hieroglyphical Figures* (V). "See that man in the shape of Saint Paul. . . He wishes to take the naked blade either to cut off his head or to do something else to that man who is kneeling at his feet. . . But do you wish to know the meaning of that man taking the sword? It means that the Head of the Crow must be cut off, the head must be cut off that man . . . who is kneeling. . . Take the head from that black man, cut off the Head of the Crow, and once it has been removed, the colour white will immediately come."

The "white" here referred to is the White Elixir, one of the substances created before the completion of the alchemical Oeuvre. What is so interesting about this passage is that traditional alchemy and the Celtic idea of correspondences both lead to the same conclusion, namely that whiteness can be paradoxically identified with the Crow. Once the alchemical Head of the Crow has been removed, it leaves whiteness in its place. Once the Celtic head of Bran has been cut off it is buried in the White Hill or Gwynn Bryn. Indeed the word *bryn* has the same analogous identity as Bran, the crow, womb, height. So, remembering that the concept crow can also be rendered by the name Lug which means white, too, we can create our own triad on the burial of Bran's head. "The head of the crow is buried in the womb of light." "The whiteness is buried in the womb of the crow." "The light is buried in the whiteness of the crow." Poetry can accomplish such remarkable transformations. And we are left with the final concept of Bran's being buried in Bran, the being remaining fundamentally one through all its superficial and contradictory variations.

We have now examined the figure of Bran, and through him the figure of Brennus. Whether or not the Gallic expedition followed the course recorded by the historians matters little; for the gold of Delphi was not merely material, it was a kind of Philosopher's gold, the gold of the Sun. Brennus may not be the same man as Bran, but he is the same mythological character, the archetypal Celtic hero. He is Bran the Blessed, the god of the dark mounds where he leads the ghosts of men to their fate. He is a god sacrificed for the good of his people, the Fisher King, the guardian of the Grail. And the expedition to Delphi is a quest for the Grail, its heroes who discover the great truth being unable to carry on living and taking their secret with them to the grave.

However, this is not the end of the story, nor yet the end of the argument. There can be no valid end to such a tale, only a temporary halting point. And that halting point has been expressed by Alfred Jarry, the 20th century heir to millenia of tradition: "This dead body . . . is not just an island but a man; he delights in being called the Baron Hildbrand of the Sea of Habundes. . . The beacon of the island of Bran is a dark beacon, subterranean and sewer-like as if after looking at the sun for too long. No waves break there, nor is there any noise to guide one. . . This beacon feeds on the pure matter which is the substance of the island of Bran; it is the soul which breathes out of his mouth and which he puffs through a leaden blow-pipe." (*Gestes et Opinions du Docteur Faustroll*, pp. 46-8.)

CHAPTER FIVE

The Celts Defeated

VER a period of years an ambitious proconsul had been looking for some means to win fame for himself and to compensate for the losses incurred by his lavish spending on political influence. Having been given command of Cisalpine Gaul and the *Provincia Romana*, where all he could find to loot were a few temples already plundered by his predecessors, he turned his sights northwards to the as yet unromanized region of *Gallia Comata*. But, although untroubled by either religious or political scruples, he was a cautious and clear-sighted man, and had decided to wait for the right moment. Indeed, he had been waiting since 61 BC, when "in the consulship of Messala and Marcus Piso, Orgetorix, the foremost man among the Helvetii had endeavoured to rouse his people and persuade them to emigrate westwards" (*De Bello Gallico* I, 2). Caius Julius Caesar could hardly contain his impatience to see what would happen. It is more than likely that he had a network of paid informers to bring him up-to-date and detailed news of events in the area between the Rhine and the Rhone, and even that he secretly encouraged Orgetorix's plan through reliable middlemen. With so much at stake it would have been a logical step to take.

Caesar's influence apart, Orgetorix began to look for friends among other Celtic tribes and concluded a secret pact with Casticos the Sequanian and Dumnorix the Aeduan, brother of Cicero's friend the druid Diviciacos. These three men agreed to unite their efforts in an attempt to seize control of Gaul and share the leadership of the land. Unfortunately for Orgetorix, however, his pact soon became common knowledge and his fellow Helvetians responded by banishing him. The desperate Orgetorix killed himself in 58 BC.

His ideas remained, however, and were to be taken up by others. The Helvetii decided to emigrate, a decision which Caesar claims was born of their hunger for power. But then he was looking for a good reason to condemn them. What he omits to mention is that the Helvetii, the Aedui and the Sequani were all subject to increasing pressure from the neighbouring Germanic tribes who, like Caesar, were only waiting for the right moment to fall on Gaul.

In order to leave their country, the Helvetii had to pass through one of two sensitive and key positions. They could either cross the land of Gex then occupied by the Sequani, or travel south of the Rhone through the area round Geneva then controlled by the Allobrages who had been under Roman protection since the Cataline conspiracy. But despite these difficulties, the Helvetii prepared to move and began to gather on the banks of the Rhone, together with various other tribes harassed by the Germans, including the Boii from Bohemia.

At this, Casear hastened to Geneva, destroyed the bridge over the Rhone and raised as many troops as he could from throughout the Province. The Helvetii then tried to negotiate with Caesar and asked him for a passage "because there was no other route open to them" (I, 7). Caesar prevaricated, asked for a delay to consider the matter and used the time to build a wall from Lake Geneva to the Jura, before finally replying that he would not allow the Helvetii to cross the Province. After trying unsuccessfully to cross the Rhone, the Helvetii asked Dumnorix the Aeduan to mediate with the Sequani, so that in return for a promise that they would pass "without harming anyone or doing any damage" (I, 9), they might march over Sequanian territory. Having thereby reached the land of the Aedui, with whom they had no treaty, the Helvetii set about pillaging the country, under the benevolent eye of the Sequani, the Aedui's eternal rivals. But the Aedui had a treaty of alliance with the Romans and asked Caesar for help. This was just the chance the proconsul had been waiting for. After a fleeting visit to Italy to collect five more legions, he attacked the Helvetii just as they were crossing the Saone, probably somewhere between Villefranche and Trévoux. Taken by surprise, the Helvetii retreated into the neighbouring forests and sent Divico, the Tigurian and former ally of the Cimbri, as an ambassador to sound out Caesar's intentions. When Caesar asked for hostages, Divico proudly replied that "it was the traditional custom of the Helvetii to demand hostages of others, but never to give them" (I, 4) and broke off negotiations. The Romans therefore spent the next fortnight following the Helvetii about in an attempt to stop them looting.

Meanwhile the Aedui appeared unwilling to supply the Romans with provisions despite their alliance with Caesar and their obvious debt to him. So Caesar summoned the druid Diviciacos and the *vergobret* Liscos and accused them of failing in their duty to him. The two Aeduan leaders laid the blame on Diviciacos' brother Dumnorix, a rich and influential figure who had married his mother to a nobleman of the Bituriges and had himself married the daughter of the Helvetian Orgetorix. Unlike the other Aeduan nobles who favoured Roman influence, Dumnorix was a nationalist with a considerable following among the people.

Caesar realized that Dumnorix would have to be immobilized. He therefore sent for him and, in his brother Diviciacos' presence, voiced his complaints. These, however, he agreed to overlook provided that Dumnorix remained under the guard of Caesar's paid informers.

Having thereby made this area more secure, Caesar and his lieutenant Labienus launched an attack against the Helvetii which ended in victory for neither side. But the shortage of provisions was becoming a major problem for the Romans, so Caesar turned towards Bibracte (Mont Beuvray), the Aeduan capital. Thinking that the Romans were retreating, the Helvetii attacked. The long and bitter battle which followed ended in a victory for the Romans. The Helvetii took refuge among the Lingones but were eventually forced to surrender through lack of provisions. After demanding that they surrender their weapons along with a number of hostages Caesar ordered them to return home.

Stability appeared to have been restored. Caesar had increased his sphere of influence and could now claim to be bringing peace, justice and mediation between rival Gallic tribes. He had established a firmer foothold among the Aedui who held the traditional passageway through the Burgundian border area and had subdued the Helvetii. Even the Sequani could be said to owe him some gratitude for overlooking the help they had given the Helvetii.

It was then that Ariovistus, the chief of the German tribe of Suevi, entered the picture; and he and Caesar began their race for the domination of Eastern Gaul. Caught between the two aggressors, the Gauls were too weak and too badly placed to be able to maintain total independence, at any rate for the immediate future. The time had come to make a choice between the Romans and the Germans.

Some years before, the Sequani and their traditional allies the Arverni had asked the Germans for help against the Aedui but had been forced to pay a high price for this assistance. For the Germans had occupied a third of Sequanian territory and, while continuing to pressurize the Aedui, had demanded a number of hostages from all the neighbouring tribes. In 58 BC Ariovistus was preparing to launch an offensive, news of which was probably spread throughout Gaul by Caesar's envoys.

Already terrorized by the Suevi, the Aedui could see how dangerous an imminent German attack might be and turned to Caesar. After listening to Diviciacos' appeal for protection against Ariovistus' depredations, Caesar reassured the Gauls with a great show of resignation and sent a delegation to meet the German leader. But he was careful to ensure that the negotiations should fail.

It should be remembered that during Caesar's consulship in 59 BC, Ariovistus had visited Rome where he had been accorded the titles of "king" and "friend of the Roman people". Caesar knew that the Suevian leader was as ambitious and arrogant as himself and that by delivering the Suevi with an ultimatum he was making war inevitable. But the Roman troops were fresh and well-positioned and a victory against the Germans might give Caesar a chance to establish himself in the newly liberated regions.

Ariovistus realized that he would have to outrun the Romans, and attacked Gaul on two fronts, with a first push across the Rhine into the land of the Treveri and a second towards Besançon, the Sequanian stronghold. Caesar hastily assembled his troops and had to make them a stirring speech to overcome their fear of the Germans. The two armies met in the southern plain of Alsace. Ariovistus tried to re-open negotiations and denied the Romans any rights over Gaul, to which Caesar replied that he would never abandon the allies of the Roman people. The battle which followed this battery of fine words ended in a severe defeat for the Germans. Ariovistus managed to flee back over the Rhine, followed by the rest of the Suevi. With his most dangerous rival out of the way and a foothold among the Sequani in South Alsace, the first round had clearly gone to Caesar.

But the Roman presence was not greeted with universal enthusiasm among the tribes of Belgica. They were justifiably disturbed by the establishment of the Roman legions along their frontiers now that the German threat had been removed, and made it their policy to prevent the Romans from intervening in their affairs. Caesar attributes this attitude to the fear that once the rest of Gaul had been subdued the Romans would take arms against Belgica, and, significantly, to pressure from "some adventurers who saw that under Roman rule they would not find it so easy to usurp thrones, as was commonly done in Gaul by powerful men, and by those who could afford to hire mercenaries" (II, 1). This comment is evidence that from the year 58 BC, Caesar had set his sights on conquering the whole of Gaul. The Belgae were well aware of this and wished to act while there was still time.

In 57 BC, therefore, the Belgae began to form a confederation. The powerful Bellovaci from the Oise region claimed the direction of the campaign. Other members included the Suessiones, who were then theoretically ruled by Galba but acutally led by Diviciacos (not to be confused with the Aeduan druid), who had proved himself in an earlier expedition to Britain. The Nervii, the Atrebates, the Ambiani, the Morini, the Menapii, the Calati, the Veliocasses, the Viromandui, the Teutonic Atuatuci and the half-Celtic half-Germanic Eburones also joined the confederation and appointed Galba their leader.

The Remi, being much closer to the Roman legions, were more cautious. They refused to join the other Belgae and made an alliance with Caesar. He took hostages to ensure their friendship and marched north of the Aisne towards la Fère with a troop of Aeduans under his command. A minor skirmish took place at Bibrax, a town of the Remi, when the Romans forced the Belgaean confederation to abandon their siege of the fortress. But the decisive battle took place on the banks of the Aisne where many of the courageous Belgae were killed. Determined to exploit this victory, Caesar hastened to the land of the Suessiones and besieged their capital, Noviodunum near Soissons. The Suessiones were forced to surrender. Then, before his enemies could mount a counter-offensive, Caesar attacked the various tribes separately, laying siege to their chief towns rather than looking for an all-out battle. The first to fall was Bratuspantium (near Beauvais) where the Bellovaci sued for peace and were spared only after the personal intervention of the Aeduan druid Diviciacos. The real reason for Caesar's magnanimity in this instance, however, was not so much his respect for Diviciacos as his hope that the Bellovaci, the most influential of the Belgaean tribes, would remain comparatively peaceful while he dealt with the others.

Meanwhile, however, the Nervii, who had a reputation for tenacity, had had time to join forces with the Atrebates and the Vironmandui and were waiting, firmly entrenched along the banks of the Sambre near Bavai, for the Atuatuci. It was then that the strange battle of the Sambre took place among the surrounding forests and marshlands, with news of the main events being relayed to both sides by retreating troops. The Nervian chief Boduognatos (Son of Victory or Son of the Crow) proved a remarkable general and Caesar was very nearly beaten. Finally, however, the Nervii surrendered. The Atuatuci, who had not even reached the scene of the battle, retreated into their stronghold (probably Namur) from where they continued to harass the Romans. Caesar besieged them, and the hungry Atuatuci feigned surrender only to attack the Romans the following night. Apparently forewarned of this subterfuge by a deserter, Caesar hastily entered the fortress and enslaved the whole population of about 50,000.

This unexpected defeat of the Belgaeans threw even the bravest of the other Gallic tribes into a terrified state of panic. A heavy and oppressive silence settled over the land from the Rhine to the Atlantic as they waited to see what would happen next.

It was under these conditions that Caesar's lieutenant Labienus managed to reach the westernmost point of Europe in Armorica with a single legion. Within a few weeks he had won promises of neutrality, if not submission, from all the tribes of Celtica living between the Seine and the Loire, including the Venelli of Cotentin, the Redones of Rennes, the Curiosolitae of the Côtes-du-Nord, the Osismi of Nord-Finistère and the Veneti of Vannes.

At the end of 57 BC, Caesar quartered his legions for the winter among the Andes of Angers, the Turoni of Tours and the Carnutes of Beauce, a region from which an eye could be kept on all the other subdued tribes. The proconsul had much to be proud of. In eighteen months he had successfully subjugated two thirds of Gaul and ensured that the remaining third lay between the Roman *provincia Narbonensis* and his new conquests. Any German threat had been removed for the time being, at least, and *Gallia Comata* looked like becoming *Gallia Togata* or at any rate a Roman protectorate.

Various reasons have been put forward to explain the ease of the Roman conquest. The suggestion that the Gauls were weak in men and equipment would seem to be contradicted by Caesar's own figures; and arguments that inter-tribal conflict divided resistance cannot be applied to this phase of the Gallic wars. The Belgaean confederation had held firm to the end, and even the age-old quarrel between the Sequani and the Aedui had been forgotten in the fight against Ariovistus. Further claims that the Roman forces were superior are hardly substantiated by the miscellaneous origins of the mercenaries who made up the legions, many of whom came from Gaul itself. The only argument in favour of Roman superiority is that the structure and command of those legions was Roman.

Far and away the most satisfactory explanation lies in the character of Caesar himself. A brilliant leader, he ranks alongside Hannibal and Alexander as one of the most remarkable generals of classical antiquity. He devoted his boundless energies to everything that came his way, and took an interest even in very minor details. He had a blind and unending faith in his own destiny and in his eventual victory. With a comprehensive knowledge of military strategy, which included the tactics likely to be employed by his enemies, he was able to take prompt and informed decisions. Tenacious, stubborn and unscrupulous, he would exploit any mistake made by his enemies to his own advantage. Another crucial element in his victories was his ability to make full and intelligent use of his network of informers and what one might call "saboteurs". During the long years when he was planning the conquest of Gaul, he had had time to study the customs, responses, qualities and defects of the Gauls. And the lightning speed of his manoeuvres and of his forced marches are eloquent proof of his familiarity with the geography of the country.

Last and by no means least, Caesar had a talent for stirring up conflict between others, following the Roman maxim "divide and rule", and for inciting people to treason, if necessary with gold. He saw war as a kind of chess game in which every move could be calculated in advance; and he never lost a pawn without winning several of his opponent's pieces.

There is little doubt that the Gauls also felt some bond with the Romans. The

Celtic and Italic peoples were descended from common ancestors and the Gauls probably felt much closer to the Latins than to the non-Aryan Indo-European Germans. Some leaders, like the druid Diviciacos and Commios the Atrebatian, believed in a kind of Italo-Celtic confederation, marking a return to their common origins.

And then, absurd as it may seem, there was the problem of wine. A number of ancient authors have testified as to the Gauls' inordinate love of strong drink and, in particular, of wine, a highly intoxicating brew then produced only in the Mediterranean area.[1] A severing of links with Italy and the *Provincia* meant an end to the flourishing trade in wine between the Mediterranean and the extreme North of Gaul, which had been handled by Greek merchants and the Massiliots since the 3rd century BC. Like any other economic consideration, the basically materialistic question of wine supplies may well have influenced the course of the war.

Even so, the submissiveness of the Gauls soon proved to be only superficial. Roman influence really only extended to the nobility, whose authority was reinforced by their alliance with Rome and who were therefore under an obligation to the proconsul. The mass of the people remained in disdainful ignorance of the Roman way, a fact which the increasingly isolated chiefs soon began to realize. The leadership was faced with a choice between relying on a more comprehensive support from the Romans or falling in with their people and heroically driving the Romans out. In 56 BC, a fair number of chiefs had opted for the second solution and it was in this climate that the Veneti raised the standard of liberation.

The ancient authors have left us various conflicting accounts of the origins of the Veneti. Caesar says that they "formed the most powerful tribe on this [the Armorican] coast" (III, 8) and their name has often been linked with that of the Adriatic Veneti. Strabo even says that they are the same people: "Most of the Celtic or Gallic peoples settled in Italy, in particular the Boii and the Senones, came from Transalpine Gaul, and I would be inclined to believe that the Adriatic Veneti are a colony of the Oceanic Veneti; it is solely the similarity between names which suggests that they originated in Paphlagonia" (Strabo, IV, 4). Elsewhere, Strabo writes of the Adriatic Veneti's migration across Thrace under the leadership of a man named Agenor from Troy (Strabo, XIII,1); and this legend is also mentioned by Sophocles in *The Fall of Troy*. Pomponius Mela describes the Veneti, the Capadocians and the Gallo-Greeks (Galatians) as Asian peoples. The *Iliad* contains a reference to the *Henetoi*, a tribe from Paphlagonia (v. 2,851) and Arrienus tells how the *Enetes* suffered during the war against the Assyrians and came to Europe where they were called *Benetoi*.

The Adriatic Veneti probably did come from Asia Minor, and had nothing in common with the Oceanic Veneti despite their common name. Polybius, a very cautious historian, specifically states, "the land bathed by the Adriatic is inhabited by a very ancient nation, the Veneti, whose clothes and customs bear some resemblance to those of the Gauls, but not their language." (Polybius, II, 17.) Since one of the established features of the Celtic world is linguistic unity, the Adriatic Veneti cannot therefore have been Gauls; and any fanciful notions that Venice was a colony of Vannes are quite baseless.

The Atlantic Veneti derived their name from the Gallic *vindu*, "white" or "blond" (Welsh *gwynn*, Breton *gwen*, Irish *finn*) and appear to have been an extremely powerful sea-faring nation since before Caesar's time. Again according to Strabo, the Veneti, like the other Armorican peoples, were Belgaean in origin, and this is partly confirmed by archaeological discoveries indicating that Sirona, a strictly Belgaean deity was worshipped in Brittany, notably at Corseul, the former capital of the Curiosolitae. Strabo attributes their hostility towards the Romans in large measure to the fact that they wanted to "prevent Caesar from crossing Brittany to Britain, which was their chief trading outlet" (Strabo, IV, 4). Contact between the South coast of Armorica and the West and South West coasts of Britain and Ireland does indeed appear to have been maintained continuously even since the Megalithic period, as the great megalithic sites of Carnac-Locmariaquer on the one hand, and those in southern England and Ireland on the other would indicate. Moreover, the fact that North West Wales was called Gwynned would seem to suggest that the Veneti had considerable influence there, if not an actual colony. Apart from their trading activities and their relations with the Britons, many of whom were also Belgaean in origin, the discovery of large numbers of Venetian gold coins demonstrates that they were also a wealthy people and clearly had every interest in preventing Caesar from colonizing their coastline in 56 BC.

When Caesar's lieutenant Publius Crassus set up winter quarters for the seventh legion among the Andes, he sent tribunes to all the neighbouring peoples to seek for corn. The Veneti took this opportunity to detain the two Roman envoys and declare that they would return them only in exchange for the hostages they had been forced to give Caesar. This was a signal for all the other tribes to follow the Venetian example and to form a hurried and probably flimsy alliance. They fortified their towns, began stockpiling provisions and assembled their fleet off the land of the Veneti, who appear to have led what was basically a maritime confederation. The tribes involved stretched from the Loire to Pas de Calais and included the Namnetes from Nantes, the Osisimi, the Curiosolitae, the Diablintes from the Mayenne, the Lexovii from Pays d'Auge, the Menapii and the Morini from the North, as well as the Veneti. They even asked for assistance from the British peoples who were related by blood and by trade to the members of the confederation.

Crassus informed Caesar, who took a serious view of the situation and immediately ordered that warships should be built on the Loire. He then sent Labienus to ensure that the Belgae did not attack from the rear and dispatched Crassus to the other side of the Loire, partly to prevent the Aquitanians from helping the Armoricans, and partly to give the Romans an entry into a region as yet unconquered. He also sent Titurius Sabinus to central Normandy and established garrisons among the Redones to watch over the activities of the confederation's rear. Having thus isolated the rebellion, he set off himself to fight its mainspring, the Veneti.

Various difficulties lay before him. For while the Veneti excelled "the other tribes in knowledge and experience of navigation" (III, 8), the Romans were inexperienced and even slightly afraid of sailing on the tidal and stormy waters of the Atlantic. The Venetian boats were flatter than the Romans' and more stable in choppy water. They had leather sails and their solid oak hulls were impervious to Roman spears.

Unsuccessful at sea, Caesar tried to take the Venetian towns, but fared no better there, for their strongholds were "so situated on the ends of spits or headlands that it was not possible to approach them by land when the tide rushed in from the open sea, which happens regularly every twelve hours: and they were also difficult to reach by sea, because at low tide the ships would run aground" (III, 12). Caesar therefore decided to wait for the new boats being hurriedly built on the Loire.

When these reinforcements arrived, a Venetian fleet of twenty units sailed out of harbour and took up stations facing the Romans.

The site of this encounter has been the subject of much discussion. Suggested locations vary from La Grande Brière to the mouth of the Vilaine, the neck of the bay of Morbihan between Port Navalo and Kerpenhir in Locmariaquer and even the mouth of the river Auray inside the bay of Morbihan.

In the first century BC the Grande Brière was still an arm of the sea with various islands and marshy areas dotted about on it. Traces of a Celtic fortress have been found at Sandun (Sandunum) and not far away there was an actual port locally identified as Corbilo[2], which is said to be the place where Caesar landed. But the land of the Veneti stretched as far south as the Loire and included the Guérande peninsula, le Croisic and Saint-Nazaire. So much is clear from the former boundaries of the diocese of Vannes and the fact that the Vannetais dialect was still spoken in the Guerande peninsula until the last century. It is more likely that Corbilo was Caesar's bridgehead and that La Brière, situated so close to the mouth of the Loire, was the point of departure for the Roman fleet.

Caesar's description of the Venetian ships sailing out of harbour on the Romans' arrival would seem to preclude the mouth of the Vilaine, as there has never been a port on the Vilaine except at Roche-Bernard which is too far away for an immediate sortie.

Everything points to the suggestion that the naval battle against the Veneti took place in the middle of Venetian territory, i.e. in the bay of Morbihan and the surrounding area. The ideal location was obviously where the Auray river entered the sea near Locmariaquer, which must have been the Veneti's largest town if not their capital, for the neighbouring creeks and inlet provided natural harbours. But in the first century BC, the bay of Morbihan was shallower than it is now, and, as the now submerged cromlech of Er Lannic shows, the water level did not rise as high as the present shore line. Morbihan was more like a fen, probably containing the inaccessible strongholds Caesar mentions, but too shallow for the Roman fleet with their deeper keels.

The battle must, therefore, have taken place in the neighbourhood of Port Navalo either in the creek or in the sea near Petit Mont. We know that Caesar watched the battle from a vantage point on the coast, presumably the 90-metre high tumulus of Tumiac in Arzon which is known as Caesar's mound and commands a good view of the ocean. The proconsul must have landed at Corbilo and marched through the Venetian lowlands along the coast to the peninsula of Rhuys, an ideal place at which to assemble his troops opposite the heart of Venetian territory.

The Roman fleet coming from La Brière must have sailed down the Loire and round the point of Croisic, hugging the coast in order to avoid Houat and Hoedic where the Venetians had watchtowers.[3] The Venetian fleet in all probability came out of Locmariaquer.

So the two enemy fleets lay facing each other. The Roman naval commander Brutus, who later conspired in Caesar's assassination, did not know what to do. Ramming made no impression on the Venetian boats, while the Veneti, from their much higher prows, could rain down a storm of arrows on the Romans.

At this point the various historians differ. Caesar (III, 1) suggests that he had ordered the Romans to prepare long poles armed with scythes which could then be used like billhooks to cut the enemy rigging and immobilize the Veneti, who unlike the Romans with their oars, were dependent on their sails. However, Strabo, who also mentions the poles and scythes, says that the Veneti used to rig their sails with chains rather than ropes (Strabo, IV, 4) and scythes, however sharp, could hardly have cut through chains. But then Strabo tends to muddle facts and Caesar to tell deliberate lies. A more likely version comes from Dio Cassius who, taking his account from a now lost passage of Livy, says that the Venetian attack came while Brutus was still lying at anchor and that the Roman victory was due merely to an amazing piece of luck; for the wind dropped and the enemy ships could neither move in nor retreat when the oar-powered Roman ships came after them (Dio Cassius, XXXIX, 40–43).

Whatever the reason, it was total defeat for the Veneti. Having lost their leaders at sea, it was not long before the whole tribe surrendered, in rather mysterious circumstances.

There is no doubt, however, of the force of Caesar's repressive measures. He executed all the councillors (III, 6) or élite of the tribe and sold the rest by auction. The total lack of any subsequent mention of the Veneti throughout the rest of the Gallic Wars gives rise to speculation about the strength of Caesar's desire to annihilate the tribe which had dared to defy him.

Admittedly there is evidence of an Armorican emigration to Britain having taken place at this period, possibly among the Veneti fleeing their country. Not all the Venetian ships were lost in battle. The others must have escaped and Britain would seem a logical place of refuge. The Veneti had a virtual monopoly of trade between the Breton peninsula and Britain, and were perfectly familiar with the old mineral merchants' routes. There is archaeological evidence to show that the Roman troops in Caesar's time never overstepped a line running from Vannes to the mouth of the river Auray, but the considerable numbers of Veneti still living within this area had now lost their leaders and, more importantly, the harbours which formed a base for their trading, and they remained content to scratch a living from the poor soil rather than join any further rebellions.[4]

Meanwhile, the defeat of the Veneti and Caesar's repressive measures had dealt a severe blow to the Armorican confederation. Viridorix, leader of the Venelli, made one last effort to reinspire the old spirit and joined forces with the Lexovii (from Lisieux) and the Aulerci Eburovices (from Evreux). But the Gauls were harassed into defeat by Titurius Sabinus, and the Aquitanians were subjugated by Publius Crassus. Only the Menapii and the Morini were still able to fight, and, although Caesar attempted to win an all-out vicotry over them, he succeeded only in driving them back into the forests and marshlands of their country from where they fought on as guerrillas. Realizing that the region offered no permanent shelter for his troops, the proconsul reassembled his forces on the other side of the Seine, after vengefully destroying and burning everything in his wake.

We have now reached 55 BC and the Gauls appear to be almost totally subdued. But behind this peaceful façade, various tribes, especially among the Belgaean peoples, were waiting only for an opportunity to take up arms again and drive the Romans back to Italy. Following the widely used practice of playing off one enemy against another, the Gauls entered into secret negotiations with the Germans who were massing on their borders. An alliance with the Suevi had obviously to be treated with caution, but the Gallic leaders apparently hoped that open war between the Germans and the Romans would weaken both to such an extent that they themselves could profit by it.

Initially this stratagem proved successful. The Suevi were encroaching on Gallic Rhineland territory where the local tribes were being sacrificed to some extent for the good of the whole. Caesar was extremely disturbed by this local conflict which threatened to bring down what he knew to be a still very shaky edifice. He therefore sent messengers to the leadership of the sacrificed tribes with assurances of Roman protection. But as he did not feel strong enough for an immediate confrontation with the Suevi, he shilly-shallied in order to gain time. Having opened negotiations with the Germans, he managed to turn the talks so that any responsibility for the conflict lay firmly in the enemy court. Then, when he had gathered enough troops, he began to look for battle. The truce he had hypocritically demanded in order to give his army time to reform, was finally broken by a German offensive.

The Romans mounted an energetic counter-attack and after various fierce skirmishes managed to put their enemies to flight. Caesar decided to pursue the Germans across the Rhine, not because he had any intention of conquering the vast and isolated area of Germania, but as part of a propaganda operation of no military value whatever to increase his prestige in the eyes of the Gauls. He had a bridge built and sent envoys throughout Gaul with details of his courage and daring. In fact the construction of the bridge passed without incident since the enemy had left the area. Once across the Rhine, Caesar fired a few undefended villages, ostentatiously paraded his troops about and crossed back over the river, cutting the bridge behind him.

But, bluster or no, this operation had whetted Caesar's appetite for further conquests and, with no urgent business to attend to, he decided to capitalize on his psychological advantage. He had realized during the Venetian campaign that the Britons and Gauls were in close contact and that an alliance between them might put him in a precarious position. He therefore needed to show the Gauls that help from Britain was out of the question; and to do this he had to land in Britain, make his presence felt and, if necessary, find some allies there. Immediate conquest of the island was ruled out: it was much too far from Rome and isolated both by the sea and by the more unreliable areas of Gaul. The first invasion of Britain was therefore a prestige operation intended only to demoralize the Gauls by showing them that no country was safe from the Romans and that the Britons could be of no use to them.

There were other considerations to be taken into account, also. Time was running out. The summer of 55 BC was drawing to a close and Caesar had no desire to remain in the Northern regions during the winter months. He sought information about Britain from merchants who surprisingly claimed to "know only that part of the coast which faces Gaul" (IV, 20). His statement that the Gauls knew next to nothing about the inhabitants and geography of Britain blatantly contradicts his previous comments on the Veneti (III, 8), the Bellovaci (II, 14), the Suessiones and Diviciacos' expedition (III, 4) and his later comments on the Gallic druids who went to study in Britain (VI, 13).

It seems more likely that the merchants questioned by Caesar were either Greeks trading between Marseilles and the British Isles, or Gauls who feigned ignorance less from patriotism than from fears of possible competition from the Romans.

Armed with a certain amount of information nonetheless, Caesar marched towards the land of the Morini (the Pas de Calais area), assembled the fleet he had had built during the Venetian War and sent Volusenus at the head of a mission to Britian. But the traders spread rumours of invasion and, in an attempt to ward off this threat, the Britons sent envoys supposedly to offer hostages, but actually to sound out the proconsul's intentions and to discover the exact size of his army.

It was then that Commios the Atrebatian entered the scene.

According to Caesar himself, Commios had already been active, although his influence as a leader was due more to his personal authority than to any real power. He appears to have maintained a friendly though firm attitude towards the Roman proconsul since the beginning of the conquest of Belgica. Caesar tells us that he was "a man of whose courage, judgment and loyalty he had a high opinion, and who was greatly respected in Britain" (V, 1). This suggests that Commios considered himself Caesar's ally rather than his servant. Indeed the courage Caesar speaks of must have been demonstrated in action against the Romans, for there is no mention of Commios' having fought the Gauls. But then, Caesar was always quick to recognize and appreciate pride and bravery in others, and to risk entrusting authority to former enemies of stature on the grounds that friendship with such men might benefit him. It would appear that Commios was such a figure, since Caesar gave him command not only over the Atrebatians but also of the Morini.

However, there is still doubt as to whether the new Commios, the powerful chief and ally of Caesar, remained loyal to Rome or played his own game.

He does appear to have fallen in with Caesar's plans, at least for a while, but his later activities suggest that he may have been merely cajoling the proconsul into a false sense of security so that he could reinforce his own authority while he bided his time. For while he remained chief, Caesar would not be tempted to assume the leadership himself.

Be that as it may, it was to Commios that Caesar gave the position of ambassador to Britain, ordering him "to visit as many tribes as possible to urge them to entrust themselves to the protection of Rome and to announce his impending arrival" (IV, 21).

So, when Caesar and his fleet came within sight of the British coast and saw "the enemy's forces posted on all the hills" (IV, 23), there were two possible explanations. Either Commios had not succeeded in convincing the Britons, in which case he lacked the influence ascribed him by Caesar and subsequently proved by events; or else he had warned the Britons against the Romans, in which case he had betrayed Caesar, possibly hoping to lure him into a trap.

The second possibility seems the more likely. Caesar later says that Commios had been taken prisoner by the Britons (IV, 27), but past and future relations between the Atrebates and the Britons, and Commios' personal friendship with the Britons would seem to suggest that this explanation was a deliberate deceit.

As it was, the Britons realized after various skirmishes that it was pointless to exhaust themselves for no reason and asked for peace, to which the uneasy Caesar agreed. He was waiting impatiently for the arrival of his cavalry on the remainder of his fleet. But by the time the boats arrived, they had been so badly battered in a storm that Caesar found himself virtually cut off from the continent and in an extremely dangerous position. He immediately tried to remedy the situation by repairing some of the damaged ships with materials from the useless ones, and sent to the continent for help.

It was then that the Britons chose to ambush the men he had sent to look for provisions, before making a direct assault with chariots, a military tactic unknown to the Romans, and surrounding the Roman camp. Caesar just managed to save the camp by bringing up all his forces and concluded a hasty treaty with the Britons, asking merely for a number of hostages. Then, under pretext of avoiding

the equinoxal storms, he raised anchor around midnight and set sail for the continent.

Rebellion was rumbling on the mainland. The Morini and the Menapii had
come out of their marshland refuges, but Caesar could do no more than drive them
back. The Romans' situation was growing increasingly precarious. Failure in
Britain had turned Caesar's prestige operation into a disaster. The Gauls knew this
and were discreetly raising their heads again.

That is why the proconsul decided to make another, better-organized attempt on
Britain in the spring of 54 BC. He ordered new ships to be built along lines more
suitable to the local waters. Then, to secure his rear he set off for the land of the
Treveri, who appeared to be straying from the Roman path. Two Trevirian chiefs,
Indutiomarus and Cingetorix, were disputing the leadership. The anti-Roman
Indutiomarus was prepared to ask for help from the Germans. Caesar therefore
lent his support to Cingetorix and, although he failed to settle the quarrel completely, he did succeed in abating the influence of Indutiomarus and ensuring that
the Treveri would remain peaceful for the time being.

Caesar then returned to his headquarters at Boulogne where he assembled the
cavalry he had mustered from all the Gallic tribes. It was an unreliable army, as he
realized when the Aeduan Dumnorix refused to take part in the expedition to
Britain on the grounds that his religious duties prevented him (v, 6). As far as
Caesar was concerned, Dumnorix's scruples were nothing more than mischief-
making, but they clearly demonstrate the attitude of Gauls, who regarded Britain
as the sacred land of druidism. An expedition against Britain was far more than an
assault on their Celtic brothers; it was an act of sacrilege. Dumnorix exploited this
religious sentiment to the full and managed to win over some of the other Gallic
chiefs. Then, one evening, when Caesar was preparing to embark, Dumnorix led
his cavalry out of the camp and headed for home.

It would be natural enough to suppose that this brought Caesar out in a cold
sweat. Dumnorix's departure not only threatened Roman plans for the expedition
to Britain; it also indicated that all the auxiliary troops might well desert sooner or
later. But the proconsul showed no hesitation. Realizing that the only way to stifle
any rebellion was by cutting it off at the source, he coolly arranged for Dumnorix to
be murdered. This frightened the other Gallic chiefs into following Caesar, however unwillingly, but it also increased their concealed hatred of him.

Nevertheless, Caesar landed in Britain and managed to establish a foothold
there. His decidedly ill-starred fleet was badly damaged by another storm and had
to be repaired. British resistance forces profited by this respite to organize themselves into any army under Cassivellaunos, an energetic and enterprising chief
later celebrated as a national hero by the Welsh bards under the name Casswallawn. With a shrewd sense of tactics, Casswallawn harassed the Roman troops and
inflicted severe losses on them with virtual impunity. Caesar was clearly wonder-
ing whether he had walked straight into a hornets' nest when he learnt that
Casswallawn had a bitter quarrel with Mandubraccios whose father, king of the
Trinoblantes, had been killed by the British commander-in-chief.

Caesar's political genius came to the fore once again. Exploiting this quarrel, he
promised Mandubraccios that he would restore him to his father's throne and
thereby divided and weakened the enemy camp. At the same time, he made a
treaty with Casswallawn, claiming that the Britons had been defeated. This
episode has clearly been embellished in Caesar's commentaries to his own glory,
for it is difficult to see why either side should agree to peace so soon, and without

any decisive battle, although the influence of Commios the Atrebatian as middle-
man in the negotiations may go part of the way to explaining it.

Caesar does admit that he was anxious to return to the continent before the
winter. He therefore demanded hostages, "fixing an annual tribute to be paid by
the Britons to the Roman government and strictly forbidding Casswallawn to
molest Mandubraccios or the Trinovantes" (V, 23), and embarked as quickly as
possible for Pas de Calais despite another storm.

The future dictator's fame at this point rested mainly on the bulletins of victory
he sent to the Senate. For, in fact, the second attempt on Britain had failed like the
first. The hostages were never delivered, the tribute never paid. Forbidding Casswallawn to molest his rival Mandubraccios was more the act of a bogyman than a
real victor. Needless to say, the British chief took no notice of it.

But by now further troubles had sprung up on the continent. The Eburones, a
tribe living between the Rhine and the Meuse and ruled by Ambiorix and Catuvolcos, began to create disturbances. The legion Caesar sent there had no effect.
Ambiorix made a treaty with the Treverian Indutiomarus, attacked the Roman
camp and slaughtered the soldiers. As undisputed victor, Ambiorix then hastened
to the Atuatuci and the Nervii, both of whom agreed to follow him in his attempt to
surprise the legion commanded by Quintus Cicero which was wintering in the land
of the Nervii. An army of Nervii, Atuatuci, Eburones and other neighbouring
tribes besieged the camp. Cicero was ordered to surrender but refused, and managed to send a message to Caesar through a Gallic traitor. Caesar mustered two
legions and proceeded by forced marches to the land of the Nervii. Although the
60,000 Gauls besieging Cicero's camp turned to face him, he avoided a head-on
battle and merely made his way through the enemy lines to join his lieutenant. The
Gauls, realizing that it was too late to achieve anything, withdrew.

The news that Cicero's camp had been relieved by Caesar spread throughout
Gaul. Indutiomarus, who had hoped to besiege Labienus' camp in the land of the
Remi, temporarily abandoned the idea and went home. The other tribes watched
and waited while Caesar, having given up all hope of making Italy, decided to
spend the winter of 54–53 BC on the Somme at Samarobriva (Amiens). From this
point in the land of the Ambiani he could keep a watchful eye on Belgica.

In fact minor incidents continued throughout the winter, both among the
Armoricans and the Senones. Basically Caesar could only rely on loyal allegiance
from the Remi and the Aedui, and even the latter were not totally behind him. The
Treveri were still prepared to fight, and Indutiomarus decided that the time had
come to take action. The Germans had refused his requests for help, but he did find
support among the Senones and the Carnutes who resented Caesar's treating them
as conquered tribes rather than as allies, and managed to muster a troop of
malcontents from all the tribes. He then had his son-in-law and rival Cingetorix
declared a traitor and crossed into the land of the Remi, intending to attack
Labienus' camp.

In the violent battle which ensued, Labienus ordered his men to seek out
Indutiomarus in particular. The Treverian chief was surprised while fording a
river, and killed as Labienus had ordered. With their leader dead the Treveri went
home. The Eburones and the Nervii then scattered and it seemed that everything
had returned to normal.

At the beginning of the sixth book of his Commentaries, Caesar admits that he
had many reasons for expecting more serious disturbances in the near future. The
Romans might have appeared to control the whole of Gaul but the entire country

could have risen against them at any moment, and Roman authority would have fallen apart at the seams. That is why he sought new recruits in early 53 BC. He wanted to impose Roman rule once and for all.

It was the Eburones, led by Ambiorix who finally launched the rebellion by talking to the Germans, now quite prepared to offer them every assistance. Caesar responded by putting down any latent opposition among the Carnutes and the Senones and making to crush the Treverian-Eburonian coalition. He crossed the land of the Menapii who again fled with all their possessions into the depths of their forests and marshes and left Commios the Atrebatian to keep them under surveillance. (Commios' authority now extended over the Atrebatians, the Morini and the Menapii.) The Treveri were routed by Labienus and power restored to Cingetorix, the Romans' traditional ally. Caesar then set off in pursuit of the invading Germans. His second crossing of the Rhine was yet another, brief, pre-stige operation before returning to Gaul. Then in the summer of 53 BC, he had the most extraordinary good luck to come across Ambiorix isolated with a small force in the middle of a forest. Ambiorix's ally Catuvolcos killed himself rather than fall into Roman hands, but Ambiorix managed to escape, ordering some of his troops to scatter into the forest of the Ardennes, some into the swamps and some to the islands and sea coast. Ambiorix clearly did not consider himself beaten and wanted to keep his army intact for a future battle.

Powerless against a guerrilla army, Caesar was content to plunder the land of the Eburones and assemble his troops and provisions in the fortress of Atuatuca. An attack on this stronghold by the Germans, who had crossed the Rhine solely to loot Ambiorix's territory, gave the Eburones a chance to recover. Once again Caesar won a pyrrhic victory. He forced the Germans to retreat but weakened his own army in the process and achieved no decisive success against the Gauls. At the end of 53 BC he set up winter quarters among the Lingones, the Treveri, the Senones and the Carnutes, and took retaliatory action against the rebellious chiefs. Acco, the Senonian, who later became a martyr for Gallic liberation, was put to death. The appeased proconsul then announced his arrival to the Senate, covered himself in glory and went to Italy to nurse his popular image at home.

The War of Independence

Over the six years or so during which this series of massacres had been taking place, the Gauls had come to realize that the Romans were intent on enslaving them. Caesar's supposed role as mediator between the tribes, and protector against the Germans had worn too thin to be believed. The Gauls now saw him for the power-hungry conqueror he was, the ambitious general who hoped to capital-ize on his foreign victories when he returned home. Even his Aeduan allies had noticed that after every campaign, successful or otherwise, the proconsul returned to Italy to parade his courage and his triumphs before the Senate and the people of Rome. Only the Remi continued to believe in him, but then they had deliberately adopted a policy of neutrality.

In early 52 BC, there were disturbances in Rome following the assassination of Publius Clodius, and the subsequent political intrigues kept Caesar at home. Presented with this apparently heaven-sent diversion, the Gallic leaders felt that the time had come to start their war of liberation.

This time the movement started in Celtica, among the Senones who could boast of their victory at the Allia and of having sown terror among the Romans. They were joined by the Carnutes, who were conscious of the strength of their position in the very heart of Gaul, and direct contact was established with the leaders of other tribes. The unfortunate Acco was held up as a symbol and as a warning. The decision to strike a decisive blow against the Romans by barring their route from the Rhone Valley to the Seine Valley and thereby cutting off the legions from their general and their supply bases had to be temporarily shelved because the Aedui who held the Burgundian approaches were still allied to the Romans. Approaches were therefore made to the Arverni, rivals of the Aedui, who had played no active part in the anti-Roman struggle over the previous few years but had retired to their mountains. They had, however, retained their independence and the economic influence afforded them by their long-standing trade with the Massiliots, and had been active at the time of the Cimbrian invasions. The Arvernian leader Celtillos had even laid claim to the supreme kingship of Gaul, or at least of Celtica, though we know nothing else about him.

We should remember that the concept of supreme kingship was much in vogue during the second Celtic Iron Age. The Bituriges were "kings of the world" (*Bitu-Rigues*, from Welsh *bydd*, world and *rix* or *rig* as in the Latin *rex*). The significantly named Celtillos, the Helvetian Orgetorix, the Eburonian Ambiorix, the Aeduan Dumnorix, the Briton Casswallawn and the Atrebatian Commios all aspired to fulfil the great Celtic dream of leadership. But it was only ever fully realized in Ireland, where the king of Tara was High King of all the island's five kingdoms. And he lived in the kingdom of Midhe, middle, a name obviously connected with the notion of the *omphallos*. The sole figure to attain supreme kingship among the Gauls and the Britons was the mythical King Arthur.

Celtillos' son, however, had inherited all his father's ideas and aspirations. This "very powerful young Arvernian" as Caesar describes him (VII, 4), was called Vercingetorix, a name which the Latin historian Florus tells us "was made to inspire terror" (Florus, III 10). Although many highly romantic meanings have been attributed to it (Henri Martin even suggesting "King of a Hundred Heads", a fearsome executioner indeed), the word Vercingetorix can quite easily be broken down into an augmentative prefix (as in the Welsh *vor* or *guor* and Breton *meur*, big), and Cingetorix, a name already borne by several figures, including the Treverian rival to Indutiomarus. Since *rix* means king, *cin* (like the Welsh *cen* or *kent*) means a hundred and *geto* or *ceto* (Welsh and Breton *cad*) means fight, Vercingetorix can be translated as Great King of a Hundred Battles. Similar appellations were given to the 2nd century Irish king, Conn Cetchatach (Conn of the Hundred Battles) and to the 8th century British leader Kyndylan, in a poem attributed to the Welsh bard Llywarch Hen.[5]

With a name like this, Vercingetorix seemed to be destined for great things. Remember that many Celtic figures were called by what amounted to nicknames, given them for specific reasons. These descriptive appellations replaced the real names which remained secret, as part of an ancient custom related to totemism and the wearing of masks. To take one example, the Irish hero Cú Chulainn's real name was Setanta, but he became known as Cú Chulainn (Dog of Culainn) after he had killed the guard dog of the smith Culainn and was required to take the animal's place. "'No,' said the child, 'I prefer my name Setanta, son of Sualtam.' 'Do not say that,' said Cathbad, 'for as soon as they hear that name, the men of Ireland and Scotland will do nothing but talk about it.'" (*Ogham* XI, 214–5)

Vercingetorix felt that his time had come. Despite opposition from his relatives, and more particularly from his uncle Gobannitio, he began to assemble an army. The Arverni did not want war and expelled him from the stronghold of Gergovia. But undeterred by this, and conscious of his mission, he raised "a band of vagabonds and beggars" (VII, 4) and sent ambassadors to all the other tribes. In no time he succeeded in winning over the Senones, the Parisii, the Pictones, the Cadurci, the Turoni, the Aulerci, the Cenomai, the Diablintes, the Lemovices, the Andes and even the former members of the Armorican confederation who unanimously elected him commander-in-chief.

A great deal has been made of Vercingetorix's courage, tenacity and patriotism. He is, after all, the first national hero of the French. But although he undoubtedly was brave and resolute, we tend to overlook the power of his own pretensions. Much of his quick-fire success among the Gauls was due to his ability to convince them that he was indeed the ultimate incarnation of the myth of supreme kingship. Once again, the myth preceded the event. And in this case the event was to be an epic on a grand scale, but an epic doomed to failure, for the Celts seemed fated always to support lost causes.

Vercingetorix speedily organized his troops and laid out the plans which he had presumably been working on for years. He sent his close friend Lucterios, a Cardurcan (from Cahors) to the Ruteni who held the Rouergue, a district whose southern frontiers bordered on the Roman *Provincia*. For support from the Ruteni would open the way to attacks on the Roman departure bases.

Vercingetorix himself then went to the Bituriges, who were unsure as to which side they should support. Distrustful of Vercingetorix they decided to ask for help from their allies the Aedui, who replied by sending cavalry and infantry on the advice of the Roman legates Caesar had left with them. Presumably, however, pro-Roman feeling did not run very high among the Aeduan troops, for they halted on the banks of the Loire and returned home. This was enough to sway the Bituriges, who promptly offered their unreserved support to Vercingetorix.

Meanwhile, Lucterios the Cardurcan had managed to win over the Ruteni, the Nitobroges (from the Agen region) and the Gabali (from Gevauden). He organized a strong army and marched into the *Provincia*, making for Narbonne. When the news reached Caesar in Italy, he rushed back to Gaul, deployed troops over a wide area to protect his rear and set off for the land of the Helvii (in the Ardeche). After a chilly passage across the Cévennes he intended to mount a direct attack on Arvernian territory, where the rebellion had started.

But there was no guarantee of victory, and rather than take unnecessary risks, the proconsul went to join the legions he had left among the Lingones and the Aedui, of whose loyalty he was justifiably unsure. When Vercingetorix realized what Caesar was planning, he marched on the Romans' other allies, a group of Boii, whom Caesar had settled under the authority of the Aedui.

Caesar was in an extremely difficult position. If Vercingetorix took the Boian stronghold of Gorgobina (La Guerche), the whole of Gaul would rise against the Romans. He therefore left a reserve force at Agedincum (Sens) and marched down the Loire to besiege Gebanum (Orleans), one of the Carnutes' richest towns, in order to create a diversion. Having made his way into the town, which he plundered and then burnt, he turned to the land of the Bituriges and laid siege to Noviodunum (Neuvy sur Barangeon). Vercingetorix raised the siege of Gorgobina and went to help his allies. The inhabitants of Noviodunum were close to surrender when the sight of Vercingetorix's advance guard gave them fresh courage. But before Vercingetorix had time to bring up his whole army, Caesar gathered all his reserves, took Noviodunum and set off for Avaricum (Bourges), the Biturigan capital.

There were two reasons for this move, of which Caesar admitted to only one. First, as the proconsul said, he thought that the capture of Avaricum would subdue the whole tribe of Bituriges. But, secondly, and this he did not admit, Caesar was running out of supplies and, as the greatest wheat-barn and one of the richest towns in Gaul, Avaricum was a tempting proposition.

Realizing that Caesar's chief concern was possible shortage of provisions, Vercingetorix did everything he could to "prevent the Romans from obtaining forage and supplies" (VII, 14). The season was in his favour; there was no grass in the fields. And a scorched earth policy ensured that the Romans found no hay in the barns either. Even the towns were to be fired so that no possible source of provisions remained.

Twenty towns of the Bituriges were burnt in this way. But it was then that the Celtic myth of kingship proved the Gauls' undoing. With the fate not merely of Gaul but also of Rome and of the whole world in his hands, Vercingetorix yielded to the appeals of the people of Avaricum to spare their town. It was a fatal mistake. With Avaricum burnt, Caesar would have found no provisions, would have been surrounded, forced to surrender. But the Great King of a Hundred Battles was primarily concerned with his role as supreme king and the myth held sway over the immediate realities. The kind of sentimentality which prompted his concession to the townspeople of Avaricum was not unlike the Celtic custom of granting an unspecified gift. Vercingetorix may even have been the victim of a *geis* or taboo which obliged him to accede to the request despite his own misgivings.

So it was decided to defend Avaricum. Vercingetorix continued to harass the Romans who could find no provisions either among the Boii, who pleaded poverty, or among the increasingly rebellious Aedui. The proconsul therefore staked everything on achieving a total victory before it was too late. During this period Vercingetorix was accused of treachery, but managed to appease the mass of the people. The men defending Avaricum proved skilful tacticians, digging pits to trap the Roman siege machines and building impregnable, fire-proof walls with a mixture of stones, burnt wood and earth. After a series of fruitless skirmishes Vercingetorix began to press for the adoption of his original idea to fire and abandon the town. But while the leaders hesitated and the Gallic army gave way to internal dissension, the proconsul launched a fierce assault and took the town. A pitiless massacre of the inhabitants followed, and the Romans were able to secure fresh provisions.

But Caesar had not wholly won the day. Vercingetorix recovered and with a speech to the effect that he had foreseen the entire event and that his initial desire not to defend Avaricum had been a right one, he gave his troops fresh confidence. He then reorganized the army, asked for reinforcements and turned towards the land of the Arverni, where he was sure that Caesar would come to attack him.

As it happened, Caesar went first to settle a political dispute among the Aedui. He then sent four legions under Labienus to march against the Senones and the Parisii and himself led the remaining six legions along the Allier towards the stronghold of Gergovia. Vercingetorix, who had been keeping the Romans under surveillance, cut the bridges over the Allier, but Caesar succeeded in crossing the river nonetheless. Vercingetorix therefore pushed on to Gergovia where he drew up his army on the neighbouring heights so that "they presented a terrifying appearance" (VII, 36).

The plateau of Gergovia lies six kilometres south of Clermont-Ferrand, and rises to a height of 744 metres. It is accessible only from the West through the pass of Goules, the eastern side being bounded by the Allier. The Gauls were in an excellent position as Caesar was well aware. There was no hope of taking Gergovia without a long siege, so he started by positioning his legions as close as possible to the fort so as to profit from any weak spot in the Gallic lines.

It was then that the Aedui, the most opportunistic and least scrupulous tribe in all Gallic history, began to cause trouble. Although their new leader, Convictolitavis, owed his position to the proconsul, he reneged on his agreement to send auxiliary cavalry to the Roman army and placed the forces under the command of a young noble called Litaviccos whom he sent to the Averni instead. But Litaviccos was betrayed to Caesar by two of his rivals, Eporedorix and Viridomarus and was forced to take refuge with his servants in the fortress of Gergovia, after surrendering his cavalry. Disturbed by this Aeduan duplicity, Caesar prepared to raise the siege of Gergovia. He openly admits as much. "Anticipating a widespread rising, however, and afraid of being surrounded by rebellious tribes, he began to consider how he could draw off from Gergovia. . . without making his departure look like a flight occasioned by the fear of revolt." (VII, 43.) Even then, he could not resist the temptation to attack what appeared to be an undefended hill. The *Commentaries* play down this assault so as to gloss over the Roman defeat, but there is no doubt that it left the proconsul in a very critical position.

He and his six legions were isolated in the middle of enemy territory. His other four legions under Labienus were in the Parisian region. He could no longer rely on the Aedui and his only means of communication with *Provincia* lay along the difficult route through the Cévennes. The Rhone Valley was no longer safe because the Allobrages had been stirred up by envoys from Vercingetorix and threatened to join the rebels at any moment.

The Gauls at Gergovia had held out. And the defeated Caesar retreated northwards after suffering heavy losses and craftily haranguing his soldiers whom he held responsible for the Roman reverse. He crossed back over the Allier and waited impatiently for Labienus' legions to join him. To make matters worse, the Aeduans Viridomarus and Eporedorix, who had betrayed Litaviccos out of jealousy, now betrayed the proconsul out of opportunism. Having feigned a reconciliation with the Romans, the Aedui evacuated their town of Noviodunum, burnt it and fell back on their capital at Bibracte. Caesar then hastened to the land of the Senones where he resupplied his army and waited.

Labienus, meanwhile, was making little progress. An attempt to take Lutetia was foiled by a tribal coalition led by Camulogenus, an old Aulercan of great military distinction. Camulogenus drew Labienus into the marshes where he inflicted heavy losses on the Romans. Labienus withdrew to Metlosedum (Melun) where he requisitioned boats and returned to Lutetia by water. The people of Lutetia fired their town and fled into the neighbouring hills. Labienus then set up camp on the present day site of the Louvre, while Camulogenus positioned his men on the other side of the Seine, near what is now St-Germain des Près.

As news of Caesar's defeat at Gergovia spread, the Bellovaci rose in open support of Vercingetorix. Labienus' only hope lay in withdrawal, and even that was none too easy. Under cover of a stormy night he crossed back over the Seine to confront the army of Camulogenus which stood in his way. The battle was fierce, for the Gauls were prepared to die rather than give ground. Finally, however, Camulogenus was killed after inflicting serious losses on the Romans. Labienus' legions reached Agedincum in a sorry condition, regrouped and hastened to meet Caesar.

At this point the Aedui publicly announced their decision to join the rebels, but only after making intolerable demands on the other tribes. They wanted to lead the coalition, a surprising step in view of their previous record. A great Gallic assembly took place at Bibracte and Vercingetorix was confirmed in his position as supreme commander by popular vote. By now all the tribes of Gaul except the Remi, the Lingones and the Treveri had joined the war effort.

Vercingetorix was well on the way to victory. His defeat of the apparently invincible Caesar at Gergovia had stirred Gaul from its apathy and his position as supreme king now seemed assured with one or two dissenting voices, notably among the Aedui. Intent on bringing matters to an early conclusion, he sent the Aedui to win over the Allobrages, either by persuasion or by force, and the Gabali and the Arverni to the land of the Helvii to cut the road through the Cévennes. Finally he set the Ruteni and the Cadurci against the Volcae Arecomici of Nimes to prevent Caesar from obtaining any help from the *Provincia*. It was an excellent plan. Caesar was now cut off from his rearguard. But the furious proconsul turned to the Germans for help; and they, delighted at a chance to play a trick on the Gauls, agreed to supply him with a number of cavalrymen and disciplined infantrymen. There is a tendency to overlook the fact that during the final phases of the Gallic war of liberation, the Germans against whom Caesar had claimed to be protecting the Gauls lent considerable support to the Roman forces.

Armed with these reinforcements, the proconsul marched southwards to force a passage through the Rhone Valley. He had now given up any hope of conquering Gaul, at least for the moment, and was concentrating on the urgent business of defending the *Provincia*.

It was then that Vercingetorix made his second mistake. His cavalry detachment was larger than the Romans', and he could have reduced the enemy gradually in a series of daily skirmishes, possibly even threatening the life of Caesar himself. But he chose to launch a premature assault and the ill-considered onslaught of Gallic horsemen ran into a compact mass of disciplined and fanatical men. With the most mobile of his forces gone and a heart-breaking number of casualties, Vercingetorix then committed his third error. He took refuge in the Mandubrian fortress of Alesia, when he could quite easily have dispersed his troops and continued to harass the Roman forces.

It is little wonder that Caesar the talented siege tactician lost no time in avenging his defeat at Gergovia and laying siege to Alesia expecially now that the enemy who had proved so formidable at large were cornered in one place.

The Gauls appeared to be doomed. Vercingetorix had made too many critical mistakes to be regarded as a hero. In fact he was only the incarnation of a myth and that myth had turned his head and led him to believe that a skilful political intriguer could be a good general as well. There is no denying that he had many good qualities. He might well have become the High King of a unified Gaul under other circumstances, but even then it would have been the concept of kingship rather than the man who governed. When the Gauls were frightened for their lives he proved a distinguished organizer, but confronted with Caesar he became merely a brave man who thought more of his own mission in life than of Gaul herself. To fight Caesar he needed more than that Gallic courage, which so often proved little more than bluster. He needed to be cunning, deceitful and cynical.

There was a man with all those qualities; Commios the Atrebatian. But he did not come to the fore until after the panicky Vercingetorix had walled himself up in Alesia, and by then it was too late.

While the proconsul was building vast siege works in an attempt to end the siege of Alesia, the Gallic chiefs held a meeting. They were tempted to muster forces from throughout Gaul with which to rescue the Arvernian leader and finish the Roman occupation once and for all. But there was a risk that an army of this kind might be too undisciplined and ultimately ineffectual. They therefore decided to ask each tribe for one contingent. This request was answered by all except the Remi who remained loyal to Caesar. The Bellovaci, who claimed to be planning their own war with the Romans, agreed to send a mere 2000 men, but only on condition that their forces were commanded by their ally, Commios the Atrebatian. It is worth noting that Caesar's list of Gallic contingents makes no mention of the Veneti although it does include their neighbours.

When these 240,000 or so men had assembled the question of leadership arose. The Aedui made a successful bid for the supreme command and the job devolved on Viridomarus and Eporedorix, who had betrayed first the Gauls and then Caesar and were now quite prepared to betray each other. Vercassivellaunos, a cousin of Vercingetorix was also appointed commander to show solidarity with the Arvernian chief. But, since it was realized that this triumvirate was incapable of leading anything at all, Commios the Atrebatian, who enjoyed considerable personal influence, was given the position of overall leader.

The name Commios, doubtless a nickname, could mean the *bow* (Welsh *cwm*), an appellation well-suited to his far from straightforward nature. For after an initial alliance with Caesar when the Germans threatened to invade Gaul, he had behaved in a decidedly suspect manner during the invasion of Britain and had since remained in the background, prudently biding his time. Although Vercingetorix had robbed him of the chance to assume the leadership of the insurgents, he probably took an active part in the first phase of the war of liberation. This emerges not so much from what Caesar says about him as from a passage in the eighth book of the *Commentaries*, which were written by Hirtius. In any case, it is safe to assume that the Gallic chiefs would never have entrusted him with responsibility for the army of rescue if he had not demonstrated some long-standing commitment to the Gallic cause.

However, it took some time to organize the relief forces and meanwhile Vercingetorix and his men were growing dangerously short of food and water in Alesia. One of their leaders, the Aeduan Critognatos exhorted the besieged Alesians to show courage and even suggested sacrificing useless mouths to make food for the fighting men, a proposal which Caesar clearly found almost too barbaric to contemplate. Vercingetorix rejected this solution and was prepared instead to send all non-combatants out of the town, but Caesar would not let them through.

It was then that the relieving army arrived. Caesar had prepared for their coming by fortifying his position both on the side facing Alesia and the outer side. According to Henri Martin (*Histoire de France*, I, 183), the proconsul started by "digging a 20 foot wide trench on Mount Alesia to prevent sorties, with a second trench 15 foot wide and 15 foot deep 400 foot lower down, and a third one of the same dimensions at the bottom of the slope, which was filled with water channelled from the Ozerain. Behind the third trench a palisaded rampart 12 foot high was erected together with a parapet surmounted by battlements and those forked branches which the Romans called 'stags' and the French *chevaux de frise*. Fortifying towers were positioned at 24 foot intervals along the rampart. This type of fortification was considered insufficient for the flatter ground where a 5 foot deep trench was dug in front of the rampart and in the trench there were five rows of tree trunks, their tops trimmed to a sharp point. In front of them were eight rows of trenches, 3 foot deep, laid out in quincunxes, 3 feet from one another. These ditches were camouflaged with shrubs and concealed sharpened stakes which projected only four fingers above ground. And to reach these the enemy had to cross a wide area of traps formed by star-shaped pieces of iron planted in the ground. Another similar line of earthworks was constructed so that the eleven-mile line round the town was defended by a fourteen-mile line facing outwards against the relieving forces. These mind-boggling defences were built in the space of six weeks by what may have been less than 60,000 legionnaires who had to face furious sorties from the besieged town".

The Gauls launched a series of violent attacks both from the outside and from the inside, fighting with great courage and daring. But the Roman pits and trenches were too much for them. In a final assault Vercassivellaunos, the Arvernian, was captured and Sedullus, chief of the Lemovices was killed. Although the day had not been entirely lost, vast numbers of men were slaughtered. With the smell of defeat in the air, the unorganized Gallic troops abandoned their positions and retreated helter-skelter.

Vercingetorix was forced to give up hope. He could not wait any longer. The starving and exhausted forces in Alesia were growing weaker by the hour. The Great King of a Hundred Battles offered himself as a scapegoat. Plutarch, in his *Caesar* Book XXVII, Florus (III, 10) and Dio Cassius (XL) all paint a marvellous picture of his surrender, with Vercingetorix, decked out in his most beautiful ornaments riding round Caesar's court, leaping from his horse, throwing his weapons at the proconsul's feet and kneeling, head bowed, before him. But this moving and noble scene belongs to the legend of Vercingetorix, the unlucky hero of Gallic freedom and independence. Its cliché-ridden and romantic tone only goes to prove that even after the conquest the Arvernian chief remained a celebrity among the victors as among the vanquished.

The less palatable truth emerges from Caesar's own account and there is no reason why he should have lied at this point. "A deputation was sent to refer the matter to Caesar, who ordered the arms to be handed over and the tribal chiefs brought out to him. He seated himself at the fortification in front of his camp, and there the chiefs were brought; Vercingetorix was delivered over and the arms laid down." (VII, 89.) As this passage makes clear, Vercingetorix and the chiefs surrendered themselves to their men and it was they who delivered them to Caesar.

Shocking as this may now seem, it was standard practice for the Celts. The highly democratic notion that the chief was responsible to his own men carried an almost sacred significance. Vercingetorix had made a mistake for which he had to pay as a sacrificial victim, that his men might be saved. In this he belongs to the same tradition as the Brennus who killed himself after the sack of Delphi and the Welsh Bran who asked his companions to cut off his head after their failure in Ireland. The religious nature of this responsibility is clearly illustrated in the story of Bran where the hero makes himself a bridge for his army and says, "Let him who is a leader be a bridge" (*Branwen*). For the bridge-maker is the Latin *pontifex*, the priest, and originally the leader was a priest with all the sacred qualities that implied.

Vercingetorix was later taken to Rome to appear in Caesar's triumphal procession and spent six months in prison before being strangled on the proconsul's cold-blooded orders. Caesar divided the other prisoners into two groups. The Aedui and Arverni he sent home free in the hope of using them to regain the allegiance of their tribes while the rest, a mixed bunch from several tribes, were given as slaves to his army, each Roman soldier receiving one of them.

However, the relieving army did not surrender but dispersed into the mountains and waited. The defeat of the Great King of Hundred Battles had dealt a severe blow to morale. The Aedui and the Arverni were therefore the first to return home. Eporedorix and Viridomarus changed sides yet again. Only Commios remained to carry on the struggle. But the peoples of Celtica did not respond to his appeals to join him despite his insistence that they were involved in a kind of Holy War, and he returned home with the Belgae. Caesar sent his legions to various areas of Gaul and went himself to his winter quarters at Bibracte.

We have now reached 51 BC. After the winter calm, insidious rumbles began to erupt again, particularly among the Bituriges and the Carnutes, and were fostered by envoys from Commios. When Gallic traitors told Caesar the news he set off on an intimidation campaign among the Bituriges before marching on the Carnutes. The latter abandoned their towns and villages and took to the forests covering much of their country before seeking asylum across the Seine among the Belgaean tribes. And it was there that the real trouble was brewing.

The Bellovaci, who had previously expressed the desire to make war on their own account, began to mobilize. Their chief Correos attached himself to Commios to form a kind of Belgaean confederation which was joined by all the refugees from Celtica. On learning of this from the ever loyal Remi and from the Suessiones whom he had placed under Remian authority, Caesar marched against the Bellovaci. The two armies surveyed each other, sent for reinforcements and set up ambushes, but the decisive battle took place near the point where the Aisne joins the Oise. There the Remi, who were fighting with Caesar, were beaten, but his German auxiliary forces marched fiercely into the attack. Correos was killed during the course of a skirmish in which he had demonstrated extraordinary courage and determination. With little hope of future success, the Belgae decided to sue for peace. "But Commios fled to the German tribes" (VIII, 21) and Hirtius, who wrote the final book of the *Commentaries*, explains why the Atrebatian did not surrender.

"For the year before, when Caesar was away holding the assizes in northern Italy, Labienus had discovered that Commios was intriguing with various tribes and plotting against Caesar, and decided that it would be no treachery to destroy such a traitor. It was useless to summon him to the camp; he would not have come, and the summons would have put him on his guard. So Labienus sent Volusenus with orders to stage a sham interview and have him put to death. Some centurions specially picked for the purpose went with him. At the interview Volusenus gave the prearranged signal by grasping Commios' hand, but the centurion who made the first sword-thrust failed to dispatch him, only inflicting a severe head wound. . . After this experience Commios was said to have resolved never to come again into the presence of any Roman." (VIII, 23.)

Meanwhile, Caesar went to lay waste the territory of Ambiorix "who fled in terror and so could not be forced into submission" (VIII, 24). Caninius, who had set off on a campaign to wipe out the remaining tribes in the Armorican confederation, was temporarily halted by Dummacos, chief of the Andes, whom he eventually defeated. Caninius then pursued the Senonian Drappes and Vercingetorix's loyal ally the Cadurcan Lucterios, who had mustered a considerable force of refugees from various tribes. Lucterios took refuge in the fortress of Uxellodunum (Puy d'Issolu), but managed to escape with a handful of men while Caninius was laying siege to the stronghold.

Concerned about continued unrest among the Carnutes, Caesar demanded that they surrender Gutuater, one of those responsible for the previous rebellion. Gutuater was probably a priest, since according to J. Loth his name was a common noun meaning "father of prayer". An inscription on a Gallo-Roman stone block re-used in the construction of the cathedral of Puy-en-Valay (under the belfrey) mentions a *gutuater* who was also *praefectus coloniae*, and whose son was a *flamen*. Another inscription found in Macon concerns a Gaul who was both a *flamen Augusti* and *gutuatros Martis*. The Carnutian Gutuater was executed in a cruel fashion on Caesar's orders.

After this satisfying act of vengeance, Caesar learnt that the men besieged at Uxellodunum were continuing to harass the Romans. He accordingly marched there with all speed and saw that the Gauls were so well positioned, with a large stock of provisions and access to water, that they might well hold out for months. He therefore made an attempt to cut off their water supply and after fierce fighting the Gauls were forced to surrender.

Caesar then decided to make an example of the defeated army in order to deter further rebellion once and for all. All who had borne arms "had their hands cut off and were then let go" (VIII, 44). Considering that the unfortunate victims probably died in any case from gangrene or loss of blood this was tantamount to a death sentence.

But at least Gaul had now been "pacified", and Caesar had done what he set out to do, a fact which does him some credit considering the difficulties confronting him. His military genius and political opportunism had brought him control of the whole country and he could therefore look forward to mastery of Rome itself. In the meantime Gaul had to be made to accept the new Roman order. Some historians have welcomed romanization as a civilizing influence on the "barbarian" Gauls. Emile Thévenot writes, "Caesar's triumph brought the Gauls into the paths of order and discipline, the only foundation on which anything great or durable can be built." (*Les Gaulois*, p. 133.) The naivety of this statement is almost disarming. For what romanization actually did was to wipe out an entire civilization, an entire religion and an entire language, replacing them with the civilization which invented the "vomitorium" and indulged all kinds of orgiastic behaviour. As the man who dug the grave of Gallic civilization, Caesar is hardly to be congratulated; and the "paths of order and discipline" sound far too much like the benefits promised by Nazi propaganda for comfort. What would have become of Gallic civilization we shall never know: there is no changing the past. But we can be sure that it would have had its own distinctive characteristics. Instead of this Gaul was subjected to the vast, oppressive machine of the Roman administration which crushed every aspect of Celtic individuality. And the ecclesiastical administration which followed continued the same repressive work, regardless of what was good and what was evil.

And yet there was one man who refused to follow the rest of Gaul into subjection and who fought on undeterred to the end. This man was Commios the Atrebatian.

With a troop of faithful followers who had fled to his command from all over the country, he continued to harass the Romans in a kind of guerrilla war. He "supported himself and his followers by brigandage, intercepting by means of raids on several convoys destined for the Roman camp" (VIII, 47).

Volusenus who had previously been ordered to kill him was sent in pursuit of him and his army, a task "which he undertook all the more willingly because he detested Commios". The Romans therefore laid a series of ambushes and managed to kill a number of Gallic cavalrymen. Finally, however, Commios and Volusenus came face to face. The Atrebatian seriously wounded the Roman, but finding himself virtually alone on the battle field he sent messengers to ask for peace, on the express condition that he should not have to appear before any Roman.

It was a strange ending to the epic of Gaul. Commios' solitary presence on the battlefield is reminiscent of all those tales in which a lone warrior returns from the war, of the great Welsh epic of *Gododin*, chanted by the bard Aneurin with its recurring image:

> Of the three score generals who hastened to Kattraeth
> a single man returned home. . .[6]

That single man was Commios. Realizing that Gaul was lost for ever, the Atrebatian set sail for Britain.[7] There, at least, the hope of a Celtic universe was still shining brightly.

CHAPTER SIX

The History of the Gaels

EORGES
Dumézil has pointed out that the Irish thought of their history in mythical terms, a comment which can equally well be applied to the other Celtic peoples though nowhere with so much justification as in Ireland. The Gaels tried to adjust what happened to them to fit what *should* have happened to them so that events originated in myth. If, therefore, the Irish have altered reality since their earliest days it is less out of a pure spirit of invention than out of a desire to re-establish that proper order of things which has been put out of joint by unforeseeable factors.

For this reason it is rather difficult to reconstruct the early history of Ireland. The only written evidence comes from mythological tales, poems and the *Leabhar Gabala* or Book of Invasions, a scholarly compilation of various oral traditions, annals and genealogies which was made in the 9th and 12th centuries by erudite monks. The whole vast epic is summarized in the *Scel Tuain maic Cairill* or Story of Tuan son of Carill, a mixture of strange prose tales and verse. The narrator is the mythological character Tuan, who has supposedly witnessed all the events recounted in a succession of reincarnations.

Five invasions were there in Ireland. Nobody came there before the

flood. After the flood nobody came for 312 years. Partholon, son of
Sera, came to Ireland in exile with twenty-four men and their wives.
They settled in Ireland and their race lived there for 5,000 years. In the
space of one week an epidemic descended upon them and they all died.
But there is never a disaster without one survivor to tell the tale. I am
that man.[1]

The people of Partholon, therefore, were the first to occupy Ireland though
where they came from we have no way of knowing. The only additional information we have about them is that they cleared the island for cultivation and that they
were shepherds. They also introduced the peculiar practice of fosterage which
survived in Gaelic Ireland for centuries, even during English occupation. The
people of Partholon had to fight the neighbouring race of Fomoré, a kind of pirate
band, more gods than men, whose favourite resting place was among the surrounding islands, and who were led by the giant Balor.

After the race of Partholon had all died, Ireland was empty for 32 years.
"Then," as Tuan goes on, "came Nemed, son of Agnoman, who took possession of
Ireland. . . When Nemed came to Ireland with his fleet he had 34 ships and they
had sailed aimlessly for eighteen months on the Caspian Sea, and many of them
foundered or died of hunger and thirst, except four couples with Nemed. Then his
race increased until there were 4,030 couples. But they all died. . ."

The race of Nemed is as mysterious as the race of Partholon, though there is a
suggestion that they were Scythians from the vicinity of the Caspian. They too
were harassed by the Fomoré and had to pay them a large tribute every year at the
feast of Samain (November 1). Other sources claim that they abandoned the
island.

"Then Senion, son of Stariath, took Ireland. From him came the Fir [Men]
Domnainn, the Fir Bolg and the Galiain; they had the island for a time." These
three groups can be equated with the British Dumnonii who gave their name to
Devon and the Breton Domnonia, with the Gauls and with the Belgae, also generally regarded as a British nation. Evidence that there was some form of British
civilization in Ireland before the arrival of Gaels lends a certain amount of cre-
dence to this part of the legend. We can presume, therefore, that there was indeed
an invasion of Belgae accompanied by Dunnonii and Gauls possibly in the 5th
century BC. These immigrants were agricultural peoples, probably of the Hallstatt
Iron Age civilization. They introduced the use of iron, notably for making spears,
and instituted a royal line connected with the fertility of the soil.

But, continues Tuan, "Beothach, son of Iarbonel the Prophet, took the island
after overcoming the peoples who occupied it. It was he who founded the Tuatha
de Danann, whose origins are said to be unknown. Their intelligence and skills
make it likely that they came from the heavens." Indeed, the Tuatha de Danann,
or tribes of the goddess Dana, were the great gods of pagan Ireland. The tale of the
Battle of Mag Tured offers the following portrait of them: "The tribes of the goddess
Dana were in the western isles of the world, learning science, magic, druidism,
witchcraft and wisdom, and they became superior to the craftsmen among the
Gentiles. The four towns where they learnt their diabolic wisdom and skills were
Falias, Gorias, Murias and Findias."

It would seem that the Tuatha de Danann came from northern Europe. If they
were the dolmen-building Hyperboreans, however, as we have suggested in the
chapter on the Cimbri, we would expect to find them in Ireland before the Celtic

Fir Bolg; and Tuan's words suggest otherwise. But poem 62 of part VII of the *Leabhar na Gabala* does say that "Iarbonel the white, the excellent prophet" was "the son of Nemed, son of Agnoman". So the Tuatha must have been a breakaway group of Nemedians who had fled to the western isles to escape the Fomoré and there reaped the benefits of a more advanced civilization. Later, when Ireland fell into the hands of Fir Bolg, the Tuatha joined with the Fomoré to fight the first battle of Mag Tured which ended in defeat for the Fir Bolg. From this point the Tuatha became masters of the island, though they had to share the land with the Fomoré. The two races intermarried, but the Fomoré became increasingly acquisitive until Nuada, king of the Tuatha, who had lost a hand during the first battle of Mag Tured, was forced to abdicate in favour of Bress, son of the Fomoré Elatha and the Tuatha Eriu (Ireland). When Bress made intolerable demands on the Tuatha, they rebelled and, led by Nuada, Lug, Ogma and the Dagda, all members of the Celtic pantheon, they fought the second battle of Mag Tured. There the Fomoré were defeated and King Balor was killed. The Tuatha were free.

The Tuatha de Danann were the bringers of civilization: Lug was a master craftsman and taught arts and crafts; the Dagda built fortresses; Goibniu the smith introduced metallurgy; Dianecht brought medicine. The Tuatha appear to have formed an intellectual and martial aristocracy unlike the beaten Fir Bolg who had to be content with working the land or the Fomoré who were a sea-faring nation.

It was then, however, that the sons of Mile, or Gaels, appeared. An ancient tale in the *Yellow Book of Lecan*, *Do Suidigud Tellaich Temra* (The sharing of the land of Tara) gives the following account of the origins of the Gaels:

> We are born of the children of Mile, of Spain. After the building of the tower of Nimrod and the confounding of languages, we went to Egypt on the invitation of the Pharaoh, king of Egypt. Nel, son of Fenius, and Goedel Glas were our chiefs when we were in the South. That is why we were called Fene, from Fenius and Gaels from Goedel Glas. . . When we were in Egypt, Scota, daughter of Pharaoh the king, was given as wife to Ne, son of Fenius. That is why she is our ancestor and why we are called Scots from her. The night when the children of Israel escaped from Egypt and crossed the Red Sea dry-footed with Moses, son of Amram, the leader of God's people, and when Pharaoh and his army were drowned in the sea after keeping the Hebrews in captivity, our ancestors did not go with the Egyptians in pursuit of God's people and therefore feared Pharaoh's anger. They feared lest the Egyptians reduce them to slavery as they had previously done the children of Israel. So they fled one night on Pharaoh's vessels across the shallow Red Sea to the boundless ocean around the North West of the world. They passed the Caucasian Mountains, Scythia, and India, crossed the Caspian Sea which lies there, crossed the Palus Maeotis and arrived in Europe; from the South East Mediterranean to the North West, right of Africa, they passed the columns of Hercules on their way to Spain and thence to this island. . . It was Ith son of Breogan who saw the mountains of Irrus from the top of Breogan's tower in Spain and it was he who came to this island leaving a path for us to follow. . . .

There is not much to be gleaned from this complicated story, except that the Gaels, like the other Celts, came from Central Asia. But it is likely that there were two Gaelic invasions, one from the South and therefore possibly via Spain, and the other from the North. With the help of the poet Amergein and of the three goddesses Eire, Fotla and Banba (the three names for Ireland), Eremon, Eber and Ir, the sons of Mile, managed to defeat the Tuatha de Danann at the battle of Tailtiu. The two races then agreed that the sons of Mile should keep the earth and that the Tuatha should have the underground and island regions. The gods therefore found themselves banished to the mounds, or megaliths, which promptly became magical and sacred places, part of the world of the *sidh*. Their memory has persisted until today in the shape of what Irish country people respectfully call "the good people".

The apparently superior sons of Mile probably represent the second Iron Age La Tène civilization. Their language was closely related to Latin and presumably therefore derives from a common Italo-Celtic base, though Gaelic is more archaic in its phrasing and vocabulary than the language of the British people, the Gauls, Belgae and Britons. The Gaels, for example, retained the Indo-European Q-sound, as the Latins did, while the Britons evolved it into a B- or P-sound. Thus, the Gaelic words for "head" and "four" are *cet* and *ceathair* (Latin *caput* and *quattuor*), unlike British *penn* and *pedwar*. Though probably fairly limited in numbers, the sons of Mile imposed their own customs, language and religion on the indigenous peoples who were themselves a very hybrid mixture. For apart from the descendants of the Belgae, there were Picts (Greek *Pretanoi*, whence the word Britons), whom the Gaels called *Cruithni*, the *Erainn*, who lived in the South and whose origins are obscure but who gave their name to the island (Eire, Iwerddon, Ierne, Hibernia) and lastly the descendants of the Tuatha.

As far as we know, there was very little difference between the Gaels' religion and that practised by the Britons and Gauls. Their priests were also druids, or seers (the Indo-European root *id* in *dru-id* being the same as in the Latin *videre*, to see). Although the druidic body as a whole was organized into a strict hierarchy, the individual druid lived alone and shared in the life of the people. The druids were well versed in all learning and had the gift of prophecy; they were masters of spells and magic and could produce enchanted mists, transformations of appearance and so on whenever required. They could also impose the *geis*, a kind of magical taboo which was both injunction and prohibition and could not be transgressed without incurring death or dishonour. Like their Gallic brothers they wrote nothing down, doubtless for the same reasons, although in early Christian Ireland there was an alphabet known as *ogham*. This consisted of horizontal or diagonal strokes grouped together in numbers from one to five and drawn from a central perpendicular line.

Such was the authority of the druids that their words were always taken as law. The king had to wait until the druid had spoken, and the chiefs to bow to the druid's ability to interpret the omens when it came to decision-making. As Caesar wrote of the Gallic druids, "They act as judges in practically all disputes, whether between tribes or between individuals; when any crime is committed, or a murder takes place, or a dispute arises about an inheritance or a boundary, it is they who adjudicate the matter and appoint the compensation to be paid and received by the parties concerned" (*Gallic Wars*, VI, 14).

The druids were also used as ambassadors and would be sent to sue for peace or war. Though Caesar claims that the Gallic druids were "exempt from military service" their Irish counterparts appear to have played their part in various wars and conflicts. At the siege of Druim Damghaire the druid Mogh Ruith carries weapons which are described in great detail (*Revue Celtique*, XLIII, 75), though the principal druidic weapon, was, of course, magic. The druids were regarded as healers. It was said of Fingen, the king of Ulster's druid, for example, that "Everyone came to show him their cuts and wounds, their injuries and their pains: he told everyone what their illness was and gave them remedies and everyone found that they did indeed have the illness he had said".[2]

It is usually supposed that the druids vanished when Ireland became Christian, particularly after Saint Patrick who "fought against the druids with a hard heart. He crushed the proud with help from the white heavens and he purified Ireland with its green plains and its great race".[3]

In fact there is evidence that the caste of druids survived at least until the reign of Domnall hUa Neill, who died in 978, while Saint Patrick's great practical achievement, the organization of the church, fell into disuse almost immediately after his death. The druids in Ireland were never hounded or banned as they were in Gaul, and to a certain extent in Britain; and it seems certain that they became absorbed into the caste of *filid*, or bardic poets, whose status was solemnly confirmed in 575 by Saint Columkill. For the *filid* were not merely poets, but to a certain extent practisers of magic, if not of sacrifice.

One aspect of the druidic religion which still remains a mystery is the question of druidesses. The lack of any historical proof has tended to cast doubt on their existence, and yet there is much evidence to suggest that there was some kind of feminine religious institution. A work written in Vulgar Latin by Numerian tells how a druidess who lived in an inn is supposed to have prophesied that Diocletian would become emperor if he killed a boar. It so happened that Diocletian came to the throne after he had killed the prefect of the *Aper* (Boar) practorium. Whether this druidess was any more than a "seer" we do not know. However, as Françoise Le Roux says "Celtic society always held women in great honour . . . in the best pieces of the Irish and Welsh cycles, where the pagan flavour is most authentic, the poetess (*banfile*) or druidess (*bandrui*) is a familiar figure. This is hardly surprising in a country where, until the 7th century, any woman owning land was bound to give military service in the same way as a man" (*Les Druides*, p. 17).

For Gaelic society accorded women a much more important role than that granted to their Mediterranean counterparts. Queens ruled as equals with kings. In the tale of the *Raid of Cooley*, Queen Medb rejects her husband Ailill's claim that marriage to him has increased her wealth and prestige and challenges him to an open display of their respective riches. The Gaelic woman could also lay claim to self-determination. If she fell in love with a man she would openly invite him to share her bed. If the man refused she cast an inescapable *geis* on him, as Deidre does on Noise, and Grainne on Diarmaid. Although Gaelic society was never the total matriarchy some writers would have us believe, the respect and authority enjoyed by women contributed in no small measure to the later restitution of woman's position throughout 12th and 13th century Western Europe during the period of Courtly Love. We do have evidence of matrilinear descent in Irish (and Welsh) tradition, where men are often called "son of such-and-such a woman", like King Conchobar mac Ness or Cú Chulainn son of Dechtire. The use of matrilinear descent must in any case have been encouraged by the custom of fosterage.

According to this practice, which survived until the 18th century, a child would be given into the care of friends or relatives until he reached the age of seventeen, the natural father relinquishing virtually all his rights over the child to the foster-father. In many cases the fosterer was actually the mother's brother, a fact which would fit in with Caesar's comments on certain British tribes where women were given complete sexual freedom and their offspring remained members of the mother's family under guardianship of the maternal uncle. It appears that this custom dated right back to the days of totemism. Welsh tales about Gwyddyon and Gilvaethwy, the sons of Don, being brought up by their uncle Math, and Lleu, son of Arianrod, being brought up by his uncle Gwyddyon, would certainly confirm that it was accepted practice.

The clan system, still in force in Scotland, is a legacy of the early Gaelic family which was related to the ancient Indo-European *gens*. There is obviously some inconsistency between the patriarchal structure of the *gens* and the use of fosterage and matrilinear descent. However, given that fosterage is attributed to the race of Partholon and is therefore pre-Indo-European in origin, there is no reason why the use of matrilinear descent may not also be pre-Indo-European, having its origins among the Tuatha de Danann, or builders of megaliths. The Gaels would appear to have assimilated the customs of the indigenous peoples and incorporated them into their own.

Legally, the Gaelic family or *deirbhfine*, an Aryan import, extended to four generations from the father or *cenn-fine* (head of the family) to the great-grand-nephew. Outside these four generations the family would be divided into various different branches, all entitled to a share of the inheritance under the law of *gavelkind*, a characteristic of Irish, British and Breton societies which appears to be related to early German (and therefore Celtic) law. The practice of *gavelkind* naturally gave rise to property being divided into endless small units, which often resulted in family disputes or attempts to repartition the legacy by force. Domestic quarrels of this kind considerably weakened Celtic society but were virtually inevitable, given the way the law was framed. Accession to the throne became the subject of similar disputes when legal succession within one family expired after the fourth generation.

The basic political unit was the *tuath* or tribe. Traces of totemism are also evident here. King Conchobar of Ulster, for example, is chief of the Red Branch; Finn is chief of the Fenians, a clan-like organization subject to strict laws; the Tuatha de Danann were all descended from the one ancestor, the goddess Dana. With each *tuath* having its own almost autonomous form of administration, inter-tribal relations could become extemely complex. Indeed, the most striking aspect of Celtic societies in Gaul, Britain and Ireland was their carefully preserved, almost built-in tendency to anarchy. Each *tuath* had its own king or chief for kingship was a concept difficult for any self-respecting Celt to accept, as witness the problems encountered by Vercingetorix. This chief was a kind of patriarch, war leader, diplomat and judge, whose authority was far more moral than material.

The chief was elected from within the royal family, every member of this one *deirbfine* being eligible. We can presume that this gave rise to fierce rivalry and intriguing among those members of the fourth generation who were last in line, for the position of *tanaisex rig* or heir presumptive was later instituted in an attempt to prevent such disputes. In fact the new institution did little to improve the situation, for as soon as a king died, fresh quarrels broke out between his official successor and the other claimants to the throne.

Even so, the myth of a world king did produce attempts to unify society. The Gaels felt that they could only survive with a single authority, but that this authority would have to be both incontestable and flexible. For the Celts would never accept the dictates of one man. During the early centuries AD Conn Cetcatach (Conn of the Hundred Battles) king of Connacht (Connaught) to which he gave his name, took the title of *Ard ri* (high king) over all the provinces of Ireland. This supreme monarch whose seat was at Tara, the symbolic capital of Ireland and a kind of *omphallos* for the Gaelic world, held a position more honourable than influential. The high kings who followed were often scorned and sometimes even dethroned to be followed by others as ephemeral as they. On his election a new high king would make a tour of Ireland providing of course that the provincial kings would allow him into their territory; and during this journey he would raise tributes, exact promises, later broken, and take hostages to ensure obedience.

As we can see, Gaelic society was structured in an idealistic, almost mythical way. At the top was the high king, a suzerain if you like, who was responsible for maintaining tradition. He was enthroned at Tara on a coronation seat called the *Lia Fail* (the stone of Fal) brought back from the islands at the North of the world by the Tuatha de Danann, which emitted a cry when each new incumbent sat upon it. Then came the provincial kings, numbering first five and later seven, who were masters in their own countries, at least theoretically, for the hierarchy was very precisely laid down. Almost on a level with the local king was his hospitaller, a high-ranking noble entitled to 800 hectares of land and countless servants, who was required to keep open house for all comers at all times. It would appear that this office was formerly allotted to the king himself, since he had retained the obligation to grant a gift to whoever asked it without even knowing beforehand what was being demanded. As the Gaels saw it, their king was to be the benefactor of the *tuath* and to serve others rather than profit by his influence. This ideal, fine though it was, resulted in his authority growing progressively weaker. The hospitaller, for example, by acquiring the king's job as provider, became a kind of second king of the *tuath* who was respected as a symbol of that hospitality which was always sacrosanct among the Celts.

Roughly on a level with the hospitaller was the bishop or abbot of Christian Ireland, or the druid of pagan times. Below them came the "professional" classes, who were divided into two categories, the *brehons* and the *filid*. The *brehons* were lawyers who fulfilled the kind of legal duties previously discharged by the druids, while the more religious aspects of the druids' work devolved on the *filid*, who were also bards and scholars. It was they who preserved Gaelic culture and taught the young, even during the Christian era when they continued their work alongside the monks, and during the English occupation. Indeed, their descendants, the wandering singers of the more farflung areas of the island, managed to keep alive the use of the Gaelic language and the memory of old traditions right up until the 19th century.

Below the king, the hospitaller, the clergy and the scholars, came the various nobles, first the king's immediate family, then his more distant relatives, the minor knights and the harpists who formed a separate, non-plebian class. The Celts in general, whether Gaels or Britons, regarded the harp as the paragon of musical instruments. The most famous harp of all belonged to the god Dagda and being magical could come down from the wall by itself. On it the Dagda could play the melodies of sleep, laughter or mourning until his audience began to doze, to laugh or to weep.

At the bottom of the social scale were the craftsmen, the vassals in the precise sense of the word (Welsh *gaws*, a servant, from the Gallic *vassos*), and the male and female slaves who were more like serfs than Mediterranean slaves and were presumably former captives unable to raise their own ransom.

The aristocratic nature of the hierarchy is proof that it was marked out by a comparitively small number of invading Gaels who formed an intellectual and warrior élite. The intellectual aspect is worth emphasizing, since few societies have ever held scholars in such honour as Irish society did. Wealth was measured in agricultural terms, with the highest status going to whoever owned most livestock: hence the cattle raids which form the subject of so many epics. This presumably meant that a large part of the non-Gaelic population was employed on the land. However perfect in theory, the nature of Irish social structure and the outbreaks of conflict in a multi-racial population made the country very difficult to govern. Indeed, before the series of battles against the English oppressors Irish history was one long succession of civil wars.

At the beginning of the Christian era the island was divided into five provinces which were actually separate states. These were Ulster in the North, Connaught and Munster in the West and North and South Leinster in the South East. Ulster appears to have been much the largest with its sphere of influence extending as far South as the Boyne, i.e. almost as far as what is now Dublin. The Ulster of the epics is a well organized and powerful state. In the *Tain Bo Cualnge* the other four provinces have to form a coalition to fight it. Underlying this epic, mythological though its characters may be, is a historical story of rivalry between Connaught and Ulster. Two of the main characters of the Ulster cycle, Conchobar mac Ness, king of Ulster and Cù Chulainn, the hero of Ulster defence against Connaught, are supposed to have died in about 20–30 AD and 2 BC respectively.

Throughout the first century AD there was a confused series of power struggles. King Cormac Conloing was killed when his fortress of Da Choga in Midhe (Meath) was destroyed. Tuathal Techtmar reigned from 76 to 106 and fell foul of the kings of Leinster. It was then that the half-legendary, half-historical figure of Conn of the Hundred Battles appeared. From Connaught where he was king he crossed the Shannon, settled in central Ireland and founded the kingdom of *Midhe* or Middle with its capital at Tara. He used this symbolic position to claim the title of high king. The new kingdom of Meath replaced North Leinster which Conn had eliminated. However the king of Munster, Eoghan Mor, nicknamed Mogh Nuadat (friend to the god Nuada) challenged Conn's position and the two men finally agreed to divide the island into two spheres of influence. *Leth Cuind* (Conn's half) was to lie North of the line of hills between Dublin and Galway, and *Leth Moga* (Mogh's half) South of that line. Conn remained a celebrated figure throughout Ireland and apart from a few interruptions the throne of Tara stayed in the hands of the *Dal Cuind*, the descendants of Conn, until 1022. Conn himself is the hero of a strange tale entitled the *Baile in sceail* (Prophetic ecstasy of the Phantom) which was written down in the 11th century on the direction of the abbots of Armagh.

> One day, Conn is walking round the ramparts at Tara when he steps on a stone which cries out. This is *Lia Fail*, the symbol of sovereignty, which continues to cry out whenever one of Conn's descendants comes to the throne. A knight then appears and asks Conn to follow him. They come to a plain where there is a golden tree and go into a magnificent house. There on a throne of crystal sits a girl wearing a crown of gold, with the god Lug beside her. The girl turns out to be the sovereignty of Ireland. She gives Conn a side of beef and a side of pork and then serves him red ale in a golden cup, asking for whom she is pouring the drink.

Lug then names each of the princes of Conn's line who are to reign after him.

Condle, one of Conn's sons, was also the hero of a magical adventure probably dating from the 8th century contained in the *Book of Ulster*. A woman appears to Condle and reveals to him that she has come from the Land of Promises (Fairy land, the land of the Tuatha de Danann). Although everyone can hear her, only Condle can see her. She declares that she loves Condle and asks him to follow her. After several attempts to do so, thwarted by Coran, Conn's druid, who tries to magic away the fairy, Condle manages to board her crystal boat and vanishes for ever. This legend is almost certainly the poetical expression of Condle's premature death, as connected with druidic beliefs about the Other World.

Another of Conn's sons was involved in the history of Munster, officially part of Mogh Nuadat's sphere of influence. Banished after an unsuccessful attempt to seize Munster, he returned to win the battle of Mag Mucrama in 195.

However, it was Conn's son Art who succeeded him and who is the hero of a strange epic entitled *Echtra Airt maic Cuind, ocus tochmare Delchaine ingine Morgan* (the Adventures of Art, son of Conn, and the Courtship of Delbchaen, daughter of Morgan) contained in the *Book of Fermoy*.

This extremely puzzling epic is of great interest, since it tells of a quest in that special world of gods and heroes where prehistoric and Gaelic ideas about sovereignty become fused together. Like its Welsh counterpart, the legend of *Culhwch and Olwen*, the *Adventures of Art* contains the two themes of the Grail-quest and of the chosen one who must come to regenerate the earth by taking up the royal office. The authors of the tale appear to have gone out of their way to make the historic parts played by Conn and Art match the myth of lost sovereignty.

> The widowed Conn is still mourning the death of his wife when he meets a marvellous woman, Becuna Cneisgel (White Skin), who is really a fairy banished from the land of the Tuatha de Danann because she committed a serious crime. She agrees to marry Conn but only on condition that Art is banished for a year. "Conn said to Art, 'leave Tara and Ireland for one year, and go now because I have promised as much.' And the men of Ireland said that it was a great shame that Art was banished because of a woman. But Art left Tara that night, and Conn and Becuna remained together for a year at Tara."

Underlying this episode there may well have been some difficulty encountered by the historic Conn in ensuring that Art was recognized as his heir. Certainly Art's exile is regarded as irregular. For "during that year, there was neither wheat nor milk in Ireland, a fact which brought the men of Ireland great problems. The druids were summoned from all over Ireland . . . that men might know what was causing this misfortune. The durids told the king of Tara that the troubles were caused by the depravity of Conn's wife. And they added that deliverance depended on the son of a faultless couple's being brought to Tara to be killed here and his blood mixed with the soil of Tara."

The druids' advice is obviously related to the fertility ceremonies of ancient times in which the blood of the sacrificial victim brought back life and growth to the barren land. Whether it is a memory of prehistoric Irish practice, or of the kind of sacrifice of the first-born related in the biblical story of Abraham and Isaac, we do not know. But the same theme recurs in the British traditions relating to Merlin the Wizard, when Vortigern is told that the blood of a fatherless child must be mixed with the mortar if the tower he is trying to build is to remain standing.

> Conn, however, cannot send Becuna away, for he is bound to her by a *geis*. He therefore sets off to look for a child born of a faultless couple. He finds a coracle and sails to a magical island where he finds exactly the kind of youth he is looking for. The young man agrees to go back to Tara on condition that he has the protection of the kings of all Ireland, of Art and of Finn. Just when he is about to be sacrificed, against Conn's wishes, a woman arrives with a cow. The woman says, "Here is what you must do: the cow must be killed and its blood mixed with the soil of Ireland before the gates of Tara. . . When the cow is dead, its two stomachs must be opened. Inside there are two birds, one with a single foot and the other with twelve feet."

Evidently there is some idea of sacrifice by substitution at work here, though the connexion with bull worship must belong to some tradition we know nothing of. Perhaps the Tarvos Trigarannos is a depiction of this theme. Perhaps the cult of the bull was related to fertility rites. In any case, the cow is killed and the two birds fly into the air and start fighting. The one-footed bird which finally gains the upper hand is clearly a symbol for Art, himself the eventual victor. This theme, too, recurs in the story of Merlin for when Vortigern sends his men to look for the fatherless child it is Merlin they find. Merlin then reveals that there are two dragons under the tower, and when these creatures are disinterred they start fighting. A similar fight between dragons also occurs in the Welsh tale of *Ludd and Llevelys*.

When the woman has sacrificed the cow, she prepares to return home with the young man, but before leaving she says to Conn, "You must put far away from you Becuna Cneisgel, that sinful and treacherous girl". When Conn replies that he cannot, the woman declares, "I desire that one third of the wheat, the milk and the harvests of Ireland be lacking as long as that girl is with you".

Conn now retires into the background. Being incapable of ensuring his kingdom's prosperity, as the Fisher-King of the Grail-quest is incapable, he has lost his power to embody the sovereignty of Ireland. It is Art who must take up the reins. Art plays and wins a game of chess against Becuna, which entitles him to demand a forfeit. Art then says to her, "A *geis* upon you. You will eat no food of Ireland until you bring back to me the wand which Curoi, son of Dare, had in his land when he took possession of Ireland and of the Great World."

As one of the Tuatha de Danann, Curoi is a remote and semi-infernal character, so Art's *geis* is tantamount to sending Becuna to the devil. Since Curoi's wand is also a symbol of the ancient sovereignty of Ireland, however, Art's request is also evidence that he is seeking the sacred and legitimate legacy of the land.

> In fact, after various adventures, Becuna returns with the wand. Art takes it and they begin to play chess again. Art notices that the invisible people of the sidh are moving the pieces about the board, but it is too late, for he loses. It is now Becuna's turn to place him under a *geis*. "I desire that you eat no food of Ireland until you bring back Delbchaen, daughter of Morgan." "Where is she?" "In an island in the middle of

the sea, that is all you can know."

As it turns out, this is all the information we need to interpret the story. For as a phallic symbol Art's wand of sovereignty represents the male, paternal patrimony. He now needs to find the female, maternal aspect of sovereignty. The girl and the island in the middle of the sea where she lives are both psychoanalytic symbols of the mother or, more specifically, of the womb. And since Art's mother is dead, a return to the maternal womb necessitates a journey to the Other World. It is evident from this that the epic of Art and the Quest for the Holy Grail are closely related.

Art therefore sets off on his journey. He discovers the coracle previously used by his father and sails from island to island until he reaches a kind of magical country where beautiful women come to greet him. One of them takes him to a crystal chamber where he lives for a month. Art's days in the egg-like room would appear to represent a period of gestation after which he is ritualistically reborn.

> When the month is over, the woman says to him, "It will be a long time before you can find the girl for the way to her is hard. There is land and sea between you; and even if your reach the sea you cannot cross it. It is a vast, unfriendly and deathly ocean. . . Crossing the forests, it is as if there were sword-points under every tree's foot. . . Then after that forest there is a dreadful firth and a sea full of vast-mouthed monsters. Then there is a huge, dense and thorny oak wood facing a mountain, a narrow path to cross it and at the end of this path in a deep thicket a dark house with seven stags and a bath of lead awaiting you, for your arrival has been foretold. And more terrible than any of these, is Ailill Dubhdedach [Black Teeth], son of Morgan Minscothach [Tender Flower], whom no weapon can injure. Two of my sisters are there. . . They bear two cups in their hands, one filled with poison, the other with wine. When you are told to drink, take the cup on your right. Then you will be near the girl's castle. This is how it looks: a bronze palisade runs round it and on each stake has been fixed a man's head. These are the heads of those who have been killed by Coinchend Cedfada [Long Head of Dog Head]. There is just one empty stake. And Coinchend, daughter of the king of the Coinchid [Dog Heads], is the mother of the girl Delbchaen, daughter of Morgan."

The tribulations Art has to overcome are evidently trials of initiation for the man seeking to accede to the throne, as represented by the well-protected Delbchaen. Other claimants have lost their heads to the palisade for only the chosen one, only the man who rediscovers the maternal tradition, can hope to reach the heart of the sanctuary. The matrilinear descent characteristic of Celtic societies is here represented by the two cups, which are the mother's breasts. But Art must drink from the right breast, he must be directly related.

Interestingly, the Welsh legend of *Culhwch and Olwen* has a similar series of trials to be undergone, though as part of a quest for objects rather than for a girl. But the palisade of severed heads with its one empty stake is also there, and the name of Olwen's father is Yspaddaden Penkawr (Large Head) who must surely be comparable with the Gaelic Coinchend (Long Head), herself daughter of Conruth (Red Head). Indeed the two characters come to similar ends, for just as Yspaddaden is executed by Goreu, so Coinchend had her head cut off and placed on the empty stake as a sign that the time has come for Art to take the throne through his possession of Delbchaen.

Art therefore returns to Ireland with Delbchaen. Becuna has to admit defeat and leaves. Conn has become a nobody. Art is now high king.

Art mac Cuind was succeeded by his son Cormac in about 250. Like his father and grandfather, Cormac is also the hero of a tale illustrating the myth of the high king, though his story was not written down until the 14th century.

> Cormac is standing on the ramparts at Tara when a warrior approaches. The stranger bears a branch from which three golden apples are hanging, and when moved these apples give forth delightful music. The warrior says that he comes from the Land of Promise and when Cormac swears to grant three wishes, the stranger gives him the branch. (Cormac has accepted the sovereignty of Ireland inherent in the magic branch, but must also accept the tradition of the obligatory gift which is part and parcel of the royal office.) The following year the warrior returns to claim first the king's daughter, then his son and finally his wife. Being bound by a *geis*, Cormac has no choice but to surrender them, but he pursues the mysterious man. Enveloped in a mist he finds himself in a magical palace where he is received by the god Mananann and a beautiful girl. Finally Cormac wakes up on the grassland at Tara with a marvellous cup which enables him to distinguish truth from lies.

Apart from this legend, Cormac mac Airt is also remembered for his excellence as a king and his attention to the political unity of the country. In Leinster he was confronted by an emergent force in the shape of the Fenians or *Fiana*. They formed a kind of warrior militia which had acquired increasing prestige since the reign of Conn and the battle of Cnucha in 174. The Fenians used to spend the winter among the local people of whichever area they happened to be in where they would ensure that justice was done and the ports defended. The summers they spent hunting in the forests, fighting brigands and collecting taxes. According to the Irish Annals, their chief Finn mac Cumail (Macpherson's Fingal) whose son was called Oisin (Ossian), died in about 252 or 286. Needless to say, Finn is a purely mythical figure and the leadership of the Fenians was probably attributed to him because of his name. The Fenians are supposed to have included some 150 chiefs and 4000 men among their number and to have extended their sphere of influence to cover the whole of Ireland except Ulster. Little wonder, then, that Cormac should have been disturbed by what amounted to a Fenian state within the state of Ireland and that he tried to reduce their prestige.

Apart from his political achievements, Cormac was also responsible for the creation of colleges for the study of military science, law, history and literature at Tara: further evidence of the throne's interest in intellectual pursuits and the Gaels' concern to preserve a peerless élite. Cormac also instituted annual assemblies at Tara and Tailtiu, where the Irish aristocracy would gather together to hold a kind of fair or olympiad. After the loss of an eye, Cormac abdicated the throne and spent his retirement composing a treatise on education for kingship and several works of law which have been preserved.

He was succeeded by his son Cairpre Lifechair who won a decisive victory over the Fenians in 283 at the battle of Cabra, where Ossian and his son Oscar are said to have been defeated. The Fenians then split into small groups which scattered over the countryside to be absorbed into the local population.

The most remarkable of the 4th century kings was Niall Noigiallach (Niall of the Nine Hostages), who reigned from 380 to 405. As the son of Eochaid Muigmedon he was descended from Conn. Niall was also the hero of a tale about the sovereignty which has been preserved in the *Yellow Book of Lecan*.

Eochaid had five sons, Brian, Ailill, Fiachra, Fergus and Niall. But while the mother of the first four was Mongfind, Niall's mother was Cairenn Casdub, daughter of the king of the Saxons. She gives birth to him out on the plain of Tara while being pursued by a wrathful Mongfind. "She did not dare take the child with her; she left it there exposed to the birds. And none of the men of Ireland dared take it for fear of Mongfind, so great was her magic power and so great the dread she inspired." It is possible to discern here the theme of the abandoned child, who is destined for great things.

> Then Torna, the bard, came to the meadow, and saw the lonely infant being attacked by birds. Torna took the child, carrying it against his breast, and it was revealed to him what was to follow. And he said, "Welcome to you, little guest, you will be Niall of the Nine Hostages. There will come a time when you will colour a whole crowd red. Seven and twenty years you will rule over Ireland and you will be heir to Ireland for ever."

Torna then brings up the child and finally presents him at the king's court as the son of Eochaid. The furious Mongfind demands that her husband choose which of his sons is to succeed him. Eochaid cautiously defers to the judgment of the smith Sithchenn, a prophet and like all people of his trade a figure connected with the Other World. Sithchenn describes all the brothers in glowing terms, but finally chooses Niall. Mongfind then tells her sons to fight amongst themselves so that Niall will try to separate them and be killed. But Torna prevents Niall from stopping the fight. During a hunting expedition, the five brothers lose their way and begin to grow thirsty. One after another they go to look for water and encounter a repellent-looking old woman.

> Each of her joints and each of her limbs, from the top of her skull to her feet, was as black as coal. Like the tail of a wild horse was the bristling grey mane which formed the top of her hair. The scythe of green teeth in her mouth reached as far as her ears and could have cut the green branches of an oak. She had two dark and smokey eyes, a hooked and hollow nose. Her body was stringy, pustulous and sickly. Her calves were twisted askew. Her ankles were thick, her shoulders wide, her knees fat, her nails green. Horrible and repulsive was the appearance of this woman.

The ugly hag refuses to give any of the princes water from her well unless they will kiss her on the cheek. All Mongfind's sons naturally refuse, but Niall agrees. "At that moment, as he looked at her, it seemed that there could have been no more beautiful, splendid and lovable girl in the world. Every part of her body from head to toe was like the snow on the edge of a ditch." This girl, who is the old witch transformed, says that her name is Flaithius or "royalty". She advises Niall not to give water to his brothers until they have each made him a gift of their rights as his elders and betters. When this is done Niall becomes his father's legal heir.

Though very much in the tone of the old druidic epics, this tale is merely an expression of the difficulties Niall had to overcome to reach the throne. It does, however, provide a record of the custom of that time by which the brothers had either to agree amongst themselves or fight to the death.

Niall Noigiallach reigned from 380 to 405. Two of his sons, Eoghan and Conall, invaded Ulster from the North West and there founded the celebrated fortress of Ailech which gave its name to the new state. Ireland was no longer the land of "five fifths" but was divided into seven kingdoms: Connaught, Munster, Leinster, Midhe, Oriel or Airghialla (Vassals of the East), Ailech (North West Ulster) and Ulaidh, the remains of the former kingdom of Ulster on the Antrim coast.

Niall's dynasty of h'Ua Neill or O'Neill (the sons of Niall) continued to reign in Ireland until 1022. His two sons shared the lands they had conquered with Eoghan founding the family of Tirone (Territory of Owen, the British version of Eoghan's name) and Conall the family of Tirconaill.

Before long the O'Neills acquired what had previously been Connaught's entitlement to the supreme kinghsip by defeating and killing Ailill at the battle of Ocha in 483. It was then agreed that succession to the high throne should alternate between the Northern O'Neills and the Southern branch of the family.

Niall himself proved a formidable conqueror. Though finally forced to withdraw from an expedition to Wales by the Roman general Stilichon, he brought back considerable spoils. He then went to the continent and is reputed to have died on the banks of the Loire after being wounded in battle by an arrow shot by the king of Leinster who had an old score to settle with him.

The taste for conquest, however, had become deeply instilled. In about 410, the sons of Niall mounted another expedition to Britain. It was a good moment to choose, as the Roman legions there had been withdrawn to the continent and the Saxons invaders were beginning to make their presence felt along the eastern coasts. It was then that the Gaels founded their settlements on the West coast of Britain, chief of which was the kingdom of Argyll (Oir Ghaedhil or Eastern Gaels) and that they imposed their generic name "Scot" on what was to become Scotland.

It was also at about this time that Christianity spread its net so swiftly across Ireland under the influence first of Palladius and then of Patricius, the celebrated Saint Patrick who died in 461. Although Patrick endeavoured to impose a Christianity which was entirely Roman in model, the institutions he established scarcely survived him and the Irish adopted a form of the religion more suited to themselves and their ideas. These we have discussed in more detail in the chapter on Celtic Christianity.

The age of heroes in Ireland now gave way to the age of saints. The monasteries so characteristic of Irish Christianity became cultural centres and political capitals often more powerful than those of the increasingly less authoritative kings. One of these kings, Muirchertach mac Erca, is remembered in a strange epic entitled the *Death of Muirchertach son of Erc*.[4]

Muirchertach is staying at the royal house of Cletech on the Boyne when he meets a beautiful girl while out hunting and falls in love with her. "He told himself that he would give the whole of Ireland for a single night with her." He invites the girl but she will only agree to come on condition that the king does everything she asks and that no priest should set foot in the house while she is there. (Presumably Christianity has not yet been accepted by the entire population.) It later transpires that the girl is a witch and therefore a druidess.

Naturally Muirchertach promises everything she asks. And when he asks the girl's name, he does so by chanting a lay:

> Tell me your name O girl,
> Thou the best loved, woman, sparkling star. . .

This lyrical request brings the highly ambiguous response, "Sigh, Noise, Storm, Wild Wind, Winter Night, Cry, Tear, Groan," and as the word for sigh is *sin*, that becomes her name for the rest of the story. No sooner has Sin moved into the house of Cletech than she drives out the queen and her children. The queen therefore goes to bishop Cairnech and asks for his protection both for herself and for the kingdom. Cairnech threatens the king in a ritual probably inherited from the druids. "He made a grave for the king and said, 'He whose grave is here is finished, and truly it is the end of his reign and of his kingdom'." He then climbs onto the tomb and recites a magic incantation satirizing the king, before finally cursing the fortress and blessing another place to show that authority has passed from Muirchertach's hands. The men of Ireland, however, refuse to follow the bishop, and side with the king. When he asks Sin what her power is, she replies that her magic enables her to work miracles and gives him some examples. But as time goes by, the king realizes that living with Sin is gradually sapping his strength. He goes to confession, but Sin bewitches him with fantastic visions and he falls under her spell again. Despite a presentiment of his own death Muirchertach can no longer escape. During the night he wakes and sees the house in flames. He tries to catch hold of a vat of wine to protect himself but drowns in it. It is then revealed that Sin is the daughter of a man the king has killed and that she is avenging her father's death. But Muirchertach's unhappy end brings her little satisfaction since in the meantime she has fallen in love with him.

Muirchertach died in 512. Two other 6th century kings have also been celebrated in epic: Diarmaid mac Cerbail (d. 544) and Aed son of Ainmire (d. 592). A relatively calm and rational state of anarchy gradually took hold of the Gaels. In 637 King Aed Slaine and his son Domnall fought a terrible six-day battle at Mag Rath (Moira) to beat back the Ulster nobleman Congal Claen. Congal had been banished and was attempting to retake Ireland with an army of Britons, Saxons, Picts and Scottish Gaels. One of those who fought in this battle was the *file* Cennfaeled who died in 678 and was the author of a number of poems celebrating the supreme kingship and the throne at Tara.

Ireland continued to prosper for another hundred years, during which time its cultural achievements far outweighed those of the rest of Western Europe. Continental scholars came to study in the Irish monasteries. Art and literature flourished. Although Christianity had come to stay, it had adapted under the influence of Columkill to include the druidic heritage still preserved by the *filid*.

It was around this time that the Irish literary masterpieces were produced. The great national epics which engraved the age of gods and heroes on the memory of the nation were developed, perhaps rather surprisingly, by the monks who worked with the *filid* to set down the most impressive and well-known stories of tradition in writing. The poetry of this period was a truly lyrical expression of man's every emotion. The art of illumination, too, reached extraordinary heights of perfection and with its interwoven and spiral patterns established a model to be followed in the later Romanesque period. As a promoter of literature and the arts Ireland had an obvious influence on the Carolingian renaissance in France. Alcuin and Scotus Erigena, who founded schools on the continent, were part of the scholarly atmosphere fostered in the Irish colleges. In view of all this, it is patently absurd to say that the Celts have given nothing worthwhile or tangible to Western civilization.

This golden age was not to last, however, for though Ireland had escaped the Roman invasions and avoided for the most part any Saxon attempts at infiltration it now became exposed to a much more fearful scourge even than these. The Norsemen were sweeping West and South and before long the whole of Europe was trembling at the mere mention of them. The Irish called them the Black People, which is significant enough.

In 795 the Danes raided the island of Rathlin and reduced it to ashes. Various monasteries were looted and destroyed. With so much of its landmass open to the sea, Ireland was easy game to the Norse pirates who roamed where they would. Although the longstanding superiority of Irish warriors had guaranteed their independence from neighbouring interference before, the new enemies were equipped with swords of tempered steel and efficient chain-mail and presented a formidable challenge. The Norsemen, moreover, obeyed their leaders' orders without question, while the Irish, as incorrigible as all the other Celts, were far too conscious of their individual importance to lose face before men whom they regarded as purely honorary commanders. To oppose the swift, uncontainable onrush of Norse tacticians, the Irish had only their old war chariots and weapons which broke at the slightest impact.

In 830 the Viking leader Torgeist settled in Armagh and proclaimed himself abbot thereby extending his authority over the area dependent on the monastery. By 841 Torgeist's wife, Ota, was playing the prophetess and delivering her oracles on the high altar of Clonmacnoise. During this period disputes over the title of high king continued among the Irish, and some Gaels even used the opportunity to imitate the Norsemen and loot the monasteries. One might argue that this at least kept the wealth of the land in Irish hands, but generally speaking the years of violence and anarchy had a disastrous effect on the island.

The Danes established settlements all the way down the East coast and sent some of their men from there to England. The Norse colonies at Wicklow, Arklow, Waterford, Cork, Limerick and Dublin (meaning Black Pool), were the first real towns Ireland had ever known. In 841 Dublin became the capital of a Norse kingdom ruled by Ivar and Olaf, the sons of the king of Norway. After Ivar died in 873, Dublin was recaptured by the Gaels and it seemed that the Norse threat had been removed. But the peace was shortlived, for in 915 the Vikings made new and more violent incursions. In the meantime there had been some intermarriage between the two races, and new dynasties known as Gael-Gall had been created. The Norsemen appear to have been converted to Christianity and some of the Gaels played along with the invaders in an attempt to eliminate their Irish rivals, as the Gauls had done with Caesar and the Britons with the Saxons. One of Ivar's descendants, Olaf Sihtricson, profited by the general confusion to seize the kingdom of Midhe.

Even so, it was from the kingdom of Midhe that effective resistance to the Norsemen first sprang. Maelsechlainn II assembled all the surviving Irish forces and managed to defeat Olaf at the battle of Tara in 980. The very site of the battle was symbolic, and Maelsechlainn became high king.

Inspired by this example, further rebellion began to erupt. Ivar, the Danish king of Limerick had imposed an overwhelming burden of taxation on the ancient

The White Horse of Uffington, more than 300 feet long, was carved into a chalk hillside in Berkshire (England). It is believed to date from the first century and to represent the horse goddess Epona.

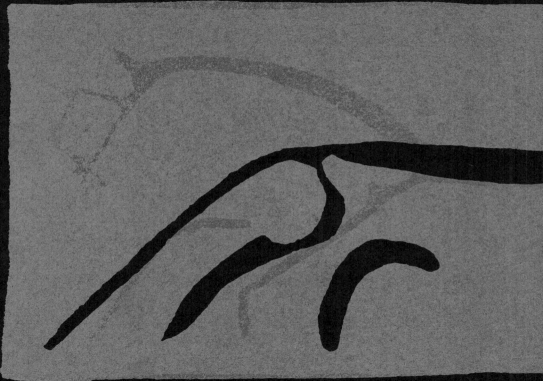

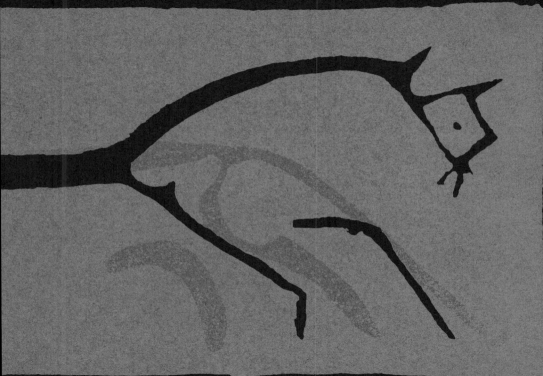

kingdom of Munster. Two minor kings named Mahon and Brian therefore took up arms against the tyrant and beat him at Sulcoit, before attacking Limerick. Mahon then reigned for eight years at Cashal, but Ivar, who had not renounced his claim to the throne, came back secretly and had Mahon murdered. At this, Brian, who had merely gone along with his brother Mahon, raised an army to avenge him. After killing Ivar in battle in 976 Brian became king of Cashel thereby depriving the dynasty of the sons of Eoghan of their legal right of accession.

Some years later, when trouble broke out in Leinster, Brian intervened and subdued both Leinster and Dublin. Justifiably afraid that Brian might prove a rival to his own throne, Maelsechlainn tried to diminish his influence, but finally had to agree to a treaty. Brian was to have power over southern Ireland, or Mogh's half, while Maelsechlainn had to be content with the North. Brian did not stop there, however. In 1002 at Tara he commanded Maelsechlainn to surrender him the throne. Abandoned by his northern allies who saw Brian as the restorer of Irish greatness, Maelsechlainn had to agree. So Brian became High King thus ending the pre-eminence of the sons of Niall who had held the title for six hundred years.

It was then that Brian acquired his nickname *Borou*, meaning "of the tributes". A man of some stature and ambition, he endeavoured to live out the myth of the high king and of the emperor, as exemplified by Caesar and Charlemagne. He had himself called *imperator Scotorum* in all legal documents and arranged that the assembly at Tailtiu should be reconvened after an eighty-year gap. He had a number of monasteries rebuilt and was lavish in his endowments to them; he also tried to rebuild the libraries which had been looted or destroyed and decreed that Armagh should be the religious capital of the island.

Even so, his reign was not entirely free of trouble. Having married Gormflaith, sister of Maelmora, king of Leinster, and former wife of both Olaf and Maelsechlainn, he then decided to divorce her. Gormflaith asked for help both from her brother and from Sitric Silkbeard, king of Dublin, her son by Olaf. Maelmora and Sitric were too weak to attack Brian alone and sought help from the Danes overseas, thereby provoking another Scandinavian invasion. Gormflaith promised to marry Sigurd, Earl of the Orkneys and to leave him the kingdom of Ireland, doubtless out of hatred for Brian Borou who had dispossessed her of the title of queen and all the concomitant privileges.

The Irish army was scarcely in any condition to withstand an attack from the Danes. Brian was too old to go into battle himself, and it was his son Murdach who led the troops of Connaught and Munster. The battle raged outside the walls of Dublin throughout Good Friday, April 23, 1014. Sigurd and Maelmora were killed. So, too, was Murdach; Murdach's son, Turloch, was found dead, still holding the hair of a Dane he had killed. Brian Borou was killed by a fugitive's axe. In fact, so great was the slaughter on both sides that neither party could be said to have won.

Nevertheless, Danish supremacy had become a thing of the past. And, ironically, the only person to profit by the battle was Maelsechlainn who survived to regain the throne of Tara until he died in 1022. His successors were the O'Briens, the descendants of Brian Borou, who had considerable difficulty in holding onto the title. For now that the Norse threat had been removed, there was little desire to obey any central authority. When the O'Briens were beaten at the battle of Moy Cova in 1103, they were forced to yield the title to the O'Connors of Connaught, distant descendants of Conn of the Hundred Battles. Turloch reigned from 1106 to 1156.

It was then that the Norse threat reared its head again, only this time under a different name. For the Normans of France had conquered England and the active new Anglo-Norman aristocracy there were casting covetous eyes on Ireland.

Things really came to a head with Dermot mac Murrough, a descendant of Gormflaith's brother Maelmora. King of Leinster and Dublin since 1126, Dermot was a man of education and refinement, who could be as cruel as he was learned. In 1141 he put down a rising of petty vassal kings with some savagery. Ten years later, during the course of a squabble, he abducted the beautiful Dervogauill, wife of O'Rourke, king of Breffni. O'Rourke retaliated by supporting another rebellion among the vassals of Leinster. Abandoned by his own men, Dermot was forced to flee. This episode became the subject of an epic tale in the French *chanson de geste* entitled *Chanson de Dermot et du Comte*.

Dermot, however, refused to admit defeat. Being unable to muster any help among the Irish, he decided to ask for foreign aid against his fellow countrymen and appealed to Ireland's powerful neighbour, the king of England, duke of Aquitaine and Normandy and regent of Brittany, Henry II Plantagenet. It was too good an opportunity for Henry to miss. He gave Dermot permission to levy an army in Wales, and the Welsh, who had been wronged by the Anglo-Normans, flocked to join him in the hope of winning new lands for themselves. In 1167 Dermot led a first expedition to Ireland which failed. In 1169 he went back with a larger force to acquire a firm foothold at Baginbun. In 1170, his ally Richard of Pembroke, to whom he had promised the hand of his daughter Aoife and the throne of Leinster, took Waterford and Dublin. It was then that Dermot died.

Richard's accession to the throne of Leinster was greeted with little enthusiasm by the Irish who were disturbed by the strength of outside influence his presence there implied. They hastily raised an improvised army which marched under the leadership of the High King Rory O'Connor to lay siege to Richard in Dublin.

Despite a near victory, the high king's army were finally forced into disorderly retreat by Pembroke's bowmen. The death knell had sounded for Ireland.

For it was at that precise moment that Henry Plantagenet, who had been observing events from a distance, made a personal move to restore order to the country and mediate between the warring factions. He used the *Laudabiliter*[5], a bull by which the pope had commanded him to reform the church of Ireland and reinstitute the payment of St. Peter's Penny in 1155, to proclaim himself *Ard Ri*. Not only did the Gaelic leaders agree to this, they were positively pleased, for they were convinced that a high king living in another country, with much to occupy him elsewhere, would require little more than formal homage from them.

Nothing could have been more mistaken. Once Henry II had something within his grasp he clung onto it. Obviously he had other affairs to attend to, but when he left Ireland, his own loyal followers stayed behind, intent on settling there. All real freedom for the Irish died then. The Anglo-Normans seized the wealthiest estates and formed a new aristocracy. The Strongbows, FitzGeralds, Birminghams, Carews and Butlers came to replace the O'Briens, O'Rourkes, O'Neills and Mac-Carthys. Strangely enough, the Anglo-Norman nobles who controlled the Irish land and economy, gradually became more Gaelic than the Gaels, even to the extent of Gaelicizing their names.

But this did nothing to lessen English supremacy. All decisions were made in London. It is fair to say that Rory O'Connor was the last real high king of a free Ireland.

From that point, a woeful darkness fell over the island. There were endless murders, rebellions, executions, famines, systematic plundering and religious conflicts. The Gaelic forces became apathetic. Large numbers of the population emigrated. Under the cruel and unjust domination of the English, the Gaelic dream faded to nothingness. Ireland received worse treatment than any of the English colonies in Africa or Asia. But despite all this, the Gaelic language survived, and Gaelic tradition was kept alive among the people by the wandering heirs of the druids. It is this, perhaps, which is the Irish miracle. Even after eight centuries at death's door, Ireland never totally gave up the ghost, and on December 6, 1921 it began a new life when the *Saorstat Eireann* was legally recognized after a violent struggle. Though sheared of Ulster, Ireland again acceded to the rank of an independent nation, to become the only purely Celtic state in the modern world.

CHAPTER SEVEN

The Ancient Poetry of Ireland

S the melting pot in which Latin intelligence and Celtic inventiveness coalesced from a very early date, Ireland has preserved its ancestral traditions better than any other Western European country. The ancient figure of Cú Chulainn composing and chanting his poems on his war chariot emerges clearer than ever as the Irish rediscover that mighty blast of destructiveness which animated the old heroes of the sagas.

Over the centuries of suffering and struggle there is a bond between Synge and Russell and the anonymous poets who gave Western European verse its principal themes and its first splash of colour. Living in a land which breathes out poetry through every spring, every lake, every valley and hill, that isolated race has been strangely treated by fortune. And there are equally strange lessons to be learnt from its poetry, as much by 20th century man as by any other. For words and images exercise a constant fascination as they become fused in an elevated desire to express life on a heroic scale, on a magical and surreal plane.

For although it is the individual word which creates the effect and which endows the poem with its basic sense, the concept of analogous images gives that word many different meanings. The whole atmosphere becomes one of initiation, not unlike that which envelops the most arcane ceremonies of the druidic religion. A sense of the miraculous, but of a pre-Christian miracle, brings life to the poem and bestows upon it the peculiar form of the popular legend developed and transcribed by an ecclesiastic. For the *file*, the poet of ancient Ireland like the bard of ancient Britain was a kind of priest who saw himself as one of the founts of wisdom in the Celtic world. The hidden mysteries of his knowledge are his verses, the words he uses are the basic ingredients of an alchemical *grand-oeuvre*.

On a more general level it can be argued that the poetical thought of the Irish Gaels represents the artistic utterance of the whole community. Most of the authors are either unknown or legendary figures. The early poems, which are very old indeed, have been re-arranged and re-worked by succeeding generations. The major themes have been used as foundations by poets whose only point in common was the poetic legacy of the Celtic tradition. There appears to have been an exceptionally well-developed collective unconscious at work for even now Irish poetry is truly the poetry of one particular race of people with the special talents and peculiarities that have given them their individuality.

The overwhelming proportion of Irish lyric poetry has had its origins in the national mythological epics since the earliest known of these great works were composed. In the middle of a battle a poet will begin to sing a war chant. During a meal a woman will start to recite a resonant anthem of love which is also a *geis* forcing her beloved to love her. In the course of an assembly a warrior will feel suddenly irradiated by poetry and the verses he declaims, whether they be prophecies or evocative yearnings for magical realms like the fairyland of Emain, will be handed on by word of mouth.

Both in Wales, the legatee of the British tradition, and in Ireland where the Gaelic tradition was preserved, the same fabulous exploits are accomplished by heroes whose names are often almost identical. And the same kinds of miracle are worked, for there is magic in Irish poetry and an inherent sacredness. More isolated and westerly than Britain, Ireland managed to retain its mythical leanings long after the rapid influx of Christianity. The new religion skimmed the surface of the myths; the mythological heroes became saints. But their weapons retained their magic properties: shields still scream when their owners are in danger. And since animals are still regarded as the reincarnations or the original embodiments of heroes, creatures like the eagle, the wolf and the raven have their own symbolic significance which is common to all Celtic countries. It is because of this that the goddess Mórrígan (the Queen of Nightmares?) continues to make her extraordinary appearances in the ever more terrifying shapes of the she-wolf, the cow or the crow.

The doctrine of transmigration acquired what is possibly its definitive form in the adventures of Tuan mac Carill, a kind of prophet whose legend has much in common with that of the Welsh bard Taliesin. Tuan claims to have led different lives under both animal and human form, and to have witnessed many of the major events in the history of Ireland since its earliest days. So, while his tale is intensely poetic, it reads to a certain extent like a historical work.

> Today I am boar,
> I am king, strong and victorious.
> My song and my words were pleasing
> to the assemblies in days gone by,
> delighting the young and pretty women.
> My chariot was rich and splendid,

my voice could sound serious and soft,
I was swift in battle,
my face was charming,
today I am a black boar . . .
Rawlinson MS. B.512.

Less politically oriented and more purely lyrical is the poetry of Amergein, one of the earliest *filid* in Ireland. His magic incantations bear witness to the Celts' mystical desire to explore the mysterious realms of intellectual speculation. Amergein seems to be saying, in fact, that he has actually taken on the nature of other things and other creatures, and that this has made him entirely at one with the universe, peaceful in spirit and great in mind.

I am the wind which blows over the sea,
I am wave of the sea,
I am lowing of the sea,
I am the bull of seven battles,
I am bird of prey on the cliff-face,
I am sunbeam,
I am skilful sailor,
I am a cruel boar,
I am lake in the valley,
I am word of knowledge,
I am a sharp sword threatening an army,
I am the god who gives fire to the head,
I am he who casts light between the mountains,
I am he who foretells the ages of the moon,
I am he who teaches where the sun sets.
Book of Leinster

The Irish sagas are full of examples of this kind of poetry. Etaine, one of the two wives of Mider, a kind of god of the dead, is changed into an insect by Mider's other wife and caught in a glass jar by Oengus, Mider's adopted son. This story belongs to the myth of the glass prison, like that where Merlin lives guarded by Vivian, and that where Tristan disguised as a madman tries to take Yseult. It is the Isle of Glass, the City of Glass, the *Kaer Wydr*, or the Glass Tower seen by the first Gaels on their way to Ireland which is mentioned in a poem entitled the "Disaster of the Power of Conan" by the 9th century Eochaid hUa Flainn.

This is the capture of the Tower of Conan, it is a mighty deed.
Against Conan the Great, son of Farbar,
the men of Ireland came,
three powerful chiefs among them.
Three score thousand, wise and splendid,
over land and over sea,
so many were those who left their homes,
sons of Nemed, for this conquest.
Three score vessels upon the sea,
so many were the ships of Muic, son of Delu.

> They met him before they had come ashore,
> the sons of Nemed with their powerful forces.
> The men of Ireland at the battle
> after the coming of the Fomoré
> were drowned by a sea-wave, all of them
> except for three times ten men.
> (*Book of Invasions*, V, 42)

Even within its most historical utterances, Gaelic poetry is wholly transfused by myths. The myth acts as a kind of corner stone for the entire poetical structure, a skeleton around which the living flesh of verse can bloom. It is myths which have given Gaelic poetry that extraordinary wealth of ideas and daring which make it so fresh and powerful.

And it is his sense of the magical which enables the poet to let his imagination run wild and free. Less or perhaps more than mere fantasy this sense of the magical is striking evidence of creative activity in men beset by all kinds of material and spiritual constraints. It is a reminder that in poetry there are no norms to be acknowledged, that poetry spurns the order and precision so essential in other literary forms.

The Irish sense of the magical is deep-rooted in the fertile soil of myth. But the marvels which cast their shadow over Irish mythological poetry are not gentle and refined. They have nothing to do with the romantic and surely spurious atmosphere of Macpherson's *Ossian*.

Forger though he was, Macpherson must have known a great deal about early Gaelic poetry. He probably had access to original texts but doubtless found them too uncivilized, too distant from the intellectual tastes of his day. He therefore extracted the major themes and dressed them up in romantic melancholy and grand inflated phrases. Although the same characters appear their names have been changed to make them easier to pronounce. Deidre has become Darthula, Oisin Ossian, Finn Fingal; while the hero Cú Chulainn has acquired the ridiculous name Clesamor. We have only to compare the poetry of *Ossian* with original Gaelic models to see where the true genius lies.

> It is night; I am alone on this hill and the storm clouds are gathering.
> I hear the winds rumble in the sides of the mountains; the torrent, swollen by rain, roars along the rock. I see no refuge which can offer me shelter. Alas, I am alone and forsaken.
> Arise, moon, torch of the nights, leave the bosom of the mountains. White stars, scatter over the veil of the skies. Will some kindly light not guide me towards the places where my beloved is? Perhaps he is resting in some lonely spot, from the exertions of the chase, his bow unbent at his side and his dogs panting around him . . .
> (*The Songs of Selma*)

There is a world of difference between this and the unsophisticated Irish incantation:

> Cold, cold,
> how cold is Lug's great plain this night,
> the snow is higher than the hills,

the buck finds no more food.
Cold as judgment
the storm has spread all around,
on the slope each furrow is a stream
and each ford a pool.
The lake overflows, it is a wild sea,
The pools are overflowing lakes,
Ross ford is too deep for horses to cross
and for men.
The birds of the island of Fal roam over the sea, there
is no shore free of breaking wave,
on the land there is no ground,
no longer can the bells be heard, no more do the
marsh-birds sing.
The wolfs of the wood of Cuan find
no rest nor sleep in their lairs.
The wren finds no more
shelter for her nest in Lonslope.
The flock of birds is battered by
the biting wind and the northern frost,
no more pleasant roof top for the blackbird
to shelter by the woods of Cuan.
The eagle of the valley of Ridi Rua
suffers the pangs of the harsh wind,
great are its misery and its sorrow,
it has ice in its beak.
(The Pursuit of Diarmaid and Grainne, *The Yellow
Book of Lecan*)

Even so, the cycle of Finn or the Fenians, as exploited and distorted by Macpherson, was to become the favourite reading of the great Romantics and to provide a link between the tradition of the ancient bards and writers like Chateaubriand.

In fact it is their treatment of love which sets the Gaelic poets apart. Though set in Britain and endowed with British and Welsh characters, the legend of Tristan and Yseult is clearly Gaelic in origin, as becomes obvious from Irish legends like that of *Baile of the Soft Words* and the *Love of Cano, son of Carthan, for Cred*.[1]

Love, as the *filid* saw it, is neither a gentle daydream nor a purely sexual act. The Gaelic concept of love (possibly even the Celtic concept, though there are no examples of this kind in Welsh literature) is much more like an extension of the Theban idea. The lovers are influenced by some inevitable destiny; their love becomes a raging torrent, fierce, absolute and unrestrained. The latent eroticism tends to be expressed through violence, for every story is tragic and ends in blood. The influence of destiny is again emphasized in all the fleeting encounters between people who are prevented by circumstance from loving each other fully and freely but who continue to seek distractedly for each other as they travel the world, their whole lives becoming a return to the beloved.

Most of the love poems are fragments of ancient legends. The poet never speaks of his own love or lays bare his own emotions as the Romantics do. Rather he hides behind his hero or heroine, so that he can express his feelings unreservedly. Diedre,

for example, will break into curses, writhe in unsatisfied desire, roll on the ground
in a fit of amorous madness.

> Dear blue eye, loved by women,
> feared by its enemies,
> across the breadth of the forest, noble meeting,
> dear, clear voice in the shade of the wood.
> I no longer sleep.
> My nails have lost their purple.
> Joy no longer fills my wakeful hours
> since the son of Usnech ceased to come.
> I do not sleep
> half the night in my bed.
> My spirit leaps out among the worlds,
> and I neither eat nor laugh. . .
> (The Exile of the Sons of Usnech, *The Book of Leinster*)

For abducted by Conchobar, chief of the Ulsterman to whom she is fated to be
wife, Deidre had fallen in love with Noise, son of Usnech who "had hair like a
raven, cheeks like blood and a body like snow". She runs away with him and his
two brothers but is betrayed and returned to Conchobar while the sons of Usnech
are killed. Unable to bear this separation from her beloved, she throws herself from
Conchobar's chariot and breaks her head on a rock. But before she kills herself
Deidre sings an unforgettable lament.

> O, Conchobar, what do you want?
> You have caused me grief and weeping.
> During my lifetime
> you have not much loved me.
> The man I thought the loveliest under the sky,
> the man who was so dear to me
> you have taken from me, it is a great sadness
> that I may only see him in death.
> Two cheeks of purple brighter than a meadow,
> red lips, lashes beetle-black,
> teeth and colour of pearls,
> noble whiteness of snow. . .
> Do not break my heart today,
> soon I shall go to my nearing grave.
> Grief is stronger than the sea,
> do you know that, O Conchobar?

In another tale, Etaine, wife of the god Mider, has been reincarnated and has
become wife to King Eochaid Aireainn. Mider leaves the darkness of the *sidh* and
comes to play chess against Eochaid, who is obliged to surrender Etaine after a
year. Before the appointed time, however, Mider appears to Etaine on several
occasions and sings her the following summons to the land beyond. It is the song of
the Harbinger of Death, the song so often sung by the beings of darkness to mortal
men.

> O lovely woman, will you come with me
> to the magical land where musicians are heard,
> where a crown of primroses is worn on the hair,
> where the body is snow-white from head to foot,
> where nobody is silent or sad,
> where teeth are white and brows are black,
> where cheeks are red like the flowering fox-glove?
> Ireland is beautiful but few countries
> are as lovely as the great plain I call you to. . .
> O woman, when you are in my mighty land
> you will wear a gold crown upon on your head,
> I will give you fresh pork to eat,
> beer and milk to drink, O woman,
> O lovely woman, will you come with me?
> (The Courtship of Etaine, *Leabhar na hUidre*)

A number of different works are based on the adventure of Diarmaid and Grainne. Grainne is furious at being married against her will to the old King Finn. Her eye falls on handsome young Diarmaid and she uses a *geis* to make him take her away. Finn relentlessly hounds the two lovers and in the end Diarmaid is killed by a boar after the old king has played a trick on him. This epic contains poems of astonishing dramatic intensity, some expressing the depth of love felt by Diarmaid and Grainne, others bringing nature to share in the lovers' sufferings.

> Sleep a little, just a little,
> and fear nothing,
> man to whom I have given my love,
> Diarmaid, son of O Duibhne.
> Sleep here, deeply, deeply,
> son of O Duibhne, noble Diarmaid,
> I will watch over your rest,
> charming son of O Duibhne. . .
> I will stay watching over you,
> a battle rampart in the West,
> my heart would break with grief
> if ever I lost the sight of you.
> To part us would be to take
> child from its mother,
> to banish body from soul,
> warrior of the lovely lake of Garman. . .
> The stag in the East does not sleep.
> He does not cease to bellow
> in the bushes of the black birds.
> He does not wish to sleep.
> The hornless doe does not sleep.
> She sighs for her spotted fawn
> she runs in the brushwood,
> she does not sleep in her den.
> The lively linnet does not sleep
> on the tree-top's lovely boughs.

The hour is noisy here,
even the thrush does not sleep.
The graceful drake does not sleep,
he makes ready to swim,
he has neither rest nor sleep, here,
in his refuge he does not sleep.
This evening the grouse does not sleep
on the wind-battered heath.
On the hill his cry is soft and clear.
Near the streams he does not sleep. . .
(*Duanaire Finn*)

Possibly one of the strangest of Gaelic love poems is that which Georges Dottin has entitled "The Meeting after Death" and dated as a 9th century work. The story behind it appears to be one of almost gothic horror, with the poet revealing an obsessive view of the mysterious world beyond and a belief in some kind of afterlife in the spirit world. The two lovers are as closely bound together in darkness as they are in daylight, and in the world of night their feelings and actions assume an even greater degree of intensity.

Silence, woman, do not speak to me. . .
My thoughts are not with you.
My thoughts are at the battle of Feic.
My blood-stained body lies
on the slope of the two banks.
My head has remained, unwashed,
among the warriors in the wild fray.
It is madness to arrange a meeting
without foreseeing death's coming.
Our meeting,
I have kept in death.
I am not the only man to have gone astray
in the heat of desire to find a woman again.
I blame you for nothing, though you are the cause.
Sad is our last meeting.
With her murderous spear Mórrígan came.
It was she who inflamed us.
Many are the spoils she washes clean.
Terrible is her hateful laugh.
She tossed her mane of hair to her back.
It takes a stout heart to stand firm before her.
Although she is near us
do not let terror freeze you.
In the morning I will leave my body
and I will follow the warrior band.
Go, do not stay here,
the end of night approaches. . .
I hear the gloomy bird
crying for its followers.
In words and in form I am a ghost.

Silence, woman, do not speak to me. . .
(*Song of Fothad Airghech*)

Henri Hubert describes the Celtic pantheon as seen in the countless numbers
peopling the underground *sidh* as "a huge cemetery". But this is a meaningless
statement, for there are no gods, only human heroes who have attained a state of
divinity and there is no pantheon or Olympus in the Mediterranean sense of the
word. The heroes are sublimated, immaterial, and with the advent of Christianity
they undergo a smooth and automatic transformation into saints. That is one of the
reasons why there are so many saints or pseudo-saints in the Christian tradition of
Celtic countries, especially in Ireland and Brittany.

In any case the inhabitants of Hubert's "cemetery" are singularly active and
alive. They have nothing to do with the grimacing skeletons of German medieval
tradition; they are no vague, unreal ghosts, but creatures of flesh and blood even if
that flesh is somehow transfigured. The glory attached to the people of the other
world explains why mere mortals hanker for everything connected with the *sidh*
and the distant isles. The quest for the land of eternal blessedness becomes a
fantastic voyage.

Bran thinks it a great wonder
to go in a ship on the clear sea,
but I, from afar in my chariot, I see him
riding over a flowery plain.
What Bran's high-bowed boat
sees as the clear sea
is a flowery, gold plain
to me, in my two-wheeled chariot.
The eyes of Bran
see the waves of the sea,
I, on the plain of Games, I see
red-headed flowers.
The sea-horses shine in the summer
as far as Bran can stretch his eyes.
The rivers pour waves of honey
onto the lands of Manannan, son of Ler.
That sea-colour where you are sailing,
that white shade of the oar-ploughed sea
is yellow and blue mixed together,
it is earth which is not hard.
Spotted salmon rise from the depths
of the white sea you see.
They are coloured lambs
gambolling to and fro.
Only one charioteer can be seen
on the flowery, gold plain,
yet there are many stallions,
but that you cannot know.
It is over the crest of a wood that your ship
floats across the peaks.
There is a wood full of fine fruit

under the prow of your boat,
a wood of flowers and fruit,
with the smell of wine in the air
a faultless, unwaning wood,
where the leaves are the colour of gold. . . .
(*The Voyage of Bran*)

A more incantatory and perhaps less spiritual facet of Gaelic poetry is to be found in the Death Songs. Like their Welsh counterparts these poems are eulogies for heroes killed in battle. Neither Irish nor British warriors had any fear of death since they were assured of rebirth. This did not mean, however, that there was no room for ordinary human responses. The following verses are Cú Chulainn's grief-stricken reaction to the death of his former friend Ferdead whom he has killed.

Sad is your golden brooch,
O warlike Ferdead,
You who struck mighty and accurate,
your hand was triumphant.
Your long, golden hair
was curled and adorned you.
Your belt, as of soft leaves,
girdled you until death.
In felling you my hand
did wrong, as I know.
It was not a good fight,
sad is the golden brooch of Ferdead. . .
O Ferdead, sad is our meeting.
I see you at once red and so pale.
I cannot use my weapon before it is washed
and you, you lie on a bed of blood. . .
(*Tain Bo Cualnge*)

Just as incantation is the poetry of sorcery, so all the Irish poets are sorcerers. Some of them had extraordinary, terrifying powers. A *file* could cast a satire on someone which would kill him. He could cast a spell and halt a whole army. The four sources of knowledge of the *filid* included magical operations like "the illumination around the hands" as well as spiritual talents and skills of judgment. The power of poetry and music is such that men listening to the harp of the Dagda will be driven to sleep, to laugh or to die. Poetry was the first form of medicine, as this incantation against insect bites shows:

Nothing is higher than the sky
nothing is deeper than the sea
before the sacred words
Christ spoke on the cross.
Take from me this pin,
the pin which has torn
my mangled flesh,
spirit of gentleness,

> the cause of this blow,
> depart,
> go, take it away.
> Mighty is the knowledge of Gobniu,
> mighty is the point of Gobniu,
> the sharp point of Gobniu,
> away![2]

Incantations might serve other purposes also, to ward off a hostile attack, for example.

> Let us set before the warriors lively naked women
> with fine, white, pointed breasts
> and young girls to welcome them.
> Open court
> defenceless fortress
> vats of fresh water
> beds prepared
> good food in plenty,
> good, strong, heady ale
> for the warriors . . .
> (*The Feast of Briciu*)

Finally, there was the poetry of prophecy, as common in the Gaelic as in any other epic tradition. The druids and the *filid* could always find an opportunity to turn soothsayer. Heroes and heroines, like the Mórrígan, are given prophetic chants to declaim, which though far from encouraging are less political in their underlying intent than the kinds of prophecy attributed to the bardic wizard Merlin in Wales.

> The ravens gnaw
> the necks of men.
> The warriors' blood spurts out,
> a wild battle is fought,
> minds are troubled,
> sides are pierced
> in warlike deeds.
> Woe to the people of Ulster!
> there will be no lack of glory
> for those who oppose them.
> (*Tain Bo Cualnge*)

The verbal violence in Gaelic poetry was further underlined by their oral recitation. As among all the other Celtic peoples, literature was first handed on by word of mouth and only came to be recorded in writing after many years. Gaelic poetry therefore offers many of the characteristics associated with oral transmission. The types of words used are easy to remember; there are refrains; certain images will be repeated, with the more peripheral words being replaced by new adjectives to suggest some subtle variation in meaning. The prose epics, which were often rich in image and atmosphere, would be spoken, while the lyric verses inserted in their midst would be sung. Some of the apparently more obscure works are obviously the result of a prose tale's being composed round an existing lyric in an attempt to explain the story behind the verse, though not necessarily with much success.

The chief interest of ancient Irish poetry, however, lies in the opportunity it affords us to rediscover that analogical system which can both define and juggle with the poetic image. It is this which gives Irish verse its incantatory quality and its unlimited freedom.

The great Celtic scholar Georges Dottin once said, "The musical charms of Irish poetry and the strangely evocative effect of epithets which the artist has no hesitation in jumbling together however curiously and contradictorily are reminiscent of our [French] symbolist poets." It would be hard to find a better definition of Gaelic poetry. For at first sight it is all strange and confusing. Indeed, a number of linguists, seeing no further than the obscurity and muddle, have denied it any literary merit whatever.

We have come to the very heart of the problem. The question of how to evaluate poetry will continue to occupy us for years to come. But an awareness of the sacred role of verse makes it easier to distinguish between what may at first appear unfathomable and what is truly obscure. When replaced in their original context and examined in the light of those principles which prevailed at the time of their creation even the wildest of images acquire a meaning. All the peoples incorrectly labelled "primitive" among whom the Celts are generally included have made deliberate use of equivocation both in their poetry and their learning in order to protect their secrets from the world at large.

In its infancy, every civilization kept its wisdom for the initiates, and for this reason concrete thought was skilfully camouflaged in a welter of ambiguity. Poetry gained a great deal from this lack of precision. The poet could use it to lay one image over another so that the name of one object became linked with that of another, totally unrelated, object. The fact that this method is now called surrealist makes it no less ancient; it is the method inherent in ritual riddles, in ready made responses and in passwords.

With this in mind there is much to be learnt from Gaelic poetry, for we can begin to assess its merits both from the purely lyrical angle and from the qualities of its symbolic imagery. Take, for example, Cú Chulainn's driver Loeg's description of the wondrous land of the fairies:

> The beds have posts the colour of blood
> and fine, gilded columns.
> The lamp which lights them
> is a radiant jewel.
> (*The Jealousy of Emer*)

or the description of Noise, son of Usnech:

> Black jet mound on a white body.
> (*The Exile of the Sons of Usnech*)

or the druid Cathba's song about Deidre:

> The treasure of her teeth
> is a winter snow.
> (*The Exile of the Sons of Usnech*)

These are just a few examples; there are too many to try to quote them all. But they reveal that deliberate intention to disguise, to modify the language so that it becomes inaccessible to those who are not receptive to poetry. The freshness or strangeness of a poem can be tasted like a ripe fruit.

It would therefore be wrong to describe these poems as the infantile babblings of an undeveloped people or as degenerate versions of classical Greek and Latin lyrics. Poetry is not a matter of fashion but of spiritual creation, and the only justification for examining the literature of the past lies in what we can learn about forgotten values and possible future means of expression. If we look back, it is not merely to satisfy some idle curiosity but to break away from the past by establishing a clean, unsullied foundation on which to build new aesthetic and intellectual norms. It is because modern Irish poets have realized this that the people of the Irish Free State would seem to be renewing an acquaintance with their oldest traditions while turning their eyes resolutely towards the future. However many centuries may separate the lyricism of the Irish *filid* from the modern reader our present day conception of poetry is so close to theirs that we must surely acknowledge ancient Gaelic poetry as one of the forerunners of contemporary verse.

CHAPTER EIGHT

The Celtic Christian Church

HE   Celts appear to have been independently-minded in every aspect of life. Their natural tendency to individualism coupled with a systematic resistance to any part of an official establishment was pushed to a point little short of mania. But though this anarchic attitude was ultimately to bring about their defeat it also produced original solutions and countermeasures to their problems. It is hardly surprising, therefore, that the Christian religion should have found a unique development in Celtic countries often along lines bordering upon the heretical.

The first apostles of Christianity reached the Gallic *Provincia Romana* at a comparatively early date, and despite considerable persecution the new religion continued to spread its net over Gaul for a period of about 150 years. These were the days of the martyrs of Vienne and Lyons. The solid foundations established by the church at Lyons made that town the metropolis of Gaul. In about 250, a group of missionaries was sent from Africa by St Cyprian, and many of these men gave their names to those places in which they preached. There was Paul at Narbonne, Trophimus at Arles, Saturninus at Toulouse, Martial at Limoges, Denis at Lutèce, Austremoine at Clermont, Gratianus at Tours. Two of these, Saturninus and Denis fell as victims of Decius' persecution in 251. The Christian communities were further decimated by Aurelianus between 270 and 275, but the most bloody persecutions were instigated by Diocletian. It was then that Saints Crispin and Crispinian died at Soissons, Quentin in the Vermandois and Victor at Marseilles.

It was not until 312, when the Emperor Constantine accorded Christianity official recognition with the Edict of Milan that the new religion came to acquire the firm basis which continues to support it to this day.

For the spread of Christianity throughout the Roman Empire followed the administrative channels which already provided a framework for Roman authority. That is why ecclesiastical administration was divided into provinces and dioceses and why the bishop of Rome immediately assumed such an important role in the hierarchy. His position at the head of the church had little to do with the legacy of St Peter (there is, after all, no evidence that Peter ever was bishop of Rome) but was based on his occupation of the seat of the old emperors. Even when the temporal power of the empire had gone the administrative establishment remained, now in the hands of the Christians. It was as if the old ideas and officials had been replaced in their entirety by a new order. Early Christianity, therefore, won its converts in the towns which as capitals of the old *civitates* benefited from Roman administration in a way which the *pagi*, or country districts, did not. The words "peasant" and "pagan" are, after all, derived from the same root.

It was not until Saint Martin was elected bishop of Tours in 372 that any real attempt was begun to bring Christianity to the outlying country areas. Indeed it is through Saint Martin that we come to the purely Celtic aspects of Christianity, since the remarkably well organized church he established at Tours was to play a major part in Western Gaul, the least romanized area of the country.

4th century Tours was the capital of the *Lugdunensis Tertia* division of Celtica which had its capital at Lyons. Tours governed the whole Armorican peninsula and the area between the Loire and the Seine. It seems likely that the missionaries sent by Saint Martin penetrated deep into the peninsula, though we have no written evidence for this. To judge from the later history of Brittany, however, it would appear that by the 4th century there were bishops at Nantes, Vannes and at *Civitas Aquilonia*, later to become Quimper. In all probability the north of Armorica remained untouched.

Purely Celtic areas were first introduced to Christianity in Britain, probably about the year 200 (though the earliest Christian inscriptions found there date from the middle of the 4th century). The council of Arles in 314 was attended by three British bishops, including Eborius (Yvor or Ifor).

There is no doubt that the new religion made rapid progress in Britain, whatever Gildas may say about the reluctance of the natives (*De Excidio Britanniae*, I, 7). Several bishops from Britain went to the council of Rimini in 359 and towards the end of the 4th century quarrels over doctrine and precedence between the island bishops had become so fierce that Saint Victricius, bishop of Rouen, had to cross the Channel to restore order.

It was also in Britain that Pelagius (Morgan), one of the boldest thinkers of his day, was born in about 360. When still relatively young he went to Rome before Alaric sacked the town, and there became a monk. He made the acquaintance of Paulinus and Augustine and in 410 went to Sicily and Africa, with a journey to the East in the following year. He died in Egypt in about 422. However, it was during his years in Rome that he expounded the bulk of his personal ideas and these were later taken up and disseminated by his disciple Celstius, probably a Scot (i.e. a man from Scotland or Ireland).

The essence of Pelagian doctrine is that there is no such thing as original sin. Being created mortal Adam was subject to concupiscence. Human nature has not been corrupted, the will of man is unimpaired and he is capable of doing good when he wills it. Baptism washes away no original sin, since none exists, but only the actual sins committed by those receiving the sacrament. (In the early days only adults were baptized.) Baptism is however a prerequisite for entering the flock, a trial of initiation which Christ himself underwent. "Grace" denotes only those natural good things God gave to man, particularly his freedom, together with the teachings provided by the revelation and the words of Jesus Christ.

According to this doctrine, then, man has complete freedom. If he has a duty to avoid sin it is because he is able by nature to do so. It would therefore be unjust to impute to him any sin which he personally is not able or obliged to avoid. If the sin of Adam is to rebound on those who have not themselves sinned, the justice of Christ must also extend to those who do not believe. In short, if we are a part of evil without committing any fault then we ought also to be a part of good without having to deserve it.

These far-reaching ideas were taken up and expanded by Celstius who stated, "Sin is not born with man. It is an act of will which he may be led to commit by his individual imperfection, but it is not a necessary result of the essential imperfection of mankind". Celstius did not want children to be baptized for fear that the administration of the sacrament would be taken as recognition of the mistaken notion that "man is wicked by his very nature before he has committed any evil," a notion insulting to the creator. Any grace which may exist in the form of supernatural succour can only influence the intelligence and not the will.

Pelagianism has been regarded as an attempt on its author's part to syncretize Christian teaching with druidism which had no concept of sin and saw individual freedom as the basic principle of its tradition. Pelagius, says Henri Martin (*Historie de France*, I, 347–48) "does not merely preserve but exaggerates the druidic doctrine of balance. God becomes no more than man's beginning and end; in between man walks alone. In his efforts to make man more important Pelagius overlooks the contribution of God, the support which is constantly needed by man. Pelagius does not see the significance of the association between creator and created, that mystery of life which seems to have enshrouded the symbol of oak and mistletoe. At the same time he exaggerates the druidic need for balance to the point of total independence and shatters tradition by denying the fall and the fellowship instead of seeking an explanation for it in freedom itself."

Certainly Pelagianism is not druidism; far from it. But there is no denying that this doctrine, with its basis in total human freedom, is very clearly Celtic in its leanings. It is also distinctly anti-Mediterranean since it emphasizes the solitude of man, while the ancient religions of Greece and Rome assume that human acts are all prompted or abetted by some divinity. The very concept of grace is Greco-Latin in origin, being an extension of the superstitious belief that man was incapable of acting alone and required the help of some impartial *numen* or divine will. By denying the power of grace Pelagius was fighting against that superstition, re-establishing the notion that man is entirely responsible for his own acts and restoring to human dignity a respect which the early Christian leaders with their erroneous ideas of evangelical humility sought to remove.

It was not long before the Church Fathers retaliated, chief of Pelagius' critics being Saint Augustine who began a violent attack on his former friend in 412. Further criticism came from Saint Jerome. Even so Pelagius was exonerated by the synod of Diospolis in 415. Augustine fought on and in the end Pelagius was condemned by councils in Carthage in 416 and 418 and in Milevis in 416. The canons of the second council of Carthage were sent to Pope Zosimus who ratified them in 418.

But Pelagius was not alone. Apart from his disciple Celstius, he had a number of sympathizers including Julian bishop of Eclanum who began to spread his doctrine and mounted a skilful attack on Augustine. In 419 the Emperors Honorius and Theodosius solemnly condemned Pelagianism. Supporters of the doctrine were banished and persecuted, though fortunately for them the Inquisition had not yet come into being. Arguments between the two sides acquired a more theological turn. Pelagius' supporters laid their emphasis on the total autonomy of man's free will, thereby obviating any responsibility for the origin of sin being attributed to God. The Lord's Prayer, after all, contains the very ambiguous phrase "Lead us not into temptation", and unless we are to conclude that the word "Lead" in this context means that God himself is making us do wrong, we must assume that He is merely presenting us with situations in which we can exercise our free will to choose between good and evil. Grace is only the primordial, divine light which enables us to acquire knowledge of good and evil.

Augustine's response was that this argument was morally wicked since it invites the individual to take pride in his good deeds. To impute all responsibility for good to man is to adopt the stoic ethics of Marcus Aurelius and Epictetes. If original sin is not passed on into each new person, then baptism is unnecessary, and the incarnation and redemption occurred to no purpose. As Saint Paul argued, man does not receive grace because of the good in him, rather he has good in him because he has received grace. Certainly our will must act in accordance with that grace but it can do so only if we have faith. And faith is the gift of God.

Saint Augustine's position was not merely a reaction to Pelagianism, but in some sense an acceptance of predestination. The quarrel between Pelagius and Augustine foreshadowed later disputes between Jansenists and Jesuits and even the quarrel between Roman Orthodoxy and Calvinism.

Pelagianism was again condemned at the council of Ephesus in 431; but, far from abandoning their beliefs, the Pelagianists now sought to reconcile their doctrine with the official position of the church. A new school of semi-Pelagianism appeared which argued that man was not morally dead, as Saint Augustine claimed, nor morally healthy, as Pelagius stated, but merely sick and in need of the healing attention of divine grace. Anyone looking for grace is sure to obtain it, but it in no way affects the exercise of free will.

This compromise position, admittedly more Pelagian than Augustinian, was upheld by John Cassian, a disciple of John Crysostom, and the Breton Faustus, bishop of Riez, and by Vincent, abbot of Lérins. Vincent fiercely refuted Augustinian beliefs in predestination. In 472, at the council of Arles, Faustus and Cassian stated that there was no other incorporeal being than God, a view not inconsistent with some druidic teaching. Through semi-Pelagianism, Celtic ideas were returning to the surface. However, in 529 and 530, at Orange and Valence respectively, the school of Lérins which taught this watered-down version of Pelagiansim was the subject of official condemnation. The idea that man might have the power to ask for grace was unacceptable. And yet these two councils also condemned the doctrine of predestination. What was to become the church's official attitude in the future was already taking shape. It was to be a modified form of semi-Pelagianism.

Before these doctrinal disputes arose, Pelagianism had made its way into Britain. It was even, as Dom Louis Gougaud says "in some sense the national heresy of the Britons."[1]

In the early 5th century, the new teaching was propagated throughout the island by Agricola, son of the Pelagian bishop Severianus; and its remarkable popularity suggests that the Celtic peoples saw it as a vessel of that druidic thought so well suited to their temperament. The triumphant progress of Pelagiansim in Britain troubled the continental church, and St Germanus of Auxerre was sent to Britain from 429 to 431 to restore orthodox beliefs. Despite apparent success on Germanus' part, the heresy reappeared as soon as he had gone and threatened to become so powerful that in 447 he was forced to return, this time with a number of missionaries. After the second visit Pelagianism was completely stamped out, on the surface at least. During later centuries there was still evidence of its after effects in Ireland, Britain and even Brittany, and its teaching formed the basis of John Scotus Erigena's doctrine. In 639 Pope John IV wrote to the bishops of Ireland, "We have learnt that the poison of the Pelagian error has reappeared among you. We urge you to reject this odious doctrine. Is it not blasphemous to claim that man can be without sin? As if this privilege had not been reserved for the mediator between God and men, the Christ who was conceived and born without sin. All other men are born with original sin and bear within them the mark of Adam's failings".

Whatever the ecclesiastical arguments, however, Britain was now firmly Christian, if a little Pelagian or even Arian in its leanings. Saint Ninian took the new religion into the Northern Border area and Scotland where he founded the episcopal see of Galloway. There is evidence that parts of the Irish coast were converted around 400, though according to Saint Patrick paganism was still rife in the centre of the island and the converts were more Celtic than Roman in their beliefs.

Patrick (Latin *Patricius*) was born around 390 in North West Britain. At the age of sixteen he was caputred by Scottish or Pictish pirates and taken to Northern Ireland. Six years later he reappeared a free man first on the continent and then in Britain. He decided to go and preach the gospel in Ireland and after studying in Gaul was ordained a deacon at Auxerre. Recognizing Saint Patrick's vocation, Saint Germanus consecrated him a bishop in 432 and sent him to convert Ireland. He began his work in Leinster at the mouth of the Boyne on the island which still bears the name Inis Padraig then moved to Ulster where he converted the chief Dichu and built a church.

At this point history becomes inseparable from legend. After the battle of Gabra at which the Fenians were finally disbanded, Cailte, one of their leaders, met Saint Patrick at Dumberg and was converted by him. He then followed the bishop across Ireland telling stories of the old days as he went. These tales were collected into the curious work known as *Acallam na Senorach* (Colloquy of the Ancient Men), in which all the old legends about lakes, forests, mountains, rivers, kings, druids and so on were brought to light once again.

After a journey to Rome between 441 and 443 Patrick returned to found the episcopal see of Armagh. Whatever quarrel he may have had with the druids and the *filid*, it was a *file* named Dubtach whom he converted and took on as adviser, and another *file* named Fiacc who became the first Irish-born bishop. Patrick also converted Conall, son of Niall, brother of King Loeghaire, who gave him the land on which the great church of Domnach Mor was built.

The stories about Patrick and the works attributed to him such as the *Confession* and the *Letter to Coroticus, Welsh prince* both written in Latin have all contributed to his image as a glorious saint who was venerated throughout Ireland. Saint Patrick's Day on March 17 is as much a national as a religious festival. Historically speaking, however, we have little clear-cut information about his life and work.

According to O'Rahilly and James Carney[2] there were actually two Patricks. The first, Palladius, is said to have converted the island and therefore to have earned the nickname Patricius; while the second Patrick, son of Calpurnius, who was born in Bannaven Taberniae in Britain and died around 461 in Glamorgan, is supposed merely to have completed Palladius' work.

Be that as it may, the ecclesiastical rule imposed by Patrick was continental and therefore Roman in nature. To an Ireland traditionally divided by quarrels of precedence as the endless conflicts in the epic tales show Patrick brought a strict church hierarchy. The bishops were to rule over vast dioceses, with authority over both parish priests and monastic orders. Rome was to be recognized as the supreme authority both for questions of dogma and for points of discipline. Patrick established four episcopal sees which he entrusted to men of great influence. His own see at Armagh he bequeathed to an Irishman named Bennen.

Patrick was undoubtedly the least Celtic of the Celtic saints. As soon as he had gone his Roman-based administrative framework began to crumble and the Irish church to develop those particularisms which continued to provoke the wrath of Rome over the next few centuries. Constant contact between Ireland and Britain meant that Irish ideas soon spread to the neighbouring island and although Rome could not manage to stamp out particularist leanings by its own efforts it eventually achieved the same end by subordinating the Britons to the Saxons who proved to be zealous devotees of the "imperial" order. Later still the papacy literally sold the Irish to the Plantagenets on condition that the rebels were brought back into the fold. When discussing the disappearance of the Celts there is very seldom any reference made to the Roman Catholic Church, its attempts to destroy the Celts politically and its intention to reduce them to a life of wretchedness. In the early days Christian dogma was still too insecure to be able to countenance the existence of free spirits like the Celts. Only Wales escaped reform, though it fell prey to other kinds of subjection. And once the Irish and Bretons had been tamed, in Ireland's case one might almost say enslaved, they became the most conservative of religious believers.

One of the reasons for Celtic particularism was the relative distance of Rome. A second was the Celts' dislike of any international authority which was not Celtic. Bearing in mind their attachment to the myth of supreme kingship, we must assume that they wished to make the new religion they had assimilated their own, to organize it as they saw fit.

The basis of Celtic Christianity and the only source of spiritual satisfaction for the Celtic soul was monasticism, which originated in the East. The monk was the Christian druid officiating in the middle of the forests. Then, when it became customary to group monks together in communities, the monastery followed directly in the footsteps of the druidic *bangor* or college.

That is why the monk took precedence over the priest, the monastery over the diocese, the abbot over the bishop. The monasteries became the cornerstone of the ecclesiastical hierarchy and of the cultural life of the new society. As there were virtually no towns in Ireland, the monasteries were both places of refuge and centres for intellectual and economic development. The abbot became the real bishop, directing and controlling Christian life in the vicinity. The custom of combining the offices of bishop and abbot spread to Britain. Saint David, for example, founded the see of Menevia; the 6th century British monk Saint Cadoc went to study in Ireland before returning to Britain to found the abbey of Llan Carvan and going to Brittany (if it is indeed the same Cadoc involved) to establish a hermitage at Morbihan. The British emigrants then took their traditions to Brittany and the diocesan abbeys of St-Pol, Tréguier, St-Brieuc, Aleth and Dol founded in Northern Armorica were very different in organization from the Gallo-Roman sees of Vannes and Quimper.

Ireland became a land of great civilization and culture which occasionally exported its ideas to the continent at that time ravaged by war and Barbarian invasion. One of the great propagators of Celtic ideas was the Irish monk Saint Columban, born in Leinster in around 540. He began his religious life at Bangor, which had been a celebrated druidic college before becoming a monastery. In 590 he went to Gaul where he was amazed at the difference between Continental and Irish church customs, particularly as far as the celebration of Easter and the wearing of the tonsure were concerned. He founded the monastery of Luxeuil which was to become a great cultural centre and lead to the establishment of convents at Remiremont, Jumieges and Saint-Omer. Not only was Columban's rule more strict than the Benedictine order which replaced it, but he insisted on the Irish date for Easter being observed and kept his own form of tonsure. Despite bitter criticism from the continental bishops he refused to bow to episcopal authority in those areas where he had founded his monasteries. In 610 he was expelled by order of Brunehaut as being too much of a nuisance and went to what is now Switzerland where he founded the convent of Saint Gall on the shores of Lake Constance. But his loyalty to Celtic beliefs provoked the animosity of the local clergy. He then settled in Italy and in 614 built the monastery of Bobbio which later became a centre for preaching in Lombardy and exerted great intellectual and spiritual influence. It was there that he died in 614 after a very full life during which he had vigorously upheld all the major principles he had brought from Ireland. He is known as a great evangelist and a great builder.

Columban, however, is not a national saint of the Irish. Another Columban, sometimes called Columba, whose real name was Columkill (Dove of the Church), is generally taken to be the most authentic representative of the Celtic church and the most typical product of Irish monasticism.

Columkill was born about 521 at Galtan in Donegal of the royal family of O'Neill. When still quite young he entered holy orders and founded the monastery of Kerry. According to his biographer Adamnan, his ninth successor, he then committed the serious crime of surreptitiously copying a precious psalter to which he had no right and thereby sparked off a war. It is clear that abbeys did fight between themselves for possession of precious objects and relics, just as Breton parishes quarrelled over exclusive rights to the remains of a saint or his grave. Whether or not Adamnan's is a true story, Columkill did leave the monastery of Kerry and went into exile. A fine 12th century poem attributed to Saint Columkill himself evokes the abbot of Kerry's farewell to Ireland. By some curious means the tradition found its way to Britain where the theme recurs in a poem of the *Black Book of Carmarthen* written in Welsh and attributed to Myrddyn (Merlin). Here the story of the book and the crime have probably been confused with a British tale about Merlin, itself a counterpart to the Irish anecdote about Suibhne throwing away St Ronan's book. The hero of the Welsh poem, Yscolan, the Scot, is easy enough to identify as Columkill. The word Scot was used to denote the inhabitants of Ireland and later came to be used for the people of Scotland also; and Columkill went to Scotland after being born in Ireland. Scot can also, incidentally, be translated as "wise". The Welsh poem reads as follows:

> Black is your horse, black is your cloak,
> black your face, black yourself,
> yes, quite black! Is it you Yscolan?
>
> I am Yscolan the wiseman [or the Scot],
> giddy is my cloud-covered mind.
> Is there no redeeming an injury to the Master?
>
> I have burnt a church, killed the cows of a school,
> I have thrown the Book in the waves,
> I am heavily punished.
>
> Creator of the created, you, of all my protectors
> the greatest, forgive me my sin,
> he who betrayed you deceived me.
>
> A whole year I was placed
> at Bangor on the dam-stake.
> Imagine what pains the sea-worms inflicted on me.
>
> If I had known then what I know now,
> as the wind blows free in the billowing treetops,
> I would never have committed that sin.[3]

In fact Columkill was exiled for political reasons. Though abbot of Kerry he never forgot that he was also of royal blood. At that time the Northern O'Neills were fighting the Southern O'Neills, and it was as a result of some clan rivalry that he was sent into exile in 563. A relative, King Dalriada then gave him the island of Iona off the West Coast of Scotland. There Columkill founded one of the most famous monasteries of the Celtic church which gave him a base from which to preach the gospel in that vast, still pagan, conglomeration of Picts and Britons now known as Scotland. Indeed it was as a result of the work of Columkill and his missionaries that the Irish word *Scot* came to be applied to the area and that the Britons became Gaelic-speakers, as they are in the Highlands and Islands to this day. Columkill's favourite disciple, Aidan, founded the monastery of Lindisfarne and undertook to evangelize the areas under Saxon domination.

The abbey of Iona became a centre of religious life not only for the Irish but for the Celtic world as a whole. Through Iona the particularist customs of Irish monasticism began to spread. Through Iona, the Celtic church's leanings towards autonomy began to make their presence felt. Indeed, during Columkill's life and for two or three centuries after, the Celtic Church was almost entirely separate from Rome. Observance of Christian ritual took a different form at Iona. Mass was celebrated only on Sundays and feast days or at the death of a friend or benefactor of the monastery. On these days, however, mass would be said both in the morning and in the afternoon and would be preceded by a ceremonial washing of hands and feet. The Celtic tonsure was worn and the monks followed a different Easter cycle from that prevailing on the continent.

In 575 Columkill returned to Ireland. The convention of Drumceat was seeking to disband the caste of *filid* on the grounds that the bards were asking far too high a payment for their work. Aed, the high king of Ireland and a supporter of the *filid* asked Columkill to judge the matter. Remembering that he was both monk and prince, both ascetic and poet, the abbot of Iona gave his judgment for the *filid* and ordered that henceforward every tribal or provincial chief should keep an official poet, the *ollave*, who was to be bard, singer of victory and defeat, joy and sadness, genealogist and chronicler. This practice found its way to Wales where, according to the laws of the 10th century Howel Dda, every chief of any importance had to support his own personal bard.

Columkill's support for the poets is important evidence that some unity between the druidic and priestly classes had been achieved by that time. Most of the druids who had adopted the Christian religion had become *filid*, and though this class of poets was supervised by the church it formed an important enough élite to have considerable influence on ecclesiastical decisions, and to impose its own almost heretical brand of theology.

Columkill founded further monasteries at Kells and Glencolumkill. He was venerated throughout Ireland and in parts of Britain; and when he died in 597 at Iona, a number of poems were written to his glory. After Saint Patrick, he and Saint Brigitte are the best known of the Irish saints.

Saint Brigitte or Bridget poses something of a problem. There is evidence to suggest that there actually was a Brigit who founded a convent at Kildare at the beginning of the 6th century. Her biographer Cogitosus even claims that Brigit ran a bisexual establishment unique in the history of the Church. Certainly the abbess of Kildare became well known and it is quite likely that people began to confuse her with another Brigit, the daughter of the Dagda, one of the Tuatha de Danann. who was still remembered in Ireland. This kind of confusion was not infrequent in Celtic countries: Saint Brendon became muddled with Bran, Saint Corneille with Cerunnos, Saint Anne with Ana.

But the story of Saint Bridget and the monastery at Kildare does raise the question of the *conhospitae*, a custom peculiar to the Celtic Church. During times of strife, Irish girls could shelter from persecution and the threat of rape by entering the monasteries and living alongside the monks, their only hope of safety. These women probably took some part in monastic worship. Certainly the custom spread to Brittany for a letter from the bishops of the province of Tours in 515 or 520 addressed to two Breton priests, Lovocat and Catihern, denounces this practice: "You continue to carry from hut to hut among your countrymen certain tables on which you celebrate the divine sacrifice of the mass with the assistance of women whom you call *conhospitae*. While you distribute the Eucharist, they take the chalice and administer the blood of Christ to the people. This is an innovation, an unprecendented superstition." (Dom Louis Gougaud, *Les Chrétientés celtiques*, p. 95.)

This custom brought down the full wrath of Rome on the Celtic Church, and yet apart from the letter quoted above, the whole subject has been passed over in chaste silence. In the Roman Church women were feared and shunned as objects of vice. They had to sit on the left, or sinister, side of the church. Christianity being the product of two patriarchal societies, the Jewish in which it originated and the Roman in which it was amended and developed, every effort was made to debase women. Like the Semites, the Roman Catholics sometimes went so far as to wonder whether women had souls. Women were given no active part to play in religious life, worship being reserved for men (and *viri integri* at that) while women were shut up in convents away from the rest of the world.

Celtic attitudes were quite different. In Gaelic and British society women played a far more important part than Mediterranean women. A wife was not merely the mother of the family but shared fully in the life of the couple. She could reign in her own right and had her own areas of responsibility, as we can see from the story of queen Medb and Tacitus' account of Boadicea. Heroes are often known as the son of such and such a woman, and this evidence of matrilinear descent is indicative of Celtic ideas about women in general. It therefore comes as little surprise to learn that many of the priestly duties were actually fulfilled by women in pagan times, though not necessarily as true druidesses, and that mythology abounds in "queens" and priestesses who were the direct forebears of our witches.

Greek and Roman sources tell of communities of Celtic priestesses, notably at the mouth of the Loire in an island which may be Bedrun, on the Ile de Sein and at Mont-Saint-Michel. These priestesses went to the mainland once a year to make love with men. They were also supposed to initiate any young man who dared go to them.

The Celts, therefore, were quite willing to include women in Christian ceremony and worship. The letter from the bishops of Tours is proof that the custom of *conhospitae* existed and that such women formed what amounted to a female deaconry. There is no documented evidence to suggest that they held any church office, but the indignant response of Roman orthodoxy to whatever position women were accorded was fierce enough to make relations with the Celtic Church very strained.

There were many other areas of friction besides. Celtic ritual remained much closer to Eastern Orthodoxy than to Roman practice. Apart from the custom of distributing both bread and wine at mass mentioned in the letter above, the Celts used to accompany their prayers with gestures and prostrations, frequently worshipping with their arms crossed. In the monasteries the monks would mortify the flesh by immersing themselves in streams or ponds where they would remain in the cold water reciting psalms. One form of penance for failing to obey the rule of poverty was to immerse the body right up to the neck. Obviously the cult of nature and of water had survived into the practice of Christianity.

The monks ate simply: no meat, a little fish, vegetables, Eastern bread and a great deal of dairy products. Many priests and bishops were married, though this was neither obligatory nor specifically allowed, the decision being left to the individual man. And where Roman canonic law demanded, and still demands, that three bishops should officiate at the ordination of a new bishop, in Ireland and Britain a single bishop could perform the consecration service on his own.

Baptism also appears to have been very different. Since Pelagius the emphasis had shifted to make the sacrement more of an act of initiation, whereas for the Romans baptism had become virtually an administrative, civil ceremony. According to a letter from Pope Zacharius to Saint Boniface (May 1 748) a synod of Saxon, and therefore pro-Roman, bishops had decreed that "whoever was washed without an invocation to the three persons of the Trinity would not be baptized." Evidently the Britons were failing in this respect. Like the early Christians, the Britons practised total immersion, though we do not know whether this meant that the person was immersed just once or three times. In 11th century Ireland, the act of annointing the convert's head with oil was omitted. In 12th century Ireland infants could be baptized at home without the attendance of a priest. The council of Cashel outlawed this custom in 1172 and condemned the practice of baptizing the infants of the rich by immersing them three times in milk.

Another subject of argument between the Celtic Church and Roman Orthodoxy was the tonsure. Until the 4th century the only rule imposed on priests was that their hair should not be too long. The tonsure originated amongst the Eastern Orthodox monks and the fashion then spread to the ordinary priesthood. This early Saint Paul's tonsure required the entire scalp to be shorn, while the Roman Saint Peter's tonsure demanded only that the top of the head should be shorn and a crown of hair left around it. Patrick tried unsuccessfully to impose the wearing of the Saint Peter tonsure in Ireland. Augustine of Canterbury, the apostle of the Saxons, introduced it into England but the Britons continued to wear another form of tonsure which Augustine's companions described as peculiar. This Briton version, in which the frontal area was totally separate, there being a semicircle of hair over the forehead and long tresses at the back, was the style which Columban took to the continent and demanded that his chief disciples wear.

The origins of the Celtic tonsure have been attributed to Simon the Magician. According to Gildas, the first man to have worn it was the swineherd of King Loegaire. It has also been claimed that this was Saint John's tonsure. But it seems more likely that it was invented in Ireland or Britain and that it may even have been druidic. For, according to the manuscript of the *Hibernensis*, the Irish druids used to shave the front of the head from one ear to the other, leaving just a lock of hair over the forehead.[4] Since Simon the Magician was supposed to have been the archetypal druid and the father of all magic and heresy, it is hardly surprising that the supporters of Roman Orthodoxy should have accredited him with the invention of the odious Celtic tonsure.

Whatever its origins, the Celtic tonsure survived for many years in Britain and Brittany as a symbol of resistance to Rome. It reached Brittany through the island emigrants and was still worn at the abbey of Landevennec in 818 when Louis the Pious tried to impose the continental rule on the monks during his expedition against Morvan Leiz-Breiz.

Another cause of controversy was the celebration of Easter. The date of Easter Day had always been fixed by scholarly computations, which meant that in the early days each Christian Church had its own date. In 314 it was decided at the council of Arles that Easter should be celebrated *uno die et uno tempore per omnem orbem*, but there was so much opposition to this decision that it was never put into practice.

In 325 the council of Nicaea ruled that Easter should never be celebrated on the same day as the Jewish Passover and never after the spring equinox. Until the end of the 3rd century, the Romans observed the 16-year cycle of Saint Hippolytus which put Easter between the 16th and 22nd day of the lunar month. The 84-year cycle of Augustalis was then adopted, and this set Easter between the 14th and 20th day of the lunar month, that is between 25 March and 21 April. It was this 84-year cycle that the Celts followed and that they continued to use even after Rome had abandoned it in 457 for the cycle of Victorius of Aquitaine. Victorius' system involved a 532-year cycle, based on multiplying the 28-year solar cycle by the 19-year lunar cycle used at Alexandria and this 532-year calculation continued to be used in Gaul until the end of the 8th century. In Rome, however, the Alexandrian 19-year cycle of Dionysius Exiguus was used from the beginning of the 6th century. With the equinox being fixed at 21 March, Easter would then fall between the 15th and the 21st day of the lunar month, i.e. between 22 March and 25 April.

When Saint Augustine of Canterbury was sent to Britain by Gregory the Great to convert the Saxons and remove them from the influence of the British, it was the Alexandrian cycle he took with him. The Saxons accepted it, of course, but the British Christians who used the 84-year cycle were very slow to adopt the Roman way.

In 602 or 603, Augustine invited the British abbots and bishops to a celebrated meeting at Saint Augustine's Oak somewhere south of the Severn, in an attempt to settle the differences between the old church and the new. But instead of adopting a conciliatory tone, Augustine immediately delivered an ultimatum, urging the Britons to join with him in bringing Christianity to the Saxons and to renounce their erroneous customs and their incorrect Easter cycle.

The Britons asked for a delay before replying and went, together with the learned men of the monastery at Bangor (another former druidic college in Wales) to seek the advice of a saintly hermit. He encouraged them to stand firm but to agree to talk. So discussions were opened with delegates from Augustine and when it appeared that there might be some area of agreement the Britons returned to meet Augustine in 605. However, he would not even stand to receive them; and deeply insulted and justifiably convinced that Augustine wanted nothing so much as their total submission, the Britons refused to make any concessions and left. A century later in 731 according to the Venerable Bede the two sides were still equally divided in Britain and a letter from Augustine's successor Laurenctius to the bishops and abbots of Ireland indicates that there, too, the Celtic Church had stuck to its beliefs.

When Columban settled on the continent he encountered similar difficulties but refused to abandon his Easter cycle. In 631 there was a whole month between the celebration of Easter in Rome and Easter Day in Ireland. Honorious I, Pope from 625 to 638, urged the Scottish church to follow the Roman rule. In 632, an Irish monk named Cummian wrote a work justifying the Celtic Easter cycle and declaring that only the Scots and the Britons were correct.

In 628 Easter was celebrated on March 27 in both Rome and Ireland. The Pope used this coincidence to make further entreaties to the Celts to give way. Finally during the second quarter of the 7th century, Southern Ireland agreed to accept the Roman cycle, but the North still obstinately refused. In 661 Colman, bishop of Lindisfarne, re-opened the Easter controversy. In 664 a conference took place at the monastery of Whitby between Colman and Wilfrid, the Saxon king of Northumbria who supported Rome. The majority of the clergy attending the synod sided with Wilfrid and Colman left with his supporters to found the monastery of Galway.

Gradually the Roman cycle came to be adopted by the Irish communities, though Iona did not give way until 716. Finally, at the end of the 8th century, the Britons and the Bretons also yielded.

The Easter controversy may seem a very trifling disagreement but it symbolized Celtic independence and the strength of resistance to Roman rule which may also have been partly due to the geographical isolation of the Celtic world in the 5th and 6th centuries. The Gaels were confined to Ireland, their only outside contact being with the Britons. The Saxon invasion of Britain merely served to reinforce the notion of Celtic unity in times of trouble; and as the Celts and more particularly the Britons regarded the Saxons as their archetypal enemies, it became a point of honour to reject anything that the Saxons had adopted. Augustine of Canterbury spoilt any chances of reconciliation with the Britons by siding so obviously with the newly converted, and to him precious, Saxons. The emigrant Britons took their hostility to Rome with them to Brittany and even to Galicia where there was a Celtic diocese at Britonnia until the year 900. This explains the traditional animosity of the Bretons towards the ruling church at Tours and their creation of a metropolis at Dol during the time of Nominoë, though it was only granted official recognition between 1078 and 1199. The Bretons kept many of the British customs, notably their form of tonsure and the particular office of abbot-bishop. Whenever the Breton bishops wanted to protest against the domination of the Frankish clergy, they would refuse to take part in the councils at Tours, a decision which almost invariably led to argument and dispute.

So long before the development of Gallicanism there existed a distinct tendency to religious nationalism. Indeed quarrels between Rome and the Celtic Church amounted to a virtual schism, less serious than the break with the Eastern Church because it had less influence on politics and economics, but nonetheless real. The apocryphal if telling words attributed to Dinoot, abbot of Bangor in 620 are a kind of summary of these differences. For, having been urged to recognize the authority of Pope Gregory, Dinoot is supposed to have replied, "I am prepared to show the pope of Rome the affection and charity which I owe to all Christian men, I owe nothing more to him whom you call the pope and who unreasonably claims to be the father of fathers. We know no other leader than the bishop of Kaerlion. It is he whom God has charged to watch over us." Clearly this statement does not ring entirely true to the 7th century. It is just a little too close to the reformatory tone of Henry VIII. But there is no reason why Dinoot should not have felt the same way.

In the end the Celtic Church was destroyed not so much by Rome as by the Norsemen. In the 9th century pirates destroyed the Welsh and Irish monasteries and undermined the whole civilization which had flowered under their roofs before going on to attack the Armorican abbeys. The years that followed were black indeed, and not only because the Irish called the Norsemen the "Black People". In 830 Armagh was sacked by the Viking chief Torgeist who proclaimed himself abbot. In 841 Torgeist's wife Ota was uttering oracles from a seat on the high altar of Clonmacnoise. In Wales Bangor was sacked and sooner or later all the other monasteries fell into Norse hands.

When the Vikings had been beaten back and order restored, the monks returned to rebuild from the ruins. But many of the old ideas had vanished during the years of exile and Rome had regained control over the independently-minded. Then, when the Irish tried to reassert their autonomy in the 12th century and refused to pay St Peter's Penny, Rome pitilessly surrendered them to Henry Plantagenet. In this case the trouble was financial rather than doctrinal, for the chief aim of the papacy was to recover the taxes which the Irish would not pay by using Henry II as collector.

In its lifetime the Celtic Church had played a considerable part in preserving and developing Western culture at a time when the continent of Europe was little more than an anarchic confusion of self-seeking nations. The Irish monasteries of Clonard, Clonmacnoise, Armagh, Bangor, Lindisfarne and Iona were great spiritual and intellectual centres. Men from many other races and lands came to study at Armagh. The Saxon Alcuin who brought a cultural revival to the Franks spent many years at Clonmacnoise. The Gallic bishop Asculf lived with Adamnan at Iona. John Scotus Erigena who was born in Ireland in about 810 was a direct offshoot of Irish monasticism. Before teaching for twenty-five years at the school of Laon under Charles the Bald he had drawn many of his daring theological ideas from the fount of old Celtic thought in which Pelagianism was again rising to the surface. His treatise on *Divine Predestination*, after all, states that evil is merely the negation of good, and that since sin does not exist for God, God attaches no punishment to it. Evil is its own punishment and the sinner will never attain blessedness for blessedness is a knowledge of the truth. John was also condemned as a heretic on several occasions for his bold statements that philisophy has a duty to prolong faith, that everything emanates from God and returns to him, that being beyond man God only exists as he is revealed to man, and that God creates himself by creating other things.

The Celtic Church also sent its missionaries into other countries. Apart from Saint Columban whom we have already examined there were Saint Fursa at Peronne, once known as *Peronna Scotorum*, Saint Fiacre near Meaux, Saint Kilian at Wurzburg and others who went as far as Southern Italy and even the Ukraine. The Irish and Britons, of course, also brought the gospel to Brittany.

Several saints are as much celebrated in Brittany as they are in Ireland. Saint Ronan, for example, is known in Ireland as a character in the story of Suibhne. Having just built a church, Ronan was met with hostility from Suibhne, son of Colman. When Ronan cursed him Suibhne went mad and had to live like a hermit in the forest. Equally familiar to the Bretons, Saint Ronan was buried at Locranon (Finistère) where he had established his hermitage and where various miracles are said to have occurred. Saint Brendan, Saint Senan and Saint Tujean are also as much venerated in Brittany as they are in Ireland.

Then there is the Briton Iltud who founded a kind of monastic seminary at Llan Illtydd, now Llantwit Major near Cardiff, and another similar establishment at Llancarvan. Iltud went to Brittany where he gave his name to the community of Lanildut (Finistère). The community at Llan Illtydd also produced Samson, founder of the see of Dol, Tugdual of Tréguier and Malo, founder of the original diocese of Aleth, which then became Saint-Malo. Legend has it that a whole parade of British and Irish saints crossed the sea to evangelize Brittany, but it is difficult to form any clear picture of relations between the mother-houses in the islands and their Armorican offshoots on the continent from the kinds of pious and ingenuous saints-lives furnished by the 18th century Father Albert Le Grand. The most we can say is that such relations did exist and that there was some concern that future generations should continue to be aware of Armorica's religious debt to Ireland and Wales.

Some of the founding saints are certainly remembered in the parish names of both Britain and Brittany. Saint Quay (Côtes-du-Nord), for example, corresponds to St Kea in Cornwall, Land-Key in Devon and Land-Tocai in Somerset. The character in question here is said to have been a bishop of Britain before founding a monastery at Cléder (Finistère) and has even been identified as the seneschal Kai of Arthurian romance. Similarly Edern, Lannedern and Louedern (Finistère) correspond to Llan Edern in Glamorgan and Bodedern in Anglesey, and Edern or Yder also appears in a number of Arthurian romances. Indeed Welsh tradition makes him the son of the god Nudd and brother of Gwynn. Saint-Tugdual (Morbihan), Landudal (Finistère), Pludual (Côtes-du-Nord), Saint-Thual (Ille-et-Vilaine) and Saint-Pabu (Finistère) correspond to St Tudwal near Pwllheli in Gwynedd, Llan-Baba in Gwent and Bryn Pabuan in Powys. Saint Tugdual, nicknamed Saint Pabu (the holy Papa) was an abbot in Britain before landing in Armorica where he founded Tréguier. He then apparently travelled on to Rome to become pope. Tugdual is one of the best known Breton saints and may well have inherited attributes from the ancient pagan gods, in particular from Dispater-Teutates.

Other semi-legendary saints which the Breton peninsula acquired from the mother country include Armel, founder of Plouarzel and of Ploërmel; Budoc or Beuzec, who sailed on a stone trough and landed at Porspoder, venerated at Beuzec-Conq and Beuzec-Cap-Sizun and Efflam, prince of Hibernia, who also appears in Arthurian legend as the tamer of a dragon on the dunes which still bear his name. Gildas, the supposed author of the *De Excidio Britanniae*, which describes the emigration, was probably confused with Gweltas, a man reputed to have studied at Armagh and founded the abbey of St-Gildas de Rhuys who is honoured in a number of parochial chapels and churches. Goneri is venerated in the region of Pontivy, which he reputedly converted, Gouesnou or Guenno in the region of Brest where he is said to have been bishop of Léon. St Hervé, son of the island bard Hoarvian, built the monastery of Lanhouarneau and is honoured on the Menez-Bré. La Villemarqué accredits to him authorship of the canticle *Ar Baradoz* (the Paradise), one of the loveliest songs of Celtic tradition. The name Cadoc or Cadeuc or Kaco, which resulted from confusion between various different characers, is reflected in St-Kado in Belz, St-Cadou, St Cast and Pleucadeuc, all in Brittany. Saint Ninoc'h is the patron saint of Scaer in Finistère. Saint Nonna or Vougay or Vio, supposedly bishop of Armagh, is venerated at Saint-Vougay (Finistère). Saint Sezeny is said to have founded a monastery at Guissény (Finistère) where he died at the age of 127. Suliau was founder of the priory of Saint-Suliac (Ille-et-Vilaine) and the patron saint of Sizun (Finistère). Teleau or Telo, who is supposed to have married the sister of a count of Cornouaille, was confused with the hypothetical saint Helo, in whom we can recognize the word *heol*, meaning "sun". Telo was probably a real person, the founder of the monastery at Llandaff in Wales as well as a preacher of the gospel in Brittany.

The fact that there are so many Celtic saints, almost none of whom were ever canonized by the official church, can be partly explained by the veneration accorded to all pious men and hermits. In this respect there is a definite link between the pagan and Christian eras for the druids, too, were solitary hermit-like figures living in the forests where they celebrated their mysteries. The religion of the dolmen-builders of which we know next to nothing may even have survived into the Christian period. There are many megalithic monuments, particularly dolmens, in the Celtic regions; and since it has been suggested that the dolmens were the tombs of ancient priests or missionaries who continued to be worshipped after their death, it is possible that the Christian hermits came to assume the same position in the minds of the local populace as those megalithic or druidic anchorites.

Besides, as Dom Louis Gougaud says (*op. cit.* p. 105), "the ancient Celts must have had a totally different concept of sanctity from ours. First of all, sanctity was very localized. A Gaul's saint was not necessarily an Irishman's saint, and the Latin church refused both the Gaul's and the Irishman's claim to sainthood."

The Celtic Church may have had its own saints, many of them undoubtedly figments of the imagination. It may have had its particularist customs, its *conhospitae*, its unique amalgam of abbot and bishop, its tendency to autonomy, its daring, sometimes even heretical doctrines, and its traces of druidism. But despite all this it played a role of the greatest importance during the first millenium of the Christian era.

To start with, it did much to preserve the old civilization which was threatened by the Germanic invasions. Within the sheltering confines of Ireland and far Western Britain and Europe, the Celtic Church continued to teach Latin literature and Mediterranean philosophy. It preserved the essence of Celtic tradition; the monks of Ireland and Wales were anxious to prove worthy of their ancestors and patiently copied a wide variety of the old tales, both sacred and profane, connected with their own culture. Druidism merged into monasticism. Ireland spread the art of calligraphy. Celtic illumination, design and stonework, in which the most ancient traditions were preserved, became models for the whole of Christian Europe in the Middle Ages. Altogether the Celtic Church made a considerable contribution to the Western world.

What it lacked however, was sufficient unity to resist external pressure; and that was inevitable, for it was the Celts' tendency to anarchy which gave their church its originality. Today very little remains, except ruined buildings and names like Clonfert, Iona, Clonmacnoise, Lismore, Kildare, Lindisfarne, Llan Illtydd, Llandaff, Bangor, Landevennec and many others. But these names and their ruins evoke an age of old, and their heritage lives on.

CHAPTER NINE

Britain

ALTHOUGH
Britain remained the only free land of British-speaking peoples after Caesar had conquered Gaul, it, too, was gradually overwhelmed by invading forces both from the South and from the North.

In fact Britain was used to invasions, since over the centuries it had absorbed a mixture of Gaels on their way to Ireland, early Britons, secondary Britons who probably came after the North Sea and Baltic disasters had destroyed their homes and Belgians, who were fleeing the Germanic threat and the dangers of overpopulation on the continent at the beginning of the La Tène III period. The Gaels also continued to make constant incursions on the western coasts, and it seems likely that the Armorican Veneti settled in North Wales in the area called Gwynedd.

Obviously such diverse, badly-organized, tribally-orientated peoples could offer no cohesive resistance to the series of invaders. For there was nothing to really bind them together apart from the druidic religion and there are other historical examples to show that whatever unifying influence druidism may have had it was not enough to avert conflict.

Strictly speaking there was no linguistic bond either. The overwhelming majority of the island Britons may have spoken a British language analogous to Gallic, but there were considerable variations in dialect resulting from the arrival of different immigrant groups. The Gaels had brought their own language which was already quite distinct from British, and North of the Tweed the land did not belong to the Britons at all but to the Picts whom the Welsh texts describe as *Ffichti* Gaels, meaning that they spoke a language of the Gaelic tradition. These were the *Cruithnig* who, after the old Celtic Q-sound had evolved into the British P-sound, gave the whole island the name *Pretannia* whence *Britannia*.

This hybrid population had been almost entirely spared by Julius Caesar, not so much because he had no designs on Britain as because he could not be sure of his rear. The two expeditions he led to the island were first and foremost reconnaissance and prestige operations. In any case the Britons had been warned about him by Gallic refugees and were determined to hold firm against him.

The first hero of British resistance to the Romans was Cassivellaunos, whose name passed into Welsh as Casswallawn ab Beli. A historical figure, he enjoyed considerable popularity in later centuries, his legend being taken up and expanded to such an extent that he became the archetypal hero of British incorruptibility (Geoffrey of Monmouth, *Historia Regum Britanniae* III, 20, IV, 2-9). In the *Myvyrian Archaeology of Wales* (402, 1), we read how Casswallawn organized an expedition of 61,000 men to recover Fflur, daughter of Mynach Gorr, who had been abducted by a Gallic prince named Mwrchan. Casswallawn landed in Armorica, beat the Romans, recovered Fflur and remained in Gwasgwyn (Gascony) where his descendants are still to be found. According to one of the Triads (Triad 80, *Mab.* II, 284) Casswallawn is one of the three lovers of the island, the two others being Tristan and Kynon. The expedition to Gascony is also mentioned in Triad 9 of the *Red Book of Hergest*: "They went with Casswallawn their uncle to pursue the Caesarians expelled from this island." (*Mab.* II, 238.)

Another triad offers a different version of the story: "Three goldsmith shoemakers in the island of Britain; Casswallawn, son of Beli, when he went as far as Rome to seek Fflur" (*Mab.* II, 273). A variant on this triad says; "to seek Fflur daughter of Mygnach Gorr, taken by Mwrchan Lleidr [the Thief] and delivered by him to the emperor Iwl Caisar; Casswallawn brought her back to Britain" (*M.A.W.*, 411). One of the two other goldsmith shoemakers is the famous hero Manawyddan (the Irish Manannan) and the two characters come together in a magical adventure in the *mabinogi* of *Branwen*, where Casswallawn is clearly portrayed as a usurper. " 'Casswallawn son of Beli has conquered the Island of the Mighty [Britain] and is a crowned king in Llundein [London].' 'What has happened to Caradawc, son of Bran, and the seven men who were left with him?' 'Casswallawn fell upon them and killed six and Caradawc's heart broke with despair at seeing the sword killing the men and not knowing who was doing it. Casswallawn had clothed himself in a magic cloak so that no one could see him killing the men, only the sword.' " (*Branwen*).

The idea of a quarrel over the throne is corroborated by Triad 10 of the *Red Book:* "There were three men of dishonour in the island of Britain. The first was Avarwy, son of Ludd ab Beli. He it was who brought Julius Caesar and the Romans to this island for the first time and arranged for a tribute of 3000 pounds of silver to be paid to the Romans to show his opposition to his uncle Casswallawn." According to the *Historia Regum Britanniae* (III, 20, IV, 3-11), Avarwy, son of Ludd, whom Geoffrey calls Androgeus, was angry that his uncle Cassibellaunos was king of the Britons in his place and wrote to Caesar. His conversation with the proconsul is one of the three treacherous conversations (*M.A.W.*, 403). Thus was there given to "Ukessar and the Romans place for the front shoes of their horses on the land at Pwyth Meinlas" (*Mab.* II, 253).

It seems likely that the character of Avarwy-Androgeus is based on the historical Mandubraccios who "had gone over to the continent to put himself under Caesar's protection, having fled for his life when his father, the king of the Trinovantes, had been killed by Cassivellaunus" (Caesar, *Gallic Wars,* V, 20).

Apart from family quarrels, Casswallawn appears to have exercised considerable authority. In the *mabinogi* of *Manawyddan,* Pryderi the Other World hero declares " 'I go to England to offer my submission to Casswallawn' .... It was during this time that Pryderi went to see Casswallawn at Ryt Ychen [Oxford], where he was received joyfully and thanked for offering his submission." Casswallawn is one of the "three legal kings of the island of Britain" (*Mab.* II, 305). It was "by virtue of the law of the land and of the nation that they were invested with the monarchy for they were not the eldest".

So, after the brief incursion of the "Caesarians", Britain remained independent. Of the various peoples living there, some are better known to us than others. The Trinovantes, who were ruled by Casswallawn, had their capital at the fortress of Camulodunum (Colchester). Londinium (Llundein or London) was the port of the Cantii who gave their name to Kent and Canterbury. The Brigantes who occupied northern England had their capital at Eboracum (Kaer Efrawc or York) and a large settlement at Combodunum (the Fortress of the Bow) or Camboritum (The Ford of the Bow, as in Chambord and Chambourcy) between Chester and York. The Iceni lived in the area North of the Trinovantes, the Catuvellauni just North of London, the Regni in the South and a colony of Atrebates in the South East. The Dobuni had settled on the Severn, the Dumnonii in Devon, the Durotriges around Salisbury and the Critani in the Midlands. The Welsh Marches were occupied by the Cornovii, North Wales by the Ordovices and South Wales by the Silures. There were also scattered settlements of Parisi and Cassi all over the island, the latter being related to the Baiocasses and the Veliocasses of the continent.

We know that Commios the Atrebatian, who led the last of the Gallic resistance to Rome, fled to Britain probably with his family and servants to join an existing colony of Atrebatians there. He certainly became king among them, and his three sons succeeded him one after the other.

As time passed, the war with the Romans faded from people's memories. The image of Caesar as an arrogant conqueror gave way to the trite picture of the defeated Roman dictator fleeing before the heroic onslaught of the British people. Any consciousness of danger vanished at a time when the Britons should have been more watchful than ever. For once the might of an expanding Roman empire had crushed all Gallic resistance and could be sure of its rearguard on the continent, it immediately took up its systematic destruction of the Celtic world.

During the reign of Caligula the Romans again attempted to establish a solid footing on the island with a large and well-provisioned expeditionary force. Again the Trinovantes led the resistance, with the half-historic, half-legendary King Cunobelinos whom Welsh tradition named Cynfelyn and whom Shakespeare dramatized as Cymbeline.

Geoffrey of Monmouth makes Kymbelinus king of Britain after Tenvantius, son of Ludd, who succeeded Cassivellaunos (*H.R.B.,* IV, 11). According to Geoffrey he was brought up in Rome by Augustus. Certainly he was a formidable warrior. Cynfelyn is one of the three valiant kings of the island of Britain (*Mab.* II, 307).

Because of this resistance the Roman expedition failed. In 43, however, during

Claudius' reign, they returned, determined to stay. Plautius who led the expedition had used the intervening years to gather detailed information about the geography of Britain and the domestic quarrels there which he hoped to exploit as Caesar had done his information about Gaul. Tacitus says that the reason given for this expedition was the Britons' refusal to hand over deserters from armies recruited in Gaul who had taken refuge across the Channel (*Agricola*, XIV).

On this occasion the Britons were led by Cynfelyn's two sons, Togodumnos and Caratacos (Suetonius *Vitellius*, XLVIII and Dio Cassius, LX, 19-23). The second of these whom the Welsh called Caradawc has remained the better known. He has been confused with a large number of quasi-legendary characters and eventually became a mythological figure of great importance. He even turns up in the Round Table romances.

The historic Caradawc held firm against the Roman assault. But his forces, composed mainly of Trinovantes, Atrebatians and Silures, were ill-prepared. Plautius managed to take Camulodunum. The future emperor Vitellius conquered the land of the Regni and took Vectis (the Isle of Wight). "The area of Britain closest to us was gradually colonized. A group of veterans was settled there. King Cogidus received several towns as his share. This prince has remained unswervingly loyal to us to this day." (*Agricola*, XIV.) For, as Tacitus adds, "It is a policy long since adopted by Rome to make use of the influence even of kings in order to enslave people."

In 50, a larger number of Britons rebelled. Publius Ostorius, the new propraetor immediately reacted, decimated the insurgents and took the opportunity to push westwards, forming a chain of military outposts along the Severn. It was then that the Iceni entered the picture, only to be beaten despite their heroic resistance. Ostorius laid waste the countryside and pushed on towards the shores of the Irish Sea. At this point the Brigantes, though traditional allies of the Romans, rose against them. Ostorius crushed the rebellion by executing its leaders and established a colony of veterans at Camulodunum to watch over the area and "civilize" his allies.

The Silures however were still in arms, and so was Caradawc. As a propagandist for rebellion he managed to persuade the Silures to make him their king and took the war into North Wales to the land of the Ordovices. Having mustered troops from among malcontents of every tribe, he then prepared to fight the Romans somewhere between Ordovican and Brigantian territory in an area of steeply sloping hills with a rampart of heaped stones near a treacherous ford. Tacitus pictures Caradawc in the midst of his warriors urging them to fight with grand words about freedom and independence. So eager were the Britons for combat that the Romans began to wonder whether it might not be better to turn back. Finally, however, the Romans regained control of the region after an exceptionally fierce battle. It was a two-edged victory for most of the Britons managed to escape although Caradawc's wife, daughter and brothers remained in enemy hands.

Caradawc took refuge among the Brigantes where he hoped that their queen Cartismandua would supply him with fresh troops. But despite her promises of help she held him and eventually handed him over to the Romans. Caradawc was sent to Rome where he boldly demanded to be heard by the Senate and managed to present a dignified and eloquent speech in his defence. Moved by the courage and stature of the British leader Claudius spared his life and granted him and his family their freedom (Tacitus, *Annals*, XII, 31-37).

It is there that the story of Caratacos, son of Cunobelinos, ends. In the Welsh traditions, Caradawc is frequently associated with Cynfelyn, though not as his son; for he has become the son of the hero Bran Vendigeit. It would appear that some conscious attempt was made to connect this hero of British resistance with the complex myth of Bran-Brennus, the conqueror of Rome and Delphi. According to the mabinogi of *Branwen*, Caradawc is a contemporary of Casswallawn who kills Caradawc's companions when rendered invisible by his magic cloak. "However he did not want to kill Caradawc who was his nephew, his sister's son. (Caradawc was thus one of the three who broke their hearts with grief)."

Caradawc was also one of the "three valiant kings of the island of Britain" together with Cynfelyn and Arthur. "They defeated all their enemies and it was impossible to defeat them except by treachery." (*Mab*. II, 307.) He was one of the "three main kings of combat", together with Gweirydd, son of Cynfelyn, and Casswallawn (*Mab*. II, 308) and one of the "three kings of assembly" when he was named war leader of all Britain to stop the Roman assault. "They were called the three kings of assembly because they received their privileges from the general assembly of all the counties and districts throughout the whole expanse of the Cymrys' lands and they held meetings in every region . . . of the island of Britain and the adjacent islands" (*Mab*. II, 308). This is obviously an idealized and utopian picture; but it seems clear nonetheless that the idea of supreme kingship continued to haunt the Britons whenever they were threatened.

Caradawc undoubtedly lived up to his reputation as one of the "three good harriers . . . hounding the oppression of the Caesarians" (*Mab*. II, 314) and he was only really defeated by the treachery of Cartismandua. Indeed her deceit was one of the "three secret betrayals" when "he was betrayed by Aregwedd Voeddawg, daughter of Avarwy ab Ludd, and was sent by her as a captive to the Romans" (*Mab*. II, 306). In the Welsh tradition, then, Cartismandua has become Aregwedd Voeddawg (the Stinking One), and is significantly given Avarwy as a father. For Avarwy, remember, can be identified as Caesar's Mandubraccios, the man who brought the Romans to Britain out of hate for Casswallawn. Aregwedd appears to be the archetypal calculating harpy, a mistress of "seduction, trickery and scheming," to be contrasted with the loyal Bran who "spent seven years as a hostage in Rome for his son Caradawc" (*Mab*. II, 309).

The *Iolo Manuscripts*, which contain many recollections of ancient traditions, have a curious tale about Caradawc who is described as king of Essyllwg. When he beats the Romans they attribute their defeat to the lie of the land, which is covered with woods and thickets. To prove that his victory was due solely to his skill in battle, Caradawc cuts down the forests. Meanwhile, Manawyddan erects a prison to hold all invading foreigners and traitors to the British cause. The prison is built from the bones of Romans killed in battle which Manawyddan mixes with lime. As it is a round building, the largest bones are placed on the outside, with the smaller ones being used inside to furnish the cells. The underground cells are kept for the traitors (*Iolo Manuscripts*, 185-87).

So famous did Caradawc become that his reputation spilled over into other legends and he gradually became confused with different characters. In the Middle Ages he was Caradawc Briechbras or Vreichvras ("Big Arm" from *breich*, arm and *bras,* big). Interestingly, however, the French Round Table romances made him Brief-bras, "Short Arm"; copyists who did not understand the Welsh had simply Frenchified his name.[1]

He thus became one of the "three favourites of Arthur's court and one of the three battle knights, none of whom could bear to have a *penteleu* [a kind of suzerain] above him. Arthur sang them this englyn:

> Here are my three battle knights
> Menedd, Llud Llurugawc [the Ironclad]
> and Caradawc, pillar of the Cymry."
> (*Mab.* II, 272-3)

Caradawc is also numbered among the "three leaders of the old men in each of Arthur's courts" (Skene, *Four Ancient Books*, II, 456) and is "chief of the ancients" (*Mab.* II, 279). An Act concerning the relics of the cathedral of Vannes mentions a certain King Caradoc, *cognomento Brech-Bras* as being involved with Saint Padern, the bishop of Vannes (B.N. fonds latin. MS. 9.003). In the First Continuation of Chrétien de Troyes' *Perceval*, Caradoc is king of Vannes and his son has the same name as himself. Here he undergoes a similar adventure to that of Cú Chulainn in the *Feast of Briciu* and Gawain in the *Green Knight*, with a mock execution following his own agreement to cut off the head of Eliavres the Magician.

Eventually Christianity also took hold of Caradawc. Just as the pagan Celtic hero Bran became the founder of a line of saints before himself being canonized as Saint Brendan, so Caradawc Vreichvras fathered a family of saints and acquired the name "son of Llyr Merini" (*M.A.W.*, 426). It is under this name that he appears in the late tale, the *Dream of Rhonabwy*. In the *mabinogi* of *Branwen*, he is one of the *seith marchawc* left to guard Britain during Bran's absence, and *seith marchawc* can mean either "seven horsemen" or "sainted horsemen". Apart from giving his name to the ancient British fortress of Ker Caradawc situated where Salisbury now stands, he was probably also unwittingly responsible for a series of places named Saint-Caradec in Brittany, notably in the Côtes-du-Nord and Morbihan regions. But then Breton saints are more often legendary than not.

Although nothing further is known about what happened to Caradawc after Claudius had released him, we do know that the Silures mounted a fresh attack on the Roman soldiers. The enemy counter-attacked but were driven back before regaining control of the area. Even then Roman domination was only superficial for the Silures continued a pitiless guerilla war in the marshlands and forests, winning a number of minor victories.

The pro-praetor Ostorius died and was replaced by Aulus Didius. At that time, says Tacitus (*Annals*, XII, 38), the best of the British chiefs was Venusius of the Brigantes. While still married to Cartismandua he had remained an ally of the Romans, but after a rift with her he took up arms not only against his ex-wife but against the Romans as well. Cartismandua managed to seize his brother and parents by a trick, but their queen's duplicity so disgusted the Brigantes that they rose against her. The Romans had to come to her aid and only just managed to re-establish some semblance of order.

Altogether, the Romans were achieving little success in their conquest of Britain, a fact which the Latin historians barely hint at. And the reason for their failure had nothing to do with British patriotism and unity, nor even with the emergence of some great leader (fame rarely came to Celtic chiefs until after they had been defeated). For the core of British resistance to the Roman occupation lay in druidism.

According to Caesar the centre of druidism was in Britain and those wishing to make a profound study of it went there for the purpose (*Gallic Wars*, VI, 13). After the conquest of Gaul and the subsequent distrust of the druids a number of them took refuge in Britain. The Romans rightly believed that the firm establishment of their authority would depend not only on their ability to impose their own law and language but also on the success with which they could stamp out druidism and introduce Latin cults, whether or not they were still adhered to in Rome. The edicts issued against the druids on various occasions, notably by Tiberius and Claudius, were therefore politically motivated. But the druids held out, even on the continent, as Pomponius Mela remarks (III, 19). Tacitus confirms this in his account of their participation in the rising in Gaul in 71 (*Histories*, IV, 54).

During the consulship of Cesonius Petus and Petronius Turpilianus, i.e. in 61 AD, Suetonius Paulinus, the commander in chief of the Roman forces, "prepared to attack the island of Mona which was inhabited by courageous men and provided a refuge for all the exiles" (Tacitus, *Annals*, XIV, 29). Presumably the reason for this Roman assault was that the exiles were directing British resistance from Mona; and these exiles, as Tacitus goes on to tell us, were druids.

In fact the island of Mona or Anglesey (Welsh Môn) was held to be the very centre of druidism. It was a blessed, sacred spot, akin to the Other World islands of Celtic tradition, more precious in mythical than in real terms. As such it was bound to be a fertile island, and the 12th century Welsh chronicler Giraldus Cambrensis calls it the "mother of Cambria". Anglesey also occupied a position of strategic importance, for apart from being an embarkation point to Ireland it was effectively a watchtower between Wales, Scotland and Ireland. Until Wales lost its independence, Aberffraw in the South of the island was principal residence of the kings of Gwynedd. The port of Gwygyr, now Cemais, on the North West of the island, was one of the "three privileged ports" of the island of Britain (*Mab.* II, 319). The renowned mythological character Gwyddyon ab Don, who was both druid and magician, was king of Môn. The druidic schools on the island are mentioned by the bard Taliesin, or the man who wrote under that name:

> There will come men to Môn
> to be initiated into the ways of wizards.
> (J.M. 79)

and he hints at the sacred nature of the island in the difficult poem entitled *Death Song of Amaethon:*

> Troubled is the isle of the glory of the Powerful One,
> the isle of the harsh distributor,
> Môn with the generous cups, enlivened with vigour,
> whose strait is its rampart.
> (*Book of Taliesin*, XLV)

Archaeological excavations on Anglesey have brought to light evidence of religious worship there. At Llyn Cerrig Bach in particular, 150 votive offerings have been found in the shape of animal bones, horses' skulls, bulls' skulls, horns, teeth, cereals and so on.

The Romans obviously regarded Mona as a stronghold which had to be taken. Suetonius therefore mustered a large force for his expedition. "He built flat boats suitable for landing on low and dangerous coastlines and transported his foot-soldiers in them, while the cavalry forded or swam across, mounting their horses in the deepest places" (*Annals*, XIV, 29).

An extraordinary, almost hallucinatory spectacle awaited the Romans, and one for which they were quite unprepared. Even Tacitus in his account of the scene could not help expressing his amazement. "The enemy army was ranged along the shore like a forest of weapons and soldiers among which women ran ceaselessly about like furies, shrieking imprecations, with black robes and dishevelled hair and torches in their hands. All around stood druids with their hands raised to the sky, howling wild curses. At this sight our soldiers were gripped by fear." (*Annals*, XIV, 30).

After some doubts, the Romans pulled themselves together and launched an attack. In fact there was no real battle. As Françoise Le Roux says in *Les Druids;* "The Romans had no difficulty in occupying an island which had not been defended presumably because it had never occurred to the Britons that anyone would dare attack it." Even so, Tacitus tries to justify the operation. "A fortress was built to contain the defeated and the sacred woods in which they practised their cruel rites were destroyed; it was their custom to sprinkle the altars with the blood of their prisoners and to consult the gods by way of human entrails." (*Annals*, XIV, 30.)

If we are to believe the Latin authors, the Roman legions were charitable organizations who came to the aid of the wretched barbarians as they suffered in their superstitions and their evil practices. But then, the Nazi propagandists sang a similar song in France from 1940-1944.

After this stupendous victory, virtually the whole of Britain rose against the Romans. Prasugatus, king of the Iceni, who was renowned for his wealth, had had such confidence in his Roman allies that he had made Nero joint heir to his property with his two daughters, convinced that his kingdom would thereby remain protected against all-comers. "In fact he was mistaken," as Tacitus admits. "His kingdom was ravaged by the Roman centurions, his home sacked by slaves. His wife Boadicea was beaten with rods and his daughters raped. Finally, as if the whole kingdom were part of the legacy, the leaders of the Iceni were stripped of their most ancient possessions." (*Annals*, XIV, 31.)

Obviously it was this outrage, coupled with the news of the sacrilege committed by the Romans at Môn which sparked off the rebellion. The Iceni took up arms and "won over the Trinovantes and other tribes which as yet unused to slavery had undertaken by a secret conspiracy to recover their freedom." Underlying Tacitus' account is a sense of outrage at his fellow countrymen's activities and he comes close to supporting the barbarians. Indeed he has more to say on this subject in his *Agricola* (XV) where he details the Britons' complaints.

> The Britons told each other of their sufferings, of the shame of their slavery, they recounted to each other the insults they had endured and as they spoke they became angry. "Nothing is to be gained by patience," they said to themselves; tyranny merely adds more over-whelming evils to those which once seemed bearable. In times past they had had but one master, now there were two oppressors; the general drained their blood, the procurator their wealth, and whether these two tyrants agreed or disagreed their burden was equally heavy. Between the greed of the one and the centurions of the other they were constantly exposed to violence and abuse; nothing was sacred in the face of their covetousness and their desires. In battle the spoils went to the strongest; and there was a handful of brigands, most of them cowardly

and effeminate taking houses, ravishing children and levying soldiers as if a Briton did not know how to die for his country. Britain had only to compare the number of its children with the number of soldiers sent by Rome. That was how the tribes of Germania had shaken off the yoke and they did not even have a river or an ocean to defend them. The Britons had their country, their fathers, their wives and their mothers to fight for; the Romans were motivated solely by debauchery or greed. The Britons had to imitate the virtues of their ancestors, to lose no heart over the outcome of battles already fought; they would see the conquerors flee as Julius Caesar, their god, had done long ago. Adversity makes the spirit more daring and more persevering; already the gods themselves had taken pity on Britain since they had arranged the absence of the Roman general and had kept his army exiled in another island; already by some extraordinary chance they were able to speak and conspire; it was more dangerous to be caught in the midst of such scheming than outside it.

Further British grievances arose when the colony of veterans established at Camulodunum ran the Britons out of their lands and their homes. A temple had been built there and dedicated to Claudius the god. This temple was regarded by the Britons as "a citadel built to perpetuate their oppression", and in a kind of religious mania they determined to destroy it as the sanctuary of Mona had been destroyed by the Romans.

The rebellion found a leader in the foremost victim of Roman "barbarity", Queen Boadicea. For, as Tacitus says (*Agricola* XVI); "women were not excluded from command." It is curious that this heroine of British resistance should have left no other mark than a purely historical one. Highly nationalistic as it is, Welsh tradition contains no reference whatever to her heroic leadership. Lacking any legendary material on which to comment, therefore, we are left with her name. Boadicea is a vaguely Latinised form of Boudicca, in which we can recognize the Welsh word *budd*, meaning "victory". Boadicea or Boudicca is then the Victorious Woman, a title she undoubtedly earned for a while, and she was probably given her name as a result of her successes.

Having won over many of the British tribes, Boadicea launched an attack. Tacitus' account of the event is worth quoting in full, since it has an atmosphere of almost epic frenzy:

> In the meantime a statue of Victory had fallen over backwards in the temple of Claudius as though fleeing the enemy. In a fit of prophetic ecstasy, women foretold an imminent disaster; and accounts of the wild cries heard in the senate at Camulodunum, or the theatre reverberating to the sound of howling, of the ocean being seen covered with blood, of the statues turned upside down in the waters of the Thames, all these marvels contributed to bring fresh hope to the Britons and further terror to the Roman veterans. As Suetonius was away the veterans asked for help from the procurator Decianus. He sent only 200 ill-equipped men. The veterans were few in number. Placing their trust in the temple fortifications and being hindered by those who had secretly joined the rebellion and were disrupting discussions, they built no ditches nor palisades to defend them; neither did they send away the

old men and the women so that only combatants remained; acting as if they were at peace rather than at war they incautiously allowed themselves to be surrounded by the host of Britons. At first everything was looted or burnt; there remained only the temple where the soldiers had crowded together, and though that held for a day it was taken on the second ... From there the victorious Britons marched out to meet Petilius Cerialis, lieutenant of the ninth legion which had come as reinforcement. The legion was crushed, the infantry cut to pieces, Cerialis fled into the camp with his cavalry and was only saved by the fortifications. Frightened by this disaster and by the ill-feeling in the province which he had pushed into war by his greed, Decianus hurriedly left for Gaul. (*Annals*, XIV, 32.)

When informed of events in eastern Britain, Suetonius led a forced march to Londinium, "a town which although not a colony was an important trade centre". But he realized that it would be difficult to defend his position in the middle of the rebels' territory and evacuated both London and the municipality of Verulam.

Certainly the Britons' revenge was violent, as we learn from the sensational account of Dio Cassius. "Having taken two Roman towns, Boadicea slaughtered large numbers there and prisoners were subjected to every conceivable form of torture. But the most terrible and inhuman deed they committed was to hang the most noble and distinguished of the women naked, to cut off their breasts and sew them onto their mouths, so that they appeared to be eating them. After this they impaled them. These atrocities were perpetrated in the midst of their sacrifices, orgies and feasting partly in their temples but mostly in the wood dedicated to Andrasta (their name for Victory) whom they held in particular honour." (Dio Cassius, XLII, 7.)

There are various comments to make on this document. First of all, the violence of the Britons can be justified as their response to the massacre of the druids at Mona and the taxes imposed on the Iceni. Secondly, the horrors described by Dio Cassius (Tacitus is more sober in his account) are curiously like the crimes being attributed to the Christians in Rome at that time, including the supposed eating of children during their clandestine orgies. Nero, after all, was quite open about his atrocities. Thirdly, any sacrifice to Andrasta can easily be explained by the fact that she was Victory and Boadicea was the Victorious Woman.

Meanwhile Suetonius had assembled an army of nearly 10,000 men, formed partly of pro-Roman Britons and partly of the remnants of his own forces, and with these he went out to meet Boadicea. The Romans took up a position at the entry to a narrow gorge which was enclosed at the other end by dense woods. Tacitus emphasizes the fact that the Roman troops were unencumbered, while the Britons "carried their women with them on chariots" (*Annals*, XIV, 34). This comment is corroborated by Caesar's descriptions of the Britons' being accustomed to use chariots in warfare and the evidence of the Irish epics where warriors are never separated from their battle chariots.

The two sides met in a decisive battle.

Boadicea had her two daughters in front of her on her chariot. As she passed before the different tribes she cried out to them that it was nothing new for Britons to march into battle under a woman's command, but that on this occasion she had not come to claim her kingdom and her might, rather she had come as a woman of the people to avenge her own loss of liberty, her beaten body and her violated daughters. Roman insolence had now reached the point of physical injury, and no account was taken of the youth or extreme age of its victims. She said that the gods were finally supporting their just act of retribution and had destroyed the legion which dared to commit this crime; that the others were still hiding in their camps or trying to flee; that they would not even be able to stand the clamour and shouting of so many thousands of fighting men, even less their physical impact; that with a cause and an army of this kind they must win or perish; that as a woman such was her unshakeable resolution and the men were free to accept a life of slavery if they wished. (*Annals* XIV, 35.)

However, the Romans were better tacticians and better positioned. Hampered by their chariots, the fleeing Britons were cut to pieces by the enemy who spared neither women nor horses (*Annals*, XIV, 37). Boadicea herself took poison rather than be taken prisoner.

In all fairness, it should be said that the rebellion led by Boadicea did not end in total defeat for the Britons. On the contrary, the Romans had succeeded only in safeguarding their settlements in the South East. An uneasy period of truce followed. The freedman Polycletes was sent to inspect the Roman colony. He travelled across Gaul with a show of pomp which made even the Roman soldiers awe-struck "but he was the laughing stock of the Britons who were too strong in their own freedom to understand the power of the freedman" (*Annals*, XIV, 39). Then Britain fell quiet. Suetonius' successor Pretonius Turpilianus was careful not to provoke the islanders and remained content to administer the colony "with the cowardly inactivity he called peace" as the righteously indignant Tacitus describes it.

After some years of stability, Roman aggression was renewed in the time of Vespasian who had fought in the island and knew it well. The Brigantes and the Silures were rendered powerless. Then Tacitus' father-in-law Agricola ruled Britain from 78-86, during which time he gradually pushed the field of Roman domination northwards to the British-Pict border at the *aestuarium Tanaum* (the Firth of Tay). He even reconnoitred as far North as Caledonia, but established no military outpost there.

Before long the emperors Hadrian and Antoninus Pius had each built a wall intended to prevent incursion by the Picts and those Britons who had fled to the North. Hadrian's wall stretched from the Tyne to the Clyde, Antoninus' wall along the Firth of Forth. Under Commodus, a rebellion was crushed by the future emperor Pertinax. Septimus Severus took an expedition into Caledonia, but we have no detailed information about it (see, *Pausanias*, VII, 31).

In fact the greater part of Britain was now under Roman domination, with only Caledonia and the Welsh area of Powys, then occupied by the Ordovices and Gaels from Ireland, still remaining free. Though occupied, however, Britain was far from romanized. Only the British nobility adopted Roman customs and chose to live in villas. Latin was the official language but it scarcely competed with British which had never been outlawed. Unlike the Gallic language, therefore, which gave way to Latin, British survived and continued to evolve.

The towns established in Britain during the Roman occupation were far smaller and fewer than those on the continent. Most of them were garrisons for the legions which can be identified by the name *Kaer* (formerly *Cair* from *Castrum*). The best known of these is *Isca Silurum* or Caerleon (the Town of the Legions), which became the Caerleon on Usk of Arthurian romances.

Most significantly of all, however, the occupying forces were content to administer the country militarily, at least until the time of Diocletian. In Gaul Roman civil administration overlapped the existing framework of *civitates* formed by tribes like the Senones around Sens and the Veneti around Vannes. In Britain, on the other hand, there were only military commandants appointed to watch over the various tribes and govern the colonies of veterans, many of whom were not Romans at all but Gauls. That is why Gallic tribal names have survived in the names of the large towns (e.g. the Parisii in Paris, the Redones in Rennes), while British tribal names had disappeared.

This military administration was in the hands of two officials who effectively ruled the island and who were quite capable on occasion of acting in their own rather than in strictly Roman interests. Of these two, the *Dux Britanniarum* was in charge of the troubled frontiers with Caledonia and Wales while the *Comes Littoris Saxonici* commanded the fleet. The fleet however was confined to the North Sea, the *Mare Saxonicum*, for the Romans never dared venture into the Irish Sea.

In 286, the *comes* Carausanus rebelled against his own countrymen and proclaimed himself emperor. He was assassinated almost immediately by one of his lieutenants (Eutropius, IX, 22). In 306 the Picts invaded the South but were held by Constantius Chlorus who died in York that same year. Another Pictish force reached London in 364 but was driven back by Theodosius the Great. In 387 the *dux* Maximus proclaimed himself emperor and left Britain with an army largely composed of native Britons. He was beaten by Theodosius as soon as he reached the continent. Later the *dux* Constantine III usurped the title of emperor and crossed to Gaul where he was opposed by Stilichon.

Strangely enough the Britons appear to have regarded the series of usurpers as true fellow countrymen to be aided in their efforts to reconquer the continental empire and avenge the honour of Britain. Works like Gildas' *De Excidio Britanniae*, the pseudo-Nennius' *Historia Brittonum* and even Geoffrey of Monmouth's *Historia Regum Britanniae* all suggest as much. This feeling is also apparent in the sometimes ultra-nationalistic Welsh traditions, in the *Triads* and specifically in the tale of the *Dream of Maxen*. For Maxen is Macsen Wledig (Maximus the king, the usurping *dux* of 387) the Roman emperor who became more British than the Britons and set out to reconquer rebellious Rome with the help of British forces.[4]

Even so, the Roman occupation was more theoretical than real, and by now there was a new race of invaders to fear. As the Goths and Franks spread over the continental Roman Empire, the Angles and Saxons began to make their way into Britain from the North East.

Britain and the Saxons

According to Welsh tradition it was British treason which enabled the Saxons to settle in Britain. And while it is difficult to discern the historical fact from the mist of mythology clouding this period, it is quite probable that the Britons had resumed the old and dangerous Celtic game of appealing to one enemy to help rid them of another. The Sequanes had called in the Germans, the Aedui the Romans. It was now the Britons' turn to call in the Saxons against the Picts and Gaels who continued their incursions on the western coasts.

The *Annals of Cambria* start from this period and end in the 10th century. They record events from "the year when Vortigern held power in Britain, Theodorus and Valentinus being consuls; in the fourth year of his reign the Saxons came to Britain, Felix and Taurus being consuls, 400 years after the incarnation of Our Lord Jesus Christ" (*Mab.* II, 371). Information from other sources suggest that this date should be emended to 449, though that does not necessarily mean that the Saxons invasions started in that fateful year. There must have been raids made from the continent over a considerable period before then, but as yet the enemy had mounted no large-scale operations and had built no settlements.

The central character of this particular story is undoubtedly Vortigern, who was evidently a *dux britanniarum*. The pseudo-Nennius gives him the title *rex*, and the Welsh texts call him *guletic (wledig*-chief). His name and its variants, Uutigerm, Wyrtgeorne and Gwrtheyrn indicate that he was a Briton. Vortigern can be broken down into *vor (guor)*, an augmentative prefix as in Vercingetorix, and *tigern* or *teyrn* derived from *tiern* (Old Celtic *tigernos* containing the root *ti*, house, patrimony) which means "head of the family, or clan". Vortigern is therefore the "Great Leader".

Triad 10 of the *Red Book (Mab.* II, 233) includes Vortigern among the three men of dishonour in Britain. He was "the first to give lands in this island to the Saeson [Saxons]; the first to marry a woman of that nation; he treacherously killed Kustennin Vychan [Constantine the Little, i.e. the usurping *dux* Constantine III], son of Kustennin Bendigeit [Constantine the Blessed, Arthur's grand-father], forced Kustennin's two brothers Emrys Wledic [king Ambrosius, a historic *dux* of Roman origins] and Uther Pendragon [the mythical father of Arthur], to seek exile in Llydaw [Armorica] and deceitfully took the crown and the throne for himself. Finally Uther and Emrys burned Gwrtheyrn [Vortigern] and his castle at Castell Gwerthryniawn 'on the banks of the Gwy [Wye] to avenge their brother."

This triad was inspired both by the pseudo-Nennius and by Geoffrey of Monmouth. In the *Historia Brittonum*, the pseudo-Nennius claims that after his accession to the throne Vortigern had to contend with continual raids by the Picts and Scots and had also to defend himself against the Romans and the *dux* Ambrosius (XXVIII). He therefore appealed to the Saxons for help and in 447 or 449 he gave the island of Thanet to the two Saxon chiefs Hengist and Horsa (XXIX). He then fell in love with Hengist's daughter and to marry her ceded Hengist Cantium (Kent) and Hengist's son the land bordering Hadrian's Wall (XXXVIII). He also married his own daughter and they had a son whom he officially attributed to Saint Germanus of Auxerre (XXXIX). The Saxons, however, proved increasingly difficult to please, so Vortigern fled to Wales where he built a stronghold at Mount Eryi (Snowdon). The fortress fell down and the wisemen he consulted told him that he would have to sprinkle the foundations with the blood of a fatherless child before the building would stand firm. The necessary child was found and was about to be sacrificed when he revealed that his name was Ambrosius and that he was the son of a Roman consul. He also showed Vortigern that there were two dragons underneath the fortress, one red symbolizing the Britons and the other white symbolizing the Saxons. Vortigern gave the child Ambrosius the West of Britain and himself retreated to the North (XL-XLV).

Vortigern's eldest son Guortemir (Gwerthevyr), a historical figure identified as Vortiporius king of the Demetae, had very different views from his father's. He beat back the Saxons, overcoming Hengist three times and putting him to flight four times. At the synod of Gwerthriniawn convened by Saint Germanus, he asked the saint's forgiveness for his father's slanderous accusations. He killed the Saxon chief Horsa and pushed the invaders back into the sea. On his death bed Guortemir asked to be buried in a port, promising that if this request were obeyed the Saxons would leave the island. But he was buried at Lincoln instead and the Saxons immediately began advancing again (XLVI-XLVIII and LIII).

After the death of Guortemir, Vortigern realized that the Saxons were taking his lands and decided to negotiate. Hengist invited the British chiefs to a feast but before they arrived he ordered his servants to kill the Britons when he gave the signal *"En Saxones enimeit saxas* (Saxons draw your knives)"*. When Vortigern therefore saw all his leaders being slain he was forced to save his own life by handing the Saxons the areas now known as Essex, Sussex and Middlesex (Saxons of the East, South and centre) which were three of his wealthiest provinces (*H.B.* XLVI).

This episode is corroborated by the *Gesta Regum Anglorum*[5]; "Hengist deceitfully invited his son-in-law and three hundred British chiefs to a feast. His guests were deliberately inflamed by drink and angered by provocative speeches until they quarrelled, first verbally, then physically. Every one of the Britons had his throat cut and gave up the ghost in the midst of the drinking. Their king was taken prisoner and paid for his freedom with three provinces."

According to the pseudo-Nennius, Vortigern then retreated to his stronghold of Din Guortigern in Diment (Dyved in South Wales). There, in answer to Saint Germanus' prayers, lightning struck the fortress and the king and his family perished in the flames *(Historia Brittonum,* L).

Geoffrey also uses the story of Vortigern in his *Historia Regum Britanniae* but his is a revised version with details apparently borrowed from other traditions. Vortigern here is leader of the Gewissei (Western Saxons) and tries to take the crown. He treacherously kills King Constans, son of Constantine. Constans' two brothers, Aurelius Ambrosius and Uther Pendragon flee to Brittany. Vortigern then asks the Saxons to help him fight the Picts and the sons of Constantine. He marries Hengist's daughter, Ronwen, but his three sons Vortimer, Kategern and Pascent quarrel with him. He cedes Kent to Hengist and the North of the country to Hengist's son. At the death of his son Vortimer he resumes the throne and tries to negotiate with the Saxons. Hengist invites him and the British chiefs to a feast. Geoffrey's account of the subsequent massacre is fairly detailed;

> When Hengist saw that a suitable moment had come for his act of treachery, he bellowed out *"Nimet oure saxas!"* He himself immediately seized hold of Vortigern and held him tight by his royal robe. The moment they heard this signal the Saxons drew their daggers, attacked the leaders standing near them and cut the throats of about four hundred and sixty counts and earls ... Afterwards the holy Eldadus buried the corpses and said the last rites over them according to the custom of the Christian Church: this not far from Kaercaraducc, which is now called Salisbury, in the cemetery beside the Cloister of Ambrius ... The Britons had all come there unarmed, thinking of nothing but the peace conference (*H.R.B.* 104).

However the pagans did not achieve their objective without loss, for many of them were slain as they tried to kill their enemies. The Britons picked up stones and sticks from the ground and struck down their betrayers in self-defence. A certain Count of Gloucester called Eldol was among those present. The moment he saw this act of treachery, he scized a wooden stake which he had found by chance, and proceeded to defend himself with it. He broke the limbs of anyone within reach whom he could hit with this piece of wood, dispatching him forthwith to Hell. He shattered skulls, arms, shoulder-blades and even legs, causing the greatest possible terror, and before he left the spot he had killed seventy men with the stake which he held. He could not resist so vast a force for long, but got away and sought refuge in his own city (*H.R.B.* 105).

After this massacre and the loss of his three richest provinces, Geoffrey's Vortigern retires to Wales where he is advised to build a fortress. There then follows the episode concerning the fatherless child and the two dragons, but Geoffrey introduces one important new element. For his child declares himself to be *Merlinus Ambrosius* (the Welsh texts call him Myrddin Emrys). This is the first written allusion to Merlin whom Geoffrey was ultimately to make one of the best known literary characters in Europe.

Constans' sons Ambrosius Aurelius and Uther Pendragon then return from Armorica. Ambrosius is crowned king and sets off to attack Vortigern in his stronghold which is eventually fired.

This last part of the story as translated by Robert Wace in his *Roman de Brut* was used as a model for the *Estoire de Merlin*: "There was in Britain a king named Constant who had two sons called Moine and Uther Pendragon. When he died, his seneschal who was named Vortigern had young Moine killed by treason and was crowned king in his place ..." Fearing Uther Pendragon Vortigern built defences but when Uther returned he fired the fortress and Vortigern perished in the flames.[6]

The legend of the dragons is certainly very old. Although Geoffrey and the pseudo-Nennius use it to symbolize the struggle between the Britons and the Saxons, this purely historical significance would appear to be very circumstantial. The legend is more likely to have been connected with the alchemical value of the dragon or with the traditional role of the dragon as the guardian of some hidden treasure, ideas not fully understood by the historians.

The ritual significance of the dragon certainly emerges very clearly from the Welsh tale of *Ludd and Llevelys*. Three plagues have fallen upon Britain: "The second plague was a scream that was heard every May Eve over every hearth in the island; it pierced the hearts of the people and terrified them so that men lost their colour and strength, women suffered miscarriages, children lost their senses, and animals and trees and soil and water became barren."

This plague turns out to be a dragon which is under attack from another, foreign dragon. In order to stop it, a whole ritual has to be performed, with a pit being dug, a vat placed in it, the vat being filled with mead and then covered with a sheet. When the dragons come to fight in the neighbourhood they fall exhausted by combat onto the sheet in the form of piglets. Sinking into the pit they drink the mead and fall asleep. The sheet is then wrapped round them and they are buried in a stone coffin. "As long as they were within that strong place, no plague will come to Britain" *(Ludd and Llevelys)*.

The place where the dragons are buried is named as Dinas Ffaraon in the Mountains of Eyri, which then becomes Dinas Emreis (the Rock of Ambrosius); and this is where Giraldus Cambrensis places his Merlin sitting on a rock as he prophesies to Vortigern.

The idea of a May Eve or May Day scourge is obviously connected with the Celtic feast of Beltaine, the fire festival celebrated on that day; and the barrenness of the land must surely be a drought. If we take the themes of drought, fire and temporary barrenness, together with the metamorphosis of the dragons into piglets and the passage from dry to wet symbolized by the vatful of mead, it would appear that there is some ancient rite underlying the story, possibly a druidic ceremony.

Certainly, it is very difficult to discern how much of the dragon story is historical and how much mythological. The two elements seem so well blended together that the whole episode may have been made intentionally ambiguous.

Dragons are included by the triads among the three things one does well to hide. The two other things are the head of Bran and the "bones of Gwerthevyr Vendigeit [son of Vortigern] buried in the main ports of the island; as long as they were hidden there was no need to fear the Saxons' coming".

However, dragons are also one of the three unlucky discoveries: "Gwertheyrn Gwrtheneu [Vortigern] uncovered the bones of Gwerthevyr Vendigeit for the love of a woman, Ronwen the Pagan. It was also he who discovered the dragons" (*Triad 15, Mab.* II, 241). According to another text Vortigern uncovered the dragons as an act of retaliation against the ill-feeling shown him by the Cymry (*M.A.W.* 406). But then, Vortigern is very much the black sheep of the Welsh tradition. He is even included among the "three drunken spirits" as the man who "being drunk, gave the isle of Thanet to Hors, in order to satisfy his passion for Ronwen Hors's daughter; he also gave the right to the throne of Lloegr [England] to the son he had by her; at the same time he spun a web of treason against the race of Cymry" (*Triad 126, Mab.* II, 310).

Nevertheless, there is no doubt that it was the treachery of the Saxons, with whom he had chosen to ally himself, that eventually brought Vortigern down at the feast of the Long Knives, as Hengist's banquet was called. According to the *Iolo Manuscripts*, this took place in 453 at *Mynydd Ambri*, or Ambresbury Hill, now Amesbury on Salisbury Plain, an area particularly rich in megalithic monuments and dedicated to the dead (as the frequent occurrence of the word *bury*, grave indicates). Even so, one triad actually accuses Vortigern of responsibility for the massacre: "It was on his advice and following a secret agreement with the Saxons that the leaders of the Cmyry were killed" (*Triad 119, Mab.* II, 306). After all, Vortigern was the only man apart from Eidol to escape death.

Geoffrey's Eidol or Eldol who managed to flee after killing seventy Saxons is undoubtedly that mythical survivor who comes through every epic disaster to tell the tale. The Welsh version of the *Historia*, the *Brut y Tywsogion* (*M.A.W.*, II, 256), confirms as much: "And there was but one man who escaped from among the knights of the island of Britain, Eidol count of Kaerloyw [Gloucester], thanks to a lever which he found under his foot and with which he killed seventy Saxons."

Altogether, myth plays a considerable part in the massacre of the Long Knives. "Eidol Gadarn [the Strong] killed 660 Saxons during the betrayal of Caersallawg, with a distaff of wild ash, between the setting of the sun and nightfall." (*Triad 137, Mab.* II, 317.) Note that the ash is a magic tree and that the fight lasts for a limited time between sunset and nightfall. A poem from the *Myvyrian Archaeology of Wales* attributed to an anonymous author (*M.A.W.* I, 164) places the massacre in the Great Circle at Stonehenge, the most venerated of all sacred spots in the Celtic world. This poem adds that it was common practice to hold a solemn assembly of three hundred men there for a feast at the equinox. Wine and mead would then be distributed by a "knight of the fortress". The anonymous poet goes on to describe the frightened guests, the interrupted songs of Eidol and the other bards, the screams, the struggling and the horrors of the fight.

From this account the feast attended by the Britons was a sacred festival, a kind of religious orgy, so that the Saxons were committing not merely a deed of treachery but an act of sacrilege. The equinox is close enough to May 1 to suggest that the feast of Beltaine may be involved. Stonehenge can only have been built for some solar cult, and as Beltaine means the Fire of Bel or of Belenos the Shining One, we can assume that some great seasonal festival based on the position of the sun was being held. Such solar festivals are mentioned in Taliesin's "Song of the Horses", a celebration of the sun's fire.

> We praise it above the earth,
> the sun, cruel meteor of the dawn . . .
> At every suitable season
> at the season of its shifts
> at the four phases of its course,
> I would exalt the violence
> of its tumult and of its intense anger.
> (*Book of Taliesin*, XXV, J.M. 83)

It so happens that the feast of Beltaine is a day of misfortune when it falls on a Thursday. A Gaelic proverb declares: Woe to the mother of the wise man's son when Beltaine falls on a Thursday. The idea of Thursday being unlucky also occurs in various lines attributed to Taliesin, such as "Thursday of murder" or "on Thursday they will be in the choir, their poverty will be wretched". The battle recounted by Aneurin in his *Gododin* lasts for seven days (a symbolic figure) and on Thursday the Britons have to concede defeat.

In fact there seems to be some trace of the tragic feast of the Long Knives in the *Gododin*. Although Aneurin was a Northern Briton and the events he describes take place in the British kingdom of Strathclyde under totally different circumstances, various aspects of it may well have been borrowed from accounts of the massacre at Stonehenge. First of all, there is a character named Eidol:

> After the feast at which wine and mead flowed,
> I know that tears soaked the mother
> of Eidol of the Plain
> (*J.M.* 22)

Then there is the fact that all the men except one are killed:

> All of them were slaughtered
> at Kattraeth, they were a clamorous army
> the warriors of Mynydawg, the great ill-fated one;
> of three score men, only one returned.

And there is even a kind of solar ceremony during the feasting:

> And now the chief lord,
> the sun is climbing,
> lord from whom the light rises

into the skies of the island of Britain ...
Shining was the horn
under the portal of Eidyn.
He had invited magnificently
to the feast of the heady mead.

After Vortigern's death, the core of resistance to the Saxons seems to have remained in Wales. "It was then," writes Henri Hubert, "that the name Kymry appears to have prevailed as the national name of the Britons. The Kymry are the tribes which fought side by side under the leadership of a *gwledy* against the Irish, the Picts and the Saxons. The land of the Kymry, known in the British language of that time as *Combrog* (the Compatriots) is called Cambria." *(Les Celtes,* II, 199). After the last of the *duces* had gone with the death of Vortigern, the *gwledy* seems always to have been a king of Gwynedd (Venedotia), the land of the Ordovices in North West Cambria.

Traditionally it was Uther Pendragon who succeeded Vortigern and avenged the honour of the Britons. And through Uther we enter the Arthurian cycle, one of the strangest amalgams ever dreamt up by the mind of man.

The Arthurian cycle can be interpreted from many different angles, but for the moment we will put aside its religious, sociological significance and confine ourselves to the historical aspect. Inevitably, however, the various areas into which the story strays will overlap.

Like the other Celts, the Britons were constantly seeking after unity, though only perhaps in theory for they never realized it in practice. The Saxon invasions were, in a sense, the last straw for a Celtic society already severely undermined by the Roman victories. The bitter taste of defeat gave the Britons a natural longing for revenge; but since there could be no question of retaliation on the material level, and since the ancient Celtic world was crumbling away, vengeance became a matter of ideas. And it was through these ideas that the Britons ultimately achieved their finest victory. In any case, myth-making was an essential characteristic of the Celtic mind, and by some process of reversal, the Britons succeeded in turning every defeat into a magical adventure where the erosion of Celtic society could be attributed only to supernatural events. In this way the myth of the supreme king or leader of the world came into being, and with it came Arthur who reigned not only over Wales where his legend was first born, but also over the kingdom of Logres or Lloegr (i.e. the whole of Britain less Scotland), over Brittany and Gaul and even over Rome.

In this way the tribal chief Arthur is transformed into a real king. But his is a theoretical sovereignty which must be shared and which is symbolized in the adulterous Guinevere whom Arthur has to share with Lancelot. Behind the medieval "courtly love" of Lancelot and Guinevere lie traces of ancient rituals suggesting that Arthur's royalty is indeed sacred. Later "King" Arthur had to become an emperor, to balance the weight of Charlemagne. And, as Charlemagne represents Germanism in triumph, so Arthur represents Celticism in contempt. As he sleeps in the isle of Avalon "from where he will one day return", so Celticism lies like the druids in the depths of the forests, hidden but not dead.

That this sense of latency is part of a collective unconscious is best proved by the fact that the whole of Celtic Europe re-emerges in the 12th and 13th century Round Table romances. All the old repressed dreams are liberated just for a moment in the marvellous adventures of Arthur, Lancelot and Gawain. The canons of Roman Catholicism form a thin veneer over the resurgent Celtic mystique in the myth of the Grail, the vaguely Christian tone being superimposed on it to ward off accusations of heresy.

Arthurian literature is animated by what seems an excess of Celtic energy, an energy later to be fostered by the Plantagenet dynasty when it assumed control of that unhappy blend of Saxons, Normans and Britons known as England. For the Plantagenets, and especially Henry II, realized how much could be gained from exploiting British pan-Celticism in the fight against continental Capetian influence. That is why so much help and publicity was given to the Anglo-Norman writers Wace, Béroul, Thomas and Gautier Map who popularized Arthurian legend. That is why the Abbey of Glastonbury was chosen as the centre of Arthurian tradition, and why the graves of Arthur and Guinevere were officially "discovered" there. The insular Celtic emperor Arthur rose to challenge the continental Charlemagne whose throne had passed to the Capetians.

Not all of the Arthurian cycle is myth, however. Some parts of the story are undoubtedly factual. There were real disputes between the various British tribes and constant incursions by the Gaels and the Picts. The Britons did resist the Saxons and were finally brought down by collusion between British traitors and Saxons, Picts and Gaels.

The earliest mention of Arthur occurs in the *Gododin* by Aneurin. In praising one of the British leaders killed in battle at Katraeth against the Saxons, the bard describes him as "sating the ravens with the enemies he killed, although he was not Arthur" (v. 1234 of the Ifor Williams edition). Although the extant manuscript of the *Gododin* dates from the 13th century, the work contains archaic elements which indicate that it was originally composed much earlier, possibly even in the 7th century and certainly no later than the 11th.[7] So, whatever the claims of early 20th century scholars like Faral and Bedier, the legend of Arthur cannot have been invented in the 12th century by Geoffrey of Monmouth. Geoffrey merely ensured that the existing legend became known outside Britain. And Arthur's fame at the time of Aneurin must have been considerable for the bard's comparison to hold any weight.

The second allusion to Arthur comes in the *Historia Brittonum* incorrectly attributed to Nennius. This work is a complex mixture of material from different writers, including the 9th century Nennius, though parts of it date back to the beginning of the 8th century.[8] Here Arthur is described as *dux bellorum*, a war leader. He fights a fierce campaign against the Saxons and wins a great victory at Mount Badon. It is this victory which the *Annals of Cambria* list under the year 516. "Battle of Badon during which Arthur bore the cross of Our Lord Jesus Christ on his shoulders for three days and three nights and the British were victorious." (*Mab.* II, 372.)

This victory at Mount Badon, which has been identified as Baydon Hill on the western fringes of Wessex, appears to have halted the Saxon advance for some time. The actual battle is also mentioned in Gildas' *De Excidio Britanniae*, though there is no reference to Arthur; for the victorious leader is named as Aurelius Ambrosius who, if not Roman, must at least have been a romanized Briton. It is conceivable that Arthur and Aurelius are one and the same, since many scholars have suggested that Arthur was Roman, his name being derived from the Latin *arcturus* or *arctus* meaning "he who reduces" or "the Rigorous". But the word *Arctus* is also used to denote the Great and the Little Bear, which brings us back to the root word *art*, a bear (Breton *arz*). And *Arcturus* is also the name of the star known as the Herdsman. All these suggestions, however, are no more than hypotheses.[9]

The pseudo-Nennius accredits Arthur with twelve battles, most of which take place in the forest of Celyddon (Scotland). This suggests that the Britons of the time were concentrating their war effort on the northern frontiers. Indeed, one of the triads actually says that, apart from the courts Arthur held at Caerleon on Usk in Wales and at Kelliwic in Cornwall, he had one in Penrhyn Rhionedd in the North (Triad 84, *Mab.* II, 285). All the names in Arthurian legend are clearly connected with people and places in Cornwall, Wales and the North. "It has been noted," says Jean Marx (*La légende arthurienne et le Graal*, 49, 50), "that the battles mentioned in the *Historia Brittonum* took place in areas which the Saxons could not have reached by the end of the 5th or beginning of the 6th centuries. However, there is no reason why there should not have been skirmishes with small groups of an advance guard. At the beginning of the 6th century, a war leader who appears to have really existed acquired a great enough reputation to be accredited with these victories."

In fact this reputation had already spread beyond history proper. The pseudo-Nennius tells how Arthur and his dog Cavall hunted the monstrous *porcum Troit* which became *Twrch Trwyth* in the tale of *Culhwch and Olwen*. A poem attributed to Taliesin, which has been dated as 10th century, describes an expedition led by Arthur to bring back a marvellous cauldron from the Other World (*J.M.* 83-4). Arthur is no longer just a *dux bellorum*, he is also, according to the pseudo-Nennius, the *mab uter id est filius horribilis*, a name the Britons had given him because of his love of war. In fact *uter* means "surprising, marvellous" and as *mab uter* Arthur becomes "marvellous son". It was confusion of the name which made him *mab Uther Ben*, or son of Uther Pendragon.

By the time we reach the tale of *Culhwch and Olwen*, the oldest of the great Arthurian texts, the myth has already been created, and the strangest traditions drawn from Old Celtic mythological sources have merged with the political and historical reality of the war leader. Even so, there is a huge gap between *Culhwch and Olwen* and Chrétien de Troyes. The Welsh court of King Arthur has none of the 12th century refinement brought to it by the French poet. It is the rough, warrior court of a British chief with all its ancient ritual and its deliberately churlish manners.

The medieval, courtly tone now associated with Arthurian romance came from Geoffrey of Monmouth. In his work Arthur is the son of Uther and the lovely Ygerne (Ingerna), wife of Gorlois duke of Cornwall, who are brought together by the help of Merlin's magic. Once king, Arthur beats the Saxons, the Irish and the Romans and conquers a good part of Europe. However, there is no reference in Geoffrey's work to the Round Table, which suggests that he drew his material from sources other than those used by the Anglo-Normans and Chrétien de Troyes.

Arthur achieves great glory. His court is a meeting place for the bravest knights of the Celtic world who turn out on closer examination to be the gods and heroes of Irish and Welsh mythology.

According to the Welsh triads, Arthur is more eminent than the three most eminent prisoners of the island of Britain; Llyr, father of Bran; Mabon, son of Modron; and Geir. He spent "three nights in an enchanted prison." (*Mab.* II, 238.)

He is also one of the "inconstant" bards, meaning that he was initiated into bardism but chose the incompatible life of the warrior (Triad 15, *Mab.* II, 238). It was Arthur who "removed the head of Bendigeit Vran from the White Hill. He did not like the idea of anyone other than himself being responsible for the protection of the island" (Triad 15, *Mab.* II, 241). Arthur is also superior to the three red fighters of the island of Britain; "where they had passed neither grass nor plant would grow for a year afterwards, whereas where Arthur had passed it was seven years." (Triad 30, *Mab.* II, 254.) Finally, he is chief of kings (Triad 71, *Mab.* II, 278), a description evidently connected with the old notion of supreme kingship.

Arthur's two nephews, Gwalchmai (Gawain) and Medrawt (Mordret), are also in some traditions his incestuous sons. The best known of his cousins are Culhwch, Gereint (Eric) and March (King Mark). His wife is Gwenhwyfar (Guinevere). His bishop is Bedwini (Bedivere); his gatekeeper Glewlwyd Gafaelfawr (Strong Grip); his foster-brother Kai (the seneschal Kay); his three mistresses Indec, Garwen (White Leg) and Gwyl; his dog Cavall; his mare Lamrei; his shield-cum-boat Prytwen (White Shape); his knife Karnwenhan; his spear Rongomyant and his sword the famous Kaledfwlch (Excalibur in the French romances and Calad Bolg, the magic sword of the Tuatha de Danann in Ireland).

It is Arthur who sends his knights in quest of the Holy Grail, though curiously enough he does not go himself. And the discovery of the Grail, the fulfilment of the quest, is a signal that the Celtic world is approaching its end. Like the great heroes Cú Chulainn, Siegfried and Achilles, Arthur is one of those who "overcome all their enemies and can only be overcome by treachery" (Triad 121, *Mab.* II, 307), and the hour of treachery is at hand.

After Arthur and Lancelot have fought their wars over Guinevere the Romans invade Gaul. Arthur drives them out but he has to leave Mordret as regent in his absence; and Mordret spreads a rumour that the king is dead, marries Guinevere and assumes the crown. When he hears of this betrayal Arthur hastens back to Britain. Mordret then forms an alliance with the Picts, the Gaels and the Saxons. Arthur has difficulty in mustering an army. He has lost many men. Gawain his "good" nephew is dead. Lancelot du Lac, his best knight, has become his enemy and stands aloof. The great high king marches to battle. Then, as *La Mort le Roi Artu* tells it,

> Arthur reached the great plain of Salisbury; it was the best and largest place to be found for a battle and he intended to wait for Mordret there. After supper, while his men were erecting their tents, he went walking in the countryside, and as he passed by a great, hard rock he saw some old-looking words carved there. These words read "This plain will be the setting for the fatal battle that will leave the kingdom of Logres an orphan". It was Merlin who had written them long ago. When the king had read them, he bowed his head for he knew that they were an unequivocal prediction of his death; however he swore not to turn back.

This passage is followed by a description of the battle in which Arcan, king of the Saxons, Yvain, son of Uryen, Heliade, king of Scotland, Carados Brebras, son of Bran and the seneschal Keu are all slain, and in which Arthur and Mordret finally kill each other.

A more prosaic reference to the battle occurs in the *Annals of Cambria* where "the battle of Camlann during which Arthur and Medrawt killed each other; and there were many killed in Britain and in Ireland" is listed under the year 537. (The Irish *Annals of Tigernach* date Camlann as 541.)

The battle of Camlann brings the Round Table to an end. Only a few heroes survive, among them Girflet, son of Do (named Kynnwyl Sant in the legend of *Culhwch and Olwen*) who witnesses the mysterious disappearance of the wounded king, and "Movran, son of Tegid, Sanddeu Bryd Angel and Glewlwyd Gafael-fawr". But these are no ordinary heroes. Girflet is the same person as Gilvaethwy, son of the Welsh goddess Don and brother of Gwyddyon. Morvran [Sea Crow] is son of Tegid the Bald and the Welsh goddess Keridwen; he survives because "no one struck him ... because of his ugliness everyone thought he was a devil help-ing, for there was hair on his face like the hair of a stag" *(Culhwch and Olwen)*. Sanddeu Bryd Angel (Angel Face) escaped "because of his beauty, everyone thought he was an angel helping" *(Culhwch and Olwen)*, while Glewlwyd Gafael-fawr, Arthur's gatekeeper, was a kind of hierophant, his rather obscure role being celebrated at some length in poem XXXI of the *Black Book of Carmarthen*.

These survivors later join with Lancelot du Lac and Bohort, the Grail hero who have remained in Brittany and they all set out to avenge Arthur's loss. But their exploits are merely the last flicker of Round Table chivalry. When we consider that Arthur and his knights are no more than the medieval versions of the ancient Celtic gods, the battle of Camlann becomes the destruction of a whole culture and relig-ion, a Twilight of the Gods without its Wagner.

Obviously it is quite possible that the legendary battle of Camlann reflects some historical event and that there was a British leader who gathered the tribes together and held the Saxons until he fell to a coalition of Picts, Gaels and Ger-manic peoples.

But the importance of this battle in Celtic mythology and the confusion which surrounds it are such as to suggest a battle of gods and heroes. On the one side there is Arthur and his clan, many of whom represent ancient gods. Girflet or Gilvaethwy is of the line of Don, or the Irish Dana, ancestor of the great Gaelic divinities Lug, the Dagda, Goibniu, the Mórrígan and Mananann. The line of Kynvarch is represented by Yvain, Welsh Owein, the son of Uryen whose totemic animal is the raven; the line of Bran by his son Caradawc who became Carados Brebras, and the line of Keridwen, the mother goddess, by her son Morvran, whose totemic animal appears to be the stag, a possible link with the Gallic god Cerunnos.

Opposing them there is Mordret-Medrawt, the god of destruction. He is also Meleagant, who lives in the Kingdom of Goore, or Verre "whence no one returns", and who abducts Queen Guinevere in Chrétien's *Lancelot*. In the *Vita Gildae*, this character is called Maelwas and reigns over the Land of Summer, the mythical land of the Dead. He also appears in Chrétien's *Erec* under the name Maheloas, "a high baron, the lord of the Isle of Glass; on this island there is no winter, nor any extreme heat; thunder is never heard there, lightning and storm never seen, and serpents do not live there".

In the Welsh tradition where names are deliberately confused and one character may appear under two or three different names, Mordret-Meleagant becomes Gwynwas or Gwynn, son of Nudd. Nudd is the Irish god Nuada Silverhand, or the Gallic Nodens of Gallo-Roman inscriptions. Gwynn (also identifiable as the Irish Finn or Fingal) belongs to the earliest mythology of Wales, and was so well known that rather than ignore him Christianity chose to make him a kind of demon guarding the exit from Hell so that no one could leave. The 14th century poet Dafydd ap Gwylym even writes "Gwynn, son of Nudd, take me" instead of "the devil take me". In the legend of *Culhwch*, Gwynn fights Gwythryr for Creiddylat, daughter of Ludd Silver Hand (a curious confusion with Nudd and Nuada).

Arthur restores order by arranging that Gwynn and Gwythyr fight for her every May Day until the Judgment. This legend would appear to be connected with the Celtic festival of Beltaine which was celebrated on the first day of May and was probably the greatest festival after Samain on November 1.

Triad 146 (*Mab.* II, 321) makes Gwynn one of the three blessed astrologers of Britain; his knowledge was such that he could predict anything one wished to know. Despite his later association with evil, the name Gwynn actually means "white", like the Gaelic *find* or *finn* and the Gallic *windos*. It can also mean "happy or blessed" as can be seen in *Gwynva* and *Gwynfydd* (Breton *Guenved*), the "white plain, or white world" as well as "blessed plain or blessed world"; i.e. the Celtic paradise. Of course Gwynfydd can be translated as "the world of Gwynn" and, Gwynn being a god of the Other World, the connotations would be the same.

Gwynn also survives outside the purely Celtic traditions, and plays a particularly active part in the French national epics, notably the *Chanson de Roland*.

In fact the *Chansons de geste* contain many traces of Celtic tradition. A number of the Saracen heroes pursued by Charlemagne are actually Gallic gods. This is easy enough to explain when we remember that the historic Charlemagne spent much of his life trying to eradicate the pagan beliefs which persisted in country areas. So it comes as little surprise that Belenos should have lived on as Balan in the *Chanson d'Apremont,* that the Tarvos Trigarannos should become the saracen idol Tervagant and that Gwynn should appear in the *Chanson de Roland* as Ganelon.

In fact, the Oxford Manuscript of *Roland* generally alludes to him as Guenes, Ganelon being the diminutive form; and Guenes would appear to be the equivalent of the Welsh *gwenydd,* "whiteness" or a Frenchified form of Gwynn, by way of the Breton *guen,* "white". In any case Guenes-Ganelon is very much the same kind of character as Mordret-Medrawt. Just as Mordret paves the way to Camlann, so Guenes, by his treachery, brings about the Frankish defeat at Ronceval. In both cases a magnificent epic is brought to an end in the only way possible, that is by the intervention of the God of Death, the all-destroyer, the dark side of Roland and Arthur.

Guenes also appears in other works of medieval literature. In the *Life of Saint Léger,* he leads the saint to an underground prison. A similar role is assigned to two characters named Guanias and Melga in the Breton version of the *Martyrdom of Saint Ursula.* And while Ursula is derived from *ursus,* "bear" (which can be compared with the name Arthur, also possibly derived from the word *art,* or *arz,* meaning "bear"), the closeness of Guanias and Melga to Guenes and Meleagant suggests not only that the original character has split into two, but that the myth has survived.[10]

The fight between Arthur and Mordret is, therefore, a battle between Day and Night, Life and Death. Indeed, when Arthur pierces Mordret, Girflet sees "a shaft of sunlight enter the body at the same time as the spear . . . which the people of the land later said was a sign of the Cross of God." This Christian interpretation is significant, for it demonstrates the divine nature of Arthur.

The shaft of sunlight is actually the Light of the Hero, the manifestation of the divine soul of a dying champion. When Cú Chulainn was about to die, his horse "the Gray of Macha came back to defend Cú Chulainn as long as there was life in him and the hero-light still shone from his forehead".

The hero-light is not lost for it changes into something else. Plutarch's strange treatise on the *E of Delphi* says that "divinity is by nature incorruptible and eternal, but it undergoes certain transformations . . . Sometimes by flame it changes its nature into fire and assimilates all substances . . . Sometimes it diversifies into all kinds of shapes . . . and it forms the world." Plutarch later adds that wise men tell of these changes in the form of mythological tales about the death, disappearance and rebirth of the gods.

Arthur does not really die, either. He is taken to the Isle of Avalon by his sister Morgan la Fée. Legend adds that the Britons believe he will one day return. Arthur falls asleep, and with him the hero-light becomes hidden. It is not merely the god, nor even the concept of divinity, but the whole of Celtic civilization which has been secreted away by the last of the druids because there is no room for it in the real world. It is this civilization which will return to invade the western world when the right moment has come. The battle of Camlann shows us that the myth of Arthur is a symbol for the Celtic world as a whole.

The Last Kings of Britain

Mythological the battle of Camlann may have been, but it is certain that the Britons were defeated in around 537 and after this defeat there followed a period of disturbance and turmoil. Various chiefs tried to organize anti-Saxon resistance but were continually fighting between themselves over questions of precedence. Now more fragmented than ever Britain fell prey to all kinds of adventurers. Some of these men have come down to posterity, though less by way of history than by way of legend, on occasion even through the Round Table romances.

One such example is Geraint, son of Erbin, the hero of the Welsh tale of *Geraint and Enid* and of Chretien de Troyes' *Erec*. There really was a Geraint, king of the Britons, who fought the King of Wessex in 710 and received a letter from Adhelm, bishop of Shiburn about the Celtic Easter and the British heresies (Bede V, 18). The 6th century chief, however, appears to have been king of Devon and Cornwall only. The triads makes him one of the three commanders of the island fleet, together with March and Gwenwynnwyn (*Mab.* II, 255). Geraint, whose name means "champion", has also been confused with the emigrant leader Waroch (Guerec or Erec) who founded the kingdom of Vanness (Browaroc'h) in Brittany. The bard Llywarch Hen composed his death song which has been preserved in the *Black Book of Carmarthen:*

> Swift and fleet were the stallions
> under Geraint's thigh, fed with fat corn,
> red and powerful like wild eagles.
> Swift and fleet were the stallions
> under Geraint's thigh, fed with hard corn
> red and powerful like black eagles . . .

Then there is Uryen Rheged, who is frequently mentioned in the Round Table romances either as Yvain's father or in strange composite forms like Mabonagrain (from *Mabon* or *Maponos*, the Gallic name for Apollo, and *Agrain* a corruption of Evrain or Uryen). One of the best known chiefs of the Northern Britons, his awe-inspiring appearances is described in a number of poems attributed to Taliesin:

> This groaning in the valley,
> is it not Uryen who strikes?

> This groaning on the mountain,
> is it not Uryen who triumphs?
> There is no one who can silence him
> there is no shelter from Uryen,
> there is no famine
> for those who plunder at his side.
> When he fights, clothed in his armour,
> enamelled in glistening azure,
> his blue spear is the hand of death
> to the slaughter of enemies.

The *Battle of Gwen Ystrat*, also attributed to Taliesin, shows Uryen defending the fortress of Katraeth, later to be the scene of a much fiercer battle. Here, too, Uryen is far more a barbarian than a Christian leader.

> The men of Cattraeth rose at dawn
> around their lord, the triumphant looter of cattle,
> Uryen, whom the bards sing,
> who joins in the feasts of kings,
> who is called the warlike Lord of Baptism
> *(Book of Taliesin, XXXI)*

As we can see, these were violent times, and though not perhaps dating from the 6th century itself, this poem is far more authentic in its flavour than the courtly combat of Arthurian romances. Another poem attributed to Taliesin says of Uryen:

> Since he has been chief,
> the sovereign lord,
> he has been a fortress against the stranger
> this fearless fighter ...
> When you go to battle
> it is vengeance you spread.
> Burning houses before dawn,
> Lord of the tended plain
> of the finest, tended plain,
> whose men are most generous.
> The Angels are defenceless
> before this bravest of chiefs.

Uryen was king of Rheged, a district in the North. According to the pseudo-Nennius, Uryen, here called Urgben, fought with his allies Riderch (Rydderch Hael), Guallac (Gwallawc ab Llenawg) and Morcant against the Saxon Deodric, son of Ida. He supposedly succeeded in besieging Deodric in the island of Metcawt but died when Morcant, who was jealous of him, betrayed him. The triads make his murderer Llovan Llawdivro (Llovan Landless Hand). Llywarch Hen claims that he was killed at Aberlleu, and writes a beautiful death song for him in which the bard imagines that he himself is bearing the head of the dead chief:

> I bear upon my cloak the head

of Uryen the generous prince.
On his white breast a raven feeds ...
I bear a head upon my shield.
Great were his deeds
and far the fame of Uryen ...
From Rhiw I have born a head
whose lips are red with blood.
Woe to Rheged this day ...
His slender white body will be buried today
under earth and blue stones.
Sorrow to me and sad disgrace ...

Both Uryen and the great Northern tribe of Kynvarch to which he belonged are mentioned in the Welsh *Descent of the Men of the North,* which claims that the 300-strong clan of Kynvarch was always victorious wherever it went (*Mab.* II, 349-50). According to the genealogies of the saints, Uryen came South to Wales where he helped to drive out the Gaels. He is listed as a saint, just as are Geraint and many other Celtic heroes. In some texts he even appears as a kind of god of the Other World, perhaps even the equivalent of Bran. He is married to Modron, daughter of Avallach (Avallon) and mother of Mabon.

Uryen's son, Owein, is the Yvain of Chrétien de Troyes' *Chevalier au Lion.* Despite his adventures at the spring of Barenton, he appears to have been a real person. His horse, Carnavlawc (Forked Foot) is one of the three horses of booty of the island of Britain. Owein himself is one of the three blessed kings and he and his sister Morvudd are numbered among the three blessed litters, being together "in the womb of Modron, daughter of Avallach" (*Mab.* II, 284). His vassals are the three hundred men of the tribe of Kynvarch and the flock of ravens mentioned in the Welsh legends. This flock of ravens takes part in a strange game of chess played by Owein and King Arthur in the *Dream of Rhonabwy.* A poem attributed to Taliesin tells how Owein killed Ida Flamdwyn or Ida Torchbearer, king of Northumbria, during the battle of Argoed Llwyfein which the *Anglo-Saxon Chronicle* dates as 560. Taliesin is also said to have written his death song, in which a nostalgic gentleness contrasts strangely with memories of the hero's violent life.

When eating he would hear the song of praise.
The wings of dew were his sharpened spears.
There was no one to equal
this lord of the flashing sunset.
He was the reaper of enemies,
worthy heir to his father and grandfather.
When Owein killed Flamdwyn, it was no greater a
task
for him than to lie sleeping.

Associated with Owein in the story of the spring of Barenton is Kynon, son of Klydno. There was a king of Anglesey with this name who died in 810, but the Kynon connected with Owein seems more likely to have been a 6th century warrior, one of the three knights of wise counsel at Arthur's court, together with Arawn, brother of Uryen, and Llywarch Hen (*Mab.* II, 291). He is also numbered with Casswallawn and Tristan as one of the three lovers of Britain, for he loved

Morvudd, daughter of Uryen (*Mab.* II, 284). Kynon is one of the many heroes of the battle of Katraeth recounted in Aneurin's *Gododin,* and one of the three who survived the battle.

> They are three kings of battle
> shining with Edyn's gold,
> three armoured forces,
> three gold-torqued leaders,
> three wild horsemen ...
> Three fearful in combat,
> lions said to have killed dead men,
> gold-crowned in battle,
> three tribal chiefs
> came from among the Britons:
> Cynri and Cynon
> and Cynrein from Aeron ...
> Has there come from the Britons
> a better man than Cynon
> a serpent against the insolent enemy.
> (*The Gododin*)

The battle of Katraeth (Catterick) took place in the middle of the 6th century between the Northern Britons and the Saxons. It ended in a crushing defeat for the Britons whose commander in chief was the Mynyddawg, king of Edyn (Edinburgh) described by Aneurin as "the great ill-fated one".

> The men of Cattraeth went out at dawn.
> Fiercely they fought against their aggressors.
> Three hundred of them against three thousand.
> Blood-stained targets they were to the spears.
> Gallantly they held their posts
> in the vanguard of Mynyddawg the Generous.
> (*The Gododin*)

Aneurin sings of Cynon again in his *Incantations for Tudvwlch:*

> Cynon, come from Môn to defend us,
> and Tudvwlch hacked out a path
> towards the fortress-heights.

Despite their courage and tenacity, the Britons were outnumbered and were forced to yield to the Saxons. Aneurin, who may well have taken part in the battle and been one of the few survivors, ends his story with the words:

> With Mynyddawg drinking meant disaster.
> I weep each year for the men of Kattraeth,
> their swords of steel, their mead and their courage ...

At this period British resistance seems to have been concentrated in Wales, and more specifically in the North Western kingdom of Gwynedd. Long before then, writes the pseudo-Nennius, the men of Gododin led by Cunedag had come *in regione Guenedotae* and had chased out the Scots [Irish] so that they never returned. Cunedag's grandson Maelgwn was one of the fiercest of the 6th century chiefs. He appears in Gildas' *Epistola* as Maglocunus who far excels the other chiefs in height, beauty and strength. Maelgwn, however, is accused of having killed and dispossessed many kings, and in his youth of having slain even his uncle, the king. Although he repents, is converted and becomes a monk, it is not long before he goes back to his old habits. Maelgwyn is king of Gwynedd and of Môn, with his capital at Aberffraw. *The Song of Mead*, attributed to Taliesin, celebrates Maelgwyn's court and his generosity:

> May Maelgwyn of Môn receive the mead and offer it
> to us
> in foaming cups, the sweet blessed spirit
> of the honey of bees which brings us delight.
> *(Book of Taliesin,* 19)

Maelgwn appears equally ruthless in the *Story of Taliesin,* written by the 13th century Thomas ap Einiawn and published in the *Myvyrian Archaeology of Wales* (I, p. 17). Having invited his nephew Elffin, son of Gwyddno, to his court, Maelgwn starts a discussion as to who is the most beautiful woman in the kingdom. Elffin has the temerity to claim that his wife is the most virtuous and his bard (Taliesin) the most skilful, whereupon Maelgwn emprisons him until his claims can be proved. Maelgwn then plans for his son Rhun to seduce Elffin's wife, but this scheme fails less through the woman's virtue than through Taliesin's efforts. It is then Taliesin's turn to challenge the king's bards whom he succeeds in ridiculing. Taliesin removes Elffin from prison, but not before roundly cursing Maelgwn.

> May there be neither grace nor health
> for Maelgwn Gwynedd!
> Because of his wicked power
> may he suffer the utmost ills!
> May all his lands be waste
> and may a long exile be the lot
> of Maelgwn Gwynedd.

The bard then goes on to cast on Maelgwn the kind of satire used by the Irish druids against kings who had committed some crime:

> From the swamps of Rhiannedd a strange creature
> will come to punish Maelgwn for his iniquity,
> its hair, its teeth and its eyes will be gold,
> it will bring destruction on Maelgwn Gwynedd.

The "strange creature" is the plague. According to the *Annals of Cambria,* 547 was the year of a great epidemic in which Maelgwn died (*Mab.* II, 372). The Irish *Annals of Tigernach* assign the same event to the year 550. A manuscript from the Havod Uchtryd collection published in the *Iolo Manuscripts* claims that, "Taliesin had his property confiscated by Maelgwn. That is why he cast his curse on Maelgwn and on his land. Then the Vad Velen [the Yellow Sickness] came to Rhos and whoever saw it was destined to certain death. Maelgwn saw the Vad Velen through a keyhole in the church of Church and died as a consequence." It sounds like a comic horror story!

There is no doubt, however, that all these fabulous tales serve to illustrate Maelgwn's basic nature and to explain his reputation. Geoffrey of Monmouth says that he conquered the whole of Britain, Ireland, Iceland, Gotland, the Orkneys and even Dacia (*H.R.B.* XI, 7). His son Rhun, who succeeded him, is regarded by the *Triads* as one of the three blessed kings of Britain, together with Owein and Ruawn Pebyr (*Mab.* II, 238). The *Laws* published by Aneurin Owen (*Ancient Laws*, p. 104) accredit him with the "fourteen privileges of the men of Arfon" who had supported him in his successful struggle to gain power against the British invaders from the North led by Rhydderch-Hael and Clyddno Eidyn. Rhun was also one of the three men of golden hobbles in Britain: "As no horses could be found for them because of their great height, they put golden hobbles around the bottoms of their legs which were then held behind them on the cruppers of their horses, and under their knees they placed a golden platter." (Triad 50, *Mab.* II, 265.) "With that they were accorded the privilege of kingship in every region and throughout the land of Britain." (*M.A.W.,* p. 403.)

Despite Maelgwn's supposed death from the plague in 547, he is also said to have fought bravely alongside Rydderch Hael and Uryen at the battle of Arderyd against another army of Britons led by Gwendoleu, son of Keidiaw, Morgant, son of Sadrynin, and Aeddan ab Gavran; and according to the *Annals of Cambria* this battle took place in 573. Arderydd has sometimes been seen as the ultimate triumph of Christianity, as represented by Maelgwn, Rhydderch and Uryen, over paganism, as represented by Gwendoleu, Morgant and Aeddan. In fact, it would appear to have been just one more of the civil disturbances so common between the Britons. One triad includes it among the three frivolous battles, since it is said to have been fought "over a swallow's nest" (Triad 79, *Mab.* II, 283).

Certainly, Morgant is generally held responsible for the death of Uryen. According to the *Life of Saint Kentigern,* Morgant also drove Rhydderch Hael from his estates and Kentigern from his diocese. Of Morgant's ally Aeddan, one triad states that Aeddan Vradawc (the Traitor) was responsible for one of the three costly raids "when he went to the court of Rhydderch Hael; after him there remained neither food nor drink nor any live animal" (Triad 19, *Mab.* II, 248).

Aeddan was king of Dalriada and therefore not a Briton, but a Scot or a Gael. For Dalriada is in the kingdom of Argyll founded by Irish emigrants where Saint Columkill established his monastery at Iona in 563. According to Bede (*H.E.* III, 34) Aeddan was beaten at Degastane in 603 by Aethelfrid, king of Northumbria. The *Annals of Tigernach* mention several battles in which Aeddan took part, including one in 581 on the Isle of Man, one in 570 at Lethigra, one in 596 at Ardsendoin and another at Circhind where he lost three of his sons. He is one of the combatants at Katraeth in Aneurin's *Gododin* and flees from the battle with his shield broken. According to the *Annals of Ulster*, he went on a piratical expedition in 579.

Whatever else Aeddan may have done, we know that he and Morgant were beaten by Rhydderch Hael at the battle of Arderyd and their ally Gwendoleu was killed. It so happened that Gwendoleu's bard was called Myrddin, and a fairly recent version of the *Annals of Cambria* says that after this battle *Merlinus insanus effectus est* (Merlin went mad). Indeed, all the poems attributed to Myrddin-Merlin mention the battle of Arderyd, Rhydderch's victory and the death of Gwendoleu. Even Maelgwn is specifically named.

> It was Maelgwn whom I saw fight.
> his warriors roared in the heart of battle.
> The army of Maelgwn will hurtle forward
> striking men with death in the bloody plain.
> At the battle of Arderyd, when the moment comes
> it will be they who lead the hero to victory ...
> Seven score generous warriors have gone to the
> shadows.
> In the forst of Kelyddon they found death.
> (Dialogue between Merlin and Taliesin, *Black Book of
> Carmathen*, poem 1)

After this battle the insane Merlin wanders aimlessly in the forest of Kelyddon (Caledonia). He, too, came to be imbued with an aura of myth which greatly assists our understanding of the Celts. For Myrddin is very much part of the tradition of druids and bards taking refuge from the Romans or Christians in the forests and being inspired by some wild sense of exhilaration to utter their seemingly crazed prophecies. Myrddin addresses the trees around him:

> Sweet apple-tree who grows in the clearing
> the lords of Rhydderch's court do not see you
> although they trample the ground at your feet ...
> I am hateful to the followers of Rhydderch.
> After Gwendoleu, no prince honours me,
> I have neither joy nor visits from my beloved.
> At the battle of Arderyd I wore a gold torc
> but now I am despised by the swan-white woman.
> (*The Apple Trees*)

Like the Irish hero Suibhne, whose legendary origins he shares, Myrddin becomes a *homo sylvester*. He talks to the pigs grazing under the oak-trees.

> Listen little pig. I have trouble sleeping
> so shaken am I by sorrows.
> For ten and forty years I have suffered so much
> that now I am pained by joy ...
> Listen little pig, it is not my purpose
> to hear the water-birds making their commotion.
> My hair is sparse, my clothes are not warm,
> the vale is my barn for I have no corn,
> my summer harvest is poor indeed.
> Since the battle of Arderyd I have lost all feeling
> even were the sky to fall and the sea to overflow ...

The battle of Arderyd is clear evidence of strife between the Britons and of the increasing frailty of the remaining kingdoms. At Deorham in 577 the Britons suffered what was possibly a worse defeat even than Camlann which gave the Saxons the strategic towns of Bath, Gloucester and Cirencester. The enemy had now reached the Severn Valley, thereby cutting off Cornwall from Wales for ever.

This severance of two Celtic areas had untold effects on later political, linguistic and literary developments.

According to the *Anglo-Saxon Chronicle*, the defeated leader at Deorham was Condidan, who together with two other British chiefs were slain in battle. Condidan has been identified with Kyndylan, son of Kyndrowen, king of Powys, who is celebrated in the *Death Song of Kyndylan*, attributed to Llywarch Hen. This is a work of great pathos and emotional intensity, in which the poet's sadness and despair are expressed through a kind of litany. The death of Kyndylan has all the proportions of a national disaster, and the poem it inspired is one of the most powerful and evocative in all Welsh literature.

> The hall of Kyndylan is dark tonight
> without fire, without light,
> and what a silence surrounds it!
> The hall of Kyndylan is dark-panelled,
> it shelters no laughing company now.
> Woe to him who comes to a sad end!
> The hall of Kyndylan has lost its splendour
> now that the shield is in the grave.
> Once this roof was never open ...
> The hall of Kyndylan is dark tonight
> without fire, without song,
> the tears furrow my cheeks ...
> The hall of Kyndylan is dark-ceilinged
> now that the Llogriens have killed
> Kyndylan and Elvan of Powys ...
> The eagle of Eli screams loud.
> He is wet with the blood of men,
> with the heart's blood of fair Kyndylan.
> The eagle of Eli guards the seas,
> the fishes no longer cross the currents.
> He howls when he sees the blood of men.
> The eagle of Eli wanders in the forest.
> At first light he feeds
> from the victims of his tricks.
> The gray-beaked eagle of Pengwern
> cries most piercingly,
> greedy for the flesh of him I loved.
> The eagle of Pengwern called afar tonight.
> He can be seen in the blood of men.
> Tren is too well named the deserted city.
> The churches of Basa are in mourning tonight
> as they hold the remains of the pillar of battle,
> of the heart of the men of the Argoed ...
> The churches of Basa are in flames tonight,
> very little remains of them ...
> The churches of Basa are silent tonight,
> and I, too, am sad.
> They are red – my grief is too great.

The white town deep in the woods,
since the day it was built,
has ever seen blood covering its grass.
The white town, since it was built,
has ever seen blood on its green courts,
under the feet of its warriors ...
Alas, Ffreuer, how sad is this night
after the loss of loved ones,
woe is me that they were killed ...
(*The Red Book of Hergest*)

It was at this point that several of the British peoples began to migrate. The Cornovii who had first settled on the Welsh borders were now in the Cornish peninsula, and some of them crossed the sea to find refuge in the Quimper region of Cornouaille (Breton *Kerneo*) in Brittany.[11] The Dunmonii, who lived in Devon, also went to Brittany, to the area of Saint-Malo and Dinan where they founded the kingdom of Donmonia; while some of the Welsh and Northern Britons found refuge in Finistère. It may well be that Wales was becoming overpopulated because of the large numbers of refugees moving there from other parts of the island.

Minor Anglo-Saxon kingdoms were being formed in Eastern England, partly from Germanic peoples coming from the continent and partly with the help of those natives who submitted to Saxon authority and assimilated the language and customs of the invader. The land of Lloegr, King Arthur's kingdom of Logres, was becoming what we now think of as England.

The Anglo-Saxons were also being converted to Christianity, which enhanced their reputation amongst some of the Britons. As the number of conversions increased Rome began to take an interest and to send missionaries to the Saxons. In their anxiety to keep their new converts, the missionaries manifested such favouritism towards the Saxons that they were immediately shunned by those Britons who had remained independent. This partiality was undoubtedly one cause of the quarrels between the Celtic Church and the Church of Rome. As one of the *Triads* says, "Three things exhausted Lloegr: resistance to foreigners, delivering prisoners and the presence of the bald man" (Triad 90, *Mab.* II, 288). The bald man was Augustine of Canterbury, apostle to the Saxons.

Some of the Northern chiefs continued to fight. Dinawd, who according to the *Annals of Cambria* died in 595, mounted a large expedition but was forced to contend with jealousy from the other chiefs. A poem attributed to Llywarch Hen describes his battle with the sons of Uryen. Dinawd has also been confused with an abbot of Bangor mentioned by Bede it being supposed that he was driven from the North and found asylum in Gwynedd where he became a monk and founded the abbey of Bangor on the Dee. In 613, according to Bede (*H.E.*, II, 2), Brochmael Ysgithrog, king of Powys, was defeated by Aedilfrid, king of the Angles, near Chester. Brochmael's son Cynan Garwyn appears to have been a famous warrior. He is celebrated in a poem attributed to Taliesin (*Skene*, II, 172).

It was then that Cadwallawn entered the scene. He was a king of Northern Wales and son of Catman, whose burial inscription was found at Llangadwaladr in Anglesey: "*Catamanus, rex sapientissimus opiniatissimus omnium regum*" (Rhys, *Lectures,* 160). Cadwallawn began his career by laying siege to the island of Glannawc (Priestholm near Anglesey) in 629, according to the *Annals of Camria*. He then

The Hallstatt Sword, recovered from a grave and now in Vienna. Warriors on horse (top left and right) and on foot (below) have been carved with immense skill and precision on the bronze scabbard. It dates from the sixth century B.C. and shows some Adriatic influence on the usually mystical images found in Celtic art of this period.

formed an alliance with the Saxon King Penda of Mercia and fought a battle against Edwin, king of Northumbria, at Haethfelth in Yorkshire, a battle which Bede dates as occurring in 633 (*H.E.* II, 20). The annals assign this battle to 630 and call it the battle of Mecein: "On the calends of January the battle of Mecein, and there were killed Edwin and his two sons. Cadwallawn was victor." (*Mab.* II, 374). A triad makes Cadwallawn one of the three "polluters of the Havren [Severn]" because of the numbers of the enemy killed and left in this river at the battle" which is here called the battle of Digoll (*Mab.* II, 274). A poem in the *Red Book of Hergest,* attributed to Llywarch Hen, corroborates the name Digoll:

> The army of Cadwallawn the glorious encamped in the heights of Mount Digoll: for seven months, seven battles a day . . .
> *(Skene,* II, 277)

Whatever the name of the battle, Cadwallawn became lord of the kingdom of Northumbria and halted the Saxon advance for a while at least. In 631, or 635, however, Cadwallawn was beaten and killed by Oswald of Northumbria at Hefenfelth which the pseudo-Nennius calls Catscaul.

By the time Geoffrey of Monmouth had finished with Cadwallawn, the Briton had become a brilliant conqueror. His Cadwallo is brought up at the court of his father Cadvan along with Edwin of Northumbria, whose mother has been banished from her own country. In accordance with the Celtic custom of fosterage, the two boys go to the home of King Salaun in Brittany to complete their education. On their return, however, Cadwallawn is unwilling to allow Edwin to govern Northumbria and the two foster-brothers take up arms against each other. This aspect of Geoffrey's story is a little too like the Irish legend of Cú Chulainn and Ferdeadh to be totally credible. The two Irish heroes also go as foster-brothers to finish their education in Scotland with the female magician Scatach, and then find themselves on opposing sides in the war of the *Tain Bo Cualnge.* But to return to Geoffrey: Cadwallo is at first beaten and forced to flee to Ireland and then to Brittany where Salaun gives him an army. He returns to defeat and kill Edwin, and to overcome both Osric, Edwin's successor, and even Oswald. Cadwallo dies peacefully at a great age and with much honour. The *Annals of Cambria,* incidentally, say that Oswald died in 644 at the battle of Cocboy or Maserfelth at the same time as his opponent Eobba, king of Mercia and brother of Penda.

When Cadwallawn died, his son Cadwaladyr took up the cause. Very little is known about him. He may have led the victorious British army at the second battle of Mount Badon in 665. According to certain traditions he and a large body of men migrated to Armorica where he is supposed to have died. Geoffrey claims that he died a holy death in Rome in 689, but then Geoffrey plagiarizes quite shamelessly from the story of the Saxon King Caedualla. The *Triads* tell how the bard Golyddan struck Cadwaladyr a blow which was avenged by a woodcutter from Aberffraw who split Golyddan's skull with an axe (Triad 18, *Mab.* II, 309). Given the additional title of Vendigeit, "blessed", Cadwaladyr is also "one of the men with golden hobbles", and one of the three inspired kings, together with Bran the Blessed because he "shared his lands and all his goods with the faithful who fled before the pagan Saxons and the foreigners who tried to kill them" (Triad 124, *Mab.* II, 309). This description would appear the most apt, since under the circumstances the Britons had little choice but to flee. Cadwaladyr died during an epidemic in 682, 678 or 677 according to which chronicler one reads.

Only three independent British regions now remained, the largest of which was Wales. A second area included Cornwall and part of Devon; while the third, the kingdom of Strathclyde or Cumbria, lay on the Pictish border. The main stronghold of Strathclyde at Dumbarton (Dun Britonnum) on the Clyde estuary was not destroyed until much later by Norsemen coming from Ireland.

For the year 722 the *Annals of Cambria* list three battles, one at Hehil or Heihin in Cornwall, one at Garhmaelawc in Glamorgan and one at Pencoet *apud dexterales Britones* (on the eastern borders). The Britons emerged victorious from all these battles and were led by Rhodri, son of Idwal, nicknamed Molwynog or Maelwynog, who died in 754, and by Elized, king of Powys, who reigned from 700 to 750.

In 750 the Britons of Strathclyde engaged in a fierce war against their Pictish neighbours. The Pictish king Talargan, son of Fergus, and the British leader Tewdur, son of Beli, were both killed at the battle of Mocetwawc. Ten years later these same Northern Britons fought the Saxons at the battle of Hereford where Tewdur's son Dyvnwal was killed. In 778 and 784 Offa, king of Mercia, wreaked havoc on the British borders. He was stopped in 795 by Meredydd, king of the Demetae, at the battle of Rhuddlann, but the British leader was killed. In 798 Caradawc king of Gwynedd was taken prisoner by the Saxons. During the years 813 and 814 Cynan Tindaethwy, king of Gwynedd, and Mowel of Môn fought a bitter war which ended in victory for Howel and exile for Cynan. It is possible that these events contributed to the legend of Conan (Cynan) Meriadek, which Geoffrey helped to make better known and which he places in the 4th century.

In 822 the Saxons destroyed the fortress of Deganwy near Conway and tried to occupy the central Welsh kingdom of Powys. King Cynnen held out against them for many years but was finally taken prisoner in 850 and is said to have died in Rome in 854. The battles over Powys are commemorated in poems attributed to the 6th century bard Llywarch Hen which have been collected in the *Black Book of Carmarthen*, and the *Red Book of Hergest*. These poems form a historically based epic cycle, only fragments of which have reached us. The Celtic scholar Sir Ifor Williams has reconstructed them in his edition of the *Canu Llywarch Hen*. Some of them are very fine and take the form of laments for lost youth as written by an old man, the author being incorrectly identified as Llywarch Hen.

> Before I bore crutches, I was eloquent at the feasting,
> I was honoured and little wonder
> for the men of the Argoed always loved me.
> Before I bore crutches I was handsome,
> I was welcomed at the assembly of Powys,
> that paradise of the Kymry ...

There then follows a dialogue of great dramatic intensity between the old man and one of his sons, Gwen, whom he orders to defend the ford of Morlas against the marauding enemy. The young man agrees but hints that he may not return alive. Later a messenger arrives with news of Gwen's death, and the old chief sings a death chant for Gwen and his other twenty-three sons who wore the gold torc, the Celtic insignia of leadership.

> By Llawen Gwen kept watch last night.

Never did he lack success.
The battle swelled on the green banks . . .
His broad thigh open, Gwen kept watch last night
near the ford of Morlas.
Since he was my son he did not flee . . .
Four and twenty sons had I
wearing the gold torc, leaders in battle.
Gwen was the best of those sons . . .

These lines gives us some indication of the heroism of the Britons as they resolutely defended their land, inch by inch, against the invader. For the Saxons were now well established in the island and determined to continue their advance. Considering that the Irish, too, kept up constant pressure on the West coast, the strength of Welsh resistance was quite remarkable. Moreover, a new enemy was appearing on the horizon in the shape of the *Dub Gint* (Black People) or Scandinavians. According to the *Annals of Cambria*, the Norsemen devastated the island of Môn in 858, though they also attacked the Saxons for in 866 Kaer Evrawg (York) which had long been Saxonized was looted by a band of Danes.

In 877 Rhodri Mawr [the Great], king of Wales, and his son Gwryat died in battle. Wales was then divided between the king's three other sons, with Cadell taking Cardigan, Anarawt Gwynedd and Mervyn Powys (*M.A.W.* 688). These were the three diademed kings of Britain (*Mab.* II, 312). In 876 Cadell defeated Mervyn and seized Powys. Mervyn was killed by his own vassals in 892. Anarawt, meanwhile, was fighting the Saxons and in 880 he won a victory at Conway which the *Annals of Cambria* describe as God's vengeance for the death of Rhodri Mawr. Shortly afterwards Anarawt turned against his brother Cadell and in 894 he joined forces with the Angles to pillage Cardigan and Ystrat Tywi. On Cadell's death in 909, Anarawt became king of all Wales and he died in 915.

Throughout this period the Danes continued to attack both Saxons and Britons and the two sides must have overlooked their differences from time to time so that they could present a united front against the invader. For although such alliances were temporary they did eventually lead to the last of the Britons paying homage to the Saxon kings. Resistance to the Saxons did not die out immediately, however, for the struggle continued during the reign of Howel Dda (the Good) from 915 to 950.

From all accounts Howel Dda was an outstanding king. As son of Cadell he was heir to the whole of South Wales and Powys; and when his uncle Anarawt's son Idwal Voel died he also assumed power over Gwynedd. Howel was one of the last kings to try to unify Wales into a single, solidly established state. For this reason he is regarded as one of the three good kings of Britain, and one of the three best legislators: "Hywell Dda, son of Cadell ab Rhodri Mawr, king of all Cymru, reformed the laws of the island of Britain, as was necessary after the revolutions and tribulations which the nation of Kymry had had to endure, to prevent what was beneficial from going to waste and to ensure that good laws found their place, their natural role and their influence on the constitution of the land and of the nation." (Triad 136, *Mab.* II, 316-7.) The laws of Howel Dda have been preserved and provide much valuable information about the social organization of the Celts.[12]

In 937 Howel Dda attempted to reunite the Britons by forming a coalition composed of Welshmen, Cornishmen, the men of Strathclyde and even Picts,

Danes and Irishmen in order to drive out the Saxons. The British forces were beaten by the Saxon Athelstan. It appears that Howel's move was supported by the Welsh bards for one of the poems incorrectly attributed to Taliesin and entitled the *Weapons of Britain*, is actually a piece of propaganda for the coalition. Some of the prophecies attributed to Merlin are very similar in tone, and we can assume that there were other works of this kind.

Even so, the achievements of Howel Dda were short-lived. After his death the Britons again began to quarrel amongst themselves and the situation was not helped by fresh incursions from the Danes. As early as 943 the Danish King Anlaf had used troops from Dublin and Irishmen already settled in the region of Gower in an attempt to take Wales. Llywalyn ab Sitsyll had forced him to retreat towards England and was then assisted by the Saxon King Edmund in driving the Danes right out of Wales after a fierce battle (*M.A.W.* 716, the Book of Ieuann Brechva). In 960 a joint Norse and Irish force invaded the island of Anglesey. Iago ab Idwal, king of Gwynedd, drove them out of Gwynedd and Môn in 966. Then, as they fled southwards towards Cardigan and Dyved, they were killed by Einiawn ab Owain, grandson of Howel Dda.

By now there was no question but that the Saxon kings were pre-eminent. In 973 Edgar, king of the Angles, took part in a kind of parade on the Dee, in which he symbolically took the helm of a boat while the British kings held the oars. The *Iolo Manuscripts* describe how Gwaethvoed, prince of Glamorgan, refused to render homage at Chester and to row the boat. When he was invited to join the other Britons he is said to have replied that even if he had known how to row he would only have done so in order to save a man's life, be he king or serf. And to a second summons he merely replied that the man to fear was the man who himself feared nobody. Full of admiration for his courage, Edgar is then supposed to have sought him out and offered him his friendship. *(Iolo MS.* p. 90).

In 972 Howel ab Jeuav defeated his uncle Iago, king of Gwynedd, to avenge his father whom Iago had dispossessed and strangled. Howel thereby became king of Gwynedd. In the same year he defeated Cystenin, Iago's son, but was treacherously killed by the Saxons in 984. Another of Jeuav's sons, named Cadwallawn, was defeated and killed in 985 by Meredudd ab Owen, prince of South Wales. Llywalyn ab Sitsyll, who had defeated the Danes and become king of Powys and the South in 998, took Gwynedd in 1015 and died in 1021 during a battle against the Irish who had joined forces with his rival Edwin ab Einiawn (*M.A.W.* 694-718). Llywalyn is said to have been betrayed by Madawc Min, bishop of Bangor, and his was one of the three acts of treason which caused the total downfall of the nation of Cymry: "Only treason could defeat them" (Triad 120, *Mab.* II, 307). This continual feuding between the Welsh leaders carried on throughout the 11th century and gradually sapped what strength still remained in the nation.

The conquest of England by William of Normandy had a profound influence on the development and future of the Celts, though in the initial stages it affected only the Anglo-Saxons. Although a number of Breton Celts came with William to avenge the Saxon conquest of their ancestral homeland, they were rewarded for their help with gifts of land taken from the Saxons and ultimately became more English than Briton. Indeed the only way in which they really assisted the Celtic cause was by contributing to the spread of Arthurian legend.

As victors over the Saxons, however, the Normans would be naturally sympathetic to the Britons, or so the latter deludedly believed. In fact William and his successors made continual efforts to encroach upon Welsh independence.

Nevertheless the struggle was a comparatively peaceful one, for Britons and Normans were able to find some areas of agreement. "There was a profound and durable interpenetration of French and Celtic ideas in Wales. The French aristocracy endeavoured to form alliances with the as yet independent Welsh ... while the Saxons were totally oppressed. It should be added that an aura of nobility and antiquity still clung to the legends of the British nation." (J. Loth, *Mabinogion*, I, 59.)

At this time the conflict between the Irish Gaels and the Welsh appears to have come to a halt. During the reign of Gruffyd ab Cynan, king of Gwynedd from 1075 to 1137, there were concious attempts at reconciliation which had a considerable influence on the development of Welsh mythological legends and on the formation of the Tristan cycle. Gruffyd's mother was Irish and he had spent his childhood in Ireland before using Irish forces to win his crown. When he was expelled by his subjects he sought refuge in Ireland and returned to defeat his enemies at the battle of Carno with the outright support of the Irish. According to a curious text in the *Myvyrian Archaeology of Wales* (p. 727), the Irishman Gwrcharci, one of Gruffyd's auxiliaries, took the body of the defeated leader, cut it into little bits and made *bacwn* (bacon) from it. In 1136 Gruffyd won a sizeable victory over a Norman force.

He was succeeded by Owein Gwynedd (1137-1169) who married a sister of Henry II Plantagenet. Owein was celebrated in a number of poems, and his death produced a whole crop of *marwnad* [elegies]. Here is one, written by the bard Bleddyn Ddu:

> Now is the season of winter, very pale is the ocean,
> the perch of the sea-birds is a raging sea,
> the Eiri is clothed in his ice-mantle ...
> Owein, son of Gruffyd, kind distributor of booty,
> fervent knight who offered his horses freely,
> swift eagle over lands where none dare venture,
> glory and honour of Gwynedd ...
> Woe to Gwynedd, he is no more,
> the resolute falcon, giver of red cloth and black ...
> (*M.A.W.* 260)

and another by Daniel ap Llosgwrn:

> He was a high chief with a fearful hand
> and a constant guide for his troops.
> Neither friend nor companion will bring me peace
> I cannot be untouched
> by the death of a man
> who was an anchor in the deep, desert sea.
> My heart burns in a long memory,
> as the fire consumes the torches ...

One of Owein Gwynedd's sons named Madawc vanished under mysterious circumstances and ranks alongside Gavran and Merlin as one of those who made a total disappearance in the island of Britain: "Madawc ... who went to sea with three hundred men on ten boats; no one knows where they went" (Triad 113, *Mab*. II, 302). A whole legend grew up around this disappearance. It was later said that

Madawc had crossed the Atlantic and discovered America, where he settled.[13] Some people even claim to have found the descendants of the three hundred men in America, speaking a language derived from Welsh.[14]

During this period Powys was ruled by Maredudd, a cruel and courageous king who fought valiantly against the Anglo-Normans and even succeeded in forcing Henry I, who had invaded his land, to retreat. He died in 1124 or 1129 and his estates were divided between his sons Madawc and Gruffyd. When Gruffyd died in 1150 his share went to his son Owein Cyfeilog who was a bard of great renown. In 1176, helped by his cousin Owein, son of Madawc, Owein Cyfeilog seized the estates of their uncle Iorwerth Goch (the Red) who had married a Norman and was an ally of the Plantagenets. Owein died in 1197. The best known of the inspired poems he wrote is the *Hirlas,* the name of his drinking horn.

It is the evening after a battle and the warriors have gathered together in the palace. Owein orders the cup-bearer to fill the Hirlas and offer it to all the chiefs in turn, devoting a few lines of praise to each one.

> Carry to Tudur, eagle of slaughter,
> the clear brew of fair wine.
> If the best mead is not in our house
> your head shall answer to me for it ...

He then addresses his brother Moreiddig and turns to greet the chiefs, but their empty places remind him that they have died in combat.

> There has been dismal mourning.
> Now I have lost them.
> Alas, O Christ! How sad I am with this grief!
> Oh, loss of Moreiddig!
> How much we miss you! *(M.A.W.* 191)

Bardic poetry was flourishing at this time, as every poet sought to glorify the British past in order to demonstrate the nobility of the last of the Cymry. But the political and military situation was rather confused, being little more than a series of local wars, broken by artificial truces. The Welsh sided against John Lackland, doubtless because of the murder of his nephew Arthur of Brittany, a claimant to the ducal crown of Armorica and a possible successor to John on the English throne. Later, in 1258, when Simon de Montfort needed help, he promised the Welsh considerable privileges in return for their assistance against Henry III.

The last of the Welsh kings was Llywelyn ab Gruffyd (1246-1282). Llywelyn spent his life trying to safeguard Welsh independence and fought a series of battles, many of which he won. For a short time Wales became a powerful state and home to great intellectual development, but in 1277 Llywelyn was forced to surrender all claims to homage from the other Welsh chiefs. He died in 1282 in a battle against the Anglo-Normans near Buelt, Radnor; and the bards celebrated him in the style of the ancient days, as this *marwnad* attributed to Gruffyd ab Yr Ynad Coch shows:

> My heart freezes with terrible greif
> because of the king, oaken door of Aberffraw ...
> Do you not see the course of the wind and the rain?

> Do you not see the oaks beating together, the sea cor-
> roding the land?
> Do you not see the sun vanishing and the stars falling?
> *(M.A.W.)*

But this was the Welsh swan-song. Edward I, king of England, accorded the title Prince of Wales to his son, the future Edward II. Welsh or British independence had had its day. All the Welsh were able to save was their language and a kind of internal autonomy which still exists and through which the intellectual capital of ancient Britain has continued to thrive.

CHAPTER TEN

The Britons and the Bretons

The Legend of Conan Meriadek

LTHOUGH
Joseph Loth's thesis "l'Emigration Bretonne en Armorique" has always been accepted as the definitive work on the subject of the British settlement of Brittany, there are still many aspects of this question which remain to be answered.

There is no valid documentation concerning the migration. The few passages of Gildas' *De Excidio Britanniae* dealing with the matter which tally with the pseudo-Nennius' *Historia Brittonum* are simply not good enough. There is, of course, a vast collection of lives of Breton saints (none of whom was actually canonized), but these are so deliberately edifying in tone that they are even less reliable than the mythological legends. We are therefore reduced to forming hypotheses of our own, though we are fortunate in having canon François Falc'hun's remarkable *Histoire de la Langue Bretonne d'après la géographie linguistique* (P.U.F. 1963) with its interesting discoveries in the fields of linguistics and phonetics to lend support to our arguments.

When the Saxons invaded Britain, Armorica was no different from any of the other Gallic provinces which had become part of the Roman Empire. The old tribal areas had been redivided into a system of *civitates*. The Osismii of Nord-Finistère had their capital at Vorigum (Carhaix), which formed a point of intersection for the Roman roads and was therefore in some sense the centre of the peninsula. The main towns of the Curiosolitae were at Fanum Martis (Corseul) and Reginea (Erquy). The Redones were grouped round Condate (the confluence of the Ille and Vilaine, which shortly assumed the tribal name to become Rennes. The Namnetes on the banks of the Loire held the great port of Condevincum (the confluence of the Erdre and the Loire) which later became Nantes. The Veneti still lived on the south coast between the Odet and the Loire, with their capital at Darioritum (Darius' ford?) which is now Vannes or Locmariaquer.

According to the Greek chronicler Zosimus, some provinces declared themselves independent of the empire at the time of Honorius and Constantine and tried to form their own government. Zosimus says that the whole of Armorica joined in this movement and formed a provisional federal republic.

There may be something to learn about these disturbances within the Roman Empire from the legend of Conan Meriadek. This tale has been the subject of much discussion and though basically Welsh it was reworked by all the Breton writers and used by all those noble families who wished to trace their origins back to some British national hero. Needless to say, most academics have regarded this tale as so much nonsense, while others have believed quite uncritically that it is totally true. But neither viewpoint is correct.

It is Gildas who introduces the subject in his *De Excidio Britanniae* (X and XI). After condemning the usurper Maximus (Macsen Wletic) as a tyrant, he goes on to say that Maximus' expedition to the continent, for which he had mustered the best of the British troops, left Britain with no defence against the Saxon invaders. One of the Welsh legends entitled the *Dream of Maxen* describes the usurper as emperor going to look for a girl called Elen whom he has seen in a dream. Being obliged to recapture his empire on the continent, he forms an expeditionary force which includes Elen's two brothers Adeon and Kynan. (The Irish *Annals of Tigernach* date this expedition as taking place in 350.) Maxen's army is such that "there were better fighters in that small band than among twice as many Romans" *(The Dream of Maxen)*. Adeon and Kynan so arrange matters that they can take Rome themselves and make Maxen beholden to them. As a reward he gives them a free hand to conquer whatever territory they will.

> The Brothers went out and conquered lands and castles and cities; they killed all the men but left all the women alive, and this continued until the young lads who had come with them were white-haired ... Kynan said to his brother Adeon, "Do you want to stay in this land or return to your country?" Adeon and many of his men decided to go home, but Kynan and another group stayed. They determined to cut out the tongues of the women, lest their own British language be contaminated. Because the women were silent and the men could speak, the men of Brittany were called men of Llydaw, and there have often come, and still do come men of that language from Brittany. *(The Dream of Maxen)*.

This part of the legend actually makes its first appearance in the work attributed to Nennius, in chapters XII and XXIII of the *Historia Britonum*. After telling the story of the women having their tongues cut out, he adds; "that is why we call them [the Armoricans] *Letewicion*, i.e. *semi-tacentes* [half-dumb] because they blur their speech". The author divides the word *Letewicion* (Modern Welsh *Llydaw*) into *let*, half and *tewicion*, silent, which can be compared to *Llediaith*, of the half language.

As might be guessed, this etymology is purely invented. *Llydaw* and *Letewicion* would seem, in fact, to come from the same root as the forest of *Litana* or *Litava*, mentioned by Livy in connexion with wars against the Gauls, and this in turn would appear to be related to *Lituus*, the ceremonial rod of the Latins.

In Geoffrey of Monmouth's *Historia Regum Britanniae* and the *Brut Tysilio*, which is a Welsh adaptation of it, Kynan Meiriadawc starts out as an enemy to Macsen. It is not until the two men have made peace that Kynan helps Macsen in his expedition and receives Llydaw as a reward. Macsen is killed in Rome and a large number of his men take refuge in Armorica with Kynan Meiriadawc. "It was then that the Britons went to Llydaw for the first time, and since then it has been called Little Britain." (*M.A.W.* 454 and *Brut Gruffud ab Arthur, M.A.W.* 512.)

This tradition is corroborated in one of the triads. One of the three expeditions to leave the island of Britain is that led by "Elen Lluydawg [Elen the leader of armies] and her brother Kynan, lord of Meiriadawc, to Llydaw where they obtained lands and territories from the emperor Macsen Wletig for having helped him against the Romans. These warriors came originally from the land of Meiriadawc [North West of Powys], from Seisyllwg [Gwent], from Gwyr and from Gorvennydd. Not one returned; they stayed in Llydaw and at Ystre Gylfaelwg where they were masters. There were so few men at arms in Cymru as a result of this levy that the Gaels and the Picts oppressed the land." (*M.A.W.* 401, 14.)

At least two aspects of this particular account change from version to version. The first alteration occurs in the *Red Book of Hergest* where the corresponding triad says that "the second expedition went with Elen Lluyddawc and Macsen Wletic to Llychlynn; it never returned to this island". As we can see, not only has Kynan been omitted, but the country to which the expedition goes is Llychlynn (Scandinavia or Scythia, according to differing traditions). Perhaps Llydaw and Llychlynn had been confused.

There is unquestionable confusion between this triad from the *Red Book* and that in the *Myvyrian*, since the third expedition described in the *Red Book* triad is led by Casswallawn in pursuit of the Caesarians, the Britons then remaining in Gwasgwyn (Gascony). It is clearly very difficult to determine which of these versions represents the original story, but it is nonetheless interesting to see what happened to the legend. Celtophiles, ever ready to see any myth which glorifies Brittany as the literal truth, have made this expedition the first migration of Britons to the continent and Conan Meriadek the founding father of the Breton nation. Celtic scholars, on the other hand, being more used to scientific evidence and more cautious in their approach, have seen the legend solely as a politically motivated fable.

What no one appears to have seen, however, is that we can learn something from the mythological aspect of the legend. Obviously the story of Conan Meriadek is based on some historical settlement of the Britons in Armorica at an unspecified date. The deeper significance of the story may lie in *Letewicion* and its translation in the *Historia Britonum* as "half-dumb". Why should the author have mentioned the way that the Britons killed the men and cut out the tongues of the women in Armorica?

Though undoubtedly very unreliable as a historian, the pseudo-Nennius is usually well informed about the mythological traditions of the Celts. In Chapter VII of the *Historia* he tells of the arrival of the first Gaels in Ireland. "They saw in the middle of the ocean a tower of glass, and on the tower something which looked like men. They spoke to them but could obtain no answer." The Irish tale of the *Voyage of Maelduin* describes a similar incident in which "They saw people on the top of that island, but they spoke to no one and no one addressed a word to them" *(Imramm Mailduin* XVII).

These silent people would appear to be the *silentes* of the Latin poets, the inhabitants of the mysterious islands in the West, or to put it another way, the people of the Other World. The translation of *Letewicion* as the half-dumb men suggests that the pseudo-Nennius saw Llydaw not as Brittany but as the kingdom of the Dead. The link between dumbness and the Other World can be clearly seen in the *mabinogi* of *Branwen*, where Bran says that the dead warriors brought back to life by his magic cauldron will not be able to speak.

The fact that the newly arrived Britons are called *semi-tacentes* means that the men are alive while the women are dead. The idea of cutting out the women's tongues is a kind of rationalization to explain the use of *semi-tacentes* and is justified as a means of keeping the language pure. In fact, as inhabitants of the Other World, the women would already have been dumb.

In the Welsh texts, the word Llydaw could be used to denote not just Brittany but also the mythical, unearthly home of the Dead and the Fairy People. The Breton peninsula has always been regarded as a land of marvels where places like the forest of Brocéliande offer a home to fairies and wizards. Similarly, the name Llychlynn could be used not only for Scandinavia in general, and therefore for the North, the land of the Dead, but also for Scythia, the distant and mysterious home of the Cimmerians and therefore the Other World. Of the warriors who left with Elen and Kynan not one returned, as the triads say.

Moreover, since all the men are killed, Conan Meriadek's new kingdom must be populated solely by these silent women, as are various other realms in the Celtic tradition. The *Voyage of Maelduin,* for example, tells how Maelduin and his companions land on a magic island inhabited only be women and are received by the queen and her seventeen daughters. "When they had eaten and drunk the queen said; 'How are our guests to sleep?' 'As you wish,' said Maelduin. 'Let each of you take the woman facing him,' said she, 'and go to the bedroom with her.' So the seventeen men and the seventeen girls went to bed with each other and Maelduin went to bed with the Queen. Then they slept till morning. When the sailors prepared to leave, the queen said, 'Stay here and old age will never overtake you. You will always be as young as you are now and you will live for ever." *(Imramm Mailduin,* XXVIII.)

A similar adventure occurs in the *Voyage of Bran son of Febal.* "It did not take them long to reach the island of women. They saw a row of women on the quay . . . They entered a big house which contained a bed for each couple, that is three times nine beds. The food put on each dish did not vanish, it seemed to them that they had only been there one year and it had been several years."

This island of women is Emain Ablach, the Irish equivalent of the isle of Avalon where Morgan reigns surrounded by her sister. It is the land of the fairies.

> Emain, wonderful facing the sea,
> whether it be near, whether it be far,
> where thousands of strange women live
> girt by the limpid sea . . .[11]

And, as the Celts saw it, these fairies needed men to propagate their race, not unlike the Amazons who are so closely related to them in myth. For the feminine divinity needs the masculinity of living men to bring fertility and prosperity to the universe which she and they create together. When Yvain, the *Chevalier au Lion* of Chrétien de Troyes' romance, kills the Black Knight guarding the Fountain of Barenton and marries Laudine who is of the Other World, he takes over the Black Knight's duties and brings renewal to his widow. It is as if Yvain is the new priest of the goddess who kills his impotent predecessor in some ancient and bloody ritual. Even today, the Catholic Church persists in according ordination only to *viri integri*.

Removed from the historical framework, the legend of Conan Meriadek therefore appears to be yet another of those expeditions to the Other World so much used by the Celts as a means of compensating for their material defeats by indulging in metaphysical speculations in their literature.

The Emigration from Britain

In 451 the church council at Tours was attended by a man named Mansuetus who is described as *Episcopus Britannorum*. But the fact that the council was confined to the ecclesiastical province of which Armorica formed a part argues against Mansuetus' being an island Briton and suggests, on the contrary, that he represented some group of Britons who had settled in Armorica. Evidently this group, however small, was sufficiently well organized and important to be assigned a bishop. A second council at Tours held in 567 clearly differentiates between Romans and Bretons. We are concerned with what happened during the intervening hundred years.

In 469, not long after he had become Western Emperor, Anthemius summoned a small army of Britons, composed of 12,000 men, to help him against the Visigoths. Their commander, Riothimus, is given the title *rex* by Jordanes, the historian of the Goths, and it is clear that Anthemius had appealed to him as an ally rather than summoned him as a subject. So presumably Britain was independent of the empire by this time. However, it is unlikely that this army came from Britain itself, since the islanders were busy defending themselves against the Picts and the Saxons and, according to the Venerable Bede (I, 13) were even asking for help from the continent. It is more probable that the force was composed by Britons already settled in Armorica, a hypothesis supported by a letter from Sidonius Apollinaris addressed to a chief named Riothamus (obviously Riothimus) in which he talks of Britons *super Ligerim sitos*.

The army was defeated at Déols in 469 by Euric the Visigoth and the Britons scattered throughout the South West. It may be that Triad 8 of the *Red Book* is referring to this event when it says that Casswallawn's Britons settled in Gascony. In fact, near enough a score of places in South West France have names like Bretenoux, Berthenoux or Bretonnière.

When it comes to delineating the progress of the British settlers in Armorica, however, we must look to place names and linguistics for there is little historical evidence to help us.

We can start by examining the names of the different regions in the Breton peninsula after the Britons had arrived; regions which roughly correspond to the pre-1789 episcopal dioceses. The former land of the Curiosolitae between Rance and Saint-Brieuc was called Domnonia, a name presumably deriving from the Dumnonii, a people originating in Devon and the South coast of England. Assuming that the Eastern Britons were either totally subjugated or prevented from fleeing westwards by the Saxons, the Dumnonii were almost certainly among the first to retreat from the invader by crossing the Channel, for the coast of Domnonia between Saint-Malo and Paimpol lies directly opposite their British home. Later Domnonia was divided into the diocese of Saint-Brieuc and the diocese of Aleth (the see later going to Saint-Malo). The diocese of Saint-Malo comprised a vast area including part of the present arrondissement of Saint-Malo, the arrondissement of Dinan (Côtes-du-Nord), North Eastern Morbihan as far as the Oust and a strip of land between the Vilaine, the Aff and the Meu stretching as far as the outskirts of Redon.

East of Saint-Malo lay the minute diocese of Dol which was once a Breton-speaking area and included parishes within other dioceses. We can therefore presume that Domnonia was a wedge-shaped region lying between Couesnon, Redon and Paimpol, and that the Britons who settled there came from South England.

It appears equally safe to assume that the diocese of Dol was the older foundation. Logically this would be the only way to explain how it came to survive alongside the much more powerful neighbouring see of Saint-Malo. The parishes which remained within other dioceses must have been too well established for later arrivals to shift or appropriate. In any case, we know that at the time of Nominöe, Dol rather than Tours was the Breton metropolis.

The region between the river at Morlaix and Saint-Brieuc-Paimpol formed Trégor or the diocese of Tréguier, a name reminiscent of an ancient *pagus* in Cornwall before that peninsula was invaded by the Cornovii in their flight from the Saxons.

The whole of nord-Finistère formed the diocese of Léon, which must have been a colony of people from Leonois or Loonois, probably somewhere near Caerleon or Kaer Llyon, Tristan's legendary home. The inhabitants of Léon were therefore descended from Welshmen who had had to leave Cambria when it became over-crowded by the arrival of refugees from other parts of Britain.

Sud-Finistère forms the greater part of the diocese of Cornouaille *(Cornu Galliae)* which is called Kerneo *(Cornovia)* in Breton. Kerneo can be compared with the Cornish *Kernew* and the Welsh *Kernyw*, both denoting Cornwall *(Corn-wealas)*. The Cornovii who had settled in Cornwall had also to flee before the Saxon advance and probably emigrated to Cornouaille.

Obviously this is only a generalized picture, giving an indication of which people predominated in any specific area. It is very difficult to exactly delineate the different regions. Immigration was fairly haphazard, with different peoples settling together in one area. *Quimerc'h* in Cornouaille, for example, could correspond to both *Cenmerch* in Wales or *Cenmerch* in Cornwall; *Quemeneven* in Cornouaille to *Cymdmaen* in Wales; *Lanvellec* in Trégor to *Llanfaelog* in Anglesey; *Langolen, Tourc'h* and *Elliant* in Cornouaille to *Llangollen, Twrch* and *Ellian* in North Wales, all suggesting that a considerable number of Welsh, and especially Northern Welsh came to Cornouaille.

It is possible to plot these migrations by way of Breton parishes, for when the Britons crossed the Channel they brought with them not only their language but also their own particular form of the Christian religion and their own ecclesiastical organization. We can therefore establish exactly which were the oldest parishes by their names; for the first British parishes bore names preceded by the words *plou*- or *gui*-.[2]

The word *plou* (from Latin *plebs*) denotes the parish as a whole, whereas *gui* (Latin *vicus*) denotes only the parochial town or headquarters. In Breton the two words become interchangeable, so that *Guitalmeze* is Breton for *Ploudalmezeau*, *Gwineventer* Breton for *Plouneventer* and *Guimiliau* used to be called *Ploumiliau*.

When the early parishes became very large; secondary settlements were founded. At first these were attached directly to the existing parish, but they later became independent and the formation of new parishes continued in Brittany until the 12th century, except in Brest and Lorient.[3] The new settlements had names beginning with *Lan* (the sacred land of a founding saint), *Loc* (sacred place, grave) and *Tre* (division of the parish). Saints' names actually preceded by the word *Saint* were Frenchified versions of a Breton word; Sainte-Anne d'Auray, for example, was once Keranna.

The one area we have left out of this overall view of Armorica is the district of Vannes, the former home of the Veneti which lay roughly between the Odet and the Vilaine and included the Guerande peninsula. This region poses a number of problems.

As we have said, a look at those parishes with names starting in *plou* and *gui* gives us a rough picture of the early British settlements in Brittany. But to do this we must obviously confine ourselves to the area which was Breton-speaking until the 12th century, which means the land West from a line known as the Loth Line stretching from the bay of Mont-Saint-Michel to Donges on the Loire. And this area did not include either Rennes or Nantes.

By examining the parish names for each pre-1789 diocese using Falc'hun's work (*op. cit.* 43) we find that Léon contained more names beginning in *plou* than any of the others (81 parishes, 35 in *plou,*, i.e. 43% of the total), and that a higher incidence of *plou*-name parishes occur in the other North Coast dioceses. In fact the *plou*-name areas in Tréguier, Saint-Brieuc and Saint-Malo are almost exclusively coastal. So we can conclude that from Mont-Saint-Michel to the roadstead of Brest, there were large numbers of British settlements.

In Cornouaille, there appear to be fewer *plou*-name parishes (21% of the total of 173), but two thirds of these lie West of Quimper in an area less than one sixth the size of the whole diocese. The rest are scattered around Carhaix. Between Quimper, Quimperlé and Carhaix there are only two, Pleuven and Guiscriff.

Plou-name parishes are equally scarce in the diocese of Vannes and along the western coastline of Brittany in general, which would suggest that there were few early British settlements in the area between the Odet and the Vilaine.

In fact, if we mark the *plou*-name parishes on the map of South Brittany (as in Map v at the end of this book) we can see that most of the few to be found are concentrated in groups, one around Carhaix (Ploerdut, Plouray, Plelauff, etc), one North West of the Gulf of Morbihan (Pluvigner, Plumergat, Plumegelen, etc) and one between Vannes and Ploermel (Plumelec, Plaudren, Guehenno, etc).

The first of these groups would indicate that the settlers came from the North along the Roman road between Carhaix and Sulim (Castennec in Bieuzy-les-Eaux), a route still frequented in later centuries.[4] The second group North of Auray appears to be the result of an immigration from the sea; while the existence of the third group suggests that the British infiltrated from the diocese of Saint-Malo.

As we can see there was very little colonization of the area between the Odet and Vilaine, the former land of the Veneti. But before attempting to explain why this was so, it might be helpful to look at the numbers of parishes already in existence before the first British settlers arrived which remained untouched by the Britons in the early years. These we can identify by the Gallo-Roman suffix *-ac*, from *acu, aco* or *acus,* which would be added to a Gallic or Roman family name to form the parish name.

As Francis Gourvil writes *(Langue et littérature bretonnes,* p. 46), the *ac* suffix "tells us two things: first that there was a native population in the places where it is found and second that the Breton language came to dominate the area later". For although the *-ac* suffix was used to form thousands of place names throughout France it developed in different ways in different regions. In the *langue d'oc* areas it can be found in its original form (Figeac, Aurillac, etc) or in an evolved form as *at* North of the Auvergne (Perignat) or as *ec* near Saint-Etienne (Aurec, Luriecq).

The various dialects spoken in the *langue d'oil* regions turned *ac* into *ieu* near Lyon (Virieu); into *y* in Savoie (Anthy); into *ey* in the East (Colombey); into *ay* in the North (Bavay); *é* in the West (Sablé) and *y* everywhere else (Fleury). The *ac* form found in Brittany is an aberration, since the phonetic evolution of the Romance language in that area should have changed it into *é.*

The occurrence of *-ac* names in Brittany therefore indicates that the British language came to predominate in that area and arrested the expected evolution of the suffix. Sévigné, for example, lies in an area where British was not spoken, Sévignac in an areas where it was. The fact that developed forms of the suffix occur even in the heart of Brittany indicates merely that both languages were spoken concurrently.

An examination of pre-1789 parishes, from Falc'hun's work again, shows that whereas no *ac*-names existed in the diocese of Tréguier, 12.8% of all parishes in the see of Vannes ended in *-ac.* This means either that the Gallo-Roman settlements were better organized and defended in the Vannes region or that the Britons came there in fewer numbers.

Some of the saints' lives suggest that when the Britons arrived the peninsula was practically deserted, and that in Léon and Trégor especially the immigrants had only to choose where they wanted to live. This argument is supported by the large number of place names indicating ruins or the remains of ancient fortifications, names formed from *moguer* (wall) and *coz* (old), for example. Ploumoguer means "the Parish of the Wall", Cozty "the Old House", Goh-Illis "Old Church", Cozmogeriou "the Old Walls". There are 236 place names of this kind, of which 89 are in Finistère, 78 in the Côtes-du-Nord and 69 in Morbihan.

However, the idea of the Britons walking peacefully into a deserted Brittany is totally at odds with the history of inter-Celtic conflict we have observed both in Britain and Gaul. "The Britons took the country by force," writes the historian Durtelle de Saint-Sauveur *(Histoire de la Bretagne des origines à nos jours,* I, 39), "all the evidence points to this conclusion, and it explains why the two races found themselves so widely separate after a short space of time."

In fact it was probably conflict between the immigrants and the native population which created the ruins on which the invaders settled and which are all too often used to support the picture of a deserted Brittany. The conquered Gallo-Romans must have fled southwards towards the land of the Veneti and the southern part of the Saint-Malo diocese, places where there are most parish names ending in *-ac.*

Then, when the Britons had virtually occupied the whole of North Western and Western Armorica, later arrivals would have been forced to go south to the Vannes region, which was further from Britain but which must have continued to trade with the island. As that area was already densely populated, however, the Britons were obliged to settle in the least productive areas, either after fighting against or after forming agreements with the indigenous peoples. Indeed, the second and third of the three *plou*-name concentrations mentioned above are still poor heath-land or patchy forest.

From all the evidence, the Britons began by settling in very confined areas and then sought to expand their territory by force. Gregory of Tours tells of the struggles of the Breton count Waroc'h who tried to gain control of the Vannetais at the end of the 6th century. In 576 Regalis, the Gallo-Roman bishop of Vannes, asked the Franks to help defend him against Waroc'h. The see of Vannes, seat of the suffragan to the bishop of Tours, which was Roman in organization, later entered into virtually open conflict with the dioceses of Dol, Aleth-Saint-Malo, Saint-Brieuc, Tréguier and Léon which were Celtic in organization and whose incumbents were abbot-bishops.

What we now have to establish is the nature of the language being spoken in Armorica when the Britons arrived, and more particularly the language spoken in the area round Vannes. It has generally been believed that here, as in the rest of the former romanized parts of France, the Romance language had entirely replaced the Old Gallic language. This belief is based on the writings of Joseph Loth:

> The Gallic language suffered the same fate in the Armorican peninsula as in the rest of Gaul. It was commonly held in the last century ... that despite the length of the Roman occupation, a Gallic idiom had remained current in the Armorican peninsula and was sufficiently revitalized by the arrival of the Britons to survive as a Celtic dialect to this day. This hypothesis is quite reasonable; not because the Armorican peninsula was less romanzied than the rest of Celtic Gaul, on the contrary, but because it appears that Gallic had still not entirely disappeared in the 4th century. Saint Jerome tells us that in his time the same language was spoken among the Trevires and the Galates ... Perhaps Gallic did not completely die in Gaul until some time in the 5th century. By then, at any rate, the process had been completed in the Breton peninsula. (*L'Émigration bretonne en Armorique*, 82-4).

Joseph Loth's argument here follows the propositions set out by Aurelien de Courson in his *Cartulaire de l'Abbaye de Redon en Bretagne* (1863). But, although Loth has done much fine and useful work on the Celts, particularly in his translation of the Welsh *mabinogion*, he appears to have gone astray here, even if he does accept as reasonable the hypothesis that Gallic survived under the influence of the British. In his book *La Langue Gauloise*, Georges Dottin, who shares a good number of Loth's theories, writes; "Suplicius Severus (363-425) describes in one of his dialogues a Gaul who apologizes for his language and is told 'Speak Celtic, or if you prefer Gallic'. Finally, it, would appear from the words of Sidonius Apollinaris (430-480) that the Arvernian nobility had only recently learned Latin and abandoned the Celtic language. The substitution of Latin for Celtic was therefore a slow process and was probably completed in the 6th century".

Falc'hun who quotes these texts rightly comments that the nobility has always been the first to abandon a local language and that the mass of the people do not follow their example until much later. So if the Arvernian nobles were beginning to give up Gallic in the 5th century, the people must have continued to speak it. And if Gallic survived in the land of the Trevires where there were flourishing Roman schools, and in the Arverne district where direct Roman influence was close at hand, then there is all the more reason why it should have persisted in Armorica. For the Breton peninsula was the most far-flung, least urbanized of the Roman provinces, where Roman military presence was at its least intensive, the bulk of the legions being posted on the borders with Germania. Moreover, as Paul-Marie Duval points out *(La Vie Quotidienne en Gaule,* 331), the small number of urban communities and important monuments found in Armorica suggests that this region was less romanized than any other; the frequent occurrence of Gallic names seems to confirm that local traditions were better preserved in the isolated regions than elsewhere.

So, as Dom Le Pelletier observed so long ago in his preface to the *Dictionnaire de la Langue Bretonne* (1752), "We should not assume that the Armoricans received the language they speak today from the Britons; like the Britons they had preserved their language ... Those who claim that the Celtic language had been abolished in Armorica and was only introduced by the Britons are overlooking the fact that if the Britons had been able to keep their language despite Roman domination, then the Armoricans could have done the same".

This is not the only example of the survival of a Gallic language, for we now know that Basque was not reimported by the Vascons from Spain in the 6th century, as was previously thought, but that it is merely a continuation of the language spoken in South West Aquitaine before the Roman invasion.[5]

As far as Brittany is concerned, we can find support for our argument in Falc'hun's work on the phonetics of Breton dialects.

Breton today is spoken by about 1,200,000 people (a larger number than those speaking Welsh and Erse), and these people are scattered throughout what is called Basse-Bretagne, i.e. the western third of the Côtes-du-Nord, the whole of Finistère and two thirds of Morbihan west of a line running approximately from Paimpol to the mouth of the Vilaine.

The Breton language can be divided into four dialects which correspond closely to the four former dioceses. These are *trégorrois* in the see of Tréguier, *léonard* in Léon, the *dialect of Cornouaille* in the old see of Quimper and *vannetais* in the Breton-speaking part of Morbihan. The first three of these differ only slightly, and when attempts were made to codify written Breton at the beginning of the 20th century, they were grouped together into what is called K.L.T. (Kerneo-Léon-Trégor.) Vannetais, however, was regarded as totally separate.

In fact vannetais differs greatly, both in vocabulary and pronunciation from the K.L.T. dialects. This difference has been attributed partly to the fact that the local people spoke Vulgar Latin at the time of the migrations, and partly to the fact that the district of Vannes, being an extension of the Loire valley and more closely connected with the metropolis of Tours, was more likely to be exposed to the infiltration of French words (Falc'hun, 123-7). The first of these two explanations seems quite reasonable, though further information is still needed about the Vulgar Latin being spoken. The second, however, is more controversial. For while the Vannes district has always offered an easy passage for French words, the vannetais dialect has survived much further to the East than the Northern Breton dialects which were less exposed to French influence.

A detailed study of the *Atlas linguistique de la Basse-Bretagne* (A.L.B.B.), has enabled Falc'hun to discover certain characteristics which suggest that in the early days of British influence the peninsula was divided into two dialect areas, the one in the North and North West and the other in the South (Falc'hun 99-114). And it is in the South that the former land of the Veneti lies.

"Northern Breton was the language of Domnonia . . . which was separated from the southern coast by vast forests and deserted moorland. For a long time the two halves of Brittany formed entities so distinct in nature that they affected the political divisions within the duchy." (Falc'hun, III.)

Indeed, if we look at the history of Brittany, we find considerable support for this argument. The influence of Alain Barbetorte, who restored Breton liberty in the 10th century, was confined to the South from Nantes to Carhaix. In 952 Alain's son's guardian relinquished the South to the Count of Anjou and kept the North of Brittany for himself. Later, in 1363, an attempt was made to avert a war between Charles de Blois and Jean de Montfort who were rivals for the dukedom, by partitioning Brittany into North and South.

If the line dividing the Channel coast from the Atlantic coast formed a kind of frontier, which is still reflected in language, then it comes as little surprise that the vannetais dialect (and to a lesser extent the Cornouaille dialect) contains distinct phonetic and other characteristics which can be compared to *langue d'oïl* idiom.

Instead of concluding, however, as so many other have done, that these characteristics are attributable to Vulgar Latin and later to French, Falc'hun thinks that they have come from the Gallic which was spoken in the peninsula at the time of the British immigrations and that Breton, especially vannetais, is a direct descendant from Gallic.

There is some evidence to support this assumption, certainly as far as vannetais is concerned, even if certain facets of the argument remain hazy and doubtful.

We can start by looking at the Loth Line which has always been regarded as the easternmost point reached by the Breton language when the Bretons took Rennes and Nantes in the 10th century. Falc'hun argues that this line could equally well mark a stage in the retreat of the Gallic language towards the heart of the peninsula.

The more interesting argument in favour of Gallic survival, however, is based on Falc'hun's observations about two types of Gallic accentuation. For, as we shall see, place names of Gallic origin have developed in different ways. In some cases two distinct evolved forms have come from a single root.

The following table lists some of the names of towns, regions or rivers in France, Britain, Switzerland and on the left bank of the Rhine, i.e. in areas where a Celtic language was once spoken. The left hand column shows how names developed when stress was placed on the penultimate syllable of the word, the right hand column showing the effects of stress of the ante-penultimate. Penultimate stress would appear the earlier and was preserved in rural areas, whereas ante-penultimate stress almost always affected urban areas and would appear to be later.

EARLY RURAL STRESS PENULTIMATE	LATER URBAN STRESS ANTE-PENULTIMATE
Bituríges > BERRY	Bitúriges > BOURGES
Parisii > PARISIS	Parísii > PARIS
Lugdúnum > LOUDUN, LEYDE	Lúgdunum > LYON, LAON
Nemaúsus > NEMOURS	Némausus > NIMES
Eburácum > YVRY, YVRAC	Ebúracum > YORK
Matróna > MEYRONNE	Mátrona > MARNE
Genéva > GENEVA	Géneva > GENES
Isára > ISERE	Ísara > OISE

Lundínium > LONDON   Lúndinium > LONDRES

If we accept, as is generally held, that any innovations are always made first in towns and only percolate through to the more conservative countryside much later, then we can deduce that the stress on the penultimate syllable, being more rural, is also older and in fact reflects the true form of Gallic accentuation.

The second type of stress must have resulted from some kind of foreign influence on Gallic. Whether this influence is Latin is hard to say, since no linguist has ever been able to define Latin stress and it is believed to have varied considerably. We can, however, compare stress of the ante-penultimate syllable with Greek usage, in which stress tended to be put as far forward as possible in certain words, including almost all proper names. Different transcriptions of Gallic names by Greek authors like Dio Cassius, show that this rule of stress was effectively applied to these names.

Even the Latin words which were borrowed by the Gauls and passed into French indicate some hesitation in choosing between stress on the penultimate and stress on the ante-penultimate syllables. Thus, for example, *íntegrum* became *entier*, while *secáte* became *seigle;* and while *recípere* became *recevoir* and *lúcere luire*, the Old French forms *recivre* and *luisir* must have derived from *lucére* and *recipére*.

It is therefore possible that there was some Greek influence on the pronunciation of Gallic before it was affected by Latin. The Greeks followed the age-old trade routes from Marseilles to the Channel and the North Sea; and if we look at some of the towns which would have been natural relay posts along these routes we discover many place names in which stress was placed on the ante-penultimate syllable:

> Némausus > NIMES
> Lúgdunum > LYON
> Sénones > SENS
> Séquana > SEINE
> Ámbiani > AMIENS
> Cárnutes > CHARTRES
> Vindósama > VENDOME
> Cambóritum > CHAMBORD
> Bellóvaci > BEAUVAIS
> Rotómagos > ROUEN

and many others. We can even extend the list along the Channel coast with:

> Catúmagos > CAEN
> Baiócasses > BAYEUX
> Abríncatui > AVRANCHES

and so on.

As the trade route crossed the Channel, so too did this form of stress as we can see in the way London became Londres and Eburacum York.

There are two areas, however, in which the names of even quite large towns have evolved in a way consistent with stress being placed on the penultimate syllable, one between the Loire and the Garonne, west of the Massif Central, and the other North of the Loire towards Normandy. It would appear that these areas were off

the trade routes and consequently remained more Gallic and less quickly romanized. Looking at their geographical position we find that these two areas virtually
shut off the Armorican peninsula from the rest of France. And if these areas were
less subject to Gallo-Roman influence, then the regions to the West of them must
inevitably have preserved the older traditions.

This is obviously an argument in favour of Falc'hun's theories concerning the
survival of the Gallic language in Armorica at the time of the British invasions, and
a Gallic language moreover which placed its stress on the penultimate syllable. For
place names which have evolved from the earlier form of stress extend into Brittany
itself, and even into Breton-speaking areas, but only in the South. And, interestingly, the K.L.T. dialect names for Rennes, Nantes and Vannes (all of which have
evolved from ante-penultimate stress being placed on Rédones, Námnetes and
Véneti) are Roazon, Naoned and Guened, which would reflect the earlier penultimate stress not usually found in K.L.T.

Our final conclusion must be that there was an area in Gaul which continued to
speak the old language while romanization was taking place, that the older stress
form survived in this area and that this area extended into the former territory of
the Veneti in South Brittany.

The Gallic language must therefore have become extinct just as it was in the
process of acquiring the new, ante-penultimate form of stress. "During the centuries which preceded this extinction, the second stress form, which had the prestige of the large towns to support it, was gradually pushing the first into the
outlying country districts, the mountains and the frontier regions, and so into
Brittany." (Falc'hun, 165.)

There is surely some connexion between the survival of Gallic and the difference in stress between the K.L.T. and the vannetais dialects.

The three K.L.T. dialects place their stress on what was the ante-penultimate
syllable before declension ceased in both Celtic and French and the final syllable
became redundant. Yet unlike French they have kept the former atonic penultimate syllable. Vannetais, on the other hand, puts its stress on the old penultimate
syllable which has now become the final syllable.

It is easy enough to explain this difference, both phonetically and historically.
Vannetais represents the language spoken in a district where the British immigrants were in a distinct minority and where the native majority can only have
spoken a Gallic language. The K.L.T. dialects on the other hand represent the
language of Northern Armorica where the Britons were more numerous. Vannetais
dialect must therefore be the direct descendant of the early continental Gallic
language with stress on the penultimate syllable, while K.L.T. is an island import.
In fact K.L.T. has all the traits of Gallic pronounced according to the second kind
of stress which spread along the trade routes and through Britain to leave its mark
on Cornish and Welsh.

Obviously a certain amount of linguistic hybridization took place. The British
immigrants and the indigenous Gauls may have been separated by a difference in
dialect, but it cannot have been very great since we know that the Gauls and the
Britons could understand each other without interpreters. And even if this difference was preserved, the two dialects borrowed freely from each other. Between the
Odet and the Loire the British language was influenced by Gallic both in pronunciation and in vocabulary, for Breton in that area has retained the stress of the
penultimate. The whole peninsula then became more uniform under the influence
of Carhaix, the capital of the Breton-speaking area as Rennes was the centre of

Romance-speaking Brittany. Gradually Carhaix evolved its own dialect somewhere between the Northern and Southern variants. It is this which appears to have survived in the present day dialect of Cornouaille, which is why there are a number of links between the Breton of Vannes and the Breton of Cornouaille. Finally, in the 16th century, the Cornouaille dialect was re-Bretonized under the influence of Morlaix, where the Northern Léonard dialect was spoken and vannetais was pushed back into its own specific area.

Whether or not we agree that vannetais is the direct descendant of Gallic we can at least trace the pattern of British immigration into Armorica through linguistic study of this kind. Armorican Brittany was populated by a mixture of Britons and Gauls who were gathered together to a certain extent in specific areas. And it was this mixture which united under the leadership of the most energetic of the Britons, those who had settled in the Pays de Vannes, to form the kingdom of Brittany.

The History of Brittany

Situated at the extreme western point of the European continent, the hybrid mixture of semi-romanized Gauls and Britons known as Brittany offered a tempting prize to the rival monarchs of neighbouring France and England. From the 6th to the 15th centuries Breton history was little more than a constant, desperate struggle to preserve the autonomy of a divided peninsula; though contrary to general belief resistance to the French monarchy was far longer-lasting, if not fiercer, than resistance to the English crown. The Bretons, after all, originally came from Britain and were bound to feel some attraction towards it. The idea of a single French nation is a comparatively recent one. Up until 1532 Brittany was quite separate from France, even if French influence was increasing by way of the metropolitan church of Tours, and the Armoricans were in no way French.

There is documentary evidence from the second council of Tours in 567 that Brittany was already regarded as an entity separate from the rest of Gaul at that date. Throughout the 7th century, writers like Fortunatus and Gregory of Tours referred to the peninsula as *Britannia,* which proves that by then there were enough British settlers to have imposed their name on Armorica.

The Merovingians were not at all pleased by Breton independence. They had no desire to see a foreign state forming on the borders of Neustria. There were frequent Frankish incursions until in 577 a chief named Waroch took Vannes and pushed the Franks back beyond the Vilaine. Waroch or Guerec, had a typically British name and was probably one of the settlers, or descendants of settlers who had formed a curving line of settlements around Vannes. Vannes itself was still a Gallo-Roman town, as we can see from a document from Regalis, bishop of Vannes, assuring a Frankish chief of his loyalty and complaining of Breton oppression.

The events of the next few years are lost in legend. For this was the time of adventuring kings and saints. In North Brittany the abbot-bishops of Aleth (Saint-Malo), Tréguier and Léon appear to have formed the only administrative bodies; while the centre and south were ruled by a number of petty chiefs, many of them short-lived and limited in their sphere of authority. Hagiography has passed on the names of some of these. In Cornouaille we find Budik, Riwawd, Miliaw, the founder of Guimiliau, Iawn Reith and Gradlon, king of Is. In Vannes there was a second Waroch. In the central region of Domnonia there were Riwal, Deroch and Conomor, the Bluebeard of Breton legend.

More precise information comes with the arrival of the Carolingians. In 753

Pepin the Short appears to have imposed a tribute on the Bretons which, like their island ancestors who ignored Caesar's demands, they never paid. Charlemagne made no direct attack on the Bretons but sent missionaries among them in an attempt to wrest them from a resurgent paganism. It is these activities which form the basic theme of the *Chanson d'Aquin*, written down three centuries later. Charlemagne did, however, organize the Breton March which he gave to Count Roland. The march included Rennes and Nantes and its western border roughly followed the Loth Line. In 786 and 799 Roland's successor Count Wido had to contend with Breton attempts to infiltrate and in 818, urged on by the Vannetais leader Morvan nicknamed Leiz-Breiz, the Bretons attacked in force. They were driven back by Louis the Pious who pushed on into Brittany and reached almost as far as Morvan's den. The Frankish poet Ermold the Black who accompanied Louis and who despises the Bretons as idle, gossiping drunkards, tells how the monk Witkar was sent to Morvan to sue for peace. Having reached Morvan's Mount on the outskirts of Langonnet, he was taken to the Breton leader and said, "I am sent to you by the Caesar Louis, the glory of the Franks and of the Christians, the leader in peace and in war, in faith and in deeds. Wandering exiles cast upon his empire by the waves, you and all your race occupy a vast territory. And yet you refuse to pay the tribute, you challenge the arms of the Franks and you threaten them with yours. It is time to end this ... Come and beg Louis for peace".

Ermold then tells how Morvan asked for a day's delay before replying and how Morvan's wife, "a venemous and perfidious soul" dissuaded the chief from agreeing to peace. The next day Morvan said to Witkar, "Go quickly and tell your king this reply: I do not till his land and I do not want his laws. Let him reign over the Franks, Morvan will reign over the Bretons. It is my right as it is his. If the Franks want war, let there be war. There is still strength in my right arm."

The war continued, but fiercely though he fought, Morvan was finally forced to surrender. Louis the Pious took the opportunity to impose the order then in use within Frankish territory on the Armorican monasteries and particularly on Landevennec, a champion of Celtic religious tradition.

Rebellious attitudes still simmered, however, and in 822 another Vannetais chief Gwyomarch, took up arms. Two years later he was defeated by Lambert, the count of the Breton March. It was then, in 824, that Louis the Pious gave the title of duke over all Brittany to Nominoë, count of Vannes, in the hope of restoring order to the region.

At first Nominoë appeared loyal to Louis the Pious, but when Louis' sons began to quarrel over the empire he found himself free to unify Brittany and earn his title of "Father of the Land". He announced that he was supporting Lothair's claim to the empire, Lothair being a distant and therefore unrestrictive suzerain, and this move placed him in open conflict with Charles the Bald. Charles mounted an expedition to Brittany and after some initial success fell ill. He was then overwhelmingly defeated at Ballon, south of Rennes, on November 22, 845 and forced to recognize Nominoë's authority over the Bretons. This was not enough for the Breton leader, however. He took Rennes and Nantes and annexed the March to give the duchy its present-day boundaries. Drunk with success Nominoë marched on into Anjou, Maine and the Vendôme. He died on March 7, 851 and was buried in the abbey of Saint-Sauveur at Redon, one of the most magnificent of the Breton monasteries which had been founded under his patronage by Conwoïon, archdeacon of Vannes. During his lifetime Nominoë had sketched the broad outlines of major political, administrative and religious reforms within the duchy. Being from

Vannes, he had shifted the political axis from Nantes to the South. He reorganized the northern dioceses of St-Pol de Léon, Tréguier, St-Brieuc, St-Malo and Dol and ensured that they were no longer so closely associated with the monasteries. Having purged the traditionally Gallo-Roman clergy in the South, he suggested that the Breton church should have its own metropolis at Dol and no longer be obedient to Tours.

Nominoë was a figure of some stature and achievement. He was one of the few Breton sovereigns who succeeded in bringing unity to a land torn by domestic conflict and quarrels of precedence, as Gaul and Britain had been. For the Celts had little sense of national identity. Unfortunately, however, Nominoë's attempts to unify the country were short-lived.

On his death, his son Erispoë resumed the struggle against Charles the Bald who was hoping to use the hiatus caused by a change in leadership to avenge his previous defeats. In the summer of 851 Charles was again beaten and forced not only to recognize Erispoë as King of Brittany but to cede to him his rights over the March, Rennes, Nantes and the Retz district in exchange for a very vague promise of loyalty. The Bretons had won more than a military victory; they had obliged Charles to acknowledge the extent of their authority.

Even so, the Bretons showed little gratitude to Erispoë, for they came out in support of his cousin Salaün whom they considered a more ardent defender of the national cause. In 857 Salaün had Erispoë murdered (legend says he killed him himself), proclaimed himself king and sought to expand even further than his predecessors. He formed a series of alliances, first with the Norsemen as they began to raid the area, second with Charles' rebellious son, third with Charles the Bald himself and finally with the Norsemen again. In 867 he forced the king of France to sign an agreement giving Brittany power over the Cotentin district. Salaün achieved considerable success and Brittany began to look not merely like an expanding nation but like a strongly based power uniting the whole of the peninsula. It was the Celts' just retribution for all the treachery and defeat they had suffered at Roman and Saxon hands over the preceding centuries.

This period marked the high point of the Breton monarchy. The peninsula was relatively prosperous, mostly because of its maritime trade with Great Britain. The Bretons had retained close links with the islanders and in particular with the Cornish and Welsh who spoke virtually the same language as themselves. They had also made peace with the Saxons, at least as far as their immediate interests were concerned. Breton wealth can be seen in the number of abbeys and castles built during this time, and the way sanctuaries were decorated. Salaün's gift of a lifesize gold statue to pope Hadrian is evidence of his desire to win prestige and display his wealth.

Cultural life was developed, particularly at Redon and Landevennec, the foremost of the intellectual centres. Curiously however, the Armorican monks chose to write in Latin, while the Irish and Welsh orders continued to preserve the best of the Celtic tradition. The only pre-15th century Breton text to our knowledge is a 12th century poem. It might appear from this absence of Breton medieval writing that the Armoricans had forgotten their ancestral tradition, but there are two other possible explanations. The first is that the oral tradition was so well established, especially in country areas as it had been among the Gauls, that clerks felt no compulsion to commit legendary tales to paper. There is evidence that travelling bards still practised their art during the Middle Ages, and it must have been they who preserved the old traditions. Secondly, it is possible that there were in fact a

considerable number of Breton manuscripts but that in the confusion following the
Norse raids they were moved for safe-keeping to Frankish monasteries. And there,
being written in a language which nobody outside Brittany could understand, they
may have been left to rot and decay.

Salaün's high-handed and authoritarian style of monarchy began to provoke
discontent among some of his vassals. It had not been forgotten that he had
murdered Erispoë, despite his public acts of penitence and his avowed desire to
lead a life of prayer. And so it was in apparent conformity with the dictum that "he
who lives by the sword will perish by the sword" that Salaün was killed by rebels in
the village of Merzer on the banks of the Scorff in 874. For some reason such an
aura of sanctity became attached to his name that he is represented on the altars of
several Breton chapels as Saint Salomon.

There is no doubt that Salaün was a great king, but he made the same mistake as
the Aedui and Vortigern in allying himself with the Norsemen. For the invaders'
sole concern was to loot as much from Brittany as they could and they exacted
large payments from Salaün in return for the services they rendered him. During
his lifetime the Norsemen kept their promises to him and remained at peace, but as
soon as he had died they attacked the chief towns. The succession was being
disputed by Pasqueten, count of Vannes and Salaün's son-in-law, and Gurwan,
count of Rennes and Erispoë's son-in-law. Pasqueten made an agreement with the
Norsemen and turned them on Gurwan who managed to drive them back some
distance from Rennes.

Pasqueten and Gurwan died within a few months of each other, but the quarrel
of the succession continued between Gurwan's son Judikaël and Pasqueten's
brother Alain. When the Norsemen began their raids again, however, Judikaël and
Alain united against the common enemy. Judikaël beat the Norsemen on the banks
of the Blavet but was killed as he pursued them. Alain defeated them somewhere
near Questembert in 890.

Alain, count of Vannes, was now sole claimant to the throne and his decisive
victory over the Norsemen had earned him the title of "Great". Apart from being
the duke of Brittany, therefore, he was also known as a "pious and peaceful king".
Alain the Great reigned from 890 to 907 and restored to Brittany some of the power
and prosperity it had known under Salaün. There were two capitals, one at Vannes
and one at Nantes, and Alain maintained friendly relations with his vassal
Bérenger, count of Rennes, a Frank from Neustria and brother-in-law of Judikaël.
He spent most of his time, however, at his castle in Rieux not far from the abbey of
Redon.

On Alain's death, fresh disputes erupted over the succession. Remember that
Celtic law admitted no right of primogeniture and held that any legacy should be
shared. Besides, the Breton monarch was an elected king, it being supposed that
the most capable candidate would thereby attain the throne. So when it became
clear that none of Alain's sons was sufficiently strong, the crown went to Gourme-
lon, count of Cornouaille.

There then followed one of the darkest periods in all Breton history. By signing
the treaty of St-Clair sûr Epte, Charles the Simple, king of France, had ceded to the
Norsemen of the Lower Seine the area which was to become the heart of Normandy and had effectively abandoned the whole of the Breton peninsula to the
Norsemen of the Loire. The invaders rushed into Brittany and many Bretons went
into exile. The monks sought shelter throughout France. Those from Landevennec
managed to reach Montreuil sur Mer, while others found refuge in Paris, Corbeil

and Orléans. The relics of Saint Korentin, the renowned bishop of Quimper, went to Marmoutier. The direction taken by the clergy is significant. For the French Church had a tangible influence on the Breton ecclesiastics, while the Breton nobility turned not towards France but, with some nostalgia, to the land of their origins across the Channel. Among the best known of the aristocratic emigrants was Alain the Great's son-in-law Mathuedoi, count of Poher, who took refuge in the court of the Saxon King Athelstan.

Athelstan was quick to see how much he could profit by the situation. For Mathuedoi had a son, Alain, who was grandson of Alain the Great and any encouragement Athelstan gave him would win the Saxon an opportunity to fight the Norsemen and become involved in Breton affairs. He therefore furnished Alain with an army of Saxons and with these and a troop of emigrants supplied by the abbot of Landevennec who had managed to safeguard the riches of the monastery, Alain landed at Dol in 936. The Bretons who had been waiting for just such a chance as this, rose to help him and in less than three years Alain had rid the country of Norsemen with victories at Plourivo, Nantes and Trans. Having acceded to the throne, Alain II Barbetorte did his best to repair the damage of war. For Brittany had been bled white, its towns destroyed, its monasteries looted and its countryside left deserted and fallow. War and emigration had almost halved the population and the new king's first concern was to repopulate the empty wastes, especially in Upper Brittany. He therefore agreed with Louis IV of France, with whom he had continued to maintain good relations, that any serfs who fled into Brittany from the surrounding areas should not be pursued but allowed to settle there.

Although the economic health of Brittany demanded that the land be repopulated, this move had a considerable effect on the development of the region. For the Celtic-speaking peoples gradually came to be replaced by Frankish-speakers even well to the West of the Loth Line. This was one of the reasons why Breton lost its supremacy to the Romance language almost throughout Upper Brittany. The other reason was that the Celtic nobility had emigrated as the Norse raids increased leaving the country severely underpopulated.

Alain Barbetorte, who is generally regarded as the last of the true Breton kings, died in 952 at Nantes. His son Drogon succeeded him, only to die prematurely in 958. There followed yet another dispute over the succession, this time between Alain's two illegitimate sons, Hoël and Guerec, and Conan le Tort, count of Rennes. Hoël and Guerec, both counts of Nantes, were supported by Foulques le Bon, count of Anjou, who had married Alain's widow. Conan, who also had authority over Vannes and Domnonia was supported by the count of Chartres. French influence was beginning to make itself felt in Breton politics. Conan took Nantes in 990 but two years later, on June 27, 992, he was defeated and killed at Conquereuil by Foulques Nerra, grandson of Foulques le Bon. In the end, however, Conan's son Geoffrey was recognized as duke and it was he who ensured that the originally Frankish house of Rennes continued to dominate. In an attempt to counterbalance the preponderant influence of his friend the count of Chartres, Geoffrey then married the sister of Richard of Normandy, hoping to establish closer relations with him. When Geoffrey died during the course of a pilgrimage to Rome in 1008 he was succeeded by his son Alain III who reigned until 1040. Initially Alain's mother Havoise acted as regent while the heir was still a minor. She had to deal with peasant revolt which ended in an almost total abolition of serfdom and with a conspiracy among rebellious vassals who were being encouraged by the count of Anjou. Alain III was never officially king though he acquired the nickname *Roebreiz* (King of Brittany). He made every effort to comply with the wishes of his Norman cousin and ally Robert le Diable and encountered some opposition from his own brother Eudes de Penthièvre, the founder of a line which was later to threaten Breton unity. For when Alain III died on August 1, 1040, it was Eudes who assumed the regency while Alain's son Conan II was still a child. When Conan reached his majority, Eudes conspired against him with Conan's brother-in-law, Hoël count of Cornouaille. Conan II died in 1066 and was succeeded by Hoël. This meant that the British house of Cornouaille had now acquired supremacy over the previous reigning house of Rennes just when the Normans were beginning to expand their sphere of influence.

A number of Bretons took part in the conquest of England. In fact, it is agreed that about one third of William's army at Hastings was made up of Breton nobility and foot soldiers. Many of them received land in Devon and Cornwall, just retribution it seemed for Saxon oppression of their ancestors five or six hundred years earlier, and a means not only of recovering their estates but of tightening the links between Britain and the continent. It was during this time, when the Bretons dreamt of rebuilding the old Britain, that the Arthurian myth came into being, and came to be seen as a kind of religious history for a people who had never accepted their own defeat.

This Breton concern in their own history and legend goes some way to explaining the subsequent turn of events. For in 1066, Brittany itself lost much of the Celtic life still left to it. After that date, it became increasingly French, although a few isolated individuals tried to ensure its survival as an autonomous nation.

An alliance with the Normans held out the possibility of fulfilling various hopes. The Bretons might be able to escape the influence of the Capetians once and for all. They might be able to use the Norman claim to England to make their own way there as conquerors, and even to rebuild a kind of pan-Celtic unity. The part they played in the Norman conquest of Wales and Ireland would suggest that such was indeed their hope.

But William the Conqueror was justifiably suspicious of his enthusiastic allies. He had his own dream of establishing a Norman empire from the Humber to the Garonne and fobbed off his allies with land he had confiscated from the Saxons. Alain of Penthièvre who commanded the rearguard at Hastings received one of the richest seigneuries in England, the Honour of Richmond. (In 1148 the title of Richmond became a traditional right of the dukes of Brittany.) William then crossed the sea to Brittany, supposedly to help his cousin Hoël of Cornouaille against a group of rebellious barons being led by the Penthièvre family but actually intending to extend his authority on the continent. He besieged Dol but was forced to raise the siege by Philip I of France who had no wish to see his vassal the Duke of Normandy and king of England acquire any greater authority. It was then that the Bretons realized that they had nothing to gain from alliance with the Normans but everything to win from playing on the rivalry between the Anglo-Norman and Capetian monarchs. From the 12th century onwards Breton history became a long and precarious balancing act between the two rivals.

In 1084 Hoël died and was succeeded by his son Alain IV. Generally speaking Alain IV was pro-Norman. He helped Henry I of England to recover the duchy of Normandy from his brother Robert Courteheuse in 1106. His marriage to Ermengarde, daughter of the count of Anjou had, in any case, already strengthened the ties between the ducal family of Brittany and the Anglo-Norman monarchy for

Henry I's daughter Matilda married the Angevin Geoffrey Plantagenet. The treaty of Gisors called a temporary halt to the war between the French and the Normans in 1113, for Louis VI the Fat solemnly accorded the king of England and duke of Normandy suzerainty over Brittany, which must therefore have been in the gift of the French crown. This agreement was the first in a series of events which marked a weakening of French influence over Brittany. Already in 1078, Pope Gregory VII had answered the Bretons' prayers by withdrawing the Breton Church from the metropolitan diocese of Tours and giving bishop Even of Dol the title of archbishop. That this was a great victory for the Bretons is undisputable, but there was more to Gregory's decision than meets the eye. For Rome was worried by the domestic quarrels in feudal France and was playing along with the Anglo-Normans who had proclaimed themselves maintainers of law and order. It was in the English king's interest to isolate Brittany from Touraine which was closely connected with the king of France, and he had therefore asked the pope to accede to the Bretons' wishes. A hundred years later, when the Plantagenets no longer needed a metropolitan bishop at Dol, they allowed Brittany to return to the hands of the archbishop of Tours.

In 1122, weary of government, Alain IV abdicated and retired to the abbey of Saint-Sauveur at Redon where he died in 1129. His son and heir Conan II was Henry I of England's son-in-law. Conan, however, proved very wary of the Anglo-Normans and more inclined to support the Capetians. He even fought for the French king in the Auvergne and wisely tried to maintain a policy of balance, making concessions to both sides. But his death in 1148 opened the way to a further period of conflict.

Although his daughter Berthe was officially recognized as his successor, there being no reason why women should not accede to the throne, his disappointed son Hoël began conspiring against her. Berthe's husband, Eon de Porhoët, managed to foil Hoël's schemes. But Berthe had a son, Conan, from her first marriage, and Conan was a tool in the hands of Henry II of England. Henry helped Conan to take the ducal crown by force and ensured that Brittany remained under English influence. For though Conan IV had his title, he deserved the nickname the "Little" being no more than a servant to Henry's will. He gave his daughter Constance in marriage to Henry's son Geoffrey and in 1166 was even forced to abdicate in favour of his son-in-law, ceding power to Henry himself during Geoffrey's minority. Henry had succeeded in achieving what William the Conqueror had hoped to do: he had acquired control over Brittany. He immediately set about reorganizing the peninsula and with the help of his own outstanding administrators developed the culture, economy and harbour facilities of the region. The Angevin links with the house of Cornouaille gave him a valid right to Brittany, which he reinforced by resurrecting the old Celtic dream of unity regained in the shape of Arthurian romance. If the myth of Arthur was to be embodied in a man, then he wished to be that man. That is why the 12th century tales transformed the British leader, a clan chieftain, into king of *Logres* or *Loegr,* the Welsh name for England, and gave him the status of an emperor over both Britain and the western continent of Europe. Marriage to Eleanor of Aquitaine and the manipulation of Conan IV had, after all, given Henry an empire stretching from Scotland to the Pyrenees.

When Geoffrey attained his majority, therefore, in 1182, he took over control of a solidly based and peaceful administration. What his father had not foreseen was that Geoffrey would become more Breton than the Bretons themselves. As soon as he had come to power Geoffrey cut all links between the Breton and English administrations and gave himself the right to govern Brittany as he saw fit. This naturally led to a quarrel with his father. Indeed Geoffrey was close to concluding an alliance with the delighted king of France when he died during a tournament in 1186. Geoffrey's legacy to Brittany was a legal document of great importance drawn up as the result of an agreement between himself and his chief vassals in 1185.

This document, the *Assize of Count Geoffroy,* was the result of concerted efforts on the part of Geoffrey and his father to update the shape of Breton society in a way compatible with Celtic tradition. For the Plantagenets, being Angevin and Norman rather than English or French, made no attempt to impose foreign institutions on the Armorican peninsula. On the contrary, they tried to give it its own unique features.

The *Assize of Count Geoffroy* was intended to safeguard Breton unity by stopping the division of baronies and fiefs. While highly egalitarian and democratic in concept, the Celtic custom of splitting estates between all the heirs, regardless of sex or seniority, was responsible for endless disputes over succession and the creation of large numbers of small seigniories. What was needed was a means of handing on the title to a single heir and at the same time anticipating the disappointment of any other claimants.

There were two kinds of fief in Brittany. Noble fiefs differed very little from those in the rest of Europe. But a concern for egalitarianism had meant that there were no quit-rent holdings for commoners. The peasants were given *fiefs roturiers* or *fiefs taillifs* in exchange for taxes but they and their lords were bound by a proper contract like that between a vassal and his seigneur which imposed obligations on both sides. In some cases, the seigneur was obliged to consult the peasant before taking any decision which might affect his fief, especially if his rights were to be alienated in any way.

The same almost democratic concern was evident in the institution of tenure *à domaine congéable,* one of the most original devices in Breton law which probably came from Britain since it was only really practised in the Breton-speaking areas. Under this law property was held under tenancy at will rather than being an absolute right. In this way ownership was split between the man who nominally owned the land and the tenant who cultivated it or had it cultivated and who owned the buildings. The tenant took out a lease on the land but was free not to renew it, in which case the tenant was entitled to compensation for his share of the property, and that included the buildings which he may have furnished, enlarged or even built himself. In an age when ownership lay at the basis of all social institutions throughout Europe, this was a singularly modern attitude to property; but it allowed for much wider exploitation of land, especially of land which had previously been lying fallow.

A similar arrangement, called a *tenure à quevaise,* was customary in some areas. Here, too, ownership was divided between landowner and tenant, though in this case the tenant lost his rights if he abandoned the land for more than one year and the youngest of the children inherited the estate, to the exclusion of all others. If the tenant had no children all rights reverted to the landowner.

The tenant was in no way a serf. Serfdom had vanished since the beginning of Alain Roebreiz's reign, although some customs associated with serfdom still persisted in certain areas. The seigneur still had the right of mortmain, for example, if the tenant had no children. Arbitrary poll-tax was noted in exceptional cases only.

Altogether, it seems extremely likely that 12th century Breton society was several centuries in advance of French or even English feudal societies. This being the case, the Bretons had nothing to gain by integration into the systems prevailing amongst their powerful neighbours.

The *Assize of Count Geoffroy* reduced the partition of land to a considerable extent. In the 12th century the duke of Brittany had many vassals but there were few large fiefs. The county of Vannes was the personal estate of the duke, as it had been the home of Breton unity. He also owned the former March, Rennes, Nantes and Cornouaille, leaving only Léon, Porhoët, Rohan and Penthièvre as fiefs to be held by his vassals.

When Geoffrey died, Henry II made himself personally responsible for Brittany until he, too, died not long after in 1189. The crown passed to Geoffrey's posthumous son, who had intentionally been given the name Arthur. Though a Plantagenet through his father, Arthur was a true Breton through his mother Constance and it was she who assumed power until her brother-in-law, Richard the Lionheart, returned from the Crusade. The king of England then invaded Brittany and took Constance prisoner, but not before she had entrusted her son to the care of Philip Augustus, king of France. In 1202 Philip Augustus proclaimed his hostility to John Lackland by solemnly investing Arthur as duke of Brittany and giving him whichever of John's continental possessions he was able to conquer. It was during the subsequent war that Arthur was captured by his uncle John who had him killed at Rouen on April 3, 1203 in circumstances which have remained a mystery. It is possible that John, who is known to have been cruel and unbalanced, actually murdered his nephew with his own hands. Arthur was just sixteen years old.

There were now two heirs, Alix and Alienor, the daughters of Constance and her second husband Guy de Thouard. Alix was eventually chosen as duchess by an assembly of bishops and barons, but since she was only four her parents were given the regency. The Bretons hoped to marry the young duchess to Count Henri de Penthièvre, but now that Philip Augustus had succeeded in removing Plantagenet influence, he had no wish for Brittany to remain independent. He therefore frightened the Bretons into agreeing that Alix should marry his cousin Pierre de Dreux, nicknamed "Mauclerc", the grandson of Louis the Fat, and being suspicious of Alix's advisers, he anticipated the marriage by giving Pierre the duchy in 1213. Brittany appeared to have fallen out of Plantagenet hands into the clutches of the Capetians.

However, just as Henry II's plans had been foiled by Geoffrey, so Philip Augustus was disappointed in his cousin Pierre. For although he never failed in his feudal obligations to the king of France, Pierre followed his own path. He treated his vassals with exemplary firmness and almost entirely dispossessed the count of Penthièvre whom he regarded as a dangerous rival. He also used the *Assize of Count Geoffroy* to appropriate any estates in which the title holder had died without leaving adult children, ensured that fortified castles should only be built with his permission so that he could restrict their numbers, and fostered Breton literature and culture. In short, he carried on where the Plantagenets had left off.

Although he could exact obedience from his vassals, however, Pierre was in constant conflict with the church, and it was his anticlerical attitude that won him the name "Mauclerc". Being unable to restore Dol to its metropolitan status, he condemned the clergy, which he saw as a loyal servant to the French crown for its privileges and prerogatives. Needless to say, the church retaliated with an impressive number of anathemas and threats of excommunication.

During the regency of Blanche of Castille, he formed an alliance with Thibaud of Champagne and even rendered homage to the king of England in order to obtain help from across the Channel. But the English king remained indifferent to Pierre's trifling worries and in 1234 Pierre Mauclerc had to yield. In 1237 he abdicated in favour of his son Jean whom he had married to the daughter of Thibaud of Champagne. Being then just an ordinary knight, he patched up his quarrel with Saint Louis and set off with him on a crusade. It was on his return from the Holy Land that he died in 1250. Despite his anticlericalism, he is remembered as a man of courage and piety. Among many innovations that he made, it is worth mentioning that he introduced the coat of arms which was to become the Breton symbol.

Jean I (1237-1286) reigned longer than any other Breton monarch. He was an excellent administrator, a shrewd business man, and a poet of taste and refinement. He restored the castle of Suscinio, one of his favourite residences and attempted to keep the balance between France and England. His son, Jean II (1286-1305) married the daughter of Henry III of England and was re-endowed with the Honour of Richmond. He had greater difficulty in parrying pressure from the English and French monarchs and came into conflict with the clergy, notably over questions of taxation. He was succeeded by Arthur II (1305-1312) who managed to reach a compromise with the clergy. Arthur married twice, the first time to the heiress of the Viscount of Limoges with whom he had three sons, and the second time to Yolande of Dreux, countess of Monfort-l'Amaury with whom he had five daughters and a son. Jean III (1312-1341), son of Arthur's first marriage, died without legal issue although he married three times; and as his two brothers had also died, the question of succession reared its ugly head once again.

In theory, the ducal crown should have gone to Arthur's son by Yolande, Jean de Monfort; but Jean III had hated both his step-mother and his half-brother and let it be known that he did not want him as an heir. Jean III's niece, Jeanne de Penthièvre, could have been named his successor, but the duke refused to make a cut and dried decision and died without making his choice known.

Jeanne de Penthièvre had been advised by the farsighted Philip VI of France to marry his nephew Charles of Blois, and when Jean III died, Philip urged Charles and Jeanne to claim the ducal throne on the grounds that Jeanne was granddaughter to Arthur, there being no adherence to Salic law in Brittany.

Jean de Montfort who based his claim on being Arthur's actual son, naturally repudiated Jeanne's claim, arguing, with some irony, that Salic law applied in France and that Brittany was only a fief of France. Jean took Nantes where he was proclaimed duke. He then hastened on to Limoges to seize the wealth amassed by his predecessor and within a few months he had acquired control of the chief Breton strongholds, where, to tell the truth, he was received with open arms. To ensure his future protection he then went to England and signed a treaty with King Edward III.

Philip VI was not best pleased by this turn of events. France and England were at one of the critical stages of the Hundred Years War and it seemed that Brittany had sided with the enemy. On September 7, 1341, therefore, the king's court assembled at Conflans declared Charles of Blois duke of Brittany in the name of his wife. Philip VI sent an army to support Charles and it was this army which took Nantes and captured Jean de Montfort. Order appeared to have been restored. In fact, the war over the succession was just beginning.

For Jean de Montfort was married to Jeanne of Flanders, a woman of remarkable courage and tenacity. Even though her husband was a prisoner, she tirelessly continued the fight for another twenty-four years. Opposing her stood Charles of Blois, a good and pious prince who was later beatified, but basically weak-willed; and since Charles was far more interested in his religious duties than in political or military matters, he was only too happy to obey his wife Jeanne, the tool of the king of France. The struggle over the ducal crown therefore came to be known as the "war of the two Jeannes", and indeed there was no love lost between the two women.

The Penthièvre faction was supported by the high-ranking nobles and ecclesiastics, virtually all of whom owed allegience to France and were in the pay of the French king.

The Montfort faction included all the petty nobility and most of the common people of Brittany, and could count on support from England.

Some historians have asserted, with apparently rabid anglophobia that the Montfort camp were traitors and that the real Bretons had sided with Charles of Blois. If anything, the opposite is true. Viewed from the impartiality of distance, the war over the ducal crown was just a domestic quarrel which happened to coincide with the Hundred Years War. And since only the Bretons were involved, there is no need to mention the English and the French. On closer inspection, however, we find that the Blois faction comprised the Frenchified nobility and Upper Brittany, that the Church had everything to gain by retaining French influence over the peninsula by way of the metropolitan see of Tours and that in fact the supporters of Charles were the least authentically Breton of the Bretons.

The Montforts, on the other hand, were supported by all the real Bretons, or what remained of them. While the pro-Blois camp were aristocratic and clerical, the Montfort camp, if not actually democratic, at least included the petty nobility and tenants who obstinately maintained their opposition to the French Church as the Bretons had always done.

Montfort was no more a traitor for allying himself with the English than was Jeanne de Penthièvre for her alliance with the king of France. Breton politics had for centuries been a balancing act between the two neighbouring powers, and Brittany had as many links with England as with France, if not more.

In 1352 Rennes fell into French hands. Seeking to capitalize on this victory Philip VI ordered Charles of Blois to pursue Jeanne de Montfort and take her prisoner. Jeanne had taken refuge in the fortress of Hennbont with her son, also named Jean, and with her faithful lieutenants Guillaume de Cadoudal, Yves de Trésiguidy, Henri and Olivier de Spinefort, the lords of Landerneau and Guingamp and the bishop of Léon, a traditional opponent of the authority of Tours. She had sent Amaury de Clisson to England to seek help from king Edward III whom she had recognized as king of France, at no great cost to herself.

Dazzled by his success at Rennes, where the people were mostly Francophiles in any case, Charles of Blois sent Louis of Spain to lay siege to Hennebont. Jeanne allowed the enemy forces to dig themselves in and prepared to defend the town. Some days later she led a commando raid on the French camp and succeeded in firing it, thereby earning herself the nickname "Jeanne the Flame". Louis of Spain found himself unable to attack the town, but the siege continued nonetheless. Fearing starvation the townspeople tried to persuade Jeanne to surrender, but she was waiting for the return of Amaury de Clisson and refused. When Amaury finally arrived by way of the Blavet with 6,000 English bowmen Louis fell back on Auray where Charles of Blois could do no more than pray for victory. Hennebont was therefore a defeat for the French, though not a very convincing victory for the

Montfort camp. Despite Jeanne's heroism, she had only really succeeded in bringing the English into Brittany.

A year after her success at Hennebont, Jeanne de Montfort signed a treaty with
Jeanne de Penthièvre at Malestroit in 1343, just as Edward III and Philip VI were
about to meet in battle on the banks of the Vilaine. It seems likely that the Bretons
were somewhat frightened by the new dimensions their struggle had acquired and
were playing for time in the hope that their dangerous allies would leave them
alone.

The treaty of Malestroit was continually being broken by both sides. In 1343
Jean de Montfort was freed on condition that he never set foot in Brittany again.
He promptly shut himself up in Hennebont where he died in 1345. During this
time the English expeditionary forces led by Thomas of Dagworth had pushed the
French back out of Cornouaille and Vannes and were pursuing them into Penthièvre. Charles of Blois tried to recapture la Roche-Derrien in 1347, but was
defeated and taken prisoner. Brittany was now in a state of total chaos and consisted merely of small pockets of land held variously by the Bretons, the French or
the English, none of whom could be said to be victors.

In August 1350, a small group of soldiers in the pay of Jeanne de Penthièvre
surprised Dagworth near Auray and killed him. In fact there were no regular
armies any more, but simply bands of mercenaries from various quarters who sold
themselves to the highest bidder. In 1351, the Anglo-Breton forces holding Ploërmel came to an agreement with the French forces holding Josselin that they should
settle their quarrels by a fight to the death between thirty knights from each side
half way between the two towns. The subsequent battle took place on March 26
and ended in a victory for the French under Beaumanoir. The "English" commander Bembrough was actually a Breton named Penvro.

In an attempt to find some way out of what threatened to become an inextricable
situation, Edward III conceived the plan of concluding a compromise agreement
with Charles of Blois. He therefore released him for a large ransom, but the talks
were interrupted when Jean II of France was captured at Poitiers in 1356. The
duke of Lancaster then laid siege to Rennes which held out for nine months before
being saved by Bertrand Du Guesclin.

"Messire Bertrand" was a strange figure. Legend has made him a hero of
French patriotism, and contemporary chroniclers obviously admired him greatly.
To put the picture straight, however, it should be pointed out that as a child he was
no more than the worst kind of rogue. With his band of adolescent brigands he
attacked everyone he met, whether they were travellers or merchants, French,
Breton or English, and made himself a small fortune by what was basically high-
way robbery. And as he grew older, he improved his technique and became more
ambitious. War was a business like any other, except that the stakes were higher;
so Bertrand hired out his services to those with most money to spend. Since the
French paid better than the English, he fought for the French. Then, when Charles
V, who was a good judge of men, heard of Bertrand's exploits, he realized that
there was much to be gained by an association with him and made him Constable
of France.

In 1360 the treaty of Brétigny brought an easing of tension between the English
and the French, but it did nothing to solve the Breton question and the dispute
over the dukedom threatened to continue for ever. It was then that Jean, the son of
Jean de Montfort and Jeanne of Flanders landed in Brittany in 1362. He was
twenty-three and as well as being brought up in the English king's court he was

linked to the English royal family by marriage. He had suffered cruelly from the war as a child and was determined to find a solution. He therefore contacted Charles of Blois and suggested that the two of them should partition the peninsula, Charles having the former area of Domnonia, i.e. Penthièvre and the northern half, and himself having the south, i.e. Nantes, Vannes and Cornouaille. Tired of a war which went against his religious convictions and unwilling to bear the responsibility for prolonging it, Charles was ready to accept this proposal. His wife, Jeanne de Penthièvre, however, refused point blank, which proves yet again that Charles was no more than a pawn in the game.

Since any agreement was now out of the question, the two sides prepared for a decisive encounter. Du Guesclin devastated Lower Brittany. The bulk of Charles's forces assembled at Auray together with a number of French nobles under the leadership of Du Guesclin to form an army of about four thousand horsemen and a further number of foot soldiers. Jean de Montfort realized that he would have to act quickly and if necessary take risks. He managed to muster two thousand men at arms and a thousand bowmen, and together with an English force led by Robert Knolles, he hastened towards Auray. There is a story that before the battle the greyhound which went everywhere with Charles of Blois deserted him and made for the Montfort camp. Whether or not that is true, the two sides met at the gates of Auray on September 29, 1364. According to Froissart both armies had promised to fight to the death and not take the enemy claimant prisoner so that the war could be brought to an end. Charles of Blois was killed by an English dagger and died shouting "Ha, domine deus!" Once Jeanne de Penthièvre's wretched husband had gone the French army broke ranks and Du Guesclin suffered the most mortifying defeat of his career.

After the battle Jean de Montfort came to pay homage to his rival's body and decided that a collegiate church should be built on the spot where he had fallen, by way of expiation. The church was to be dedicated to Saint Michael, the battle having taken place on Michaelmas Day. His orders were immediately carried out and the church is now known as the Chartreuse of Auray.

The war over the succession had ended. On April 12, 1365 a treaty was signed at Guerande making Jean de Montfort duke of Brittany as Jean IV. It was understood that Jeanne de Penthièvre would retain control of her county but that no woman would be able to lay claim to the ducal crown ever again. Brittany was to continue to pay homage to the king of France.

However, Jean de Montfort's adventures did not end there. At first he tried to make good some of the damage done by the war. Brittany had been badly battered and its resources were severely depleted. He had the towns rebuilt and established a magnificent castle at Vannes which became his favourite residence, though it has now disappeared. He also instituted the order of the Knights of Ermine and made the ermine the sole element in his coat of arms. But Jean had interests in England. He owed everything to the English sovereign and hoped to resume the Honour of Richmond. Edward III of England exploited the situation by forcing Jean to sign a treaty of alliance in July 1372, under which English forces were to remain permanently in Brittany.

This imposition irked the Bretons, even those who had supported Jean. They were prepared to accept English aid against the French, but in peace time they cared little for their burdensome allies. The Bretons therefore appealed to Charles V who could hardly believe his good fortune and promptly sent Bertrand Du Guesclin to take his revenge. Jean IV had to flee hurriedly to England. In 1373 the only towns left in English hands were Derval, Bécheral, Auray and Brest.

Charles V decided to push home his advantage and imitate the tactics Philip Augustus had used against John Lackland. He therefore summoned Jean IV to answer to parliament for his felony, i.e. his treaty with Edward. Naturally, Jean did not answer the summons and on December 18, 1378 parliament announced that he had forfeited his fief which thereby became the legal property of the king of France.

It was then that Charles, thinking he had won the day, made an unhappy discovery. For though the Bretons would always turn to the French when they wanted to get rid of the English, the prospect of being absorbed into France sent them running to the English again, as their only hope of remaining independent. Even the old and ever intransigent Jeanne de Penthièvre joined with the other barons in recalling Jean IV who landed at Saint Servan on August 3, 1379 to a rousing welcome.

This time the Bretons were wholly united. On March 1, 1380 Jean IV concluded an offensive and defensive alliance with Richard II, the new king of England. As the duke put it, he had "risked his life and his honour". The treaty was unanimously accepted by the Breton nobility, but before a full blown war could develop Charles V died in September 1380 and Charles VI's uncles were anxious to settle the affair. On April 4, 1381, therefore, a second treaty was signed at Guérande, under which Jean IV promised to ask Charles VI's pardon, to recognize him as his liege lord and to expel his English advisers.

Even now the struggle continued. For when Du Guesclin had died in 1380, his position as Constable had passed to Olivier de Clisson, formerly one of the Montforts' most ardent supporters. Clisson distrusted Jean IV whom he accused of anglophilia though he spent much of his time among the duke's followers. But then Clisson was paying court to Jean IV's pretty, young, third wife, Jeanne of Navarre. The quarrel between Clisson and Jean erupted into violence when the duke arranged that his rival be killed in an ambush at Vannes in 1387 and when that failed in Paris in 1392. It was to avenge these unsuccessful attempts on his Constable that Charles VI mounted an expedition to Brittany, during which he went suddenly insane in the forest of Le Mans.

Clisson, meanwhile, had extricated himself from the situation by marrying Marguerite de Rohan, and his sister Margot had married Charles of Blois' son, the count of Penthièvre. Jean IV's emotional quarrel with Clisson now became a political matter as well, for the duke invaded the county of Penthièvre. In the end, the two rivals were solemnly reconciled in 1395 and on November 1, 1399 Jean de Montfort died at Nantes.

The Montfort dynasty was firmly entrenched. Although Jean IV had only ever borne the title of duke he had acted like a king. Despite his recognition of the French king as liege lord he had assumed control of the courts which should by rights have remained with the French crown. Brittany negotiated directly with foreign powers, which was clear proof of its virtually total autonomy. Indeed the 15th century marked the height of Breton independence, with the country managing to keep out of the terrible conflict which scarred the end of the Hundred Years War. It seemed that Brittany had at long last found the correct balance and that it was on its way to becoming a great modern state.

Despite the fact that his mother Jeanne de Navarre married Henry IV of England, Jean de Montfort's son, Jean V, managed to remain totally neutral as far as the Anglo-French conflict was concerned. The Bretons intervened only to help their Welsh brothers who had rebelled against the English, and despite promises to send a contingent to the king of France they arranged for this force to arrive after the battle of Agincourt, so that they were not involved in the French defeat. In 1423 Jean V made an alliance with Philip the Good, duke of Burgundy and with the English regent, the duke of Bedford, so as to forestall any attempt on Brittany by the supporters of Charles the Dauphin. As Margot de Clisson, a worthy heiress to the Penthièvres, had been plotting against him, he finally confiscated the Penthièvre estates.

Within the dukedom, Jean V did much to encourage the arts and it was during his reign that all the churches and chapels of which Brittany has every reason to be proud came into being. Jean died at Nantes on August 28, 1442, leaving three sons, François, Pierre and Gilles. François I (1442-1450) quarrelled with the English and hounded his younger brother Gilles who he thought had sold out to them. Gilles died of starvation in a dungeon in the castle of Hardouinaye. As François had no sons, he was succeeded by his brother Pierre II (1450-1457), and when Pierre died, also without male issue, the ducal crown passed to his uncle Arthur III of Richmond, brother of Jean V, who was Constable of France.

Arthur III was on very good terms with the French king, whom he had served on several occasions, and despite his advanced age he proved an excellent prince. He profited by his happy relations with France to further his policy of Breton emancipation from the French crown and when he came to pay homage to the king of France on October 14, 1458, he stood before the French monarch with his sword at his side. This lack of obeisance was contrary to normal practice and placed Brittany virtually on an equal footing with France. In December 1458 Arthur died and was replaced by his nephew François II, son-in-law to François I.

François II was a champion of Breton independence and built on the political achievements of his predecessors. He succeeded in winning the pope's permission for a university at Nantes, though it should perhaps be pointed out that the papacy was unhappy about the Gallicanist tendencies of the French Church and anxious to remove the peninsula from the influence of Angers and Paris. François called himself "Duke by the grace of God" and based his actions on the activities of Charles le Téméraire, duke of Burgundy, who was continually rebelling against the authority of the French crown. The treaty of Arras had exempted the duke of Burgundy from paying homage and François may well have wished that the duke of Brittany might enjoy similar privileges. In 1468 he signed a treaty with Charles and Edward IV of England. On Charles' death he drew even closer to the English, and in 1481 he agreed that they and the Bretons should be eternal allies and that his daughter Anne should marry the Prince of Wales. At this, Louis XI, who considered Brittany just as great a threat to him as Burgundy, bought the rights to the succession from the heiress of the Penthièvres.

François II had two important ministers. The first, his chancellor Guillaume Chauvin, supported the idea of an agreement with France. The second, his treasurer Pierre Landais, opposed this view, and it was he who eventually won the day. Landais had Chauvin arrested in 1481 but himself fell to a conspiracy among the nobility in 1485. With his right hand man gone and the English prudently waiting to see what would happen next, François promised the hand of his daughter Anne to Archduke Maximilian of Austria, King of the Romans, heir to the Habsburg empire and son-in-law to Charles of Burgundy. He then took part in the celebrated "mad war" against the regent Anne de Beaujeu. She sent an army to take Nantes in 1487, but despite a defeat in that year she persevered and on July 28, 1488, the French army under La Trémoille won a victory at Saint-Aubin du Cormier. This was the beginning of the end. On August 19, François II signed the treaty of le Verger by which he undertook not to marry his daughters without the king's consent. On September 19, he died heartbroken.

There were now no male heirs to the house of Montfort and the only possible successor was Anne, then aged eleven, a cripple but an intelligent and stubborn girl who was well aware of the responsibility falling on her shoulders. Obviously her choice of husband was to be crucial. She already had two official fiancés, the Prince of Wales and Archduke Maximilian, and now the king of France was preparing to enter the ranks. Despite her advisers' counsel, and the treaty of Le Verger, Anne decided to marry Maximilian and in December 1490 a wedding by proxy was celebrated.

This was a slap in the face for the king of France who immediately sent an army to Brittany under La Trémoille. Rennes fell into French hands on November 15, 1491, and with it came Anne. An assembly of legists and bishops in the pay of the French king promptly declared Anne's marriage to Maximillian null since it had not been consummated, the couple never having seen each other, and Anne was married to Charles VIII.

Anne had no choice but to agree, though in all fairness it should be said that she had mustered all her considerable intelligence to retain some control over her future. It was agreed that if the very sickly Charles VIII should die without children then Anne should marry his successor and that she and her husband should have equal rights over Brittany which should pass to the other in the event of one's death; Charles having inherited the rights to Penthièvre.

The Viscount of Rohan rebelled at the news of the marriage but was defeated. Then on April 18, 1498, Charles VIII died and was succeeded by Louis XII. Louis, however, was already married and therefore unable as Charles' successor to marry Anne. She therefore returned to Brittany as her own mistress and mistress of the duchy, for by virtue of her agreement with Charles she had inherited his rights to Penthièvre on his death. Anne was now therefore duchess in her own right and had coins minted in her name. The Breton problem appeared to have been solved, for the time being at least.

Meanwhile the French king's advisers were racking their brains to find some solution advantageous to the French. It was conveniently discovered that Louis XII's previous marriage had been contracted by force, not true, of course, but the only way out of the situation. Some of the Breton nobles murmured that if that was the case then Anne's marriage to Charles could equally well be described as forced. But they were silenced and Louis' marriage was declared canonically null and void, a decision assisted by the fact that he had no children.

Lacking any further reason for refusal, Anne married Louis XII at Nantes on January 8, 1499. But she was older now, and wiser, and demanded various conditions. She was to keep the title duchess of Brittany in her own right and Louis was to solemnly promise to respect the liberties, institutions and customs of the duchy. In no way was the king of France to be master of Brittany, at least in theory, and the duchy was to remain the property of Anne.

In 1501 Anne went even further and succeeded in getting the king to agree that her daughter Claude should inherit the duchy and should marry Maximilian's grand-son, later Charles V. Louis XII later realized that he had been foolish to agree to this and demanded that Claude marry François of Angoulême, the heir presumptive to the French throne. Anne was furious. She left court and returned to Brittany where she was received with great ceremony. Once again she sought to retain Breton independence and forced Louis to agree that if she were to marry again and have a son, then Claude would lose all rights to the duchy. Unfortunately Anne died on January 9, 1514. A year later, Claude's husband François became king of France as François I. Though Claude was still duchess of Brittany in her own right, she, too, died in 1524 and the title passed to the dauphin. Realizing that this unsatisfactory form of succession might continue for some time, François decided to force the situation. By spending lavishly in the right places he ensured that the Breton body politic would request a total union with the kingdom of France on August 4, 1532, at Vannes. On August 13 the king published an edict approving this resolution by which he was officially recognized as the person of a Brittany *united under certain conditions with the kingdom of France but not subject to it* which was to enjoy special rights and privileges.[6]

Independent Brittany, the last of the Celtic principalities, had had its day. It gradually merged into the developing state of France. Throughout the pre-Revolutionary period the treaty of Union was more or less respected, but after the Revolution it became clear that Brittany was a second-class region. Though favoured by Napoleon III, by the end of the 19th century Brittany was a byword for backwardness, a laughing stock to the average Frenchman. Doubtful jokes about the Bretons were made, such as "Potatoes for the pigs, peelings for the Bretons" or "The Bretons are born and die in cupboards" (a reference to their cupboard-beds). The Breton in his big clogs was the archetypal simpleton who *"baragouinait"* when he joined the army, meaning that he could only ask for bread *(bara)* and wine *(gwin)*. Little wonder that the Bretons themselves formed demonstrations and separatist movements. A more serious example of discrimination occurred during the Franco-Prussian War of 1870 when an army of Bretons was formed only to be abandoned without provisions to the cold and mud of the camp at Conlie, for fear that they were insurgents. Even so, the Bretons continued to fight for the French. About 300,000 of them were killed in the First World War, fully justifying the claims made by the marquis of Estourbeillon, supported by Marshall Foch and the Breton bishops, that the treaty of 1532 should be revived. This move provoked considerable response and led to the founding of a Breton Nationalist Party in 1930 and the announcement of an autonomist national council in 1940.

The trend has now been reversed and Brittany today appears to enjoy a privileged position, in some areas at least. There has been a rebirth of folk-lore in the area; Celtic studies are now recognized at university level and the Breton language is respected once more. We have come a long way since the days when Francisque Sarcey condemned himself out his own mouth with the laughable statement that "the Lower Loire is the most reactionary district because Breton is spoken there!"[7]

And we have come a long way since the days of the late 19th century when children were punished for speaking a single word of Breton, when Jacques Le Maréchal, a poet born in Pluvigner in 1877 who adopted the pen-name *Blei-Lannvaus* (the Wolf of Lanvaux) and wrote the celebrated song *Kousk Breiz-Izel* (Sleep, Lower Brittany) was prepared to admit in a poem:

> *A oe oen me en armeien,*
> *Pautred Paris doh me cheleu*
> *e lare d'ein get fal seleu:*
> *— Ma tahlet de gonz brehonek,*
> *ni ia de hrouait t'oh peg.*

(When I was in the army, the lads in Paris who heard me disparaged me and said "If you don't stop speaking Breton, we'll shut your mouth for you!")

But then, with the humour so characteristic of the Breton, the poet quietly adds:

En Diaul n'en des bishoah disket
konzein er breton a Huened;
a ben bras e zou ré galet.
Lavar ker spis pautred Paern
n'zn de ket konzet en ihuern

(The devil could never learn to speak the Breton of Vannes. His big head is much too thick. The pure, clean speech of the lads of St-Patern is not spoken in hell.)

CHAPTER ELEVEN

Taliesin and Druidism

Sacrifice

THE act of sacrifice occupies an important position in every religion, but our present day conception of it appears to be a modification of its original meaning which has gradually altered over the centuries.

For the word sacrifice actually derives from *sacrum facere* which means "to make sacred" and was used to describe any act of self-transcending through which the individual sought to attain the divine. It has now come to denote very little more than the killing of an animal or a man as an offering to the divinity either by way of supplication or thanksgiving; and Christianity has further devalued the word by associating it with notions of austerity and self-denial.

To regard sacrifice as a synonym for mortification is a serious error, since it totally alters the nature of that spiritual process by which the Ancients sought to fulfil their destiny. Ritual sacrifice was never intended to deprive creation for the sake of the creator. The Gallic chief Brennus gave a lucid and accurate account of its real meaning during the Celtic expedition to Delphi when he uttered the supposedly impious comment that "The gods had no need of treasures since they showered them upon men" (Justin, XXIV, 6).

Sacrifice was first and foremost a psychic procedure in which the sacrificial "victim" threw off the burden of earthly dross and rose through a series of stages in his attempt to reach the divinity. This divinity might be the Perfect Being, the Great Mother, an objective god or some concept of the ideal which was inherent in the individual.

It is this sense of sacrifice which motivates the Courtly Love of the 12th and 13th century Round Table romances, a subject brilliantly explored in Denis de Rougemont's *L'Amour et l'Occident*. The sacrifice of Lancelot, as described by Chrétien de Troyes, is a series of acts through which the hero seeks to win favour with Guinevere, his Lady or *Domina*, the feminine aspect of the divine powers which the Hindus call *sakti*.

Every sacrifice, however, presupposes some kind of initiation or beginning and this initiation is deliberately given an outward sign in baptism, the starting point of the sacrificial process. The baptism of Jesus by John the Baptist is both a transmission of the sacred powers which stretch back in a golden chain to the dawning of mankind and the first step on the road to Golgotha. Perceval's crossing the bridge as he leaves his mother's house is the first act in a ritual which will lead the hero to the Grail.

Traditionally the models to be followed are always divine. Whether he be a god-made-man or the archetypal sacrificial hero-made-god, the divinity stands as an example to mankind. "I am the light of the world," said Jesus. "He that followeth me shall not walk in darkness but shall have the light of life." (*St John* VIII, 12.) The legendary hero is the man who comes through the initiatory journey to complete the sacrifice and in so doing directs others in the path they must follow.

The original act of sacrifice, then, was a process of self-identification with the divinity. It is this act which the Catholic priest performs during the mass. As Plutarch points out in his treatise on the *E of Delphi*, however, wise men seek to hide the truths from the masses and resort to fable as a means of preserving a tradition accessible only to the initiate. For the truths are not always to be lavished upon the common herd, and the means used can be both positive and negative in their effect. They may lead those who use them thoughtlessly and clumsily to unforseeable disasters. They way to hell is paved with good intentions.

The need to follow the correct procedure underlies the sin committed by Adam and Eve. "If you eat of this fruit," says the serpent, the initiator, "you will be as gods." First Eve and then Adam allow themselves to be persuaded, but because they are too impatient to properly observe the ritual of initiation they fail. Their crime is not that they wished to be god's equal but that they acted heedlessly. The importance attached to this, the original sin, and the myth to which it gave rise are evidence of the wise men's desire to prevent the masses from considering any such error themselves.

For sacrifice requires the total gift of self, an offering which man has never been prepared to make. The fulfilment of this gift makes the victim or offering divine and enables him to discover himself transcendentally and to reveal himself to others. In his last hours Jesus appears to have failed. He is no more than a heaving body on the brink of oblivion. But when he dies, the earth quakes, darkness falls, the veil of the temple is rent in twain. When the Irish mythological hero Cú Chulainn, victor over so many armies, eventually falls under the blows of enemies weaker than himself, the hero-light shines on his forehead at the moment of death. Fulfilment is always made manifest in some extraordinary phenomenon.

Plutarch says as much in his *Dialogue on the Disappearance of the Oracles* (XVIII).

The narrator has landed on one of those island at the ends of the earth where strange people live. "Soon after his arrival, there was a great disturbance in the atmosphere . . . the winds roared and the storm raged. When calm had returned the people of the island said that one of the higher beings had just died . . . Just as a lighted lamp causes no trouble but can inconvenience many people when it goes out, so great souls, while they still shine, have a brilliance which is not harmful but beneficent, but when they are extinguished and die, rouse the wind and storm.

The human victim burnt at the stake, whether in Gaul or elsewhere, was, therefore, made sacred and divine, and those who sacrificed him knew this. It is wrong to suppose that they were trying to appease an angry god or win divine favour; for there was a more complex process involved. The victim was a messenger for the community fulfilling the ritual, a messenger whose association with the divinity would make him a link between that particular god and mankind. The same appeal to an intercessor is evident in the worship of Christian saints.

This kind of sacrifice is also part of the traditional alchemy practised by men like Nicholas Flamel, Raymond Lulle or Basile Valentin. The quest for gold by way of the Philosopher's Stone is only a material cover for the real *Oeuvre,* the metamorphosis of the individual. The many people who have practised alchemy solely in the hope of material gain have inevitably failed. The sceptical would seem entitled to claim that alchemical science is so much nonsense.

Legend contains many illustrations of sacrifice. The myth of Osiris offers possibly the clearest image of that metamorphosis which takes place in the sacrificed man. Osiris is dismembered by Set and the pieces of his body are scattered throughout the world until Isis, the Universal Mother and *Natura Naturans,* reconstitutes his body and restores him to a new life. Osiris the setting sun, the material sun, becomes Osiris the black sun, the spiritual sun of the Other World.

According to the indiscreet revelations of Apuleius, the dismemberment and reconstitution of Osiris formed the basis of initiation into the mysteries of Isis. The neophyte had first to undergo a period of preparatory retreat with daily attendance at the services held in Isis' honour, and to dream every night of the goddess. The high priest would then read him the sacred books and give him instructions "which the human voice cannot express". Similarly, in the Celtic world, Taliesin speaks of his initiation into the mysteries of Keridwen by saying;

> While I was a prisoner, sweet inspiration filled me
> and my laws were given to me in a language without
> words.
> (*The Hall of Keridwen,* J.M. p. 96)

Once his education was complete, the novice in the religion of Isis received baptism and spent ten days fasting. Then came the final moment when the new member was led into the heart of the sanctuary where he put on a linen robe. And there a mysterious ceremony took place. What follows is spoken by Lucius, Apuleius' mouthpiece and the hero of *Metamorphoses or the Golden Ass.* "I approached the bounds of death, I trod the threshold of Proserpine and I returned through all the elements. In the middle of the night I saw the sun shine in its dazzling brightness. I looked the gods of hell and the gods of heaven in the face. I worshipped them from close by. That is all I can tell you. But there is no use your hearing my words, you cannot understand them." (Apuleius, *The Golden Ass,* XI.)

Taliesin also speaks of metamorphoses through the elements:

> I have adopted a multitude of appearances
> before acquiring my final form ...
> *(Cad Goddeu)*

Apuleius' work contains much that is of interest. The narrator, Lucius, who has come to Hypata to learn about magic, asks his mistress Photis to let him watch his hostess Pamphilia at her spells. Carefully hidden, he sees her cover her body with ointment and turn into an owl. He begs Photis to get him some of this ointment but she, like Brangwen in the romance of *Tristan,* chooses the wrong vessel, and Lucius is turned into a donkey. After various trials and tribulations the donkey Lucius arrives in Egypt where he prays to the Great Goddess: "Queen of Heaven, whether you be Ceres the nurse ... who now haunts the Fields of Eleusis; or celestial Venus ... or the sister of Phoebus ... or terrible Proserpine with her nocturnal howls and her triple face ... you who spread your female light over all the city walls, who nurture with your damp rays the fertile semen and who dispense in your solitary evolutions a dim radiance, by whatever name, by whatever rite, in whatever form it is lawful to invoke you ..." The goddess Isis grants Lucius' prayer and eventually regains human form and devotes himself to her worship.

There are three aspects of this tale to be considered. The first is Lucius' migrations after his unfortunate transformation into a donkey. For migrations of this kind also occur in the poems and legend of Taliesin. Secondly there is Isis, the great universal, female face of the divinity who is both herself and all other goddesses. Lucius' devotion to her is the devotion required of a knight to his Lady by the rules of Courtly Love. By restoring him to human form Isis becomes Lucius' mother just as she becomes Osiris' mother by giving him new life. Taliesin, too, owes his rebirth to Keridwen who is actually his mother. Lastly there is the sacred vessel which is not intended for Lucius. For just as Tristan and Yseult drink a potion which was not meant for them, just as Taliesin drinks the three drops of the cauldron which were not meant for him, so Lucius covers himself with the wrong ointment.

The ways of achieving sacrifice, or metamorphosis, are endless, though two in particular seem to stand out. The example set by the saints and elders of all religions show that it is possible to sacrifice oneself through meditation and patience, through a slow psychic transformation process. The monastic life is one road to sanctity, and sanctity is the highest form of sacrifice. The alchemists call this the *Long Way.*

Totally different is the *Ars brevis,* or alchemical *Short Way.* This, the most dangerous of all paths, is also the Royal Way, the Heroes' Way. Though the speediest form of sacrifice, it necessitates external intervention and is bound to end in bloodshed, either actually or by proxy. The sacrificial victim journeys along the Short Way. When Galahad cures the sick, old King Evallach, he kills him; and this death is material proof of the metamorphosis taking place.

For, as all world religions have held, sacrifice is no more than metamorphosis. The true problem posed by the nature of the change is summarized in the treatise on the *E of Delphi,* by Plutarch, himself a Delphic priest. "The divinity is by nature incorruptible and eternal, but it undergoes certain transformations under the influence of fate and of an ineluctable law. Sometimes it is enflamed into fire and assimilates all substances into itself. Sometimes it diversifies into all kinds of different forms, qualities and conditions as is the present case, and it then constitutes what we call world ... When the transformation of the gods ends in the ordering of the world ... wise men describe the changes undergone by innuendo as being a tearing apart and a dismemberment ... and they tell of certain divine deaths and disappearances, then of rebirths and regenerations, all mythological tales which are merely obscure allusions to the changes of which I have been speaking."

Plutarch's ideas are very close to the Hindu concept of creation as being a rhythmic cycle, starting with *Akâsa,* the infinite substance from which *Prâna* or energy is drawn, and ending in *mahâ-pralaya,* the great decomposition in which the world is reabsorbed into the divinity until a new cosmic egg can be hatched. This pattern of creation can be seen in a wide variety of traditions, and not necessarily in cases where one civilization has influenced another or shares a common origin with another. Apart from the Indo-European language, the Celts had no direct links with the Indians, and any attempt to compare the two might lead to artificial syncretism.[1]

Wherever Plutarch found his ideas, they do highlight the essence of all metaphysical traditions. The sacrifice of a god, or of a hero, as described in every mythology, is merely the accomplishment of certain metamorphoses. Since death is merely a phase of the metamorphosis, ritual sacrifice is a re-enactment on the individual level, of the divine transformations taking place on the cosmic plane. This appears to be the underlying significance of all the metamorphoses to be found in the poetry and legends of the Celts. We should not take such incidents solely as evidence of a Celtic belief in metempsychosis, as so many have done[2], for what they really show is that myths were used to illustrate realities almost too difficult for the human mind to grasp. That is why God tells Moses; "Charge the people, lest they break through unto the Lord to gaze, and many of them perish." (*Exodus,* XIX, 12.) That is why when Galahad is allowed to see the Grail he cries; "All the veils are rent, the secret of universal life is revealed," and dies, unable to bear the blinding truth.

The Story of Taliesin

All the Celtic myths concerning unearthly migrations and metamorphoses acquire a definitive form in the story and in the very person of Taliesin.

If we think of Taliesin as a real man we imagine him to be a poet or bard who had given his name to a number of poems described by Joseph Loth as "in some respects possibly the strangest in Welsh literature". An examination of the language used in these poems makes it clear that the verses attributed to Taliesin were written at widely differing periods, which suggests that none of them is authentic. In fact there is no strictly historical proof that a man named Taliesin ever existed.

And yet he remained a figure of extraordinary renown in Wales over several centuries. The texts gathered together in the *Iolo Manuscripts* (a collection of ancient manuscripts published by Iolo Morganawc in the 19th century) which vary considerably in age, suggest that Taliesin was a 6th century bard. Allusions to Irish mythology in his verses are taken as proof that he was captured by Irish pirates and spent some time among the Gaels. Then, having escaped, he is supposed to have come back to Wales where he became bard to Elffin, son of King Uryen Rheged, or possibly, to judge from the poems in praise of Uryen, bard to Uryen himself. Taliesin was then given the supreme title of *pennbardd,* "chief of bards", and is also said to have been a member of the quasi-mythical court of King Arthur.

He is even supposed to have been converted to Christianity by St David, apostle to the Welsh.

Some authors claim that after Arthur's death, Taliesin sought refuge in Armorica with St Gildas who had just founded an abbey on the Rhuys peninsula. This particular tradition was reworked by Geoffrey of Monmouth, the originator of Arthurian romance, in his *Vita Merlini*, where he makes *Thelgesinus* Merlin's disciple. Folklore, too, has contributed to the legend by placing Taliesin's grave in Wales on the Machynlleth road near a hamlet called Tre-Taliesin. The supposed grave itself is a mound surrounded by two circles of stones and the local inhabitants were said to have claimed that whoever spent a night on the mound would wake up either a poet or a madman.[3]

Attempts to give Taliesin a historical background are fairly vague and limited and prove nothing at all. They may well have been made *a posteriori* by rationalistic scholars who wanted to explain the bard's legend and sought information from the poems.

When it comes to the point the legend itself is much more interesting, partly as an aid to examination of the "Taliesin myth" and partly because it matches the poetry attributed to the bard so closely. It matters little that the poems themselves were written at different times and by different authors, for what is important is that they all rose from the idea of the *pennbardd* Taliesin, "a personification of human knowledge and, more particularly, of a great religious, poetical and scientific organization: he is druidism made man".[4]

The legend of Taliesin is contained in an 18th century manuscript,[5] and though composed at a later date than the poems it is based on, may be regarded as an authentic representation of the traditions prevailing in the Middle Ages. The "Story of Taliesin" is therefore a valuable aid to any study of druidism, or certainly of the medieval view of druidism which belonged to a time when relatively unadulterated traces of ancient Celtic thought could still be found in predominantly Celtic countries.

The *Story of Taliesin* starts with a scene of classic witchcraft. "At that time there lived at Penllyn a man of high rank named Tegid Voel [The Bald], whose house was in the middle of Lake Tegid. His wife, Keridwen, gave birth to a son named Morvran ab Tegid, and a daughter named Creirwy who was the loveliest girl in the world. Now they had a brother, Afang-Du, who was the least favoured of all men. The Keridwen, his mother, thought that it was unfitting to send him into noble society because of his ugliness unless he had some great merit and some rare knowledge ...

> Keridwen therefore decided to follow the art of the books of Fferyllt [Metal-Worker], and boil up a cauldron of inspiration and knowledge for her son, so that his entrance into human society would be honourable because of his knowledge of the mysteries of the future state of the world. Then she began to boil the cauldron. It was not to cease boiling for a year and a day until the three magic drops of grace and inspiration were obtained.
>
> She told Gwyon Bach, son of Gwreang of Llanfair in Kaereiniawn in Powys, to watch over the cauldron and a blind man named Morda to keep the fire going beneath it. She asked them to ensure that it continued to boil for a year and a day. She herself went out every day during the hours of the planets to gather all kinds of magic herbs in

accordance with the books of the astrologers. Now one evening towards the end of the year, as Keridwen was gathering plants and uttering incantations, three drops of the magic liquid happened to spill from the cauldron and fell on the finger of Gwyon Bach. Because they were so hot, he put his finger to his mouth, and the very moment the magical drops reached it, he could see the whole future and knew that he would have to beware Keridwen's tricks, for she was very cunning. Seized by an irrepressible fear, he fled towards his homeland. And the cauldron broke in two because all the liquid it contained, apart from the three magical drops, was poisoned.

There are a few minor points of interest in this first part of the story. Keridwen, or Ceritwen, or Cyrritwen, is reminiscent of the Roman Ceres and Greek Kore. The name itself may come from *ceres,* meaning "head", or *cerus,* an ancient word meaning "god" which would make Keridwen *cerrita,* the woman possessed by god. It is equally possible that the name is linked with the Indo-European root KER meaning "to grow, to become powerful" which has given us Cerunnos and crown.

Of Keridwen's children, Creirwy ("Jewel") is one of the three lovable women of Britain (Triad 87, *Mab.* II, 287), her lover being Garwy, son of Gereint; Morvran ("Sea-Crow") is one of the three survivors of the battle of Camlann, and Afang-Du ("Black Beaver") is the mythological monster already mentioned in an earlier chapter on the Submerged Town.

Morda's blindness may well mean that he is a druid, since legendary tales contain frequent references to blind druids. Like the priest the druid is a "seer" of the Other World.

When we return to the *Story of Taliesin,* we find that the tone changes at this point from one of fairy-tale to one of epic.

At this point Keridwen returned and saw that her year's work had been wasted. She snatched up a block of wood and struck the blind Morda with it until his eyes fell out onto his cheeks. And he said; "You have disfigured me for no reason, for I am innocent." "You are right," said Keridwen. "Gwyon Bach is the guilty one." So she ran after Gwyon Bach as fast as she could. He saw her and changed into a hare so that she could not catch him; but she changed into a greyhound and caught up with him. Then he ran towards the river and became a fish. But Keridwen chased him under the water in the form of an otter, so that he had to change into a bird of the air. She then followed him in the form of a falcon and harassed him in the sky. And just as he was about to fall upon him and he thought his end had come, he saw a heap of corn which had just been threshed on the roof of a barn. He hastened there and changed himself into a grain of corn. But Keridwen took the form of a high-combed black hen and swallowed him. And, so the story goes, she became pregnant. When the time came for her to be delivered, she did not have the courage to kill the child because of his beauty. That is why she put him in a leather bag and threw the bag into the sea, thanks be to God, on April 29.

Two days later, on May 1, the great Celtic fire festival of Beltaine, young Elffin, son of Gwyddno, joins in the traditional angling expedition held on that day, although his reputation for bad luck makes it certain that his net will be empty. Indeed, he does not catch any fish, but he does find the leather bag containing the infant Taliesin who though newborn can speak and prophesy. And it is Elffin who rears the child. The explanation given for this episode is that Taliesin escaped from the Irish pirates by jumping from their boat into a little leather coracle he had noticed floating empty on the sea. He rowed for shore and caught the coracle on a piece of wood from which he was rescued by Elffin *(Iolo Manuscripts)*.

Naive as it may at first appear, the tale of Taliesin's birth does contain a number of themes common to other traditions. Firstly there is the cauldron-cum-container of wisdom. Secondly we find metamorphoses on land (the hare), in water (the fish), in the air (the bird) and finally in fire (the corn). For the sheaf of wheat is analogous with divine fire and the black hen is she who devours the fire in order to transform herself through the elements. Lastly there is fertilization by mouth (a common feature of other Celtic tales) which leads on to the future hero's unusual birth and the theme of the child on the waters which belongs both to obstetrics and psychoanalysis, and even to the biblical Moses.

> For nine months I was flat
> in Keridwen's womb.
> I was Gwyon once
> and now I am Taliesin
> *(Former Lives,* J.M. 99)

Gwyon Bach, the "Little Wiseman", is therefore dismembered, torn into several parts. Like Apuleius' Lucius he passes through all the elements after the initiation of the magic drops. Once purified, his nature transcends itself and is reabsorbed into the unity represented by the grain of corn, the first element and the last, life and death. Then Keridwen, the Mother Goddess and Mother Earth, swallows him. He decomposes only to be reborn as the New Being, the infant who is rescued by Elffin on the festival of the sun god Belenos (the Shining One) and receives the name Taliesin (Shining Forehead?) as he becomes the wisest and most skilful of men. In one way, Gwyon's sacrifice has given him an identity with the divine fire or spirit of god as symbolized by the corn. The spirit fertilizes Keridwen, the earth goddess and thus mother of the wheat, and so becomes both her husband and her son.

The cauldron theme, which foreshadows the myth of the Grail, provides a basis for many Celtic tales and is reflected in historical references to sacred cauldrons like that of the Cimbri. Taliesin makes constant allusions to the cauldron of inspiration:

> Eminent when they sprayed from the cauldron,
> the three inspirations of Gogyrwen.
> (The King's Seat, *Book of Taliesin,* XV)

> I was gifted with genius
> by the cauldron of Keridwen.
> *(Former Lives,* J.M. 95)

But this cauldron does not merely provide inspiration:

This was the first word uttered from the cauldron.
It was gently heated by the breath of nine girls.
Is it not the cauldron of the Master of the Abyss?
(*The Spoils of the Abyss,* J.M. 84)

The Master of the Abyss is Pwyll, the Other World hero whom Arthurian romance transformed into Pelles, the wealthy Fisher-King and guardian of the Grail. Pwyll also bears all the features of Teutates whom Caesar and the Romans called Dispater, and Teutates is the Father God, the Lord over Life and Death. Both Teutates and the cauldron theme are depicted on the famous Gundestrup Cauldron found in the land of the Cimbri and now housed in the National Museum of Copenhagen. Marginal comments on one of the manuscripts of Lucan's *Pharsalia* tell how sacrifices to Teutates were made by immersing a man's head in a basin until he was asphyxiated.[6] And the Gundestrup Cauldron contains a remarkable illustration of this act of sacrifice, with additional elements which offer further indications as to its meaning.[7]

In the bottom right hand corner of one plate on the cauldron stand three men facing left and blowing trumpets shaped like horses' heads. To the left of them a man is depicted walking towards the left with his sword on his shoulder and a boar on his helmet. In front of him there are six men also walking towards the left, their swords raised in their right hands and their shields held diagonally across their bodies in their left hands. These six have nothing on their helmets but a sunlike circle in the centre of their shields. All these figures are half the height of the actual plate.

On the left hand side, the whole height of the plate is taken up by an enormous figure who stands plunging a warrior head down into a kind of cauldron. Under the cauldron is an animal, almost certainly a dog or wolf, with its two front paws raised. Above the walking figures, four horsemen ride towards the right of the plate, as if returning from the place of sacrifice. The first and third of these carry spears in their left hands, and all of them have something on their helmets, one a kind of letter "M", the second a horned emblem, the third a boar and the fourth a bird. The horses have lotus-like leaves on their trappings. In front of the horsemen is a snake with a ram's head, apparently leading the procession.

Horizontally across the middle of the plate, between the two sets of figures there is a tree with seven three-petalled flowers or three-lobed leaves on its upper side, six on the lower and one at the end. To the left the tree has three roots which seem almost to be growing from the cauldron.

The significance of this scene is fairly clear. The walking warriors with nothing on their helmets are moving leftwards towards the sinister side. The large figure, the lord of the cauldron, is Teutates or Pelles, or Pwyll, or Bran, who is immersing them in the basin. The resuscitated warriors then ride off towards the right led by the ram-headed snake which is a symbol of reproductive fertility. We can even identify the flowers of immortality on their horses and the Tree of Life and Death which recurs in the strangest of all Taliesin's poems, the *Cad Goddeu*.

This cauldron which restores to life belongs to Bran. "I will give you a cauldron, the property of which is this: take a man who has been slain today and throw him into it, and tomorrow he will fight as well as ever, only he will not be able to speak." *(Branwen.)* It is the same cauldron which amazes Peredur, the Welsh Perceval. "He saw a horse approaching with a body laid across its saddle. One of the women rose and took the body from the saddle and bathed it in a tub of warm water that was near the door and then she rubbed it with precious ointment, whereupon the man rose alive and went to Peredur, greeting him and making him welcome." *(Peredur.)*

The cauldron of rebirth is also part of other Indo-European traditions. Pindar tells how Pelops was cut into pieces and boiled up in a cauldron then put back together again before Clotho, the god of birth, brought him back to life from the cauldron *(Olympics* I, 40). Even in Rome there was a story about a man named Valesius whose children were dying during an epidemic. Valesius heard a voice saying to him; "Make them drink the hot water on the altar of Pluto and Proserpine". And this remedy cured them *(Valerius-Maximus* II, 4).

Even closer to the tale of Taliesin is the story of Kvasir as told in Germano-Scandinavian mythology. When the Aesir and the Vanir seek to end their war, they all spit into the same vase and from their saliva a man, Kvasir, is born so wise (like Taliesin) that there is no question in the world he cannot answer. But two dwarfs kill him, collect his blood in two pitchers and a cauldron, add honey to it and made a mead such that whoever drinks it becomes a poet and a man of learning *(Skaldskaparmal* IV).

The origins of such cauldrons are always shrouded in mystery. At the beginning of the *Battle of Mag-Tured* we are told that the Tuatha de Danann who came "from the islands at the north of the world" had brought with them magic talismans. "From Falias was brought the Stone of Fal which was at Tara; it cried out under every king who ruled Ireland. From Gorias was brought Lug's spear; no battle could be won against him who had it in his hand. From Findias was brought the sword of Nuada; when it was drawn from its sheath, no one could escape it . . . From Murias was brought the cauldron of Dagda; no company left without being grateful to it . . ." (G. Dottin, *L'Epopée Irlandaise,* 37.)

Some memory of the ancient sacrificial rites attached to the cauldron appears to have been preserved in the *mabinogi* of *Branwen:*

> "I was hunting in Ireland one day, at the top of a mound which overlooks a lake called the Lake of the Cauldron, and I saw a huge man with yellow-red hair emerging from the lake with the cauldron on his back; he was a great monstrous man with an evil thieving look about him. His wife followed, and if he was huge she was twice as big . . . I took them with me and maintained them, and they stayed with me for a year. For that first year I kept them willingly, but thereafter they became a burden to me. By the end of the fourth month of the second year they had caused themselves to be hated and detested throughout the land . . . In these difficult circumstances it was decided to make a chamber entirely of iron; when this was ready all the smiths of Ireland were summoned to bring their hammers and tongs, and charcoal was piled up to the top of the chamber. Inside the man and his wife and their children were served with great quantities of food and drink until it was clear that they were all drunk, whereupon those outside began to fire the charcoal round the chamber and work the bellows round the house. There was one man to each bellows, and these men blew until the house was white-hot round its occupants. The strangers inside held a council in the middle of the chamber; they waited until the wall was white-hot, and then the man, by reason of his great strength, was able to rush it and break it down with his shoulder, so that he and his wife

alone escaped. After that I suppose the couple came over to you, lord."
"Indeed he did come here," said Bran, "and he gave the cauldron to
me."

This ritual of the white-hot house, like that of the sacrifice by asphyxiation in the
cauldron appears to be attached to the feast of Samain, the Celtic New Year and
festival of the Dead. The kings Diarmaid mac Cerbhail and Muirchertach mac
Erca both die by drowning in a basin, as does Fjolnir, son of the Scandinavian god
Yngvifreyr, who is drowned in a barrel of mead. In the Irish tale of the *Adventures of
Nera,* the hero releases a hanged man during the night of Samain and takes him to
drink in a strange house. "There were basins to bathe and wash in and a brew in
each of them ... Then the prisoner drank a mouthful from each of the vats and
blew the last drop out through his lips over the people in the house so that they all
died."[8]

We have mentioned the fact that the cauldron foreshadows the Grail, and we
know that the Grail is a female solar image. "When she had entered with the Grail,
there came such great brightness that the candles lost their lustre like the stars
when the sun or the moon rises." We also know that the unfertilized Grail is the
cause of the barrenness and aridity of the *Gaste Pays* which has been overheated like
the white-hot house. Nera's basin full of liquid, on the other hand, is the fertilized
Grail which can bring rebirth, though not through resurrection or reincarnation
but through a new life in the Other World. The bodies which emerge from the
cauldron seem to be alive again, but they cannot speak; and the inhabitants of the
other world are *tacentes*.

Bran's cauldron, like the Dagda's, is also a provider of food and nourishment for
no company leaves it unsatisfied. In *Culhwch and Olwen,* Arthur sets off to win the
cauldron of Diwrnach the Gael which has the same properties, and it is this
expedition which appears to underlie Taliesin's poem the *Spoils of the Abyss*.

> Is it not the cauldron of the Master of the Abyss?
> At its top are rings of pearls.
> It does not boil the food of a coward, that is not its
> role.

An Irish poem inserted into the tale of the *Death of Curoi* was inspired by the
same expedition and alludes to the same cauldron:

> There was a cauldron in that fortress.
> It streamed with gold and silver,
> what a splendid discovery!
> This cauldron was given to us
> by the king's daughter ...
> (*The Fortress of Shadows*)

In the *mabinogi* of *Branwen,* however, the cauldron comes to a peculiar end
during Bran's battle against the Irish. "The Irish, however, began to kindle a fire
under the cauldron of rebirth; corpses were thrown in until it was full and next
morning the warriors sprang forth as fierce as ever, except that they could not
speak." One of the Britons decides to sacrifice himself for his fellow countrymen.
He pretends to be dead and lies down among the Irish bodies to be thrown in with

the others. He "stretched out inside the cauldron until he broke it into four pieces, and then his heart broke also." *(Branwen.)*

The white-hot house and the cauldron are identical in that they are broken when they become too dry, a causal relationship analogous to certain present day theories concerning the sun and the stars and an eventual explosion of the sun when it has been reduced to its barest state by maximum condensation. In this respect the nature of Bran's cauldron and of the Grail open out interesting new fields of speculation. Through them we can see how Plutarch's ideas about the transformation of the divinity by way of dismemberment can be applied to the cosmos. Solar myths have been much abused and consequently disparaged in recent years, but the fact that the Celtic sun was feminine means that we can learn a great deal from such myths as far as the Celts are concerned.

The theme of fertilization by mouth, and thus of the migration of the soul, is connected with the theme of metamorphosis in a number of Irish tales. In the *Two Swineherds*, the heroes Rucht and Rucne undergo various transformations from swineherds to crows, to sea-monsters, to champions of Ireland to worms living separately in two springs. One day one of them says to king Fiachna who is feeding them, "Tomorrow one of your cows will swallow me while it is drinking the water and one of the cows of queen Mebd will swallow my companion. Then two bulls will be born and there will be a great war in Ireland over them." *(Book of Leinster)*. The war in question forms the subject of the *Raid on Cooley*.

In the tale of the *Birth of Conchobar*, Nessa gives her husband Cathba the druid some water to drink. He notices that the water contains two worms and forces his wife to swallow them. In this way Nessa becomes pregnant and gives birth to the famous King Conchobar.

The traditions concerning Etaine, the Gaelic archetype of Queen Guinevere, provide us with a similar episode. Etaine and Fuamnach are both wives to Mider, god of the Dead. Jealous of Etaine, Fumnach magically changes her into an insect. After various tribulations the insect lands in the house of Etar, an Irish nobleman, falls into a cup of wine and is swallowed by Etar's wife. She becomes pregnant and gives birth to a daughter also named Etaine, who becomes the wife of Eochaid Aireainn, high king of Ireland, before being abducted by Mider *(Eriu, XII)*.

In other tales we find examples much closer to the story of Taliesin. Tuan mac Cairill, for example, takes on various forms before being changed into a salmon. "But a fisherman caught me and took me to the wife of Cairill, king of that country . . . The woman wanted me and ate me whole. And I was in her belly. I remember the time when I was in the belly of Cairill's wife, I remember also that after that time I began to speak like men. I knew everything that happened in Ireland, I was a prophet and I was given the name Tuan son of Cairill" *(Leabhar na hUidre)*. This legend is easy enough to interpret, for the fish is undoubtedly a symbol of the penis, and Tuan, being both husband and son to his mother, is committing incest.

Following quite naturally from such odd forms of fertilization, we find the theme of the child upon the waters, an image primarily of the foetus, of the cosmic egg. The idea of the world gestating in the womb of the primordial mother before it acquires its diversity through birth is common to all Genesis stories. "The Spirit of God moved upon the face of the waters." The Finnish *Kalevala* tells the story of the birth of the world and of the bard Vainamoinen in a very similar way.

The virgin Ilmatar is fertilized by the wave. She bears her burden "for seven hundred years", a complete cycle. The virgin Mother of the Waters, who can be likened to Mary's mother St Anne, is borne floating on the waves. A duck lays its eggs on her knee and the eggs fall to the bottom of the sea where they break and hatch out the earth, the sun and the moon. Then the mother of the waters begins to fashion the world, but she cannot give birth to the infant which spends another thirty years in its mother's womb. The child begins to think for itself and appeals to the moon to free him. In the end he is delivered by his own efforts.

> He fell head first
> arms outstretched among the waves;
> he was at the mercy of the waters,
> remained a prey to the high billows.
> He stayed there five years ...
> then finally he landed
> on a nameless headland
> on a land without green growth ...
> This was how Vainamoinen was born
> how the eternal bard appeared,
> child of a divine mother
> issue of the virgin Ilmatar.

All the forms of birth we have examined are preceded by some peculiar death for the former person who decomposes into different shapes before being gathered together in the womb of a woman personifying the mother goddess. This whole process suggests that the druidic religion practised some cult of sacrifice by transubstantiation, which necessarily involved bloodshed if only on a mythological level. Such a cult would certainly explain the bloody sacrifices attributed to the Gauls by the authors of antiquity. It would also explain the bloody aspect of the Grail legend and the ritual of severed heads which is attested not only by legends but also by historians like Livy and Diodorus Sicilus, and by sculpture.[9]

To sum up, then, the act of sacrifice works on two levels. On the individual plane, it is the act by which man reaches for the divine; on the cosmic plane it is the regenerative act of a creation threatened by exhaustion. To achieve both aspects there must be identification with all parts of the cosmos. That is what Taliesin is saying when he writes:

> I have been sow, I have been he-goat,
> I have been a sage plant, I have been a boar,
> I have been a horn, I have been a wild sow,
> I have been a shout in battle,
> I have been a stream on the slope,
> I have been a wave on the stretch of shore,
> I have been the damp gleam of a downpour,
> I have been a tabby-headed cat on three trees,
> I have been a ball, I have been a head,
> I have been a she-goat on an elder-tree (?)
> I have been a well-fed crane, a sight to see ...
> (*Book of Taliesin*, XXV)

Amergein, one of the great mythical bards of Ireland, expresses the same idea:

> I am the wind which blows over the sea,

> I am wave of the sea ...
> I am bird of prey on the cliff-face ...
> I am lake in the valley.

So, too, does Tuan mac Cairill, whose story is so like the tale of Taliesin:

> Vulture today
> I was once a wild boar ...
> I first lived in the flock of pigs
> here I am now in the flock of birds ...

There are obvious comparisons to be made between such writings and the ancient Egyptian *Book of the Dead* which includes a number of incantations to be sung by the soul of the departed once it has crossed the boundaries of death. It is the duty of the departed to announce that he is of divine essence because some part of his body belongs to a particular god or goddess:

> The hair of my head belongs to the god Nu,
> my face is the solar disc of Ra,
> the strength of the goddess Hathor lives in my eyes,
> the soul of Up-Uaut resounds in my two ears,
> in my nose live the forces of the god Kenti Khas,
> my two lips are the teeth of Anubis,
> my teeth are the teeth of the goddess Serkit,
> my neck is the neck of the goddess Isis ...
> My spine is that of Set,
> my phallus is the phallus of Osiris ...
> The forces of the eye of Horus flow at the base of my back.

The same theme would seem to lie behind the *Song of Songs*

> Thy hair is as a flock of goats ...
> Thy teeth are as a flock of sheep ...
> As a pomegranate are thy temples ...
> The joints of thy thighs are like jewels ...
> Thy navel is like a round goblet
> which wanteth not liquor ...
> Thy belly is like an heap of wheat set about with lilies ...
> Thy neck is as a tower of ivory.

The lyrical and the metaphysical are combined in an incantatory form that is close to magic. One of the strangest adventures undertaken by mankind is here revealed, an adventure which has so haunted the imagination of men that it recurs in the realm of pure poetry, where all-powerful analogy can transform reality. This we can see in André Breton's poem *l'Union Libre*.

> My wife with tresses of wood-fire
> with thoughts of flashes of heat

the height of sand
my wife the size of an otter between the tiger's teeth
my wife with the rosette mouth of clusters of the
largest stars
with teeth of white-mice prints on white ground
with the tongue of polished amber and glass ...
My wife with lashes of children's pencil strokes
with the brows of the rim of swallows' nest ...

The Cad Goddeu

Lyricism is one form of the sacred. But the sacred makes its own demands and has its own secrets, which are sometimes well kept. The poetry of Taliesin is a flame burning in the darkness, a flame slicing harshly through the shadow to leave no intermediary area of twilight. The flame rises from some unknown source and cuts through the night in strange and fantastical shapes. To identify himself the author of the poems writes:

I am he who brings life to the fire
in honour of God the Master ...
I am a bard versed in astrology
who recites
his inspired song at the setting
of a fine night of a fine day.
(The Seat of Taliesin, *Book of Taliesin*, XII)

The only way in which the bard can have acquired this divine fire or sacred inspiration is by undergoing some metamorphosis, some poetical descent into hell.

The inspiration that I sing
I bring back from the depths
(*Hostile Conjuration*, J.M. 60)

It is this inspiration risen from the depths of the man which created the *Cad Goddeu*, or Battle of the Shrubs, one of the most extraordinary poems ever conceived, and certainly the most puzzling of all the poems attributed to the bard Taliesin.

Basically the *Cad Goddeu* is an extremely confused poem centred round a battle between an army of Britons, which includes Taliesin himself and the hero Gwyddyon son of Don, and an army of anonymous enemies apparently led by a woman. As the Britons begin to fall back, Gwyddyon is forced to resort to a magic trick.

I was at the battle of Goddeu with Lleu and Gwyddyon
who changed the elemental form of the trees and the
rushes.
(*The Three Seats of Taliesin*, J.M. 76)

Gwyddyon therefore turns the Britons into trees and other plants, thereby giving them the victory and Taliesin a reason for writing some dazzling and rapturous lines on the subject of metamorphoses. The following version of the poem, here quoted in full, has been slightly emended in translation by the present author.

I have taken on a host of shapes
before acquiring my final form,
the memory of them is clear to me.
I have been a narrow, gilded spear,
I believe in what is clear,
I have been raindrop in the air,
I have been the furthest star,
I have been word among letters,
I have been book in the beginning
I have been light of the lamp.
For a year and a half
I was a huge bridge
spanning three score creeks.
I have been path, I have been eagle,
I have been fisherman's boat on the sea,
I have been food at the feasting,
I have been drop of the shower,
I have been a sword gripped in the hands,
I have been shield in the battle,
I have been string of a harp,
in this way for nine years.
In the water, in the foam,
I have been sponge in the fire,
I have been tree in the uncharted wood.

I am not he who will not sing
of the fight, although I am small.
I will sing of the battle of the shrubs
before the leader of Britain,
guardian of the swift horses
and master of so many fleets.

There was a beast with gaping jaws,
with a hundred heads.
A battle was fought
on the root of its tongue,
and another fight fought
on the back of its head.
It was a black toad
stalking on a hundred claws,
a spotted serpent ridged with a crest.
A hundred souls of sinners
were tortured in its flesh.

I have been at Kaer Vevenir
where trees and plants grew in riot.
The musicians used to sing,

the men of war were amazed:
a resurrection of the Britons
was brought about by Gwyddyon.
They appealed to the Creator
and the Christ to judge the trial,
until the Eternal One
was prepared to help his creatures.
The Lord replied
through the voice of the elements:
Take the form of trees,
stand in battle line,
send away all those
who are unskilled at close quarters.

Then they were spellbound into trees,
and while waiting to be trees no longer
the trees raised their voices
in four waves of harmony.
The fighting ceased.
Let us end the days of violence!

Then, controlling the tumult, a woman
advanced in challenge.
At the head of the army was a woman.
The qualities of a shameless cow
will not make us yield!
The blood of men will gush up to our thighs!

The greatest of the three warrior hopes
was staked on the world
and there was no more thought
of the flood
of Christ crucified
and of the impending judgment day.

The alder-trees, at the head of the army,
formed the advance guard,
the willows and the service-trees
lined up behind them,
the plums which are rare,
astounded the men.

The new medlars
were a pivot to the battle,
the bushes of thorny roses
struggled against a great mass,
the raspberries, ranged in thickets,
showed as no others
how fragile is life.

The privet and the honeysuckle
with ivy on the front line
set off into battle with the gorse.
The cherry-tree handled the aggressors,
the birch, despite his noble mind,
was placed at the rear,
not because of his cowardice,
but because of his height.
The golden clover proved
to the stranger how wild was its nature.

The pines stood at the front
in the centre of the fray
which I exalted greatly
in the presence of the kings.
The elm and his followers
did not move a foot.
They fought against the centre
against the flanks and the rear.

Of the hazel-trees, one could see
that their warlike rage was most great.
Lucky the privet's role,
he was the bull of battle, the master of the world.
Morawg and Morydd
did great deeds in the shape of pines.
The holly was spattered with green,
he was of all the most valiant.

The hawthorn, watching to right and to left
was wounded in the hands.
The aspen was pruned,
he was pruned in the fray.
The fern was despoiled.
The broom at the forefront
was wounded in a ditch.
The gorse was not unscathed
although he filled the whole field.
The heather triumphed, watching to right and left.
The mass was enchanted
during this fight of men.

The oak marching swiftly
made heaven and earth quake.
He was a stout guardian against the enemy,
his name is much revered.
The bluebells fought
and caused great pain;
they crushed and were crushed,
others were pierced through.

The Cardonagh Cross, found in Donegal (Ireland), and dating from the sixth century. It is an early example of the interlaced ribbon pattern which became a widespread feature of Christian Celtic art.

The pear-trees were the great firebrands
of the battle on the plain,
because of their violence.
The forest was a stream of ashes.
The timid chestnuts
gained littled triumph.
Jet became black,
the mountain grew stunted,
the forest was full of holes
as once the great seas were
as soon as the war-cry was heard.

Then the birch-top covered us with his leaves
and transformed our withered shape.
The branches of the oak enchanted us
with the incantations of Mael-Derw[10]
smiling by the rock.

The Lord is not passionate by nature.
He has neither father nor mother.

When I came to life,
my creator fashioned me
from the fruit of fruits
from the fruit of the primordial god
from the primroses and the hill-flowers
from the flowers of trees and bushes
from the earth and its terrestrial course,
I have been shaped
from the flowers of the nettle
from the water of the ninth wave.
I have been marked by Math[11]
before becoming immortal,
I have been marked by Gwyddyon
the great purifier of the Britons,
by Eurwys and by Euron,
by Euron and by Modron,[12]
by masters of wisdom numbering five times five,
by the wise children of Math.
At the time of the great separation
I was enchanted by the master
when he was half consumed by fire.

By the Wiseman among Wisemen I was marked
before the existence of the world,
at the time when I received life
worthy were the people of the world
the bards were heaped with favours.

I have bowed before the glory-chant,

I have played in the night,
I have slept in the dawn.

I have been in the ship
with Dylan, son of the Wave,
on a bed, in the middle
between the knees of the kings,
when the waters like unexpected spears
fell from the sky
to the depths of the abyss.

In the battle there will be
four score hundred.
They will do as they see fit.
There are neither older nor younger
than me in their armies.
A miracle: a hundred men are born,
each of the nine hundred was with me.
My sword was stained with blood.
A great honour was accorded me
by the Master, and protection wherever he went.
If I go to where the Boar was killed[13]
he will compose, he will decompose,
he will compose praises,
he whose name is glittering and whose hand is mighty:
with a lightning flash he controls his troops
who spread like a flame across the heights.

On the heights of the mountain have I been a spotted
snake,
I have been viper in the lake
I have been star with a curved beak,
I have been an old priest
with my chasuble and my chalice.

I do not make false prophecies.
I predict in four score fumes
the fate alloted to each man:
five times five troops at arms.
I have broken under my knee
six stallions of yellow.
But a hundred times better is my horse Yellow-Ehite.
It is gentle like a sea-bird
which never leaves
the peaceful shore.

I have been the hero of the blood-stained meadows
in the midst of a hundred chiefs.
Red is the stone of my belt
my shield is rimmed with gold.

> They are not yet born in the abyss
> those who have visited me
> except Goronwy
> from the meadows of Edrywy.
>
> Long and white are my fingers.
> Long ago I was a shepherd.
> I wandered a long time over the earth
> before I was skilful in the sciences.
> I have wandered, I have walked,
> I have slept in a hundred islands,
> I have grown restless in a hundred towns.
>
> O you, wise druids,
> ask of Arthur
> who is older
> than me, in the chants!
> Someone has come
> to think of the flood
> and Christ crucified
> and the judgment day to come.
> Golden gem in a golden jewel,
> I am splended
> I am skilful
> in metal work.

This poem is far from easy to understand and certain passages are totally incomprehensible. In fact it is more like a combination of three poems: the first could be entitled "Migrations" and concerns the various transformations undergone by Taliesin himself during his adventures with Keridwen; the second is the *Cad Goddeu* proper, an account of that mysterious battle; the third seems to be connected with the adventure of Gwyddyon, his son Lleu Llaw Gyffes and the strange Blodeuwedd "Born of flowers" by means of Gwyddyon's magic.

Familiarity with the story of Taliesin makes the first of these three poems relatively the most accessible, since it describes the series of metamorphoses through which Gwyon Bach passes before he finally becomes Taliesin. As if in a process of initiation, he journeys through all the elements to identify with the cosmos. But these transformations are not to be taken literally. This section of the poem is far more like the reflexions of the individual as he performs a kind of return into the womb of *Natura Naturans* as represented in her outward forms. There is no allusion whatever to any kind of belief in metempsychosis. Rather the poet is singing his love for all things in existence and using this love as an excuse to indulge in a flight of wondrous lyricism.

The account of the battle itself poses a number of problems. There have been various attempts to provide it with some kind of historical basis, to see it as a skirmish between Saxons and Britons in the 6th century when Taliesin is supposed to have lived. For this reason, it has been likened to one of the few poems by Taliesin which can be described as historical and which concerns the battle of Argoed Llwyfein. But any comparison between the two does not prove that the *Cad Goddeu* refers to a real battle.

A much more attractive theory is propounded by Robert Graves in *The White Goddess*. He suggests that this was a battle over the necropolis of Salisbury (which included the megalithic monument at Stonehenge) between the previous occupants, priests who had lived there since the Bronze Age and were allied to the island British tribes worshipping Beli on the one side, and the British tribes who had come from the continent on the other. Any such event would have taken place during the first or second Belgic invasions of Britain, i.e. in 400 or 500 BC.

There is some evidence to support this theory. We have already discussed the existence of pre-Celtic solar cults at Stonehenge and Delphi, both being connected with the Hyperboreans or megalithic peoples. The whole area round Salisbury is a vast necropolis, whose use dates back into distant pre-history. It is the land of the Dead and therefore very much a place of the Other World.

A slightly different picture of the battle may emerge from a reading of Geoffrey of Monmouth's *Historia Regum Britanniae*. Here Belinus and Brennius the two sons of Dunvallo quarrel over the succession to the kingdom of Britain. Brennius goes to Norway and comes back with a fiancée and an army. After various adventures Belinus captures Brennius' fiancée and refuses to return her. Brennius then engages his brother in a great battle "in a sacred wood called Calaterium". Brennius is beaten and takes refuge in Gaul only to return with yet another army. The two brothers are about to do battle again when their mother, Conwen, intercedes to bring about a lasting reconciliation. Belinus and Brennius then set out together to conquer Gaul, take Rome and demand a tribute from the Romans (*H.R.B.* XXXV-XLIV).

The end of this episode, as Geoffrey describes it, suggests that Brennius and the Brennus who took Rome in 387 are one and the same. We have already shown that Brennus was the hero Bran, a fact confirmed by the Welsh version of the *Historia* which calls Brennius and Belinus, Bran and Beli respectively. A text from the *Myvyrian Archaeology of Wales* sheds further light on the subject, and on the *Cad Goddeu* in particular.

> There was a man in that battle who could not be saluted unless his name were known ... And Gwyddyon son of Don blessed the name of the man and sang these two *englynion*:
>
>> Sure is the shoe of my stallion pricked by the spur.
>> The high branches of the alder-tree are on your shield:
>> Your name is Bran, of the dazzling branches.
>> Sure is the shoe of my stallion, the day of the battle.
>> The high branches of the alder-tree are in your hand.
>> Bran you are by the branches you bear.
>> (*M.A.W.* 127)

Bran therefore takes part in this battle as an alder-tree, quite naturally in fact since all the Britons have been changed into trees or plants. For all we know, Belinus-Beli may well be fighting on the other side. Beli is the mythical ancestor of the Welsh, the son of Mynogan and father of Ludd and Casswallawn (Caesar's Cassivellaunos). The 10th century Welsh genealogies copied in Harley MS 3859 trace the forebears of two famous families back to a Beli who may well be the same man, here shown as the husband to the goddess Ana. And Ana, supposedly cousin to the Virgin Mary, is probably the Irish goddess Ana or Dana, mother of the

Tuatha de Danann and known to the Welsh as Don, mother of Gwyddyon.

Among the bushes taking part in the battle is the broom or genista, known in Welsh as *banadl* and in Breton as *balan*. And if we look at the *Chansons de geste*, where so many of the supposed Saracens are actually Celtic heroes, we find a character named Balan, the hero of the *Chanson d'Apremont*, of *Fierebras* and of the *Chanson de Balan*. Saracen though he is, Balan is depicted as having fair hair, light-coloured eyes and a white horse. He is the archetypal solar hero and the broomflower being golden yellow, his name merely adds to his basic character. Balan's country has much of the Other World about it. To reach it people must cross a mountain and a magic bridge belonging to the purest Celtic tradition. Balan's daughter is called Floripar ("Born of a Flower"), a name to be compared with Blodeuwedd, whose legend forms the last part of the *Cad Goddeu*. All the evidence suggests that Balan is a sun god of the same type as Belenos and it would seem, though it can only be a hypothesis, that the broom in this fight is the Beli-Belinus of Welsh tradition.

The only problem is that the broom seems to be fighting on the British side which means that we have to rule out any suggestion of a battle between Bran the Alder and Beli the Broom. However, there is no reason why Bran's enemies should not also have been fighting in the form of trees. Indeed, the text from the *Myvyrian Archaeology of Wales* quoted above claims that the battle was fought "because of a white stag or a little dog", animals from Annfwn, the abyss, and says that "on the other side was a woman called Achren and her army could not be saluted unless her name were known". It so happens that *achren* means trees, which would indicate that both armies were composed of trees and bushes. That the idea of a battle between plants was part of Celtic tradition, we have already established in the chapters on Rome and Delphi.

Further examples occur in the Irish tales. The "three daughters of Calatin ... the black witches, create a mirage of a battle between two armies, between magnificent moving trees, fine leafy oaks, so that Cú Chulainn heard the noise of a fight" (The Death of Cú Chulainn, *Ogam*, XI, 200). During the battle of Mag-Tured, the Tuatha de Danann plan a similar trick. "We will spellbind the trees, the stones and the mounds of the earth which will appear to them like an armed force." There are even echoes of this tradition in the *Chansons de Geste*. The *Prise de Cordes* and the *Chronique du Faux Turpin* both tell how the Franks planted their weapons in the ground where they began to grow like trees.

The underlying motives for the battle are difficult to determine. It may be that there is a struggle in progress between two families of gods, of the kind found in virtually every mythology. A rational explanation would suggest some sort of sectarian conflict between the followers of the old religion and the new. A metaphysical explanation would suggest that the battle represented the tribulations and transformations of the divinity.

In this sense, the Battle of the Shrubs would be an eschatalogical battle like the struggle between Chronos and Zeus for sovereignty over the universe, and similar in some respects to the struggle between Arthur and Mordret at Camlann and to the confrontation at Mag-Tured between the ancient Fomoré gods led by Balor and the new Tuatha de Danann led by Lug.

The great battle of Teutonic mythology, which was developed in the Scandinavian *Ynglingasaga*, takes place between two divine races, the Aesir and the Vanir. Each side lays waste the land of the other until, exhausted, they make peace. Similarly in the *Gylfaginning* (XXXIII-XXXV), the struggle between Loki and the other gods, following Loki's murder of Baldr, ends in the final battle marking the end of the world. The *Edda* tells how the forces of evil represented by the wolf Fenrir, the great serpent encircling the earth named Hrym, the giant dog Garm and Loki the god of Death, were put in chains, but escaped to fight a battle against Odin, Thor, Freyr and all the Aesir. When everyone else had been killed, Heimdall, the primordial god, was left alone to face Loki. They killed each other and Sutr the fire burned up the whole universe. But from the wreckage of the world are born gods who will find "the marvellous golden tablets which the ancestors had owned in the early times ... The fields will be covered with fruit although they are not sown". This will be the reign of Odin's son Baldr, the new and ultimate incarnation of beneficent divine power.

The *Cad Goddeu* also appears to be an eschatalogical war, which ends in resurrection, in renewal in a new life. In this battle the trees represent opposing forces which each have their specific personalities and their own part to play, although it is very hard to determine exactly who all of them are. Take the plum-tree, the medlar and the privet, for example. There is nothing in the poem itself to suggest what their true significance is or whom they represent.

The alder-tree is certainly Bran. He is the Fisher-King, the Bron of 13th century French romance, also called Pelles from Pwyll Penn Annfwn, Master of the Abyss. He can be identified, too, as Uther Pendragon or Uther Ben ("Terrible Head"). He is Ban of Benoic, Lancelot's father. He is Teutates for whom men were immersed in a cauldron.

The willow or *helig* (Breton *haleg*, Latin *salictum*) is a solar tree whose long drooping branches are reminiscent of the sun's rays and of the hair of solar gods. In a number of languages the esoteric process of phonetics relates the word for willow with the word for sun (Lat. *sol*, Greek *helios*, Breton *heol* or *sul*, Welsh *haul*), and, strangely, with the word for salt (Lat. *sal*, Bret. *holen*, Welsh *halen*) a commodity of great symbolic value.

The service-tree appears to have been used by the druids because of its magic powers. "Nothing will shake you except a druidic fire ... Let the armies go into the woods and bring back the branches of the service-tree for it is with that wood that the best fires are made." (*The Siege of Druim Damgaire*, R.C. XLIII, 105.)

The wild rosebush or briar is a kind of magic barrier against danger. "Using a magic more often maleficent than beneficent, a druid would build an impenetrable hedge; Fraech made the druids' hedge for Diarmait. Diarmait's army was defeated after his magic hedge had been destroyed." (Francoise Le Roux, *Les Druides*, p. 90.)

The honeysuckle is a symbol of fidelity. In Marie de France's lay, the *Honeysuckle*, this plant is indissolubly bound to the hazel tree. "Tristan cut down a branch of the hazel by the middle and squared it. When he had peeled the branch he carved his name with his knife." This action is connected with the rite of the magic wand. "The pair of them were like the honeysuckle which attaches itself to the hazel; when the one has seized the other and twined round its trunk, they can endure together, but if attempts are then made to part them, the hazel soon dies and the honeysuckle perishes as swiftly."

The ivy is a symbol of tenacity and also of a kind of immortality. In another poem Taliesin writes; "I have owned the ivy branch", doubtless alluding to some sort of initiation. The gorse is a blustery, fussy plant whose yellow flowers suggest links with the sun. The riddles behind the cherry, the clover, the elm, the bluebell or the chestnut are impossible to decipher.

The pine was rather rare in Great Britain and Brittany in ancient times, being introduced on a widespread basis much later. In the legend of the spring of

Barenton, it is specifically stated that there was a pine growing near the spring, and that it was on this pine that the birds sang so magically after the storm.

The hazel tree was also used by the druids. By cutting a wand and carving his name on it Tristan was performing a magic gesture. "Cú Chulainn ... saw two men fighting and near them a satirist with a hazel wand." *(The Death of Cú Chulainn.)*

In Ireland the hawthorn is the sacred bush, the home of the fairies, a fact which even the government has to take into account when mapping out new roads which may involve destroying hawthorn bushes. The druidic curse known as the *glam dicin* was an appeal to the hawthorn: "the poet had to go with six companions ... They turned their backs to a hawthorn bush ... With the wind blowing from the north each of them held a sling shot and a hawthorn wand in his hand and chanted a verse against the king over these two objects ... Each of them then put down his stone and his branch on the root of the hawthorn bush." *(Book of Bally-more*, quoted by Le Roux, *op. cit.* p. 84.) Clearly this was a prayer to the fairies, to the world of the mounds, for help against the enemy, and it is quite likely that the same idea is evident in the *Cad Goddeu.*

The holly, like the ivy, is a symbol of permanence. In a Welsh tale about Tristan, Arthur is asked to judge how Essyllt should be shared between March and Tristan. "Arthur decided that the one should have Essyllt while there were leaves on the trees and the other when there were not. Her husband was to choose. March chose the time when there were no leaves on the trees because the nights were longer. Arthur went to tell Essyllt, who cried; "Blessed be this judgment and blessed be he who gave it." She then sang this *englyn:*

> Three trees are generous in kind,
> the holly, ivy and the yew ...
> They keep their leaves throughout their life
> I am Tristan's while he lives ..."
> *(Peniarth MS* 96)

The aspen or poplar appears to have had some magical significance, for a literal translation of its Welsh name is "mistletoe-tree". In fact mistletoe does usually grow most profusely on the poplar, and the druidic religion made much of mistletoe, though why we do not know. As it happens, the druids used only mistletoe which had grown on the oak, which must have been extremely rare as there is only one variety of oak on which the parasite will grow.

The fern and the heather were familiar plants to the Celts, but what part they played is hard to determine. The broom as we have already said, may have represented Beli the sun god, as he fought his brother Bran the alder. The pear-tree can be compared to the word for cauldron which is *peir* and to Peredur. But more interesting than any of these trees are the oak and the birch.

According to Maximus of Tyre (VIII, 8), the oak is the "Celtic representation of Zeus". In the *Cad Goddeu,* the oak does indeed appear to be the commander, though which human character he represents is another matter. It cannot be Bran since he is the alder. The text of the *Myvyrian Archaeology of Wales* already mentioned attributes the victory to Amaethon son of Don and brother of Gwyddyon and Arianrod, who is fighting against Arawn, king of the Other World. It is thus that "Amaethon the good triumphed". We know that Arawn was Pwyll's predecessor and as Pwyll can be identified with Bran, the battle of Goddeu becomes the replacement of one god by another. Obviously we cannot say for certain that Amaethon is the oak. In his *Death Song for Amaethon*, Taliesin calls him "the loyal lord of Britain, the dragon-headed chief", but apart from these two texts, Amaethon appears only once in Welsh literature in *Culhwch and Olwen*. Here he is seen as the great labourer, his name being derived from *Amaeth* (Gallic *ambactos*) which means "labourer". The same concept of work on the land is connected with the name Arthur (from the Indo-European root *ar* which occurs in virtually every language). As we have seen, the *Cad Goddeu* mentions a place called Kaer Vevenir which also appears in *Culhwch and Olwen* as Nevenhyr. When Arthur's gatekeeper reminds him of all the expeditions in which he has taken part he says; "I was at Kaer Nevenhyr; there we saw nine mightly kings, fine-looking men". This would seem to indicate that Arthur was among the Britons at the battle of Goddeu. It would be tempting to identify Arthur with Amaethon and to give him the form of the oak, whose role and symbolic significance would certainly match the character of Arthur.

The *Death Song for Amaethon* tells how Gwyddyon and Amaethon fought Math and Hyvedd and made a shield to contain the sea unleashed by their enemies' spells. Considering that Math represents the most ancient of British magic and that his nephew Gwyddyon was his heir, their struggle also appears to be based on the substitution of one god for another.

The birch tree is undoubtedly Gwyddyon himself.

The birch (*bedw*, Bret. *bezv*) is the Tree of the Dead, a significance first accorded it in the far North where it is the only deciduous tree to grow. The Tuatha de Danann came from islands in the north and are known as the sons of Dana or Ana, i.e. the sons of the Welsh Don. In Breton the word *anaon* means the "departed" and denotes the people of Ana, the people of the Dead.

The Latin name for the birch is *betulla*, a word reminiscent of the *bétylles* or standing stones representing the divinity. The Celtic name for the birch is related to the word for grave (Welsh *bedd*, Bret. *bez*), to the word for life (Welsh *buhedd*, Bret. *buhez*), to the verb to be (Welsh *bod*, Bret. *bezan*) and to the word for the world (Welsh *bydd*, Bret. *bed*). So it is both the tree of the Dead and the tree of Life, like the tree described in the *Quête du Saint-Graal*. "Eve the sinner plucked the mortal fruit of the tree which the creator had forbidden and the branch came with the fruit hanging from it ... When God later expelled them from the garden of delights Eve was still holding the branch in her hand ... She planted it in the ground ... it took root. It became a speading tree; and branches, leaves and even the trunk were all white as snow. One day Adam and Eve were sitting under this tree and Adam, looking at it, began to bewail the suffering of their exile ... Eve said that the tree bore in itself the recollection of suffering; it was the tree of Death. Scarcely had she uttered these words than a voice spoke to them from the high heavens, 'O wicked ones, why do you speak thus of death? Do not prejudge fate but have hope and comfort each other, for Life will triumph over Death'." (A Pauphilet, *La Quête du Saint-Graal*, 80-81.) When Eve loses her virginity the white tree turns green, and when Cain kills Abel it turns scarlet. It was always called the Tree of Life.

The same concept underlies the episode in the Welsh *Peredur* concerning the myth of the Ford of Souls. "On one bank there was a flock of white sheep, and on the other a flock of black sheep. When a white sheep bleated a black sheep would cross the river and turn white, and when a black sheep bleated a white sheep would cross the river and turn black. On the bank of the river he saw a tall tree: from roots to crown one half was aflame and the other green with leaves."

According to Caesar (VI, 18), the god of Life and Death in Celtic mythology was Dispater. But Dispater is a Roman name for the god and opinion varies as to his Gallic name. It has been suggested, though without much evidence to support the hypothesis, that Dispater was Sucellos (Hard Hit), the god with the mallet found in so much Gallo-Roman statuary (P. M. Duval, *Les Dieux de la Gaule*, 60-62). It would seem much better sense to identify Dispater with Teutates. For although the official, rather unsatisfactory argument is that Teutates is the "god of the tribe" (from *Teuta* meaning tribe), we believe that the name is formed from *Teu* or *Deu*, meaning "god", and *Tat* or *Tad*, meaning "father". Teutates would then be a Gallic form of Dispater, God the Father, rather than just a common noun as so many people have believed. The ritual depicted on the Gundestrup cauldron with its resurrected warriors and its tree lying halfway between life and death would appear to prove this identification beyond any doubt.

And in the *Cad Goddeu* it is Gwyddyon the birch who plays the part of Teutates, changing the Britons into trees, transforming their withered aspect and bringing them back to life. The birch is also described as occupying a special position in the battle not because of his cowardice but because of his size. The one fault in this argument is that the rold of Teutates is elsewhere ascribed to Bran or Pwyll; but then the characters of Celtic stories are frequently superimposed one upon another.

In any case, Gwyddyon is definitely represented as the god of Life and Death throughout the story of Blodeuwedd, as told in the *mabinogi* of *Math son of Mathonwy*. Here Gwyddyon, Math's nephew, helps his brother Gilvaethwy to consummate his love for the young virgin in whose lap Math has to keep his feet during peacetime or die. Gwyddyon robs Pryderi of his pigs by a trick. The pigs are animals of the other world exactly like the bitch, the roe deer, the lapwing, the white stag and the little dog which start the battle of Goddeu and come from Annfwn (*M.A.W.* 127).

The trick is a simple enough matter for a magician like Gwyddyon:

> The cleverest man of whom I have heard tell
> was Gwyddyon, son of Don, with terrible powers . . .
> who stole the pigs of the south
> for it was he who had the greatest knowledge.
> From the earth of the court
> with curved and plaited chains
> he formed horses
> and remarkable saddles.
> (*The Seat of Keridwen*, J.M. 78)

Gwyddyon exchanges these magic objects for Pryderi's famous pigs; and when Pryderi realizes that the horses are only tufts of grass he declares war on Math and Gwyddyon. During wartime Math can live without the young virgin, which leaves the field free for Gilvaethwy. The war ends in single combat between Pryderi and Gwyddyon. Pryderi is killed, but Math, who has learned of the deception in the meantime, takes his vengeance by turning Gwyddyon and Gilvaethwy into animals for three years. After this period all is forgiven. When Gwyddyon suggests his sister Arianrod as a replacement virgin for Math, Math makes her jump over his magic wand to see if she is really a virgin (a clear enough indication of the true significance of the wand and its relation to the cult of the phallus among the Celts).

As she jumps over the wand Arianrod drops two new born children, Dylan who is brought up by Math, and Lleu Llaw Gyffes whom Gwyddyon snatches up and himself brings up in secret. Other works suggest that these two children were the fruit of an incestuous relationship between Arianrod and Gwyddyon.

When Lleu Llaw Gyffes, as yet unnamed, becomes a handsome lad, Gwyddyon takes him to Arianrod who refuses to recognize him as her son or give him a name. Gwyddyon then tricks his sister into naming Lleu and providing him with weapons despite the *geis* she has placed on him. Furious, Arianrod then declares, "I will swear a fate on the boy: he shall have no wife of the race that is on earth at this time."

Gwyddyon goes to Math, who says "'Let us use our magic and enchantments to conjure up a woman out of flowers ...' Math and Gwyddyon took the flowers of oak and broom and meadowsweet and from these they conjured up the loveliest and most beautiful girl anyone had seen; they baptized her with the form of baptism that was used then, and named her Blodeuwedd [Face of Flowers]."

It is this adventure which probably forms a basis for the last part of the *Cad Goddeu*. Taliesin's claim to have been formed from "the primroses and the hill-flowers, from the flowers of trees and bushes" is very like the tale of Blodeuwedd.

In the *Three Seats of Taliesin* the poet writes, "I was at the battle of Goddeu with Lleu and Gwyddyon." So Lleu was present at the battle. The mention of the horse Melygan or Yellow-White is also significant since this is Lleu's horse. Finally, we learn from the end of *Math, son of Mathonwy*, that when Blodeuwedd took a lover, Goronwy or Gronwy Pebyr (also mentioned in the *Cad Goddeu*), he killed Lleu. Gwyddyon manages to conjure Lleu back to life under an oak tree, thereby confirming his role as god of life, and arranges for Lleu to kill Goronwy, incidentally demonstrating that he is also the god of death.

As we can see, the extremely confused final section of the poem seems to be a complex mixture of the history of Taliesin and his metamorphoses and the story of Blodeuwedd, the girl born of flowers. But this does nothing to detract from the importance of Gwyddyon, whose final appearance in the poem marks him as a repository for the great secrets of the world, not the divinity iteself but a servant of the divinity.

The name Gwyddyon comes from *Gwydd* meaning "wood" (Gallic *vidu*, Bret. *coad*), but curiously enough *gwydd* is also linked to the Latin *videre* "to see", and in *videre* we find the root *id* which serves to form the word druid. For druid comes not from the ancient word for the "oak" (Greek *drus*, Welsh *derw*) but from an ancient *dru-wid-es*, the "all-seeing", the very wise. The fact that the druids always officiated in the depths of the forest and that their temples were merely an extention of nature itself, only serves to emphasize the link between them and the tree. Trees have a symbolic significance in every tradition. But in this case the oak, which is usually taken to represent the supreme divinity, appears to have been eclipsed by the birch. The birch is a tree of northern origin, after all, and the druidic cults seem to have been Hyperborean in origin. While the oak represents strength, the birch as tree of life and death doubtless represents knowledge. The peculiarly Celtic relationship between the word for knowledge and the word for wood suggests that specific conclusions can be drawn from the *Cad Goddeu*.

It appears that this poem is a synthesis of druidic beliefs, a synthesis at once extremely obscure and much adulterated. And yet there does emerge from it the idea of a resurrection into another life which is not necessarily corporeal but spiritual. The battle it relates is not real but mythical: a contest of ideas, man's reflexions on his origins and his destiny. The *Cad Goddeu* is also the *Cad Gwyddyon,* Gwyddon's battle, the fight of the Wiseman, the druid, who draws his strength from wood, from nature itself. He is the man who must always ask questions.

Through this peerless poetry, Taliesin achieves uncommon heights of intellectual intuition, though unfortunately for us many of them remain too enigmatic to be grasped.

CHAPTER TWELVE

Celtic Mythology

LTHOUGH
the Celtic myths are relatively familiar to us, we know virtually nothing about
Celtic gods and even less about the cults practised throughout the druidic area. In
a passage of the *Pharsalia* which has given rise to much comment (I, 444), Lucan
mentions "cruel Teutates, horrible Esus and Taranis whose altar is as bloody as
that of the Scythian Diana". Lucan, however, was very much of a sycophant to
Julius Caesar, and it is only to be expected that he should have emphasised the
savagery of Gallic cults so as to justify the massacres ordered by the bald dictator
and his successors, and their policy of systematically exterminating druidism. The
manuscript of Lucan's work is covered with notes and comments by a zealous
medieval christian, who also had something to gain from pointing out the barbarity of paganism; and it is from these that we learn that men were hung from trees
and torn into pieces in honour of Esus, that men were immersed in basins until
they asphyxiated in honour of Teutates and that the victims sacrificed to Taranis
were burnt in the hollow trunk of trees. The last of these three confirms Caesar's
words about certain tribes who placed their condemned men in huge cane dum-
mies and burnt them (*Gallic* Wars, VI, 17). Anxious to demonstrate his knowl-
edgeability, Lucan's commentator identifies Teutates with Mercury, Esus with

Mars and Taranis with Dispater, whereas Gallo-Roman inscriptions identify Teutates with Mars, Esus with Mercury and Taranis with Jupiter. Obviously this kind of discrepancy is very little help. And then there is Caesar (VI, 18) who says of the Gauls that "the god they reverence most is Mercury ... next to him they reverence Apollo, Mars, Jupiter and Minerva."

Up until now all commentators on Gallic religion have based their arguments on Lucan, Caesar and the many anthropomorphic images of supposedly "Gallo-Roman" gods. There is considerable contradiction between these sources and yet it is they which lie behind recent attempts to classify Celtic divinities in some rational way. Interesting though such attempts may be, they rest on the false premise that all Roman or Gallo-Roman sources can be totally relied upon. In fact, the contradictions are evidence that even in Gallo-Roman days there was confusion about Celtic gods. It would seem that the Romans knew next to nothing about them but being unwilling to admit as much blithely identified any one god with any other. More seriously still, it would appear that from Caesar's time onwards, the Romans did not even know about their own gods any more.

In his *Aspects du Mythe* (pp. 181-198), Mircéa Eliade has clearly shown how Greek and Roman myths were rationalised. Early Greek mythology is virtually unknown to us. Everything that we do know has been codified into literature by Homer and Hesiod, and then reworked by subsequent writers and artists until it became rigid and fixed. It is this literary mythology which was logically and rationally criticised by the philosophers and which the 3rd century BC Euphemerus described as a series of adventures concerning men made gods or men made heroes. The Greek mythology gradually swamped Rome, driving out the religious ideas of ancient Latium to become the vaguely synchretised mythology we know as classical Greco-Roman. Jupiter was assimilated to Zeus, although the Capitoline Jupiter was very different from the Olympian Zeus. Saturn is no Chronos, the Latin Mars no Ares and the real Latin gods Janus, Quirinius and Vesta have lost their original character.

It is also worth emphasising the fact that ancient Greek mythology had become literary rather in the way that European folklore became fossilised when it was written down in the 19th century. "Classical Greek myths are already evidence of the triumph of literary works over religious belief," writes Mircéa Eliade. "There is a whole, vital, popular area of Greek religion of which we know nothing simply because it was never written down in a systematic way." Even so, it was this mythology, in its most stereotypic form, which spread through the Roman empire as part of the new cultural and political administration. The worship of Rome itself and the Emperor are further evidence of the way religion was sacrificed to meet the fashion of the day and the need for some cohesive force to bind together the vast areas conquered by the legions.

By Caesar's time the official religion was Hellenistic rather than purely Greek since some synchretism between Greek and oriental beliefs was already at work, and it had become a political and patriotic show, totally unconnected with the religious wealth of ancient Latium. No intelligent man could possibly believe in the kinds of idiocy with which man had saddled the gods, which explains why some Romans were attracted to the mystery religions which offered them a real basis for meditation. "It was possible for Christianity to accept and absorb this mythological heritage because the myths were no longer encumbered with any living religious values," as Eliade says.

Given the state of Roman religion there is nothing to be gained by comparing it or assimilating it to Gallic cults. There was no Gallo-Roman religion, only a Gallo-Roman culture in which attempts had been made to relate the two systems. There are very few Roman gods reflected in French place-names, while Gallic gods' names abound, if only through the names of spurious saints.

For at the time of the Roman invasions, the popular, unwritten and therefore living mythology of the Celts was the only mythology prevalent in Western Europe. Indeed the strength of Celtic mythology survived well into the Christian era. Resolutions passed at various church councils (Tours in 567 and Nantes in 568, for example) prove as much; so, too, do Charlemagne's edicts of 789 against the worshippers of stones and those who practised their superstitious forms of worship by trees and springs.

When Christianity proved powerless to repress the old beliefs, it simply followed in the footsteps of all previous religions and assimilated aspects of the existing paganism. That is why there are so many springs dedicated to saints or to the Virgin, so many sanctuaries built on what had been sacred mounds, and why we can still find so many inexplicable and sometimes even improper practices which turn out on examination to belong to the very distant religious past of the Western world.

The Christian religion is one of the basic sources for any study of Celtic divinities.

For, being still vital and developing, Celtic beliefs survived through Christianity, particularly in rural areas. Obviously it is very difficult to reconstruct these beliefs accurately. There is no Gallic writing about them because the druids had quite reasonably forbidden the myths to be divulged in writing, thereby allowing them to retain their strength and to evolve naturally. The ban on writing was the *sine qua non* of the druidic religion. As Lévy-Bruhl says, "If the sacred myths were to be divulged, they would be profaned and would thus lose their mystic qualities. Their deeper meaning and efficacy were revealed only to the initiate. Non-initiates regarded them merely as amusements" (*La mythologie primitive*, 1935).

In fact, it is these "amusements" which help us to discover the Celtic divinities. For although the Gaelic sagas, the Welsh *mabinogion*, the *Chansons de geste* and the Round Table romances were destined to divert an audience which never really understood them, they are actually codifications of the mythology which must have existed in Gaul, Britain and Ireland at the time of the Roman conquests and which ceased to develop them.

Irish literature provides us with the earliest documents. The three cycles of Gaelic epic, the mythological cycle, the Ulster or Red Branch cycle and the Ossianic cycle of the Fenians, are stamped with an originality and an archaism which remain virtually unaltered by the medieval copyists. There are some spurious insertions and interpretations but the basic concern of the Christian monks was to safeguard their national heritage as a fount of culture for future generations.

Welsh literature suffered more from the effects of Romanization and Christianity, but certain passages of the oldest of those tales known as the *mabinogion, (Pwyll, Branwen, Manawyddan, Math*) as well as *Culhwch and Olwen* reflect extremely ancient traditions. The poetry of Wales also contains strange mixtures of tradition which are worthy of examination.

The *chansons de gests* were composed in quite a different spirit. But even in their basically anti-Celtic attitude they are valuable documents. For their basic subject matter is the struggle of Charlemagne (and consequently of the Church Militant) against paganism in all its form which becomes dressed up under the generic term of "Saracen". The supposed Moslems of the *Chanson de Roland* who worship images and pray to Mahomet, Apollo and Tervagant, have nothing in common with the true practisers of Islam. *Roland* also gives us an emir Baligant who is as alarming as any primitive god, a king Marsile who like the Irish Nuada Silver Hand and the Germanic Tyr has lost his right arm and cannot reign any longer, and a Ganelon (Guenes) identical in name and nature to the Welsh Gwynn son of Nudd (Nuada) who became the watchman of the Christian hell. Then there is the pagan Balan of the *Chanson d'Apremont*, who is one of the versions of the Gallic Belenos, and the giant Corsolt, eponymous hero of the tribe of Curiosolitae, who became Fierebras. Surely, too, the *chanson d'Aquin* is merely a transposition of the Carolingian struggle to rid Brittany of the last traces of paganism.

The most recent form adopted by the Celtic myths is the Round Table cycle which grew up around Arthur. Here we can identify the whole Celtic pantheon under one name or another. The Arthurian romances were first written at the direction of the Plantagenet dynasty which sought to glorify the English (and therefore British) monarcy in order to counterbalance the popularity given the Continental Capetian (and therefore Carolingian) dynasty by the *chansons de geste*. A figure had to be found who could match the stature of Charlemagne, and when Arthur became that figure, the attitudes of a conquered race found their way back to the surface and through him conquered Western Europe throughout the Middle Ages.

Even so, the Celtic mythology in all these literary works is extremely confused and entangled. Because of the way the tales are told, one particular character may appear under different names and be divided into two or even three. But this is only to be expected; for though the authors themselves are little more than enthusiasts, the story-tellers who supplied them with their material deliberately confused the tales as any well-bred mystic would. It is also true that heroes' names varied from one region to another.

It is right that we should establish at the outset that the heroes of these stories are actually Celtic gods who have been slightly altered and humanised. This process by which the early gods reappear in later legends under human or semi-human form (as monsters or supernatural beings) can be observed in many parts of the world, notably in India and Scandinavia. There is no question of historical characters being invested with divinity. A detailed examination of all ancient religions, not to mention the new ones (e.g. Christianity with its legions or warrior saints), shows that the gods were originally far more abstract and general forces which gradually degenerated and became anthropomorphic or zoomorphic. We can also observe how relatively integral faces of the divinity tended to divide into polymorphism and eventually to polytheism. Christianity itself has become unofficially polytheistic by accepting the three persons of the Trinity and admitting the worship of the Virgin, certain archangels and well-known saints. And when we look at the cult of the Virgin alone, we find that she has acquired a myriad of different names, from Our Lady of Lourdes to Our Lady of the Road, and so on. It is gradually reaching a point at which every believer has his or her own Our Lady, emotionally different from the Virgin of his neighbour even if intellectually the same Mother of God.

Every religion in the world has allowed its divinity to become polymorphous, for the process reflects the analytical rather than synthetical nature of the human unconscious. In this the Celts were no different from any other race, as we can see in the medieval romances where Bohort, Perceval and Galahad, the three knights of the Grail for example, are actually a single person, probably identifiable with the Teutonic Baldr.

Nevertheless, any systematic study of Celtic divinities, however summary and of course hypothetical, requires the use of some method of classification. Celtic mythology is such a quagmire that we might otherwise sink into it and never re-emerge. The only viable method, it would seem, is that based on a study of the Indo-European background. There is too much of a tendency to forget that the Celts were members of an Indo-European branch very closely related to the Latins through common Italo-Celtic ancestors, and to the Germanic peoples who were probably not Indo-European but became Aryanised through contact with their neighbours the Celts. This method of classification was determined by Georges Dumézil whose remarkable research[1] has proved the existence among all the Indo-Europeans of an early structure of divinity. Dumézil shows that the heirs of Indo-European civilization used "words evolved in a regular fashion from a single prototype *deiwos* and used both in the plural and the singular" to specifically denote "personal, superhuman beings, conceived in the image of men. The Indo-Europeans together had therefore already completed a long religious development which had taken them away from the forms of representation over-hastily classified as elementary or even primitive" (*Les Dieux des Indo-Européens*, p. 5).

Having established this general point, Georges Dumézil goes on to define the three basic functions which characterise both divine and human society: the function of sovereignty, attributed in Vedic India to the *Adityas*, the gods Varuna, Mithra, Aryama and Bagha who correspond to the Brâhmana or priestly caste; the function of force or strength represented by Indra who belongs to the same race as the *Adityas* and corresponds to the *Kshatriyas* or warrior caste, and the function of fertility attributed to the *Asvins* or *Nasatyas* who correspond to the *Vaisya* or agricultural and merchant classes.

In theory, then, it should be possible to classify the Celtic gods according to these fundamental divine functions. Given the fabulous nature of the works in which they appear, however, and the lack of available information about the early Celts, any such classification can only be provisional and hypothetical. But even guesswork of this kind would seem to be of some value in attempting to understand more about the Celtic phenomenon.

Sovereignty

According to Dumézil, the first function, that of sovereignty, is divided into four divine entities known in the Indian Rig Veda by the names Varuna, Mithra, Aryama and Bagha. Varuna is the great god of the firmament, of the invisible fire. He is the supreme and fearful magician, the Binder, he controls the will and confers intoxication. He is lord of the Night and of the Other World. His Greek equivalent is Uranus (the sky), whose name comes from the same root. In early Rome he was Jupiter. Among the Teutons he was Odin or Wotan.

The Gallic god most close to Varuna appears to have been the Esus whom Lucan describes as *horribile,* and whose name still means horrible or terrible in present-day Breton. Esus is represented on one of the bas-reliefs of the Nantes altar at the Cluny Museum as a forester pruning a tree with a bill-hook. His Welsh equivalent is Math son of Mathonwy, the central character of the *mabinogi* bearing his name. Math is the terrible master of magic and owner of the power-giving wand. In peace time he can only live if he keeps his feet in the lap of a virgin, a sign

The Wandsworth Shield found in the River Thames in London and dated to the third century B.C.

that the sovereignty inherent in Odin and Varuna has in some way degenerated. Math probably means "terrible" as does the Irish Uath, a giant who appears in the Irish saga the *Feast of Briciu* where he is seemingly a supreme force. Math can also be compared with Wotan, which would give him some connexion with the word for wood (Welsh wydd). Math seems to be aided in his function by his nephew Gwyddyon, also a magician, whose name is always linked with his. Together they create a woman from flowers and perform a number of other magic acts, notably the building of a rampart against the waves. Taliesin says in his *Cad Goddeu* that he was marked by Math before becoming immortal, and tells in the same poem how Gwyddyon saved the Britons from defeat by magically turning them into trees. Elsewhere Taliesin cites Gwyddyon as the "most skilful man of whom I have heard tell" and gives him "terrible powers". As we have already seen Gwyddyon is the lord of the Living and of the Dead. In Wales Kaer Gwyddyon (the citadel of Gwyddyon) also means "the galaxy", suggesting some affinity with Uranus, though the Uranian aspect of his nature may well be inherited from his uncle Math. For the Celts practised matrilinear descent and as the son of Math's sister Don, Gwyddyon would be both his adoptive son and his heir. It is also quite possible that king Mark (Welsh March) of the Tristan legend is the same person as Math. March shares Yseult with Tristan just as Math shares his magic with Gwyddyon. March or "horse" (whom certain versions of the legend depict with horses' ears) is definitely a god of the Other World, while Tristan ("Oak-fire") from *drus-tanos* appears to have links both with the tree of Esus and with the horse on which Math is able to live in war-time.

Varuna's function as the Binder, on the other hand, is associated with the Gallic Ogmios, or Irish Ogma of the *Battle of Mag-Tured*. The character of Ogmios has given rise to a considerable number of comments. A superficial reading of the work of Lucian of Samosata (2nd century AD) has led to Ogmios' being identified as the Gallic Hercules. What Lucian actually wrote is "The Celts call Herakles Ogmios in the language of their country, but the image they paint of the god is quite strange. For them he is an old man at the end of his life, with his hair receding and what hair he has being white, and with his skin being rough and sunburned ... one would take him for a Charon or a Japhet from the underground Tartary, in fact anybody rather than Herakles. Even in this state, however, he has the trappings of Herakles ... But I have not mentioned the most extraordinary aspect of this portrait, which is that this old Herakles is represented pulling along behind him a mass of men all kept together with gold and amber chains through their ears ... Not knowing what to do with the other end of these chains, since the god's right hand was already holding the club and his left the bow, the painter has perforated the end of the god's tongue so that it appears to be pulling along the men, while the god turns smiling towards them" (Lucian, *Herakles*).

It is clear from this that any attempts to identify Celtic gods with Gallo-Roman models must be quite arbitrary. In his comments on the passage quoted above, P. M. Duval wonders whether "the myth related here which is no part of the legend of Hercules, could belong to Celtic mythology" *(Les Dieux de la Gaule,* pp. 83-84). Duval even suggests that this portrait might be depicting some kind of *dance macabre* in which the souls of the dead are being drawn into an infernal ring by a leader-cum-wizard, though he soon rejects this idea by concluding that "Any infernal quality in Ogmios is only conjecture." Conjecture it may be, but there is considerable evidence to support it.

In the *Battle of Mag-Tured*, Ogma, who is also the divine woodman responsible for supplying the court with timber and building fortresses, is shown to be a powerful magician, which would make him an obvious counterpart to Math, Gwyddyon and March, the gods of the Other World, and to Esus, the woodman god. Ogmios-Ogma is supposed to have invented oghamic script in Ireland and from Lucian's description we can also classify him as the Binder-god of the Galatians (these being the Celts whom Lucian is describing), since he is the god of eloquence who can bind men by his words. This latter characteristic reinforces his connexions with Varuna.

Of the other figures who might be included in this category, we should mention the Tuetonic Odin, who is one-eyed because he is a seer. As Dumézil says, "The gift was guaranteed him and is symbolically expressed by deliberate mutilation, or so it would seem; he is one-eyed because he has given one of his eyes into the honeyed source of all knowledge" (*Les Dieux et les Germains*, p. 41). There are two one-eyed characters in the epic literature of Ireland. The first, Balor, is "King of the Isles", a Fomoré. "Balor had a destructive eye which only opened during combat. Four men raised the lid with a well-polished hook which they pushed into it. Any army which looked at this eye was powerless to resist it, were it to contain several thousand men." Balor is killed by his opponent Lug, a Tuatha de Danann who is also his grandson and represents the Mithra side of the sovereignty function. Balor's death is further evidence of the decline of the Varuna aspect of sovereignty among the Celts. The same myth is also related in the Welsh romance of *Culhwch and Olwen*. Here the giant cyclops is Yspadadden Penkawr, whose daughter Olwen Culhwch is trying to win. It takes two forks to raise Yspadadden's eyebrows, and he finally loses his eye to Culhwch before he is killed. The idea of Balor's eye opening only in battle is to a certain extent reiterated in the notion of Math being able to walk only in war-time.

The other one-eyed figure of Irish epic is Goll who appears in the Leinster cycle as rival to Finn mac Cumall, a character classifiable in the Mithra category. Goll is the chief of the clan Morna. He has conquered Britain and the land of Lochlann (Scandinavia) and the tribute he receives from his conquests provokes the jealousy of Finn, the leader of that strange association of knights-huntsmen called the Fenians. For Goll is only Finn's vassal although he has killed Finn's father Cumall at the battle of Cnucha. In the end Goll is murdered by men sent from Finn. Goll must therefore be the Varuna side of the deity, once powerful but now supplanted by the Mithra side, since Finn is obviously one of the Mithraic sun gods. Cumall, Finn's father, whose name means "powerful" (Gallic *camulos*) seems to be yet another Celtic incarnation of Varuna.

The Mithra of the *Rig Veda* can be rather loosely described as the solar hero. At the time of the Roman empire, his name and nature had been so widely spread by the Indo-Europeans that the cult of Mithra achieved almost greater proportions than Christianity. Strictly speaking the Indian Mithra is the god of visible fire. He is lord of the Day, of whiteness, and is therefore the daylight sun as opposed to Varuna, the black sun. Mithra is the patron of contracts. Like the Hebraic Yaweh, he forms alliances with the race of believers, but he is not fearful. On the contrary he is the god of gentleness, benevolence and intelligence. He provides the basic nourishment of milk. Mithra is therefore a more human god than Varuna. His Greek equivalent is undoubtedly Apollo, but not the classical Apollo, the Hyperborean for want of a better term. Among the Romans, the god most like Mithra is the Mercury honoured on a number of rocks and mountains which became known as Monts-Saint-Michel. For the Teutonic peoples he was Tyr, the one-armed god.

In Gaul, Mithra was the Mercury of whom Caesar speaks, but he has many different names, including Grannos-Moritasgos, Vandannos, Abelio and, more especially, Nodens, Lugos and Belenos, this last being feminised into Belisama.

Nodens is attested by inscriptions in Britain. He is the Nuada of Irish epic, the chief of the Tuatha de Danann who loses his hand at the first battle of Mag-Tured against the Fir-Bolg. But "with the help of Credne the smith, Dianecht the doctor gave him a silver hand which had the strength of any other hand" and which earned him the name Nuada Silver Hand. The one-armed god of Teutonic mythology is Tyr who lost his hand to the wolf Fenrir when the gods were attempting to bind the beast. For Tyr was the only one prepared to put his hand in the wolf's mouth when Fenrir demanded proof of the gods' good intentions, and lost the hand when Fenrir realised that he had been tricked.

Dumézil notes the existence of two quasi-legendary Roman epic tales which describe the exploits of Horatio Cocles (the one-eyed man) defending the pontus Sublicius against the Etruscans, and of Mucius Scaevola (the left-handed man) who deliberately held his right hand in the fire to prove a false point. Dumézil adds, "When Odin and Cocles dazzle the enemy forces they have already become one-eyed in some previous incident; when Tyr and Scaevola lose their right hands it is an actual part of their legendary tale and the hands are given as a pledge in a heroic act of perjury. The only comparable, if considerably more remote, example of this kind occurs in the epic of the Irish, a people related both to the Teutons and the Italiots" (*Les Dieux des Germains*, pp. 72-3). Obviously Odin and Tyr, the one-eyed and one-armed men, belong to an early Indo-European tradition which also recurs in Ireland in the form of Balor and Nuada, who are allies during the first battle of Mag-Tured. The Welsh equivalent of Nuada is Ludd Llaw Ereint (Ludd Silver Hand). We can assume that Ludd is a corruption of Nudd, especially as Nudd is attested as the father of Edern, one of Arthur's knights, and of Gwynn, a character who became christianised in Wales as gateman to hell.

When Nuada loses his hand he can no longer reign over Ireland and the throne passes to Bress, who is half Fomoré and half Tuatha de Danann. But Bress's heavy taxation provokes the hostility of the Tuatha who then fight the second battle of Mag-Tured against the Fomoré. To prepare for combat Nuada enlists the help of the giant Dagda, the doctor Dianecht, and Ogma. He also gives the position of commander to Lug Lamfada (Long Spear), elsewhere known as Lug Samildanach (Sym-poly-technician). Lug is undoubtedly the most widely known of the Celtic gods, since his presence is also attested in Gaul (as Lugos or Lugu) in place names like Lyon, Laon, Loudun, Leyde, etc., which are all derived from Lugdunum (Lug's citadel).

Lug is both Tuatha and Fomoré. He is the grandson of Balor whom he kills at Mag-Tured with a slingshot in Balor's single eye. Lug is the universal master craftsman. When he wishes to enter the palace at Tara, the gatekeeper, a powerful figure among the Celts, refuses to admit him until he declares his skills. Lug then replies that he is a carpenter, a smith, an athlete, a harpist, a warrior, a poet, a magician, a cup-bearer and a bronze-worker. The gatekeeper says that they already have specialists in all these fields in Tara, to which Lug retorts that there cannot possibly be one man capable of practising all the skills. He is therefore admitted to the castle and wins a chess game which the king makes him play as a trial. He then sits in the seat of knowledge. He is the Samildanach, the all-round expert.

Lug is clearly identifiable with Mercury, the patron of travellers and merchants of whom Caesar speaks. But Lug is also the god of skills, of music and poetry which makes him partly Apollonian as well. Moreover in the Irish epics he is represented as being a radiant and luminous character, suggesting that he is a "sun god", whatever help that term may be. Lug means "white, shining" and is connected with the Greek λευκος. He owns a magic spear reminiscent of the arrows of Apollo which can both kill and cure. The spear is called Gai Bolga, and is an emblem of lightning. It comes from Assal, one of the northern islands (an allusion to Hyperborea) where the Tuatha de Danann originally lived. To moderate the poisonous and destructive power of this spear its point has to be immersed in a cauldron full of poison and "black fluid" or blood.

> The spear of Assal ...
> dead is he whose blood it spills.
> Its quality is such that it does not strike in error
> if one simply cries out 'ibar'.
> If one cries out 'athibar'
> it comes back
> to the hand of he who threw it.
> (*Leabhar na Babala*, poem 66).

Lug's renown was not confined to the Celts. The Romans themselves appear to have been impressed by the versatility of the Gallic god and likened him to Mercury. Indeed the emperor Augustus wished his own festival of *mensis augustus* (August 1) to be celebrated at Lyon, partly because Augustus was a great devotee of Mercury, and deliberately allowed himself to be associated with the god, and partly because August 1 was the great Irish feast of Lugnasad, the marriage of Lug, on which the triumph of the sun god was celebrated.

Perhaps even more surprisingly, Lug came to acquire quite remarkable fame throughout the post-12th century West of Europe as Lancelot du Lac, one of the best known characters of Arthurian legend. However audacious the identification of Lug with Lancelot may at first appear, it is based on fact and has been ably demonstrated by the eminent Arthurian scholar R. S. Loomis. To start with, the character of Lancelot, whose name is in theory French, does not appear in the Welsh texts pre-dating Chrétien de Troyes, whereas later texts do mention Lawnslot dy Lac. This absence is quite astonishing considering the importance of Lancelot. We then find that there is no mention whatever of Lug in any Welsh text, and must presume, given his pan-Celtic renown, that the Welsh called him by another name. There is a very minor character in the romance *Culhwch and Olwen*, one of the oldest Arthurian tales, who qualifies. This is Lleenleawg the Gael, prince of Britain. During a battle over the magic cauldron of Diwrnach, "Lleenleawg the Gael seized Kaletfwlch, swung it round in a circle and killed Diwrnach and his entire retinue." Kaletfwlch or Kaled wulch, "Hard steel", is Arthur's sword, known as Escalibor in the French romances. It has an Irish equivalent in *calad-colg* (cutting hard), the sword brandished by Ogma in the battle of Mag-Tured and owned by the hero Cú Chulainn, son of Lug. Nobody except Gawain in Chrétien's *Perceval* ever had the audacity to brandish Kaletfwlch; and when Arthur realises that he is going to die after the battle of Camlann, he says to Escalibor, "My good and magnificent sword, the best in this world apart from the sword with strange sheaths [the sword of Solomon, given to Galahad who discovers the Grail], you are going to lose your lord. Where will you find another master who can use you as well as I, unless you fall into the hands of Lancelot" *(La Mort du Roi Arthur)*.

It is clear from this that only Lancelot will be able to have the sword. So, if Lleenleawg the Gael has taken it, it is because he is worthy to do so. And to see Lancelot and Lleenleawg as the same character requires very little imagination. Further clues come from Taliesin's poem the *Spoils of the Abyss* which describes how Arthur wins a magic cauldron. Here the man holding the sword is Llymninawc, a character of whom we know nothing else. It is quite likely, however, that bad spelling or misreading led to errors on the part of copyists. For in other texts we do find a Llwch Llawwynnyawc (Llwch Whitened Hand or Silver Hand) who is father of Gwalchmai, the Welsh name for Gawain. But Llwch or Lloch is also the Welsh form of Loth, and Gawain is the son of King Loth of Orkney. As we weave our way through these characters we find that they are all connected with the sword, and Loth or Llwch is the phonetic equivalent of Lug.

Since Lug is known as Lamfada meaning "Long Spear or Long Lance" we must presume that he is the same person as Lancelot or Lance-Loth. Childish as it may seem, puns were used a great deal in mythological writings, and the authors of the Arthurian romances were always quite prepared to indulge in dubious etymology and to frenchify names however haphazardly. They even went to far as to qualify Lancelot as "du Lac" and to explain this name by describing how he had been brought up by a mysterious lady of the lake. Since the Welsh word for lake just happens to be Llwch, the identification of Lug with Lancelot becomes a foregone conclusion. It is perhaps worth pointing out that the Welsh made Nuada into Ludd Silver Hand, which would seem to indicate some conscious confusion between Nuada and Lug.

Lastly we find that both Lug and Lancelot lose their fathers in some clan quarrel, Lug's father being murdered by the sons of Tuirenn and Lancelot's father, King Ban of Benoic (an erroneous translation of the Welsh Bran Vendigeit) dying when his castle is taken. In both cases it is the sons who avenge their fathers' deaths. Like Lug, Lancelot is supremely versatile. He is the best and most skilful knight in the world. Like Lug, he is radiant, he destroys monsters, removes the spells from the castles of the Dolorous Garde and from the *Val sans Retour*. He is the light which combats the forces of darkness. In this sense, Lancelot is the Persian Mithra, also a young and handsome god, a dragon-killer, or the Saint Michael and St George of Christian mythology. His failure to win through the quest for the Grail is not due to his state of sin, but to the fact that the mithraic sovereignty he represents has degenerated. Having then failed to find the Grail, Lancelot becomes an incomplete cripple, a Nuada Silver Hand, a Tyr. In some ways the character of Lancelot is a synthesis of Nuada and Lug.

The purely solar aspect of Mithra, however, is more closely personified by Belenos, whose name means the Shining One. The worship of Belenos is attested by a number of inscriptions and by place names such as Beaune and the christianised Saint-Bonnet. The fact that Mont-Saint-Michel was once called Tombelaine, a name which has now passed to the neighbouring island, shows how the solar cult was carried on from Belenos to Saint Michael. One of the highest points in Brittany, the mountain of Bel-Air, is also known as the Signal of Bel Orient (Bel rising), and another high point, the Mont St-Michel de Braspart, must also have been consecrated to the worship of Belenos. Similarly, the presence of Mercury is attested at Saint-Michel-Mont-Mercure in the Vendée. In the Welsh tradition Belenos occurs under the name Beli, father to a line of saints. It was Beli who gave his name to one of the strangest springs in Celtic paganism at Barenton, formerly

Balenton (*Beli nemeton,* "the clearing of Beli"). Belisama, the feminine version of Belenos, is a superlative meaning "the very brilliant", and occurs in place names like Bellême, Blismes and so on. The idea of a solar divinity being female is natural enough since the sun in both the Celtic and the Germanic languages is feminine.

Another character we might include in this category is Finn, the hero of the Irish Fenian cycle. His name means "white" and he, too, is a solar hero, a defender from monsters and a hunter as well as a righter of wrongs. The association of men he commands is a very curious one and foreshadows some of the medieval chivalric societies, including orders like the Knights-Templar. From November 1 (the feast of Samain or feast of the Dead) until May 1 (feast of Beltaine, new fire), the Fenians would live among the local people, overseeing the application of justice, guarding the ports and defending widows and orphans. Then, from May 1 to November 1, they would hunt the stag and the wolf, while keeping down bandits and helping to collect taxes. To put it more bluntly, they rid the land of brigands only to take their place. There were strict conditions for entry into Fenian ranks. A warrior was not to marry a woman for her dowry, but for her good qualities; he was never to assault a woman, never to refuse anything to anyone who asked for a precious object or for food (as the obligatory custom of the gift demanded) and never to run from less than ten of the enemy. The warrior had also to be admitted into the order of *fili* (wisemen and poets). He had to undergo extremely rigorous endurance tests, proving himself able to stand with a shield and a hazel stick against nine warriors all hurling spears at him together, able to escape through the woods from the combined force of the Fenians, able to keep his weapons always steady in his hands, to walk without breaking any twig beneath his feet, to jump the height of his own forehead and bend to the height of his own knee, to take a thorn out of his foot while still running. With entry requirements like these, the Fenians were obviously an elite, and it is their adventures that are recounted in the many sagas which inspired Macpherson's *Ossian.*

Finn, the leader of this intrepid force, is represented as a kind of magician. He has only to put his thumb in his mouth to know secrets beyond the reach of common mortals. He can cure a wounded man by bringing him water in his own hands. He is also a poet and father of the poet Ossian. So, as well as being a dragon-killer, he is also skilled in poetry and healing like Apollo, and his knowledge of the secrets of the gods makes him Mercurial also. All the evidence suggests that his Welsh counterpart is Gwynn, son of Nudd, whose name also means "white', although Gwynn was gradually altered by external influences to become a kind of god of death belonging to the Aryama side of the sovereignty function.

Etymologically, Aryama is the protector of the *Aryas,* or early Indo-Europeans. He is the lord of nourishment, both spiritual and material. It is he who gives, but also he who takes away. As patron of roads, he is the god of crossroads. Finally, he is the divinity of the ancestors and thus the lord of the Other World, but not as the supreme master like Varuna, more as what we might call the "manager". Being both benevolent and fearsome, he is essentially two-sided in nature, and it is this ambiguity which led the Persian Mazdeans to make him the anti-Mazda or anti-god, lord of the shadows, a concept which then passed into christianity in the character of the devil. Aryama is the Greek Hades, but he is also Cerberus and Thersites. According to Dumézil he is the Juventas of ancient Rome, who later came to be replaced by Orcus and Dispater. He is probably the Teutonic Loki.

In the Celtic world he appears under a multitude of different names, which suggests that he was the chief god of the Gauls. Caesar certainly thinks so: "The

Gauls all claim to be descended from Dis Pater, declaring that this is the tradition preserved by the druids. For this reason they measure periods of time not by days but by nights" (*Gallic Wars*, VI, 18). Caesar, however, alludes only to the god's Latin name, and attempts have been made to identify him with a number of known Gallic gods. In fact there can be no doubt that he is Teutates, and his Welsh equivalents are Pwyll (Pelles), Bran the Blessed, Maelwas (Chrétien's Meleagant), Medrawt (Mordret), Evnyssen, Gwynn or Gwynwas. In Ireland he becomes Dagda, Briciu and Mider, all of whom reappear during the Middle Ages as the Ogre (Orcus), St Blaise (or St Loup), St Roch and St Tugdual.

In his *Les Dieux de la Gaule* (pp. 25-6) P. M. Duval states that Teutates was a common noun, though surely all the names of gods are common nouns or epithets of a kind. Teutates has also been regarded as the patron god of the tribe, a role perfectly compatible with his other activities. As we have seen in the chapter on Taliesin, however, there is a strict similarity between Teutates and Dispater, and the form of sacrifice in which victims are said to have been offered to him is actually a means of achieving resurrection or passage into the Other World by immersion in the cauldron of rebirth.

The cauldron or cup is therefore the essential attribute of Teutates. There is evidence of a cult based on the cauldron in all Celtic countries, and the two-sided nature of Aryama is reflected in the way Christianity turned the cauldron both into the beneficent Grail and into the satanic pot in which the medieval devil boiled the damned.

The Irish lord of the cauldron is Dagda, one of the Tuatha de Danann and a kind of monstrous giant. His spoon is large enough to hold a man and a woman, the forked branch in his hand big enough to carry eight men. His harp is a magic object which reflects his ambiguous nature, for by playing it he can make people weep or laugh. He is also called Eochaid Ollathair (Eochaid Father of All), which makes him clearly identifiable with Teutates. His cauldron is inexhaustible and can satisfy whole armies. Dagda himself is an extraordinary glutton: before the battle of Mag-Tured he stupefies the opposing Fomoré by devouring the contents of an immense pot of porridge in which goats, sheep and pigs are floating.

In the Welsh texts this cauldron is *Peir Penn Annfwn* (Cauldron of the Master of the Abyss). The title "Master of the Abyss" belongs to Pwyll, king of Dyvedd and hero of one of the oldest *mabinogion*. During a stag-hunt Pwyll meets Arawn, king of Annfwn, who demands that in compensation for a wrong Pwyll has done him the two of them should exchange identities for a year during which time Pwyll will have to fight Arawn's enemies in Annfwn. Pwyll is victorious and the two kings eventually resume their own names and places. Later Pwyll marries Rhiannon, an incarnation of the mother-goddess.

It is very likely that Pelles, the wealthy Fisher-King, was based on Pwyll. Pelles also has all the marks of a lord of the other world. He guards the sacred Grail and clearly has control over the future, since he gives his daughter to Lancelot in order that she may give birth to Galahad, the hero predestined to accomplish the ultimate act in the Grail quest. Arawn's brother, the semi-historical Uryen, father of Owein and husband of the mother-goddess Modron, also plays the part of an other world divinity.

Bran can be assimilated to Teutates in two respects, both as owner of a cauldron of rebirth and as divine patron of the tribe, or in Bran's case of the nation. For we learn from the *mabinogi* of *Branwen* that his head is taken home by the survivors of the expedition to Ireland and that it protects them for seven and then for eighty years before they bury it in the White Hill at London on his orders. This head is "one of the three things it is well to keep hidden ... while it stayed there, the Saxons did not come to oppress this island" (Triad 14, *Mab*. II, p. 240). In the end Arthur exhumes the head because "he does not like the idea of the island being protected by any force other than his own" (Triad 15, *ibid*. p. 242). As protector of the nation, Bran guarded the countryside and the roads which led to it, and we can recognise him in all the many tricephalic gods of Gaul. In this he shares the same duties as the Roman Janus, the descendant of a much earlier god to whom we shall return later. It is worth noting in passing, however, that the Capitol *(caput-toli)* is the site of a buried head. Bran is also the Blessed, the giver and the patron god of the gift. One of the later triads would make him a saint, claiming that "he was the first to bring the Christian faith to the nation of the Cymry, from Rome where he spent seven years as a hostage for his son Caradawc" (Triad 124, *Mab*. II, p. 305). It is hardly surprising, therefore, that Bran should have become Christianised into the St Brendan of medieval legend. The Round Table romances made him Lancelot's father, Ban of Benoic, Bran de Lis and Brangore d'Estragore. As Bron, he is one version of the Fisher-King. He also appears in various of Gawain's strange adventures, notably in a city under the water (a symbol for the Other World). Later texts betray an increasing tendency to confuse the giant Bran with the Ogre, for though the latter is part of folklore rather than mythology he nonetheless belongs to the myth of the divinity who gives life and takes it away. A tale like "Hop O' My Thumb", for example, is evidence of remarkable continuity in popular belief. When the ogre is deceived into killing and eating his own children, he is merely fulfilling his basic function. The fact that romanesque sculpture portrays so many man-eating monsters based on the moster of Gallic epic known as Tarasque de Noves serves to remind us that Aryama is by nature ambiguous, both creator and destroyer.

Dagda, Pwyll, Pelles and Bran represent the beneficent side of the function. Teutates is a more alarming figure and the maleficent side of the god which he goes part way to portraying is to be found in the more minor characters of Celtic or related legend. Gwynn, son of Nudd, as we have already said, was originally a Mithraic sun god but became the guardian of hell and therefore the devil of Welsh Christian mythology. In other Welsh texts, he takes the name Gwynwas ("White Servant"), a name analogous with *Gwynnva* or *Gwenved* ("White World") the word for the Celtic paradise or other world, there being no heaven and hell in the Christian sense. This Gwynwas became the Ganelon of the *Chanson de Roland*. In Chrétien's *Erec* he is Maheloas, "A high baron, lord of the island of glass; in that island it is neither very cold nor very hot, thunder is never heard, lightning never strikes and snakes do not live there." In the same author's *Chevalier à la Charette*, Lancelot pursues the abductor of Queen Guinevere into the kingdom of Gorre (Voire-Verre) "from where no stranger returns but is forced to stay in servitude and exile." The abductor is Meleagant, son of King Baudemagu who reigns over that land and Baudemagu could be Bran-de-Magu or "Bran of the Plain". He is a benevolent lord, while his son is capable of all kinds of treachery. In a medieval Welsh poem we find Meleagant as Maelwas O Ynys Wydr (Maelwas of the Glass Island), and the *Vita Gildae* calls him Melvas and says that he reigned over the land of summer, in a well-fortified castle sheltered behind reeds, a river and marshland. Apart from the fact that the land of summer denotes the kingdom of the dead, Maelwas' territory bears all the hall marks of the typical entrance to the other world. In the middle of the Monts d'Arrée region of Brittany there is a large area of sinister-looking marshland called Yeun Ellez, which is the subject of a number of legends about souls in purgatory. The church at Brennilis (possibly meaning Bran's Church or the Marsh of the Ellez) holds a statue of Our Lady of Breac-Ellis, Breac meaning "marsh" and *Ellis* or *Elles* being comparable to the Anglo-Saxon word hell. A number of Breton villages and rivers have similar names. Brocéliande, which was called Brecheliant in the Middle Ages and is Bro-Hellean in Breton, obviously means the land of hell, the land of the other world.

When Chrétien's Meleagant abducted Arthur's wife Guinevere, it was simply the god of death taking her. In the *Mort du roi Arthur,* it is Mordret who abducts Guinevere and seizes the throne, and Mordret, or Medrawt as the Welsh texts call him, effectively sounds the death knell of Arthurian chivalry. He is Arthur's nephew, but also his incestuous son, and he kills the old king.

The Irish equivalent of Medrawt is Mider, one of the Tuatha de Danann and hero of the story of Etaine. Like Medrawt he steals the king's wife and takes her to his land, the mound of Bri Leith. All King Eochaid's attempts to recover his wife fail. The Irish Mider also appears to have been known to the Gauls, since there is a stone in the Strasburg Museum showing a warrior carrying a spear and leaning on a bull's head with the dedication *Deo Medru*[2]. Be that as it may, the name Mider, like the name Medrawt, is obviously derived from the root *med* which is linked in Indo-European languages to the concept of the middle (*medium*) and to the idea of drunkenness (Welsh *medw*, "drunk", *med*, "mead" and Indian *mada*, a huge monster whose name means drunkenness). This would make Mider the intoxicator, the man who brings the drunkenness of immortality in the depths of his underground palace, just as he is the mediator between the worlds of the living and of the dead.

It is these characters who belong to the infernal aspect of the divinity, to the myth of Hades who abducted Proserpine. And it is this myth which gave rise to all the tales in which the devil steals the soul of a man or a woman, either with or without their consent, as in the Faust story. The Aryama aspect of the sovereignty function is also inherent in more obviously unpleasant characters like the Greek Thersites and the striking Teutonic Loki. Loki is a trouble-maker and a traitor. It is he who causes the death of Odin's son Baldr, who starts the battle of the end of time and who kills the primordial god Heimdall. As Dumézil says, he is "similar in all respects to the inspirer of the great misfortunes of the world, of the diabolical spirit" (*Les Dieux des Germains,* p. 90).

In Ireland he is undoubtedly the sharp-tongued Briciu, an Ulster nobleman who entertains warriors and kings in his home with great ceremony only to make them quarrel amongst themselves. In Wales he is Evnyssen, Bran's half-brother, who is responsible for the loss of the magic cauldron and the fatal quarrel between Bran and his brother-in-law. This maleficent quality also recurs in the medieval Satan.

The final category of the sovereignty function is symbolised in Vedic India by Bagha. It is he who presides over the partition of goods. He is the lord of wealth, or rather of future wealth, a kind of god of the Promised Land, or a Golden Age to come. This role appears to have been fulfilled by the Greek Dionysus, the Roman Terminus and the Teutonic Baldr. In Gaul he becomes Maponios, in Wales Mabon.

According to the Triads, Mabon, son of Modron, is one of the three eminent prisoners of the island of Britain. The romance of *Culhwch and Olwen* also makes him a prisoner who has to be rescued before Arthur can hunt the boar Twrch Trwyth.

In their search for him Arthur's knights Kai and Gwrhyr "rode on the salmon's shoulders until they came to the prisoner's enclosure and they heard moaning and wailing from the other side of the wall" (*Culhwch and Olwen*). The *legend* says that Mabon was held captive at Kaer Loyw (Gloucester) and describes how, once freed, he was able to take the vital razor and comb from between the boar's ears so that the rest of the adventure might be completed.

Mabon's imprisonment is explained in Chrétien de Troyes' *Erec et Enide*, in the episode entitled *La Joie de la Cour* which also appears in the Welsh tale of *Gereint and Enid*. Gereint comes to a magical orchard and "a clearing within; there stood a pavilion of *paile* and a red canopy and the entrance open, and next to that an apple tree with a great hunting-horn hanging from a branch. He dismounted and entered the pavilion and inside there was nothing but a girl" *(Gereint and Enid)*. When Gereint sits down a knight appears and challenges him. Gereint beats him and learns that this knight (whom Chrétien calls Mabonagrain) had promised to remain a prisoner in the orchard because of his love for the girl and that he cannot leave until he has been overcome by another knight. In another medieval tale, the *Bel Inconnu* by Renaud de Beaujeu, the hero rids the *Gaste Cité* of the spell hanging over it by killing two fearful knights: "The first is Evrain, the other his brother Mabon, the great wizard" (A. Mary, *la Chambre des Dames*, p. 301). When we call Mabon and Evrain by their Welsh names, *Mabon ag Euryn*, it becomes clear that they and Mabonagrain are the same. Indeed Euryn, as in Gwri Wallt Euryn is Mabon. In Chrétien's version of the story, the king who owns the castle of Brandigan where the magical orchard stands is himself called Evrain, while the Welsh tale names him as Owein.

Mabon ("Son") has been regarded as a kind of Celtic Horus, a youthful sun held captive by the night. While he is still a prisoner the day cannot dawn and all life is halted in its tracks. Mabon's mother is Modron, one aspect of the mother-goddess, and consequently analogous to Demeter. It is therefore possible that there is a connexion between the imprisonment of Mabon and the captivity of Demeter's daughter Proserpine.

Apart from Mabon there are two other famous prisoners in British tradition. One of them is the Gweir mentioned in Taliesin's poem the *Spoils of the Abyss*. "Total was the imprisonment of Gweir at Kaer Sidhi . . . Nobody before him had been able to make his way into the city. A heavy blue chain holds the brave lad who sighs sadly among the spoils of the abyss." Apart from the common theme of lamentations, Taliesin's poem is very similar to *Culhwch and Olwen* in that it tells an epic tale of a quest for objects belonging to the other world. R. S. Loomis has identified Taliesin's Gweir with Gwri Gwallt Euryn (Gwri Golden Hair); and Gwri is Pryderi, son of Pwyll and Rhiannon, yet another version of the mother-goddess. She is accused of having killed her child and is condemned to carrying passing travellers on her back, as if she were a mare. Indeed Rhiannon is the same person as Epona, the horse goddess of the Roman empire, though her name is distinctly Gallic (from *epos* a horse). When Rhiannon eventually finds her son, who has been brought up by a fine man, she calls him Pryderi (Care) while his foster-father calls him Gwri Gwallt Euryn.

The theme of the prisoner or of the young man who is shackled in some way, material of spiritual, occurs in the *mabinogi* of *Math*. Here Arianrod, another face of the mother-goddess, has given birth to a son whom she refuses to recognise. Gwyddyon, Arianrod's brother and lover who brings the boy up, manages to trick the child's mother into naming him Lleu Llaw Gyffes. Then when Arianrod condemns Lleu to symbolic impotence by declaring that he will never be able to marry any daughter of man, Gwyddyon and Math conjure a woman, Blodeuwedd, out of flowers and marry her to Lleu. Blodeuwedd, however, falls in love with a hunts-man and makes him kill Lleu. Lleu flies away in the form of a bird, but Gwyddyon manages to find him and restore him to human form after turning Blodeuwedd into an owl. Lleu then kills his murderer in the same fashion as he had himself been killed.

The name Lleu means "lion" and is undoubtedly connected with the early practice of totemism. The constant companion of Yvain-Owein is a lion, and he is also said to be son of Modron. The fact that Owein is never described as Mabon's brother although they supposedly have the same mother, suggests that they are the same person.

Owein is one of the three blessed kings of the island of Britain (*Mab.* II, 238). Both he and his father Uryen are frequently confused with the British leaders who fought against the Saxons, but Owein is undoubtedly a partly mythical figure, as we can see in the strange Welsh tale of the *Dream of Rhonabwy*. While Owein is playing chess with Arthur, Arthur's servants attack Owein's ravens. He asks the king to stop the fight but Arthur changes the subject. So Owein raises his standard and the ravens massacre Arthur's men. Wherever he goes with his flight of ravens, they are victorious.

In a number of texts Owein and Uryen are saved by the intervention of Mod-ron's ravens which can be compared to the birds of Rhiannon singing the song of immortality. In the *mabinogi* of *Manawyddan*, Pryderi is out hunting a boar when he comes to a castle. There he sees a fountain with a golden cup fastened to it by chains, the ends of which cannot be seen. When Pryderi grasps hold of the cup his feet become stuck to the stone round the fountain and he is a prisoner. Later his mother Rhiannon tries to free him but the same thing happens to her. Then there is a clap of thunder and the castle, Pryderi and Rhiannon all disappear. *(Manawyd-dan, son of Llyr)*. An imaginative scientist might explain this episode in terms of electrical phenomena. For anyone touching a high tension cable immediately becomes stuck to it, and would-be helpers suffer the same fate. The thunder clap could be a symbol for the volatilising effects of lightning. In this case, however, the fountain itself is magical, like the Barenton fountain in the forest of Brocéliande. The Welsh tale of the *Countess of the Fountain* describes the second of these two as follows: "You will see ... a great tree with branches greener than the greenest pine. Beneath that tree is a fountain and beside the fountain a great stone, and on the stone a silver basin and a silver chain so that the bowl and stone cannot be separated."[3] And Chrétien, who tells the same story in his *Chevalier au Lion*, goes on to say, "If you want to take some water from the bowl and sprinkle it on the step you will see such a storm that there will remain neither beast, goat, does nor stag, nor pig in this wood, the birds will fly away for you will see everything caught up in wind and lightning, trees blown to pieces, rain, thunder and lightning, and if you can survive it without great trouble and suffering, you will be luckier than any other knight" (G. Cohen, *Chrétien de Troyes*, p. 51). Then, says the anonymous Welsh author, "A shower of birds will come and sit in the tree and in your own country you have never heard such singing as theirs."

However the adventure is not yet over. A great moaning and groaning is heard and any man rash enough to have come this far will have to fight a Black Knight mounted on a black horse. Only Owein-Yvain succeeds in killing the black knight, and having then married the man's widow, he himself becomes guardian of the fountain, in one way bound to it and kept apart from the world.

It is possible that this adventure contains some allusion to alchemy. The façade of Notre Dame de Paris which is full of alchemical allegories contains the sculptured image of a spring flowing from between the roots of an oak-tree. Opposite it there is a representation of an alchemist dressed as a knight who stands defending the *athanor*, or alchemical furnace. The spring at Barenton also flows at the roots of an oak, and in alchemical writings the hollow oak is one of the most frequently used symbols for the *athanor*. The fountain or spring is also an ideal place in which to keep secrets. In the *Désir désiré*, by Nicholas Flamel, the author writes of "a secret stone, hidden and buried deep in a fountain." It is said of the fountain of Barenton, too, that it is "boiling like hot water though it is colder than marble."[4]

On the mythological level, however, the fountain like the Grail is a symbol of the female divinity. The black knight like the Fisher-King remains content to guard it simply because he is black, or powerless to use it to fertilise his land. When the black knight has been removed because he is weak, Owein-Yvain is able to regenerate the land with his new powers. The fact that Laudine, the knight's widow, prevaricates for so long before agreeing to marry her husband's murderer shows that the function which Yvain is to regenerate is basically sterile. Having tasted the fruits of the other world represented by the fountain, Owein must stay there a prisoner, like Mabon, Pryderi or Lleu.

Strictly speaking there is no Irish equivalent for Mabon, except perhaps in Oengus, one of the Tuatha de Danann. He is not actually a prisoner, but he does live apart from the world although he is the favourite child. Oengus is frequently alluded to as Mac Oc "the young Son" and is the most handsome and most lovable of his race. His kisses change into birds which come and hover over the young in a way reminiscent of Owein's ravens and Rhiannon's birds. Oengus is the patron god of heroes and of unhappy lovers like Diarmaid and Etaine.

The story of Etaine, one of the strangest in the Irish epic cycle, describes how Oengus was the son of Dagda and the fairy Boann, after whom the river Boyne was named, who is presumably a kind of mother goddess like the Gallic Matrona (goddess of the river Marne). But Boann was already married to Elcmar, king of the *sidh* of Brug (the tumulus of New Grange). Dagda arranges for Mider to kidnap the child, and when the Mac Oc grows into a young man he takes the *sidh* of Brug by a trick and drives out Elcmar. Now lord of the Brug, Oengus helps Mider to win Etaine, the loveliest girl in all Ireland, and when she is changed into a butterfly by the jealous sorceress Fuamnach, it is on Oengus' cloak that she comes to land. He then takes her to his house "and to his sun room which had shining windows to go out of and come in through. He decorated the room with purple. Every night the Mac Oc slept with her in the sun tower and comforted her until her joy and her color returned. Then he filled the sun room with beautiful green plants, and the insect thrived on the flowers . . ."

The theme of the sun chamber, which is probably linked to the myth of the Hyperborean oasis, occurs fairly frequently in Celtic legend. In the *Folie-Tristan* Tristan disguised as a madman tells King Mark that he wishes to take Iseult to a chamber of crystal where all the colours of the sun are reflected. Then there is the kingdom of Gorre or Voire where Meleagant holds sway. Finally we have the prison of air in which Merlin is held by the fairy Vivian, a kind of mysterious castle in the depths of the forest of Brocéliande. One of the triads talks of the three total disappearances from Britain and includes that of "Merddin" the bard of Emrys Wledig and his nine Cylveirdd (possibly "Lost Bards") who journey across the sea to Ty Gwydrin ("Glass House") and were never heard of again (Triad 113, *Mab.* II, 301-2). Whether this means that Merddin is also a similar kind of person to

Owein is hard to say. It is possible, but there are so many other themes caught up in his legend that no hard and fast statement can be made.

The *ty gwydrin* also occurs in the *Historia Britonnum* attributed to Nennius. Having left to conquer Ireland, the sons of Mile "saw a tower of glass in the middle of the ocean, and on the tower something which looked like men. They spoke to them but received no reply." The Irish tale of *Conle the Red* is part of the same myth. Here a woman from the race of the fairies falls in love with Conle, son of King Conn of a Hundred Battles. After many speeches, she invites Conle to follow her in her glass boat to the magical land where there are only women and girls (Emain Ablach or Avallon). Conle leaps into the crystal ship and is never seen again.

The story of Conle is not very far removed from the story of Mabon. For whether he be called Owein, Oengus, Lleu or Pryderi, our hero has retired into the other world, like the youthful sun held captive by the darkness. All these characters are in some sense prisoners of destiny. Mabon is held in an airy castle; Lleu is killed but survives in the form of a bird; Pryderi is removed from the world first as Gwri and then with his mother; Oengus appears to be a captive of his sun chamber. It is as if fate had overtaken some character in whom the world had placed its hopes, so that he is forced to wait for the day of his return in a dormant state. The role of the sleeping hero is also given to Arthur, or rather to the mythical Arthur who should be differentiated from the quasi-historical figure belonging to the prosperity function of the divinity. It is possible that the name Arthur derives from an ancient *Artaios* or *Artos* (Breton *arz*, Welsh *arth*) meaning "Bear", and as we know the bear is a hibernating animal. Legend has it that Arthur has been sleeping in the isle of Avallon since he was wounded at Camlann. According to two of the triads (11 and 56), there was one prisoner more eminent even than Llyr, Mabon and Weirr, and that was Arthur who spent three nights in an enchanted prison under Llech Echymeint (*Mab.* II, 238).

Arthur will return however, and the key to his return and to the whole Bagha aspect of the sovereignty function lies in the Teutonic myth of Baldr. According to the *Gylfaginning* of Snorri (Chapter XI), "Baldr, so of Odin, is the best of men and everyone praises him. He is so handsome in appearance and so bright that he radiates light, and there is a meadow flower so white that it has been compared to Baldr's eyelashes. He is the wisest of the Aesir, the most eloquent and the most merciful. But there is a condition imposed on him that none of his judgments is to be realised." This description could equally well be applied to Mabon, Pryderi, Lleu, Owein or Oengus. Unfortunately Baldr is killed by the blind god Hodrh, who is tricked into throwing a branch at him by Hodrh's wicked brother Loki. After his death, or rather his disappearance, Baldr finds himself in the domain of Hel, the other world, since the fact that he was not a warrior prevents him from being admitted into Odin's feast. All the gods send messengers throughout the world to ask men to weep so that their tears may draw Baldr from the power of Hel, but Loki disguised as a giantess refuses to mourn and Baldr must remain where he is. When the great battle at the end of time is fought, the gods and demons will all kill each other and the sons of the dead gods will assume power. In this new era Baldr will leave the kingdom of Hel and will reign over a reconciled universe.

So, like Mabon, Arthur and the rest, Baldr is not only the young son held in the other world, but also the long awaited hero who will restore the vital flame to a dying universe. For all the gods of the sovereignty function have grown powerless. They no longer rule the world, and without them everything has gone adrift. Their decline goes hand in hand with the process of polymorphism and is taken to be the cause of all the troubles and instability affecting mankind. Man therefore places his hopes in the hero who will set the world to rights, although he is now prevented from doing so. We can recognise this belief in the original myth of Christ who descended into hell for three days as Arthur was imprisoned for three nights. And when we return to the Celtic sphere, we find the myth inherent in the relatively recent legendary figure of Galahad, who discovers the Grail. It has been argued that the pure and spotless Galahad was created by 13th century Cistercians in order to bring the pagan legend of the Grail to a proper Christian conclusion, and for this reason he has been compared to Christ himself.

Such a comparison is quite justifiable when one considers that both characters belong to the same myth. But to assume that Galahad is a Christian creation is to misunderstand the sense of the myth. For Galahad is the ultimate but perfect incarnation of the Mabon-Baldr character.

The name Galahad is obviously Hebraic, though it goes without saying that attempts have been made by the over-enthusiastic to derive it from the root *Gal* which has given us Gaul and Galatia. And it is this name which gives the character his Christian veneer. Fears of religious persecution meant that pagan Celtic myths were revived with considerable caution in the Round Table romances. Galahad is the son of Lancelot and Elaine, daughter of the Fisher-King. He is therefore linked by birth with both the Mithra aspect and the Aryama aspect of the sovereignty function. Elaine or Helen, whose name is Greek in origin, is a lunar symbol representing the mother-goddess.

Galahad is the predestined and long awaited hero who will regenerate the sovereignty function. His role was originally allotted to Perceval who proved too naive to be successful. So Galahad is presented as being an idealised Perceval figure, taking his father Lancelot's place in order to revitalise the race of gods and re-establish some cosmic balance. "For as each day dawns, the miracles wrought by the Grail increase in number and grow more alarming. At river crossings and crossroads, unknown warriors appear to halt the travellers, and to shame them, the castles house armed bands of men who terrorise the countryside ... institute infamous customs ... Violence, betrayal and spells reign over the whole country. The very earth, once so fertile, seems to be cursed. The fields no longer give the labourer any return for his toil, there are no more fruits on the trees nor fish in the waters. The fatal enchantment of the Grail spreads over the whole of Britain" (A. Pauphilet, *La Queste du St-Graal*, 17-18). As we can see, the Grail can be as deadly as it is beneficent. For anything sacred is always two-sided. The world of the sacred is a world of forces, as opposed to the world of the profane which is a world of objects. "While an object is by definition constant in nature, a force can bring good or evil according to the particular circumstances of its successive manifestations. It is good or evil not by nature but by virtue of the direction it takes or is forced to take" (R. Callois, *L'Homme et le Sacré*, p. 33). Galahad the chosen one, for whom mankind is waiting, will ensure that the force of the Grail is directed towards good. Though the Grail is housed in a castle "to which the road is unknown and which can only be found by chance", Galahad was born and brought up there and must know the way. And this is the essential element of the whole adventure, that only a hero of the same nature as the Grail can put an end to the enchantments. Only a hero of the race of gods can regenerate that race, just as only a crucified god like Christ can regenerate the world. And since the Grail, the symbol of femininity, represents the mother-goddess, Galahad's achievement is the son's return to the mother, a *regressus ad uterum*. Paradise lost is a memory of the intra-uterine state and human activity tends unconsciously to seek after this state however symbolically and indirectly. Galahad's journey, then, is part of the myth of mother-son incest which underlies the concept of imposing order upon the world. The Grail mother goddess which is solar (the sun being feminine for the Celts and Germans) is withering in the fire. Her dryness and sterility will cease when the son who is lunar (the moon being masculine among the Celts and Germans) brings his fertile mois-ture to her. For he has been separated from her by the accident of birth, the cause of the most terrible disasters. In this sense, the story of Galahad is close to the story of the Prodigal Son.

And Galahad the Prodigal Son has his own special seat, the perilous seat where no other man can sit unscathed. The perilous seat is obviously reminiscent of the Lai Fail of Irish legend which "cried out under each king who governed Ireland". The Lia Fail is the stone of sovereignty. By sitting in the perilous seat Galahad is affirming his right to the sovereignty he intends to regenerate.

This is the essence of the Galahad myth. He will be lord of the Grail castle, just as Pryderi will inherit the kingdom of Pwyll, just as Owein will take Laudine's fountain, just as Oengus will live in the sun chamber, and just as Mabon will regain his solar power. It is then that the end of the world will come, that Galahad will die when he finds the Grail, that the knights of the Round Table will be slain at the battle of Camlann in an almost Teutonic twilight of the gods. And then that Arthur, or whoever he may be, will return from the isle of Avalon, and sovereignty will reign anew.

Strength

As Georges Dumézil writes of the Teutonic divinities: "The gods who form the second and third divisions of the functional triad raise fewer problems than the sovereign gods." This statement certainly holds true of the Celtic divinities belong-ing to the second function of strength and to the third function of prosperity.

Strength, which is symbolised in Vedic India by Indra, is also the execution of the higher will. Indra is the agent of the sovereign gods. His Greek counterpart is probably Hercules, his Roman counterpart the original Mars, and his Teutonic equivalent Thorr the Hammer-God. We can recognise him in the Gallic thunder-god Taranis and in Sucellos, whose name means "Hard Hit". In Ireland he is the hero Cú Chulainn, in British legend the anonymous Giant, sometimes called Kawr or Gurgunt.

Taranis's name makes him thunder, as does Thorr's name (from Thonraz). Like Indra's *vagra*, his hammer is a symbol of thunder. When the significance of the hammer was no longer understood, the god became the striking divinity, the mallet-bearing Sucellos. Sometimes he is represented with a wheel, that also being a symbol for thunder as one of the scenes on the Gundestrup cauldron shows. It seems very likely that the horseman with the snakefoot so frequently depicted on North Eastern Gallic monuments is Taranis, although inscriptions call him Jupi-ter. Certainly this figure of a rider felling a giant or leaning against him is pecul-iarly Celtic.

Cú Chulainn is the son of the god Lug and of Dechtire, King Conchobar's sister. His original name was Setanta, his nickname being given him after he had killed the god of the smith Culann (Cú-chulainn, "Culann's dog"). He takes part in the celebrated battle of Cooley where he stands alone against the combined armies of

Ireland which have united to fight Ulster. He goes into warlike trances, contorting his eyes, arms and legs in curious fashion. He casts a spell over his enemies, then kills a hundred of them, while a hundred more die of fright at the sound of his weapons (thunder). After three days fighting he kills his foster-brother Ferdead who is fighting on the opposing side. He slaughters nine battalions. A vase from the Rhone Valley depicts Sucellos armed with a mallet and accompanied by a dog with the inscription: *Sucellum propitium nobis!*, a figuration clearly reminiscent of Cú Chulainn. In the *Feast of Briciu*, Cú Chulainn argues with Loegaire and Conall Cernach over which of the three champions should receive the Hero's Piece. Cú Chulainn is eventually declared the winner after a strange incident in which he has to cut off the head of a giant on condition that he allow his own head to be cut off the following day. The next day the giant simulates decapitation and proclaims Cú Chulainn greater than all the heroes in Ireland. In another tale the goddess Fand falls in love with him and makes him come to the Land of Promise. A poem telling virtually the same story as Taliesin's *Spoils of the Abyss* shows Cú Chulainn stealing a magic cauldron from the Fortress of Shadows. In the *Death of Curoi* he takes that god's wife, Blathnait. Cú Chulainn finally dies as the result of scheming among his enemies who trap him in a series of taboos which he cannot transgress.

Like Indra, Cú Chulainn is in some senses the protector of his people. He goes into battle in place of the other Ulstermen who are suffering from the effects of a curse laid upon them and cannot fight. He dies to prevent his people being dishonoured. Cú Chulainn is the actual agent of power. His physical strength and his courage are linked to the symbol of the bull. Indeed it is possible to compare the name Taranis with the word Tarvos meaning "bull". The Tarvos Trigarannos or Bull with Three Crows in the Cluny Museum, a figure also depitcted on some Gallic coins, is the marvellous Brown Bull of Cooley, for whom the Raid on Cooley is made; and by defending Ulster against the raiders, Cú Chulainn becomes identified with the bull. There is a confused mixture in this tale of ancient totemism and traces of bull-worship.

However, the basic characteristic of Cú Chulainn, Thorr and Indra is their gigantic size, or their capacity for becoming giants.

It is scarcely surprising that various versions of the god should have found their way into Welsh literature and the Round Table cycle where they tend to occur as minor characters. These are the giants encountered by Arthur and his knights; the giant Corsolt of the *chansons de geste*, whose name comes from the tribe of Curiosolitae; the many faces of Fierebras. In Wales we find Gwrnach Gawr (Gwrnach the Giant) in *Culhwch and Olwen*, and Gwrgant Varyf Twrch (Gwrgant Boar-beard) who physically resembles Thorr and whom Geoffrey of Monmouth turned into Guurgunt Barbtruch in his *Historia Regum Britanniae*. Gwrgant is no literary invention; he appears, rather, to be descended from an ancient British and Gallic tradition, for we find him in place names like Mount Gargano, Livry-Gargan, Garges, etc. Eventually, though, it was through a literary work that he came back to life and that he reached a new audience via the pages of folklore. For there can be little doubt that Cú Chulainn, alias Taranis, alias Sucellos, grew by way of Gwrgant into the good giant Gargantua, the traditional character so successfully reworked by Rabelais.

We might also include in this category the warrior goddesses like Andarta or Andrasta whom Tacitus mentions in connexion with the British uprising of 61. Andrasta appears to have become the Saint-Victoire worshipped on the mountain near Aix-en-Provence which still bears that name. In Ireland she is the goddess

Bobd ("Crow or Raven") who became confused with Mórrígan at a fairly early date. As her parentage implies, Mórrígan is she who rouses the warriors to fight and stirs up murderous disputes among them. For she is the daughter of Ernmas or "Murder".

Prosperity

While the first two of the divine functions are represented by Uranian gods of the air, the third function includes the gods of earth, fire and water. (The differences between the air-group and the earth-fire-water-group can be observed in the Teutonic Aesir and Vanir respectively).

Like the second function, the third raises few problems, except perhaps for the enormous number of names under which the relevant gods appear. Even in Vedic India we find a pair of gods, the Asvins or Nasatyas who are associated with a goddess. These figures can probably be identified as the Greek Castor, Pollux and Dione (the early name for Aphrodite). In Rome we have the third member of the Capitoline triad Quirinos (Co-Virinos), i.e. Romulus (who is known to have a twin brother in Remus), protector of the human community. The Teutonic gods in this category are Njorthr and his children Freyr and Freyja.

When it comes to the Celts, we can include in the third function all those gods and goddesses who are connected with prosperity, health, agriculture, hunting, peace, water, love and fertility.

First among these is the god Kernunnos as represented in the altar in the Cluny Museum. Kernunnos is always depicted with horns, usually with antlers. His name clearly evokes the horn (Breton *Korn*, plural *Kern*) but is also connected through similarity in the sounds with the Breton word for stag which is *Karu*, plural *Kervi*. Rather far-fetched arguments have also been made to equate the name Kerunnos with the name Carnac, mostly because the god was Christianised at Carnac and because he became assimilated to the difficult figure of St Corneille or St Cornely, the patron saint of horned animals who is always depicted with a bull. In fact Carnac comes from a pre-Indo-European root *car* meaning "stone" and its Breton name is Kerreg, the stone town. Even so, local legend attributes St Cornely with the construction of the famous standing stones at Carnac. Pursued by an army, he is said to have changed all the soldiers into *menhirs*, the stones being called Soudar Sant Kornely (the soldiers of St Cornely) to this day.

Invented though these etymologies probably are, they do betray a real relationship from the mythological viewpoint between the stag, the stone and the horn. But when it comes to Kernunnos himself, it seems far more likely that his name derived from the Indo-European root *ker* which gave rise to the Latin *creare*, to create, and *crescere*, to grow. This would certainly establish Kernunnos as the god of plenty, a status amply demonstrated by various representations of the god. On the altar at Reims he is shown pouring out the contents of a bag full of coins and grain, watched by a stag and a bull and surmounted by Mercury and Apollo. At Somecourt (Vosges) he is accompanied by a goddess bearing a horn or plenty. At Autun he has three faces and holds two ram-headed serpents, symbols of earthly fertility. One of the positions in which he is most frequently represented is the buddhic posture, sitting with his legs crossed in front of him, as at Roquepertuse.

The goddess of plenty often found accompanying Kernunnos has various different names. Sometimes she is the goddess Artio (She-bear), who can be compared with the bronze sculpture in the Beren Museum of a clothed woman sitting in front of a large bear by a short-branched tree. Beside her there is a basket of fruit on a little pillar. All the indications are that she represents fertility of the soil rather than being a bear-goddess. As a hibernating animal, the bear is an image of the earth sleeping through the winter and producing fruit in the summer. Similarly, the fact that the goddess Arduinna (who gave her name to the Ardennes) is represented as a Diana riding a boar does not prove that she is a goddess of the hunt.

The goddess Rosmerta, whose name means the "Great Provider" also bears a horn of plenty or a basket of fruit. She is known as Damona, Nehalennia and Bergusia as well as several other names which vary from region to region. Rosmerta, however, appears to have a male counterpart in Smertrios (the Provider) who is represented on the altar at the Cluny Museum striking a serpent. This may mean, of course, that he is a god like Belenos-Lug, a dragon-killer, or a divinity like Taranis-Sucellos, a giant who guards against monsters. It would seem more likely, however, that Smertios' gesture is a symbol of the way the god masters the earth, here represented by the aboriginal serpent. We should remember that the Celts were great cultivators of the land, and that their whole civilisation was based on agriculture. G. Dumézil expresses surprise that there is no god typifying the agricultural worker in Gaul and explains this by suggesting that such work was left to slaves or women. He goes on to say: "Those responsible for milk and corn were doubtless demons or lesser spirits, subject to the will of the great gods" (*Jupiter-Mars-Quirinus*, p. 173). As we have seen, Kernunnos was a god of husbandry, despite the fact that he is shown without the sheaf of corn or the spade usually associated with such figures. For the Gauls plenty and labour were synonymous, since the one was impossible without the other. It is unthinkable that an agricultural people should have omitted to worship a divinity of this kind.

When it comes to the Welsh, we do have evidence of an agricultural god in Amaethon son of Don who appears in *Culhwch and Olwen*. He joins Gwyddyon in leading the Britons to their great victory at Goddeu. He is also the hero of Taliesin's *Death Song for Aeddon*, Aeddon being a contracted form of Amaethon. The early Arthur can also be regarded as an agrarian god.

It is possible to derive his name either from *arth*, meaning "bear", or from the Indo-European root *ar*, meaning "labourer", or even from the Sanskrit word which gave rise to the Persian *arta*, meaning "order". Having established that the bear represents the earth, these three very different etymologies are not necessarily contradictory. The Arthur of so many obscure traditions is the god of stability and peace; the Round Table he is said to have founded is an image of an ideal world, an agricultural society in which everyone has his own place, equal to his neighbour and shares the earth with his fellows honestly and faithfully. Just as Arthur has a magic boat in his shield Prytwen, so too does his Teutonic counterpart the god Freyr. Just as Arthur owns a magic sword, so too does Freyr. Whenever the prosperity of the kingdom is threatened, it is Arthur who brings peace and order, notably by sending his knights to seek the Grail which has caused barrenness and disturbance in the land.

The Irish counterpart to Arthur is Eochaid Aireann, one of the heroes of the *Tale of Etaine*. Just as Arthur's wife Guinevere is taken by Mealagant, or Mordred, so Eochaid finds that his wife Etaine has been abducted by Mider, who takes her to the other world. Eochaid pursues the lovers through the mounds in which they have taken shelter and in his attempts to trace them he has all the mounds in Ireland hollowed out, one after another, thereby earning his nickname *Aireann*, the ploughman.

Attempts have been made to identify Arthur and Finn as gods of the hunt like the Gallic figures found at Effignex (a god accompanied by a boar), at Mont St-Jean (a god holding a bow and a bill-hook), and at Mont Domon (a god accompanied by a stag and armed with a spear, a cutlass and an axe) and like the god name Vosegus who is armed with a bow. There can be little doubt that the Gauls did worship a god of the hunt, therefore; but it is hard to find exact equivalents for him elsewhere. Finn and Arthur may be huntsmen but they are huntsmen of a very particular kind. When they set out in pursuit of a boar, the animal is usually supernatural, like the celebrated Twrch Trwyth, and their activities are unlikely to be merely a sacred version of ordinary, human hunting.

Water has produced a number of divine figures, including all the rivers with names like Dive or Divonne (meaning divine). The best known of the Gallic water gods, however, is Borvo whose name has been preserved in the names of hot springs like Bourbon-Lancy, Bourbon l'Archambault, Bourbonne les Bains, la Bourboule. Borvo is very much a river god, being linked with springs and certain rivers, and we have no way of knowing if the Gauls had a sea-god comparable to the Greek Poseidon. Considering the skill of Gallic navigators, particularly the Veneti who had a virtual monopoly of Atlantic and cross-Channel trade, it would seem quite likely that there was such a god but apart from the Vesperious (Western) or the Breton coast, his name remains unknown. The Irish definitely had a sea-god in Mananann son of Ler (the Waves), one of the Tuatha de Danann who reigned over the isle of Emain Ablach. In the tale of the *Voyage of Bran, son of Febal*, the hero Bran sets sail in search of Emain, the land of the Fairies. "When he had been at sea for two days and two nights, he saw a man in a chariot on the ocean. This man ... made himself known as Mananann, son of Ler." Mananann owns a herd of magic pigs from which he feeds the Tuatha de Danann. His wife Fand falls in love with Cú Chulainn and brings him to Emain, in an episode reminiscent of the abduction of Blathnait, wife of Curoi Mac Daere by Cú Chulainn himself. In fact Curoi is merely another name for Mananann, and he too is very clearly connected with the sea.

The Welsh equivalent for Mananann is Manawyddan son of Llyr, hero of the *mabinogi* bearing his name. He is Bran's brother, and after the disastrous expedition to Ireland he is one of the seven survivors to enjoy the hospitality of the head. Pryderi marries him to his mother Rhiannon and it is Manawyddan who frees Pryderi's land from the spell affecting it.

Mananann, then, appears to be a lord of the sea like the Germanic Njorthr, god of navigation and fishing whom Tacitus identified in a female form as Nerthus, a kind of mother-goddess living in an oceanic island.

There is no fire god among the Celts. The only figure we can place in this category is the technical goddess whom Caesar equates with Minerva and who was probably called Brigantia. In Ireland she became the three-faced Brigit, worshipped by poets, smiths and musicians, before being christianised into the Saint Brigitte who is patron of present day Erin. The Gauls also had a smith god of whom we know nothing, perhaps rather surprisingly considering the importance of metallurgy in Gaul. This god is however identifiable in Wales and Ireland as Govannon, one of the brothers of Gwyddyon and Amaethon, the sons of the goddess Don. Govannon was later christianised to a greater or lesser extent to become St-Cov and gave his name to the parish of Plogoff in Brittany. In Ireland he is Gobniu, a Tuatha de Danann and one of the victorious warriors at the battle of Mag-Tured. The oldest traditions speak of a "feast of Gobniu", a kind of feast of immortality like Odin's. Gobniu is famed for his skill. If the weapons of the Tuatha de Danann "deteriorated one day, they would be renewed the next day, for the smith Gobniu was at his forge making swords, javelins and spears, he would manufacture these weapons with three blows."

There is evidence of warrior gods all over Gaul, especially in the vicinity of hot springs, for the Gauls were exploiting the curative effects of the waters long before the Romans arrived. At Fontaine-Salle, near Vézelay (Yonne), for example, there is evidence of some native constructions existing under the Roman baths.

Sources of rivers and streams were frequently dedicated to some divinity. A number of votive offerings have been found at the sources of the Seine. The traditions attached to sacred fountains grew from the worship of such gods. The Fountain of Barenton is said to cure madness, and other fountains are attributed with particular healing properties. Such places were later christianised and given the names of saints, some of them more real than others. Brittany has large numbers of healing saints of this kind who are merely Christian substitutes for the gods worshipped over many centuries in the same places.

The only real evidence we have of a Celtic god of medicine is in Ireland and here, too, the divinity is connected with a cult of the spring. The Irish god in question is Diancecht, one of the Tuatha de Danann. "This is how warmth was restored to warriors who had died so that they were full of life the following day. Diancecht, his two sons and his daughter, would sing a spell over the spring called Health. In it they would throw the fatally wounded men they were nursing, and as they came out they lived. The wounded men were cured by the song of the four doctors who stood round the spring."

This spring is obviously reminiscent of Bran's cauldron of rebirth, and the reviving tub in the Welsh tale of *Peredur:* "One of the women rose and took the body from the saddle and bathed it in a tub of warm water that was near the door, and then she rubbed it with precious ointment, whereupon the man rose alive ..." While Bran's cauldron is truly miraculous, however, Peredur's tub requires an ointment and Diancecht's spring the incantations of the god and his children to be wholly curative. Indeed Diancecht's spring is medical in an obvious sense: "The spring bore another name, lake of herbs, since Diancecht had placed in it a sprig of every herb to be found in Ireland."

It is none too easy to find a god or goddess of love among the Gauls. There are fertility goddesses, but they belong to the very different mother-goddess category, and there is no equivalent for Eros or Aphrodite. The worship of Venus did become established in certain places (as we can see in Port-Vendres, from *Portus Veneris*) but any traces of such worship which still remain are vaguely Christian and deviant. There are, for example, a number of saints called Venerand and Foutin. Saint Guigner or Gwiner who gave his name to Pluvigner seems to have been a Venus in disguise, as is Sainte Agathe of Langon, patron saint of a chapel formerly dedicated to St-Venerand which is actually a Gallo-Roman temple complete with a fresco depicting Venus rising from the waves.

It is possible that the Gauls had their own love goddess who was later concealed behind the name Venus. Arthurian epic, and indeed Welsh and Irish literature in general, contain many girls whose sole interest in life appears to be love, even if theirs is a Celtic love, ardent, unfettered and amoral. Very often they are damsels of the kind who woo Gawain. Another damsel keeps Mabonagrain in the orchard of the Joie de la Cour. There is Vivian who holds Merlin in her prison of air; Branwen, "white crow", Bran's sister and heroine of a *mabinogi*. Branwen's role as a goddess of love has been amply demonstrated by Joseph Loth who uses an ancient Welsh poem from the *Black Book of Carmarthen* to identify her with Yseult's maid Brangwen or Brengwain. It is she who brings Tristan and Yseult together by giving them the fatal love potion. Love of this kind is in some sense predetermined and ineluctable, it is connected with feelings of death for it is stronger than death. The amorality of Celtic love, its lack of ceremony, the freedom with which women offer themselves do not mean that the basic emotion is any less strong and serious. We can in no way compare it with the delicate and refined eroticism of Hellenic civilisation. When Ness, daughter of the king of Ulster, sees the druid Cathba passing by, she asks him "What is the right thing to do now? It is right to make a king with a queen, said the druid ... Then the girl invited him to come to her, for she could see no other man around."

This extraordinary openness is a direct result of the *geis,* the force of a taboo which may affect anybody. The female characters whom we might reasonably identify as goddesses of love always use the *geis* as if imposing an element of fatality. Brangwain's *geis* is the potion, Ness' *geis* the druid's prophecy against which she is powerless. Grainne, daughter of King Cormac is married to the much older Finn. During the wedding festivities she is moved by the beauty of young Diarmaid to place a *geis* of destruction on him unless he immediately takes her away with him. As Diarmaid cannot refuse he finds himself being fiercely pursued by Finn. Finally the two men feign reconciliation and Diarmaid is killed during a boar hunt because he has transgressed another taboo.

Deidre, the national heroine of Ireland, is also a kind of love goddess. She is destined to marry Conchobar, king of Ulster, but she actually loves Noise, son of Usnech. When she meets him Noise does not recognise her and says "The heifer passing us is very fine." Deidre replies "You need large heifers where there are no bulls." "You have the bull of the province with you," said he, "the king of Ulster." "I would like to choose between you," said she, "and I would like a small young bull like you." "No," said he. Then she rushed at him and took him by the ears and said "There are two ears of shame and ridicule if you do not take me with you." The weight of the *geis* prevents Noise from escaping and a great epic tragedy follows. Noise is finally killed and Deidre throws herself from a chariot.

The character of Morgan la Fée offers a number of problems. She is not mentioned by name in any of the Welsh tales, except in a masculine form as Morgan-tut, Arthur's doctor and magician who occurs in *Culhwch and Olwen*. In Breton folklore she becomes the Mary-Morgan, a kind of siren connected with water. Indeed her name actually means "born of the sea" *(Mori-genos,* Irish *Muir-gen)*. It is possible therefore that she is a water goddess. But she may also be a goddess of love, since the Round Table romances portray her imprisoning all those knights who have deceived their ladies in the Val Sans Retour. Like her Irish counterpart, Mórrígan, she appears to have the same nature as the Teutonic Freyja, a warrior, a witch and a passionate lover. Her position as mistress of the Isle of Avalon, however, would suggest an analogy with the warrior Nerthus (a feminine version of Njorthr) mentioned by Tacitus, who is a *terra mater* living in an oceanic island.

Tacitus' definition of this goddess and the very specific atmosphere and significance of the Avalon legend would suggest that Mórrígan-Morgan is not a goddess of love at all but a mother-goddess. In the Celtic sphere, the mother-goddess played a part of considerable importance and had little to do with the fertility goddesses which can easily be identified with the third of the Indo-European divine functions. For this mother-goddess belongs to the myth of the primordial divinity and though the myth is recognisable among the other Indo-European peoples, it is most fully illustrated in the mythology of the Celts.

The Mother-Goddess

"When compared with the uniform organisation of the universe," writes Roger Callois, "the gods appear to be principles of individuation. They have a personality. They embody a type" (*L'Homme et le Sacré*, p. 168). But above the gods there is always something else which ensures that the gods are never total masters of their own destiny. Like mere mortals, Zeus obeys some higher power variously named as *fatum* or *moira*.

This higher power is the primordial divinity recognised by virtually all religions but rarely named and deliberately forgotten, being only addressed in cases of exceptional danger. It is as if this superior being had delegated its powers to its ministers the gods, the Indo-European *deiwos*. Only when the *deiwos* fail, therefore, is supplication made to the Supreme Being. In this respect there is no polytheism, but only recourse on the part of weak men to personalised and vaguely anthropomorphised divinities who are to act as intermediaries between mankind and an over-distant or over-abstract *deus abascons*. We learn from Jewish history that during times of peace and quiet the Hebrews sacrificed to a number of gods, but that during times of trouble they destroyed their idols and returned to the monotheistic cult of Yahweh.

Yahweh is therefore the most meaningful representative of monotheism, though how old the concept of Yahweh may be is another matter. The Jewish religion, after all, was created by Moses, who also wrote or inspired the early books of the Bible. And Moses was half Jewish and half Egyptian, as the myth of the infant floating on the waters clearly indicates. The fact that the child was found by Pharaoh's daughter means that she was actually his mother, and if she could not admit as much it must have been because the child's father was Jewish.

Moses despised the Egyptian idols and wished to reform his people. Having no father himself he also sought by way of compensation to emphasise the importance of the father or of the male element in society. He therefore defeminised the sacred tradition which still accorded an important role to women. It was then that woman became seen as ambiguous, if not evil. As a result, Yahweh was to be male and warlike, a jealous god, and the myth of Genesis was turned on its head. Obviously the original story must have been that Adam was formed from Eve's rib, that he came from her belly. The first human in the world had to be a woman, or conceivably a hermaphrodite. The name Eve remains to remind us of the aquatic nature of the Mother, despite all the later Mosaic meddlings in the myth.

It still remains to be answered whether this primordial divinity is male or female. Freud, and many others besides, have said that the oldest religions refer to male gods. A psychoanalytical approach to the sacred myths, however, would appear to prove the contrary. For given that the whole impulse of mankind is a semi-unconscious return to the mother, it is reasonable to ask whether the Mother is not indeed the ideal Original Being, on both a divine and a human level. Using Freudian interpretation, the Garden of Eden is the Mother's womb in which life is entirely pleasant and carefree. The expulsion of Adam and Eve from this garden is the drama of birth.

The Freudian school, however, is very much constricted by the Oedipus complex, or the rebellion of the Son against the Father, which Freud takes to be the cause of the original sin and therefore of the explusion from Paradise. Freud's arguments on this point are worth examining in some detail.

He has taken the totem meal as a point of departure. "Thus we have the clan which on a solemn occasion kills its totem and eats it raw" (Freud, *Totem and Taboo*). But "after the act is accomplished the murdered animal is bewailed and regretted ... Psychoanalysis has revealed to us that the totem animal is really a substitute for the father." Obviously an explanation has to be found for the fact that it is both forbidden to kill the animal and permitted to do so on certain occasions, and for the outburst of grief and then of joy which follows the killing. And Freud's explanation is that in the primal horde all the sons were subject to the father who jealously guarded for himself both his authority and the mother, and doubtless all the daughters as well. "One day the expelled brothers joined forces, slew and ate the father and thus put an end to the father horde. Together they dared and accomplished what would have remained impossible for them singly ... The totem feast, which is perhaps mankind's first celebration, would be the repetition and commemoration of this memorable, criminal act with which so many things began, social organization, moral restrictions and religion."

Every mythology shows the son taking the father's place. Even within Christianity Jesus is often regarded as more important than God the Father. "With the introduction of agriculture the importance of the son in the patriarchal family increased. He was emboldened to give new expression to his incestuous libido which found symbolic satisfaction in labouring over mother earth. There came into existence figures of gods like Attis, Adonis, Tammuz and others ... who enjoyed the favors of maternal deities and committed incest with the mother in defiance of the father."

This is obviously a basic theme of some importance. When we look at Greek mythology we find that Zeus succeeds in toppling Chronos with the help of his mother Rhea, and that Chronos himself had dethroned his father Uranus. Instead of killing his father Zeus is content to emasculate him. The Saturnalia in Rome were held in memory of this act of aggression against the father and of the change in power, for Saturn was the Roman version of Chronos. In the Middle Ages the celebration continued in the form of the Fools Feast. When we attempt to determine the meaning of symbols from a psychoanalytical viewpoint, we find that the castration complex is represented by the tearing out of eyes (as in the actual Oedipus story), by drawing teeth and also by uprooting trees or plucking leaves and fruit from a tree.

In the light of such symbolism, the Genesis story takes on a whole new significance. When they commit the original sin, Adam and Eve, by plucking the fruit of the forbidden tree (for which read the totem) are emasculating the father. And by eating this fruit they are fulfilling the primal totemic meal symbolically reduced to the father's genitals. While the totem or tree represents the Father-God, the Garden of Eden represents the womb of the Mother in which the male tree is planted. The Genesis story is then simply a symbolic transposition of the rebellion of the sons against the Father in their attempt to win possession of the Mother. When the serpent, itself a sexual symbol for the son's desire, says that he will make Adam and Eve as gods, he might easily add that they would have the same rights as God to the mother, the object of their desire.

As Freud says, however, "A process like the removal of the primal father ... must have left ineradicable traces in the history of mankind and must have expressed itself the more frequently in numerous substitutive formations the less it itself was to be remembered ..." and "we let the sense of guilt for a deed survive for thousands of years, remaining effective in generations which could not have known anything of this deed" *(Totem and Taboo)*.

It is from all this that the cult of a male divinity has arisen. Freud says, "Thus the bitter feeling against the father which had incited to the deed could subside in the course of time, while the longing for him grew ... as well as the willingness to subject themselves to him." Freud continues his argument by suggesting that the father became deified, which is by no means certain, but his emphasis on the role of the rebellion against the father which became reversed in men's mind into love is surely correct. That is why god is male and why the primordial female deity has been replaced by the image of a father-god, in some attempt to atone for the incestuous desires now repressed in the collective unconscious.

We can now look at the original myth in some detail and examine it from the perspective of a Freudian interpretation. In the beginning the Spirit of God (the male element) moved upon the face of the waters (the female element). The two elements came together and there was creation. The human race came into being but it enjoyed a privileged, paradisial existence, feeding on fruit. Obviously humanity was still at the intra-uterine stage. Humanity then rebelled; presumptuously claiming the authority of the father, it left the mother's womb and was born. The transition from a moist and nourishing place to a dry and hostile environment is disastrous. Man had to adapt to aridity and to find food. In Genesis the drought is symbolised by the flaming sword with which the angel bars the way back into paradise. To the man God says "In the sweat of thy face shalt thou eat bread" or "Your labours, the product of your inventive mind, will bring you that moist fertility again;" while to the woman he says "In sorrow thou shalt bring forth children" or "You will perpetuate the species by perpetuating the catastrophe of birth."

From that point onward, mankind lived in fear of the father (God), but it was a fear tinged with a vague sense of god's goodness and hope survived. This hope was for a *regressus ad uterum*, or a return to the bosom of Abraham, symbolised by the mission of the Son of Man, or more accurately the Son of Woman. For salvation can only come through woman. In this way the myth of the Virgin came into being alongside the myth of the original mother.

All primitive civilizations regard woman as in some way sacred because of her ability to give birth. Primitive peoples, writes Gustave Welter, "find it hard to accept that an act so short-lived and in their eyes so natural and common as copulation should result in the birth of a new human being: such an extraordinary event cannot come about from an ordinary cause" *(Les Croyances primitives et leurs survivances*, p. 59). This cause has therefore to be the spirit which introduces the seed into the woman's body. The husband is redundant, except as a provider of food. "That is why the husband has so often to continue relations with his wife until her confinement" *(ibid.* p. 60).

It is beliefs like these which created the myth of fatherless children who proved to be exceptional men. The mystery of the Incarnation belongs to the same myth, for the Virgin is fertilised by the spirit and Joseph assumes the role of provider.

For the Virgin is very much the Mother. Motherhood has been the object of a cult since darkest pre-history, since the days of the cave-dwellers. We can therefore presume that the primordial divinity was a Mother-Goddess. This supposition would certainly agree with the mythical process found in most traditions.

For the Hindus of the Vedic era, Varuna, Mithra and Indra were only intermediary gods, personalised manifestations of a primoridal divinity which was ambiguous in that it represented both good and evil. Georges Dumézil has identified this divinity as Vayu, the wind or breeze, which would correspond with the Hebrew Spirit moving upon the face of the waters. The primordial god of the Germanic peoples was Heimdall, who is known as "the son of Seven Sisters". Among the Romans Dumézil finds this god in Janus, *bi-frons* (two-faced to show his ambiguity), a god which later became much altered and limited to the function of gatekeeper.

It is worth looking at Janus more closely since he summarises all the complexity of the Indo-European primordial god. Janus has no equivalent among the Greeks. He is the god of beginning *(initia)*, the god of essences *(prima)*, the god of the first manifestations *(primordia)*. He is initiator, introducer, heavenly gatekeeper *(janitor)*. In his *Fasti* (v. 125) Ovid places the following words in Janus' mouth: "I sit before the gates of heaven with the gentle seasons: at his comings and goings Jupiter himself has need of men, whence my name Janus." A character like this is clearly reminiscent of the gatekeeper of the Tuatha de Danann who will not admit Lug until he has demonstrated his skill, or of Arthur's gatekeeper Glewlwyt Gavaelfawr (Strong Grip) or of the gatekeeper of the Christian paradise, St Peter himself.

Janus always takes precedence in some way over Jupiter. Of the hills of Rome only the citadel was dedicated to Jupiter while the hill overlooking the gate was dedicated to Janus. Roman legends make Janus the first king of Latium, the king of the Golden Age (Ovid, *Fasti*, I, 247), of an earthly paradise. As Dumézil writes, "He is the absolute *primordium*" and Ovid tells how "the ancients called him Chaos since he was the ancient thing *(res prisca)*" *(Fasti*, I, 102).

The most remarkable aspect of Janus, however, is his ambiguity which is shown in his two faces. He opens the way to peace but also to war. He is both good and evil. With their cautious legal minds, the Romans always approached the names and sexes of their gods with some care. When the Pontifex Maximus addressed Jupiter, he always added "sive quo alio nomine volueris (under whatever other name you wish to be called)." According to Servius (*Ad. Aen.* II, 351), there was a shield on the Capitol bearing the inscription *"Genio Romae, sive mas, sive femina* (To the spirit of Rome, whether male or female)."

This last formula could equally well be applied to Janus. Dumézil sees his name as being derived from "a root word Ya also attested in Indo-Iranian and in Celtic and meaning: go somewhere, pass by" (*Les Dieux des Indo-européens*, p. 91). However, without wishing to discount his etymology, the Latin J may well have led to some confusion, since it could be used both as a vowel and as a consanant. It is quite likely therefore that the early form of Janus' name was *D-yanus*, as in Dianus, which can be broken down into *Di-Anus*. Anus means "old woman", which would wholly confirm the idea of the primordial divinity being a woman, and naturally enough a very old woman. The *-us* ending is also confusing, because in the second declension it applies solely to masculine people and things, whereas in the fourth declension, to which *anus* belongs, it can be feminine as well. So the goddess became a male god. The realisation that Janus-Dianus is actually a female divinity, the *res prisca* has brought us to the essence of Indo-European mythology.

Further evidence that a *deus mas* came to replace a *dea femina* can be found in the goddess Diana. She appears to be a Latin form of Artemis and therefore a comparatively recent creation. But the choice of the name *Di-Ana* can only mean that there was still some memory of a female divinity once inherent in the concept of Janus. Then there is the goddess Anna Perenna, who tends to be overlooked. She was worshipped in an orchard at Rome, *virgineus cruor* being scattered in her name. Anna Perenna is the archetypal goddess of nourishment, and obviously closely related to the Indian Anna Purna (from Sanskrit *anna*, meaning "food").

This worship of a goddess brings us back to the purely Celtic field. In Gaul the cult of the maternal divinity reached considerable proportions, as we can see from the impressive number of *Matres*, *Matrae* and *Matronae*. As P. M. Duval says "In their varied forms, their name is both Gallic and Latin: *mater* is Latin but its use in the plural to denote goddesses is not." The statues depicting these mother figures, either singly or in groups of two or three, always show a woman carrying a child on her arms or her knee, clearly foreshadowing the Virgin and Child so frequently portrayed in Christian iconography.

Surprisingly enough there are no Irish names which can be compared with the Gallic *matronae*. Wales, on the other hand, appears to have inherited all the devotion to the mother found in Gaul. To start with there is Modron, the Welsh equivalent for Matrona, mother of Mabon and Owein. She is the daughter of Avallach or Avallon, which may mean that we can identify her with Mórrígan. In the *mabinogi* of *Math* she bears the name Arianrod, daughter of Don. When Math wishes to check that she is a virgin he makes her jump over his magic wand (a clear allusion to the phallus). She then gives birth to two infants. One of them runs to the sea and is later called Dylan Eil Ton (Son of the Wave) or Dylan Eil Mor (Son of the Sea). The play on words between *Modr*, "the mother", and *Mor*, "the sea", suggests that Dylan accomplishes his *regressus ad uterum* immediately, or that he is born dead. The second child is secretly snatched up by his uncle Gwyddyon and later becomes Lleu Llaw Gyffes. Arianrod lives in a castle in the middle of the sea, another symbol for the womb, and this fortress *Kaer Arianrod* is traditionally used in Wales to denote the constellation of *Coronae Borealis*. We might therefore compare Arianrod with the Gallic goddess Sironna or Dironna in whose name we can identify the word *ser* meaning "star".

The mother-goddess is also personified under the name Rhiannon (Rigantona, meaning "Great Queen"), heroine of the mabinogion of *Pwyll* and *Manawyddan*. Rhiannon has to be identified with Epona, since she is linked with the myth of the Mare who loses her colt and finds him again after a series of adventures. She is the goddess who receives the dead into her bosom and who gives them immortality through the singing of her marvellous birds. She recurs in the Provençal romance of *Jauffrè* under the name Brunissen, a strange queen who lives confined in an enchanted orchard, consoled by the song of birds. We can also find her in the neolithic burial caves of Coizard (Marne) and in megalithic dolmens like those in Morbihan.

In the *Story of Taliesin*, she appears as Keridwen, who swallows the former man (Gwyon Bach) to give birth to the new man Taliesin. Taliesin can be taken as an image of the man who has successfully accomplished his return to the mother. He comes out of the trial a grown man, the powers he enjoyed before the disaster of birth restored to him. His story is the myth of the Grail and the drama of the world. The Grail is a symbol of the abandoned and arid mother goddess who needs the Son, now gone from her in the catastrophe of birth. Her divinity withers, the world is falling to pieces. Only the son of woman can bring new life to the goddess by acting as husband to the mother. Freud's discoveries concerning the Oedipus complex and sexuality in general are confirmed by legend.

The most likely incarnation of the Indo-European mother-goddess concept is a deity continually mentioned by both Welsh and Irish although she is never the heroine of any story and appears only to give her children a name. This figure is the Welsh Don, the Irish Dana or Ana.

Don is the sister of Math and mother of Gwyddyon (a double for Math), Amaethon (the ploughman), Gilvaethwy (the Girflet of the Round Table romances), Hyveidd, Govannon (the Smith) and Arianrod. She is first in a line of gods and heroes.

In Ireland Dana or Ana is mother of the race of the Tuatha de Danann, or men of the goddess Dana. She is the *mater deorum hibernensium* and is mentioned in all the Irish legends. A hill in Kerry is actually called Paps of Anou, an unambiguous allusion to her maternal role. The folklore of Leicestershire has stories of Black Annis, a kind of man-eating witch and guardian of the dead. Before the town of Puy acquired the name Podium, it was called Anicium, "town of Ana", suggesting a connexion with the age-old cult of the Black Virgin.

For Anna reigns over the dead and her people are called *anaon* ("the departed") by the Bretons. Indeed the figure of Dana-Ana comes most vividly to life in Brittany, for the Breton mixture of paganism and Christianity transformed her into Sainte-Anne.

It was in 1625, when a Breton peasant from Pluneret, near Auray, found a statue of Saint Anne and claimed to have seen vision there that the cult of Christ's grand-mother gained widespread acceptance. There had been a previous discovery of a similar nature at Commana (Anna's Hollow) where a pregnant statue had been found and the second incident occured at Keranna (Anna's town). The peasant claimed that the saint had told him of a chapel which had been dedicated to her in times gone by, a rather curious revelation in view of the fact that the official worship of the saint did not develop in the West until the 14th century. Certainly neither the Scriptures nor the Early Church Fathers make any mention of Saint Anne. In 550 Justinian erected a church which was dedicated to her at Byzantium, but nobody in the 6th century could be really sure that the Virgin's mother was called Anne. She first came to be included on the Christian calendar in 1382, though no particular festival was assigned to her until 1584.

The fact that one of the discovered statues was pregnant, and that the Capucine Fathers of Auray who were the first to benefit from the miracle and begin pilgrimages to the statue should have recarved and repainted it is suspicious to say the least. The figure in question was probably a statue of the Gallic mother-goddess, like so many of the Black Virgins miraculously discovered since. Being found in Keranna, the statue had to be given the name Anne, and with pilgrimages being a source of income a need must have been felt to compete with Commana.

There were good reasons for faking the Saint Anne of Auray, nevertheless. Unconsciously the flock was always ready to return to a cult of the woman, and by ensuring that the faithful turned their attention to the mother of the Virgin, whether or not her existence could be proved, such a cult would remain Christian. Memories of the goddess Anna must have lived on in the outlying areas of the Breton countryside and could now be channelled into worship of the Virgin's mother.

There is actually a Breton tradition concerning Saint Anne and a building which the mythical King Gradlon is said to have built on the strand of Sainte-Anne la Palud after the submersion of the town of Is. The tradition has it that Saint Anne was herself Breton, that she married Joachim who proved to be a tyrannical and wicked husband and that she came back to the land of her birth not to die but to sleep.

Obviously this legend appears very childish and characteristic of the Breton mind, ever ready to assume that the saints can only have lived in Brittany. Childish or not, however, this legend is not merely the product of some over-zealous Breton imagination, it comes from much further back.

If we look at the Welsh genealogies we find that historical figures, like people everywhere, had sought to trace their families back to mythological characters and to saints. One of these genealogies now preserved in the Harleian manuscript number 3859 which dates from the 10th century looks at the forebears of Owen, son of Howel Dda *"Run, map Mailcun (Maelgwn) ... map Aballac, map Amalech qui fuit Beli magni filius, et Anna mater eius, quam dicunt esse consobrinam Mariae virginis, matris domini nostri Jesu Christi"* (Loth, *Mab.* II, 326, 329). Another tracing the genealogy of Morcant follows a line back to *"Aballach map Beli et Anna"* (Harleian, 3859, *Mab.* II, 335, 336).

Evidently Welsh tradition agrees with Breton tradition. The precise way in which Anna is described as mother of the Virgin Mary is a Christian addition to a much earlier belief, proving that the Christians were unable to merely omit the embarrassing figure of the Mother of Gods and transformed her either into the Virgin Mary herself as the Black Virgin or into the Virgin's mother, the ancestor, the old woman.

The cult of Sainte-Anne which has reached considerable proportions in Brittany is therefore simply a christian version of the pagan, Celtic cult of the Mother-Goddess.

The fact that Anna is wife of Belenos or Beli and that she is also his mother in the sense that she is mother of all gods brings us back to the myth of mother-son incest, the basic myth of regeneration. The genealogies also tells us that Anna is mother or grandmother of Avallac or Evallach who appears in the Quest for the Grail and is obviously linked with the isle of Avallon. His daughter is Morgan, yet another personification of the mother-goddess.

The figure of Morgan brings us into pagan folklore. For while Saint Anne represents the official, christian, permitted aspect of the goddess who has become an integral part of the new myth, Morgan is the dangerous, diabolical aspect of the divinity, relegated to the ranks of the fairies and ultimately to being a mere witch. In the last analysis, the witch is simply the ancient priestess who has strayed into a Christian world. She retains all the old attributes but emphasis is laid on her potential for evil. The old, ugly, bad-tempered fairy Morgan comes into being.

Originally she was quite different. The Round Table romances, which are a compromise between druidism and Christianity, portray Morgan as authoritarian and deliberately mischievous.

The same description could be applied to the *femme fatale*, the fact that Morgan is a fairy only accentuates this. Boldly choosing to love Lancelot, impossible though it is, she keeps him prisoner in her mysterious castle as shamelessly as the Irish Mórrígan offering herself to Cú Chulainn during the battle of the *Raid on Cualnge*.

> She was very cheerful and playful and sang very agreeably: otherwise she was brown in the face but pleasing in the body neither too fat nor too thin, with lovely hands, perfect shoulders, skin softer than silk ... in short miraculously seductive; and added to that the most wanton and passionate woman in all Great Britain. Merlin had taught her astrology and many other things ... She was more good-natured and attractive than anyone in the world when she was even-tempered. But

when she was angry with someone it was hard to quieten her . . .(J. Boulenger, *Les Romans de la Table Ronde)*.

Altogether, Morgan was a woman of mettle. The 12th century portrait of her quoted above follows the same broad outlines as a description of the Irish Mór-rígan. Her passionate nature conforms perfectly with the picture of the mother-goddess waiting for the man to flood her aridity. Like the Queen Mebd of Irish epic who gives herself to any man who wants her, or the supreme kingship she represents, she is the Sacred Prostitute, a figure familiar in the East but intolerable to present-day Western minds labouring under twenty centuries of Judeo-Roman tradition. And yet no one can be shocked by hearing that Morgan, or Modron, or Arianrod, or Don, or Ana is the *Matrona,* i.e. she who incites the procreative act, for the divinity must be creative.

The memory of the fairy-goddess lingers on in a small valley not far from the Fountain of Barenton in the mysterious forest of Brocéliande, now known as the Val-Sans-Retour.

According to the legend, Morgan was deceived by her lover Guyomarc'h and laid a spell over the valley so that any knight unfaithful to his lady who dared to venture into it would have to stay there, a prisoner for ever. There, in what was also called the Val des Faux Amants, a number of knights led an artificial existence girt about by spells and guarded by dragons, giants and imaginary flames.

The only man to break the spell was Lancelot du Lac, the best knight in the world, and the only knight faithful to his lady Queen Guinevere. He succeeded in passing four series of trials strangely like the four stages of the ancient initiation ceremonies which passed through the four elements, the four planes (vegetable, material, intellectual and spiritual) and like the Christian mystic of the symbolic steps to the altar.

Looking behind the legend, it is easy enough to identify Morgan as mistress of the world, abandoned by her lover and therefore unable to continue the process of creation. When the infidelity of Guyomarc'h threatens her with drought, she arranges that her lost lover should be replaced by knights whose infidelity is all too obvious since they have left their ladies for Morgan. The theme of Supreme King-ship as represented by a prostitute appears here as it does in the stories of Lancelot and Guinevere, Tristan and Iseult, Diarmaid and Grainne. In this case, however, Lancelot plays the part of the kill-joy. The hero refuses the goddess because his initiation is incomplete, just as he comes close to the Grail without being able to see it.

Morgan's kingdom is the isle of Avalon, the mythical isle somewhere in the sea, the island in the middle of the world, a kind of navel but also a matrix, an inexhaustible store of energy. There Arthur stays until he can be reborn and return to the world. There Queen Morgan reigns, as Geoffrey of Monmouth says in his *Vita Merlini.* For when the bard Thelgesinus (Taliesin) returns from Armorica, he says: "The Isle of Fruit is also called the Fortunate Isle . . . The only things grown there are grown by nature herself. There people live to a hundred and more; the laws are kept by nine sisters . . . of which one, the eldest, is expert in the art of medicine. She is more beautiful than all her sisters . . . She can change her shape and fly from one place to another: Morgan is her name."

This island, and its Gaelic equivalent Emain Ablach (The Isle of Apple Trees) is the paradigm of the sacred kingdom, but it is also the Garden of Eden, the image of the maternal womb. As mistress of Avallon, Morgan must be the Mother of Gods, or at the least a transposition of a mother-goddess myth into medieval times. Psychoanalytically speaking the journey to Avallon is the *regressus ad uterum*, which appears to motivate most human activity and which finds its most poetical expression in Celtic legend.

The Heritage of the Celts

HE Celtic art which originated somewhere in Europe around the 5th or 4th centuries BC has long been regarded as non-existent or very crude, and yet it is very much a reality. At first symbolic and schematic in a way probably inherited from dolmenic art, it later expanded into a kind of linear explosion which was used to express the imaginings of minds totally bound up in the fantastic and the unreal. The ancient patterns of triskel, concentric circle and chevron are so arranged that they turn in every direction, unfurling their long tresses into animal and human forms which are always idealised and never realistic. The greatest of Celtic art was undoubtedly developed in their coins which apart from being both practical and religious objects were also works of art mirroring their basic intellectual leanings. Considering the variations we can find in the gold, silver and bronze coins of Gaul which were struck and engraved before being moulded, there is no doubt that Gallic numismatic art was rich indeed.

Most of the stonework in Gaul is to be found in the South where the statuary has clearly been influenced by Mediterranean civilization. Even so, it is possible to discern visible differences in expression and line between Roman and Greek statues and the statuary usually called Celto-Ligurian. In any case Gallic stone monuments tend to be rather crude, which suggests that the Gauls were not much interested in masonry and sculpture. Metallurgy, on the other hand, was well developed. Gallic jewellery offered craftsmen an opportunity to give free rein to their abstract fantasies and the results they achieved so altered some of the Mediterranean ideas about ornamentation that Celtic adornments formed a pattern for future centuries. In fact there was a continuity of ideas. "The so-called Barbarian, pre-Romanesque (Merovingian and Carolingian) art which succeeded Gallo-Roman art and the Romanesque art which followed it form a slender yet tangible link between Celtic and Gothic art" (Andre Varagnac, *L'Art Gaulois*, pp. 279-80).

It would seem that the "Barbarian" arts, which have so often been compared with the Scythian art of the steppes, are simply Celtic and were drawn from the same original source, since the Celts and the Scythians were early neighbours. During the great period of Gaelic monasticism, Barbarian art became Irish art, which then crossed back over the sea with the foundation of the Colomban monasteries on the continent and made a considerable contribution to the Carolingian renaissance.

Perhaps even more importantly, it would appear from recent research that Romanesque art itself is very much of the Celtic tradition. Obviously Coptic and Byzantine art exerted their own considerable influence, but the depth and darkness of Romanesque sanctuaries must have more than a little to do with the Irish mounds in which the Gaelic gods and heroes lived. Romanesque capitals must have something to do with Irish interlaced decoration, with Celtic spirals and with the old myths of the man-eating monster, a symbol of Teutates father of mankind and destroyer of all. "The spirit of the classical world is well-matched by Greco-Roman figurative art. The spirit of the Barbarian world is matched by the styles of Central Asia, the Germanic and Celtic peoples. Here we find glorious expression of the constant need for drawn-out and expanded shapes, for complex and symmetrical protusions, as well as a stylised depiction of man strained to convey energy" (A. Varagnac, *ibid,* p. 324).

Romanesque art, with its elements of fantasy and its continual search for a living dynamism would appear much closer to Gallic and Irish art than to Gothic art. Ogival architecture has far too often been defined as the paradigm of Western art. That it was influenced by Gallic art would seem clear enough, if only in its apparent instability, its unwritten challenge to all the laws of balance. However, this instability in itself provides no link between the Gallic mind and Gothic art, for the latter is essentially Mediterranean, wholly given over to light and to a respect for form. Gothic art is confined by a classical system which must have originated in ideas brought from the East; it is the product of a Romano-Oriental synchretism and its connexions with Celtic art can only be observed in its variant forms. Gothic statuary is actually a step backwards in which everything is sacrificed to balance, to the search for a human dimension in keeping with the grandeur of the divine. Leaving aside any progress, nothing could be more Greek. The pointed arches so obstinately described as slender and well-made are merely a moment of time congealed into stone. Gothic faces are the perpetual definition of some mystic ecstasy. There is a world of difference between them and the disturbing depth of Romanesque faces, between the pointed arch and the gradual curves which unfold into the shadow and extend into forms of ornamentation which express a complex symbolism.

Purists will be shocked by this attitude. But any close examination of a Gothic cathedral like Chartres, for example, will reveal a sense of dimension, an aesthetic concern and a precision which are in no way Celtic. Turning to Saint-Nectaire, St-Julien de Brioude, Notre-Dame du Puy and, especially, St-Michel d'Aiguilhe, however, one can see behind the apparently rigid mass, a gigantic outburst of shapes, a systematic desire to turn inwards and to pass into the twining whorls of the mind. And that is essentially Celtic.

In some cases Gothic art moved closer to Gallic ideas, particularly in England where the adaptations of the Norman style enabled a new aesthetic to develop. But it was not until the 15th century that the underlying forces of Celticism really re-emerged to touch Gothic art and wholly transform it into what is called the flamboyant style. Here the Gallic tradition re-asserts itself. The shapes are no longer enclosing frameworks for man, but lines which seek to burst through the confines of the real, darting violently from their point of origin like a world bursting into flame. The old part of Rouen is remarkable evidence of that Celtic renaissance which preceded the Renaissance proper by nearly a century and which was to last until the 17th century in the outlying areas, especially in Brittany.

There is no great distance between this art and the paintings of Hieronymus Bosch. The wildly irrational fantasies of this brilliant painter, which were little understood in his day, perfectly convey the metaphysical concerns and the quests into space which always excited the Celts. In fact the great changes of the Renaissance which are usually and superficially regarded as a simple return to Greco-Roman antiquity owed their existence to very different and diverse antecedents including Celtic art. This was especially true of the pictorial arts in which artists now felt themselves wholly free from former restrictions.

This resurgance was merely a passing breeze, however and before long Celtic spirit appeared to have totally faded from official art, although provincial art, architecture and the ornamentation of churches and chapels became so wildly and furiously complicated as to appear positively curious. The means of expression used in the Baroque period are so ambiguous that some Breton reredoses are almost beautiful in their ugliness. Most Baroque art, however, is merely degenerate.

It was not until the late 19th and early 20th centuries that the vanished current of ideas resurfaced. Despite its development in form, the spirit of Romantic painting is purely classical; but Impressionism gave back to landscape a sense of inner movement, looked at the countryside not as an apparent reality but as an individual interpretation of outside objects.

People have forgotten that the artistic process is one of transformation and metamorphosis, of digestion if you like. Unconsciously all the painters of the 16th, 17th, 18th and 19th centuries sought to impose their personal view of reality, but they were all fundamentally restricted by the narrow framework of the rationalist tradition. To suggest that art was not an attempt to imitate reality was unthinkable. Though the Romantic poets were the first to convey the difference between reality and the developed work of art, it was some time before this idea really acquired any substance among artists imprisoned in stolid academic convention.

Because of this, the final break with the past was a great deal more violent. Although Victor Hugo's drawings opened the way, it was the Impressionists who demonstrated the immense possibilities of the inward image as opposed to the objective view of nature. Thus Gauguin and Van Gogh attempted, as Cezanne would never dare, to express the inexpressible. Picasso took up the torch and passed through all the stages of painting, like an embryo in the womb, to achieve a measure of revolution, though this revolution was far more highly valued by the general public than by other artists.

The true innovators were those who rediscovered the old Celtic rhythm and adapted it to the modern world; and they had a decisive influence on their contemporaries. Chief among them were Kandinsky and Marcel Duchamp. Kandinsky sought pure graphic form in the abstract. Art became a science. But as it was recognised that the complex sciences could all be traced back to the simple science of mathematics, art came quite justifiably to be accorded its mathematical values. This new attitude was very much in the Celtic spirit since it made everything relate to the symbolic movement of the internal dialectic between real and self, a dialectic which could be resolved by movement between two extreme points. And this movement could be toned down or rendered completely non-existent. The kind of contemporary art usually described as scientific, cerebral and intellectual is basically philosophical and can be validated from a reading of the works of Bergson, of Psychoanalysis, Marxism and Structuralism.

The direction Marcel Duchamp followed was different in application at least, since it, too, was based to a certain extent on Marxist concepts, as was the work of all the Surrealists. But Duchamp gave over a far greater part of his work to dreaming and the unconscious than the Abstract artists. In this respect Futuristic art was to look to Duchamp rather to Kandinsky. For the art of Kandinsky like the writing of Marllarmé is a blind alley, while Duchamp, like Rimbaud, provided a foundation on which many other offshoots could be grafted. Kandinsky closes doors; Duchamp opens them.

The doors opened by Duchamp led not only to Surrealism and the art of between the wars, but much further besides. For by bursting through the basic framework of painting he took his art out to the spectator. A Duchamp painting is like a piece of Gallic coinage from the Osisimi, the Carnutes or the Bellovaci, in which "real" shapes are drawn only to be extended into space by the imagination of the onlooker. Art returned to its old definition as an interplay between the work or object and the spectator or subject. Simple as this definition is, it has been largely disregarded by the general public who have therefore little understanding of modern art. For lack of education has meant that the vast majority of people have never progressed beyond the false classical definition of art as something which is pleasant to look at and easy to understand.

Similar problems exist in the world of music. Originally music was the transposition into sound of a continually changing universe, as we can hear from Gregorian Chant. From Beethoven onwards, however, Romantic music with its sentimentality and its sense of aesthetics distorted the public's ear so that we now think of music as something that is pleasant to listen to. The experiments of Schoenberg, Berg, Webern, Ives and Varèse, the electronic music recently composed, have been rejected by a public unaccustomed to new sources of sound. We need to find new definitions for music and noise, and to remember that sounds were originally a raw material which gradually came to be confined within the artificial bounds of conventional instruments. The first manifestations of music were ritual and the energy or magic they expressed must surely form the basis for music in the future.

Art is necessarily an attempt to go beyond the real. It demands no great effort to look at a natural landscape, whereas the contemplation of a work of art requires a relationship, a judgement, some process of thought, whether it be intuitive or logical, that will enable the work in question to extend, to become alive, to speak. Like every other language, the language of art is symbolic and needs some interpretation, however unconscious. By deliberately shocking, by breaking the natural rhythm that it might be recreated in the mind of the spectator, Surrealism demands of its audience that an effort be made, pleasant or no. Beauty is not an unchanging form, but the result of a dialectical relationship between the object and the subject. No work of art is beautiful in itself but becomes so for the spectator who discovers his own synthesis between himself and the object. This is the Celtic definition of beauty, never transfixed in a state of non-existence, but always alive. At the end of *Nadja*, André Breton exclaims "Beauty will be convulsive or it will not be at all!" The Celtic convulsion symbolised by the spiral is perpetual motion, unconcerned with the moment and seeking to express the destiny of mankind.

For the narrow sphere in which man lives is stifling. It is a sphere which his conceptual imagination has done more to create than basic reality. Having realised that classical Euclidian geometry formed an unreal prison around him, man discovered that the universe was quite different. Riemannian geometry then extended our vision by moving outward from the only possible basis, a sense of the dynamic.

This is what much of contemporary art is doing. It is returning to that original explosion of form and extending the Celtic rhythm of life.

Language

Even after the Celts vanished as a political body, the Celtic language remained live and has done to this day. At first it withdrew into the least Romanized areas of the Empire, then shrank still further into the Western islands and peninsulas of Europe. Although Gallic disappeared completely, the British linguistic group to which it belonged survived in the form of Cornish, Modern Welsh, Breton and its four dialects, Trégorois, Léonard, Cornouaillais and Vannetais. Gaelic developed into Modern Irish or Erse, Manx and Scots Gaelic.

The Gallic language did leave its mark on French, however. Some words, such as *bruyère, alouette, braie, vassal, savon, bec*, etc. are entirely Gallic. A large proportion of French place names are Gallic. In many cases we can find an explanation in Gallic phonetics for the way Latin words evolved into romance languages. There is the French U-sound, for example, the tendency to drop atonal vowels when they fall next to the main accent, the special pronunciation of certain consonants and the development of diphthongs. As Henri Hubert wrote, "French is Latin pronounced by Celts, and altered to suit the Celtic mind. The analytical nature of the French verb, the use of demonstrative and demonstrative particles, the flow of the spoken phrase are all common to the Celtic languages as well" (*Les Celtes*, I, p. 18).

Possibly one of the most unusual practices to have passed into French is the Gallic custom of numbering by "twenties" which has also been preserved in Breton and Welsh. The only evidence of this usage in modern French lies in *quatre-vingts* (four score), but in the Middle Ages it was possible to find *douze-vingts* (twelve score) and *quinze-vingts* (fifteen score). In Breton *ugent* meaning "twenty" is multiplied by other numbers to produce forty, sixty and so on, while the Welsh versions are *dengain* (forty), *trigain* (sixty), *pedwar-gain* (eighty).

When it comes to examining the evolution of the Celtic languages, we know more about Irish than about any of the others. Irish is also the closest of all Celtic languages to its early form. It has preserved the oldest form of inflexion with three cases (genitive singular, nominative and dative plural) for its nouns. The early Indo-European S has survived in Ireland while it became H in British languages. So the Irish *"sean"* ("old"), *sior* ("long") and *samail* ("similar") (Latin, *senex, serus* and *similis*, respectively) correspond to Breton *hen, hir* and *henvel*. In many cases the Irish T remains as it is, with the preceding vowel being lengthened, while it is nasalised in British languages. The Irish *cêt* ("a hundred"), for example corresponds to the Welsh *can* (from which the T has recently disappeared) and the Breton *kant*.

Similarly the Indo-European Q has survived in Irish while developing into P in all the British languages including Gallic. The word for "five" (Latin *quinque*) is thus *pemp* in Breton but *coic* in Ancient Irish. The word for "head" (Latin *caput*) is *pen* in Welsh and Breton but *cen* in Modern Irish.

As the Romans made their way to Ireland, it is tempting to assume that Latin had no influence on Irish. Certainly Irish vocabulary seems to have remained generally untouched, but the language was very influenced by medieval ecclesiastical Latin even if the words it borrowed are easy to recognise.

English exerted a much greater influence since Ireland was actually subject to England between the 12th and 20th centuries and is still within the English-speaking area. Even so, the Irish language did survive and was still spoken by 500,000 of the island's four million inhabitants in 1911 (with 20,000 speaking Gaelic to the exclusion of English).

Since Ireland achieved independence and the Saorstat Eireann was created Gaelic has come into its own again. The language is taught in schools and universities and there is a developing Gaelic literature. There are even Gaelic newspapers and magazines. But it is hard to fight against English especially now that it has become the language of international trade. It is very unlikely that there will be much increased numbers of Erse speakers in the future, but it should be possible to ensure that the use of the language survives by making it official, by intellectualising it and by synthesising the three main dialects of Munster, Connaught and Donegal. In this way we can be sure that an especially rich and interesting national language will continue to exist in the far distant future. The written language is that used in the old manuscripts of the monastic golden age which has been codified into some kind of unity. The spelling is rather complicated because the vowels have no inherent value.

The Manx language is a form of Gaelic, written and spoken according to English spelling and phonetics. There are few Manx-speakers even within the Isle of Man and none outside it. And most of these are intellectuals who deliberately cultivate the language so that it may survive in a slightly artificial way.

Scots Gaelic or *gaidhelach* is spoken by about 130,000 inhabitants of the High-lands and Islands, of whom about 5,000 speak Gaelic to the exclusion of English or the various Scots local dialects which are based on English. *Gaidhelach* has produced some of the finest works of Gaelic literature, notably the poems of the Ossianic cycle collected in the *Book of Lismore* (1512), and the language is presently being taught in schools and on the radio though it does not appear to have grown beyond its 19th century boundaries. But we can at least be sure that it will be preserved.

The glories of the Welsh and Breton languages are all that remain of the language which was once spoken over virtually the whole of Britain.

The Britons, like the Belgae, spoke a language very close to Gallic. All the historical evidence confirms that the Gauls, the Belgians and the Bretons could understand each other perfectly. In fact it is possible that they spoke exactly the same language with various dialectical differences acquired from the indigenous peoples.

The Latin brought to Britain by the Roman legions had virtually no influence outside the towns. Once the legions had gone in 410, Latin ceased to be common currency and left traces only in religious, medical and technical vocabulary. Briton might well have evolved into a great modern language at that point had it not been for the Saxon invasions. When they forced themselves upon the Britons, the Saxons also imposed their language and Briton gradually vanished from the greater part of the island, withdrawing into the Welsh mountains, the Cornish peninsula and, after intensive emigration, into Brittany.

Welsh, or *cymraeg* as the Welsh themselves call it, has always been spoken and taught. No other Celtic language has been so well protected and so little attacked. Even within the kingdom of Britain the Welsh have maintained a kind of domestic autonomy which has enabled them to express themselves freely and to develop their language in a natural way. It is even possible to claim that the population of Great Britain would be speaking *cymraeg* today were it not for the arrival of Anglo-Saxon. Welsh literature has continued to flourish through the ages and there is nothing to prevent its present course being pursued into the future. The language is taught in schools and the University of Wales with its four colleges has an international reputation. Welsh-language books, magazines and newspapers are all being published today.

It is worth emphasising the fact there is also a popular language existing along-side literary or official Welsh. It is divided into four dialects, Gwynedd in the North West, Dyfed in the South West, Powys in the North East and centre and Gwent in the South East, and is spoken by about one million people concurrently with English.

Over the centuries the Welsh language has been considerably enriched by the formation of new words from basic roots. It is this process which has given rise to a certain number of relatively complicated and very long words which remain virtually unpronounceable for anyone unfamiliar with Welsh spelling.

Cornish was spoken in Cornwall until 1777. The few remaining literary works in this language show that it evolved in a slightly different way from Welsh. It is generally agreed that Cornish marks a kind of intermediary stage between Welsh and Breton, since it contains variations peculiar to both languages.

Breton was imported from Britain by islanders fleeing the Saxons who settled in Brittany between the first half of the 5th century and the second half of the 7th. The British language gained a firm footing especially in the North of the peninsula, while it tended to absorb traces of Gallic in the South. By the 9th century Breton was spoken over an area which included the present departments of Finistère, Morbihan, Côtes-du-Nord, and parts of Ile-et-Vilaine and Loire-Atlantique. Having now shrunk back to behind a line running from Paimpol to Damgan which takes in Finistère, the western third of Côtes-du-Nord and two-thirds of Morbihan, it is spoken by about one and a half million people. Of this theoretical number about one hundred thousand speak only Breton and no French. The rest are all bilingual, some of them preferring Breton and others French. Even so Breton is now the most widely used of the Celtic languages and not only in the Breton-speaking part of Brittany but by Breton emigrants all over the world.

Obviously the development of Breton is very unstable. Breton emigrants may still be speaking their own language but their children no longer do so. Even within the Breton-speaking area of Brittany the language is receding before French, mostly because nothing has really been done to preserve it, rich and expressive as it is. Indeed in the last century every effort was made to eradicate Breton and it is something of a miracle that it still exists. Nevertheless there is evidence of a local resurgence and of a modest desire to see Breton taught in schools. There are a number of Breton-language magazines and a chair for Celtic studies at the University of Rennes. Altogether there is a great deal of good will towards Breton particularly among intellectuals but nothing compared to what is happening in Ireland and Wales.

The basic reason for this is not French contempt or animosity towards what is considered a "barbaric" language, but the almost total lack of Breton literature. Apart from some remarkable popular verses, there have only been a few Breton writers since the 19th century and even they were often what might be called "second-hand" Breton speakers in that they wrote in French first.

Toponomy

There are most Celtic place names in France, and their existence is due to the firm and lasting roots established by the Gauls over that vast and potentially productive area of Western Europe. The Celtic peoples who arrived in the 5th century BC were traditionally sedentary farming peoples, fiercely attached to their land and they left their own ineradicable mark on the soil of France long after the Gallic language had disappeared.

Although the Loire *(Liger)* appears to be pre-Indo-European, the bulk of French streams and rivers derive their names from Gallic. The Rhine may be linked with the Celtic **renos*, "rushing stream" and the Irish *rian*, "waves". The same root can be recognised in the Reins (or *Rhins*) a river which flows into the Loire at Roanne. The Seine and the Saône get their names from Sequana which also gave the tribe of Sequani their name. The river Lot comes from an ancient *Olt* which occurs in the names of villages set in the upper valley of that river. The Charente comes from **Carenta*, meaning "lovable, charming", the Marne and the Meyronne from *Matrona*, one of the names of the mother-goddess. The Sambre and the Somme derive from *Samara*, "quiet", the Mayenne and the Mionnaz from **Meduanna*, "gentle". The Moder is a **Matra*, "mother", the Dive a *Diva*, "divine" the Vienne a **vinda*, "white". There are countless other small rivers which have names describing their colour or strength, like the Doubs from **Dubis* meaning "black".

The Celtic word **dubron*, "water" which can be recognised in Breton *dour* created a number of names including the Douro in Spain, the Thur in Switzerland and the Dore, the Dordogne, the Drance, the Drome, the Droue and the Douvre in France. The Durance came into existence by way of a **Druentia*.

The word for *beaver* (**bebros*) has remained linked to marshes and streams and can be found in the Beuvron, the Beuvronne, the Bièvre, and, of course, Bibracte the Aeduan capital which became Mont-Beuvray. The word **wabero*, "a stream", as in the Irish *fobar* and the Breton *gouer* formed names for a number of rivers like the Vosvre, the Vaure and the Voivre, and uncultivated land and gulleys like the Woëvre, the forest of Vièvre and villages like Vabres, Vaour and Vouvray.

*Nanto, the word for valley was used as a basis for a number of names. The Namnetes were the people of the Loire valley and gave their name to Nantes. But there are other such names scattered all over the Gallic area, including Nant, Nant le Grand, Nansouty, Nantua, Nanteuil and Nantuel.

The valley-dwelling Gauls often made their settlements at the confluence of two rivers, which they called the *condate* or *comboro*. Condate was actually the original name for Rennes and can also be recognised in all the various places named *Condé*,

Candé, Cosne, Condal and *Condat. Comboro*, on the other hand became Combre or Combres.

Settlements of this kind invariably had bridges (Gallic **briva*), and can be seen today in Brive, Brives, Brioude, Chabris (from *Caro-briva*, "bridge over the Cher) and Brissarthe. There was otherwise a ford (Gallic **rito*), whence names like Bedarrides ("Four fords), Niort ("New Ford) and Chambord ("Ford over the Courbe").

Territorial boundaries can be discovered in words derived from *Equoranda*, "a frontier", such as Ingrande, Aygurande, Eygurande, Iguerande, Ingrannes and Yvrandes. By Gallo-Roman times this word has often translated as *Fines*, whence the name Feings.

Any settlement not located on rivers were given the name **magos*, which later came to denote a "market" and was used for any place in which trading took place. *Rotomagos* ("Plain or market of the Roue"), for example, became Rouen, while *Noviomagos* ("New Market") became Noyon, Nouvion, Noyen and le Nouvion. Argenton and Argentan are "Silver Markets", Riom the "King's Market", Carenton and Charenton "Markets of Carentos" or "charming plains". *Magos* was also used in conjunction with various proper names to form words like Billom, Usson, Caen, etc. The sites of old forts are indicated by words derived from **rate* (Argentre, Carpentras, "Forts as white as silver", for example), but more often from *briga* and *dunum* which originally meant "hill" and later "Fortified hill". *Briga* can be recognised in Brigue, in Briançon, Vandeuvre (Vindo-briga, "white fort") and the Swiss Brig. *Dunum* became Dun; *Lugdunum* became Lyon, Leyde, Loudun, Laon Laudun and Lauzin; **Noviodunum* became Nevers, **Augustodunum* Autun and *Metlodunum* Melun and Meudon.

A group of houses was known as a **durum*, whence names like Jouarre (from *divo-durum*, "divine village"), Briare ("Bridge Village") and so on. The Gallic word for a house was **trebo*, which can be compared to the Irish *treb* meaning "a town". It was from *trebo* that the tribe of Treveri acquired their name to pass it on to Trier. In the Armorican region *treb* was used as the first in a series of names denoting secondary settlements within an original parish, as in Trehorenteuc, Tredion and so on.

The word **ialo*, Welsh *ial*, was used for an open space in conjunction with the names of people, trees, geographical situations, and most of all with adjectives. Valvejols comes from *aballo*, "apple tree", Casseneuil from *Cassano*, "Oak tree", Argenteuil from *arganto*, "silver", Nanteuil from *nant*, "valley". Chanteuges means "a shining place", Mareil, Maroilles and Marvejols a "big place" and Vendeuil a "white place".

*Barro (Irish *barr*, Welsh and Breton *bar* meaning a "summit" or a "top") created names like Bar-sur-Aube, Bar-sur-Seine, etc. **Cambo*, "a bend" created all the Chambons and Cambons. **Borva*, "mud" and *Borvo*, the name of a Gallic water made names like Bourbon, la Bourboule, le Bourbouilloux. Words for trees are remembered in names like Ver (from **devros*, "oak"), Verneuil, Vernay or Vernet (from **vernos*, "alder"), Avallon (from **aballo*, "apple") Limours, Limeil, Limeuil and Lake Léman (from *lemo*, "elm") which also gave the tribe of Lemouices their name.

*Mediolanum, which means "middle ground", was much used. The Italian town of Milan appears to be the oldest of those places derived from this word, but there are many others in France such as Moliens, Meulin, Meslan, Miolans and Meylan.

*Novientum, like Villeneuve, meant "new town" and gave rise to Nogent, Noh-

ant, and Noyant. *Nem*, "the sky" and its derivative *nemeton*, "sanctuary", formed Nanterre (from *Nemeto-duro*, "the fortress of the sanctuary"), Arlempdes (from *Are-nemeton*, "near the sanctuary") and Vernantes, "the great sanctuary". Nîmes and Nemours are both *nemausus*, "consecrated".

Most of the names for mountains are pre-Indo-European, though the Vosges come from a Gallic god Vosegos, the Jura from the Celtic word Juris "a wooded hill". The Ardennes, also, are definitely Celtic, being derived from *Arduinna* whose root is *arto* meaning "bear". Originally therefore they must have been Bear Mountains.

By far the most interesting of those names which derive from Gallic, however, are the names of the oldest towns. Some of them still bear the Celtic name they were called by in Caesar's time. We have already mentioned Nîmes and Nemours and to these we can add Avignon *(Avenio)*, Cavaillon *(Cabellio)*, Arles *(Arelate)*, Toulon *(Telonia* from the Gallic god Telo), Lyon *(Lugdunum)*, Rouen *(Rotomagos)*, Nevers *(Noviodunum)* and many others.

Even so, the largest towns kept neither their original Gallic names nor the names which the Romans chose in some instances to give them. For these towns were the capital cities of the *civitates* or tribal areas and ultimately they were given the names of the peoples who lived there. This applied not only in Gaul, but also in Britain, Belgium and Germany west of the Rhine. By looking at a map of modern Europe, therefore, we can redraw the map of ancient Gaul and discover where the tribes of Britain, Gaul and Germany lived.

Riez was the capital of the Reii, Chorges the capital of the Caturiges, St-Paul-Trois-Châteaux the capital of the Tricastini. Paris abandoned its own old name *Lutetia* to adopt the name of the Parisii, Rennes changed from *Condate* because it was the capital of the Redones, Arras from *Nemetocenna* because it was the home of the Atrebates, Amiens from *Samarobriva* because of the Ambiani and Reims from *Durocrtorum* because of the Remi.

The tribal names were descriptive. The Parisii, for example, were the craftsmen, the Redones the running men or men with four-wheeled chariots, the Ambiani the men of the river. The list of towns with tribal names is long indeed and covers the whole of modern France from Troyes (of the Tricasses) to Soisson (of the Suessiones) to Beauvais (of the Bellovaci) to Tours (of the Turones) to Angers (of the Andecavi) to Poitiers (of the Pictavi) to Limoges (of the Lemovici) to Périgueux (of the Petrocorii) and many others besides.

In Britain, the tribe of Dumnonii gave their name not only to Devonshire but also the Armorican Dumnonia, the Cantii are remembered in Kent and Canterbury, the Cornovii in the Breton Cornouaille. It goes without saying that almost all the place names in Wales are Celtic in origin, since the Welsh language is still spoken there. As in Brittany it is possible to find a large number of towns beginning with *Llan*, ("an enclosed or sacred land"), such as Llandudno, Llanfair and so on. Former forts are characterised by names starting with *Caer* (Breton *Ker*) a Celtic corruption of the Latin *castrum*. *Caer* has given us places like Caernarvon, Carmarthen, Cardiff as well as less evolved forms like Chester, Gloucester, etc.

Dotted throughout Britain are names indicating that a large proportion of local inhabitants were once Celts. Carlisle is a British name as are Dumfries (from *dun*, "a fortress"), Lanchester and Lancaster, York, Colchester, Dover and Dorchester. Devon and Cornwall are full of such names: Torquay, Lynmouth, Lynton (both from *lyn* "a lake"), Ilfracombe, Bude, Tintagel, Bodmin, Penryn, Redruth, Truro, Penzance and many more.

Naturally enough Scotland has its share of Gaelic names like Aberdeen, Glasgow, Inverness, all the Lochs, Argyll and Rothesay (from *rath* "a fortress"), but it also has British names like Dumbarton (from *dun-Briton,* the "Britons' fort").

The most Celtic of all toponomies, however, remains the Breton, mostly because the Breton language has always been spoken over a wide area of the region and because it is still the most widely spoken of all the Celtic languages. Apart from names derived from Gallic there are also a large number of Breton names even in the French-speaking areas where the names have been developed from an originally Breton word. Paimboeuf, for example, comes from *Penvro,* meaning "head of the land".

Most Breton names have been formed from words denoting territorial limits like *plou, tref, gwik, lan, lok, ker, kastell, ilis.* Then there are geographical names partly created from words like *men* meaning "stone" (Menbihan, Penman), from *mené,* "a mountain" (Maneguen), from *pen,* "head" (Penmarc'h), from *ros* "mound" (Rosporden, Roscoff), from *bren* "hill" (Brenedan) from *koad* or *coet* "wood" (Coetlogon, Kergoat, Penhoët, Porhoët). All the names of rivers, coastal inlets, lakes and marshes are also typically Celtic.

The complete list of Celtic names would be long indeed. Celtic toponomy has extended its reach into America where a number of towns are called after existing places in Europe. Dumbarton Oaks has a strangely Celtic ring. New York itself, the largest city in the world, is actually derived from the humble Gallic tribe of Eburovices and protected by the totemic symbol of the yew-tree.

Philosophy

It is very hard to find any traces of druidic philosophy. We know that it existed but its essence has been lost. By looking at the mythological writings, however, and the modifications which Celtic attitudes brought to bear upon Christianity, it is possible to discern some of the broad lines of druidic thinking.

There appears to have been no dualism based on good and evil. Before the introduction of Christianity the Celt was essentially amoral, preferring to believe that the inner motion governing his own life was also leading the universe towards some justified end. According to Lucan, the Celts saw death as merely the middle of a long life, but there was no idea of reward or punishment in the after life. Man could either live here on earth and then elsewhere or be reincarnated again to infinity. Any judgement as to whether an action were good or evil was to be made with due regard for the circumstances surrounding it by man himself. There was nothing fearful about life. The Celts had none of that morbid seeking after annihilation which can be found among the Hindus and the Buddhists. The non-being of Nirvana means immobility and unchangeability, a condition of no interest to the Celts who based all their behaviour on movement and change. With no fear of death they could envisage the future with serenity and devote their thoughts to imagining the world beyond. It was concerns of this kind which gave rise to the Celtic love of extra-terrestrial voyages and expeditions into the Other World, to the relations between the world of the living and the world of the dead so frequently described in Celtic tradition.

This state of mind had fatal repercussions on everyday behaviour. With their well-developed sense of imagination the Celts had an extraordinary ability to fly above the real and even to despise it. No other race has ever refused so determinedly to confront the material realities besetting it. Although they were continually being conquered by more logical races, or races whose logic was different from theirs, the Celts continued to behave as if nothing had happened, rejoicing in their proud ignorance.

Practically speaking, this meant that there was a general tendency to anarchy and individualism, to a hatred of all authority. The Celts were actually excellent farmers, warriors and metal-workers but they were quite capable of rejecting any activity from one moment to the next on the grounds that they were no longer interested. The bravest fighter would flee before the enemy, the farmer would stay at home rather than work his land, the craftsman would decide that his labours were useless.

Naturally enough, this attitude weakened the nation. The Celts fell before enemies who were better organised than they, but consoled themselves by inventing victories and dreaming of the day when the King of the World would return, perhaps in the form of the mythical Arthur. Being convinced that there was some deeper reality beyond appearances, the Celts were free to think whatever they would. They could not accept the kind of strict analysis which demanded that elements which they knew to be dependent upon one another should be separated.

The taste for freedom is also evident in the teachings of Pelagius and of Johannes Scotus Erigena. Man is free to determine his own destiny regardless of what others may think. The essence of Celtic philosophy would appear to be a search for individual freedom, not based on any egoism but founded in the belief that each man is special and therefore different from any other, that behaviour cannot be modelled on patterns created by others.

There is evidence of that search for a reality beyond appearances in the theories of the 18th century Bishop Berkeley, an anti-Cartesian. The world does not exist except insofar as we create it in our imagination, says Berkeley, and this idealism, or immaterialism is surely suggesting that our entire behaviour is determined by the imaginary. Diderot regarded Berkeley's ideas as an affront to reason but had to admit that he could not attack them logically. If we follow Berkeley's argument through we find that the dream is more real than life, that life itself is a dream and the dream is life. Everything becomes confused and jumbled together in another universe where all apparent contradictions can be finally resolved.

It was with a view to resolving contradictions the Hegel formulated his dialectic. Like the Celts, Hegel refused to accept dualism, and the concept of synthesis which he hit upon is no different from the Celtic sense of movement.

Hegel marks an important stage in the history of philosophy, the beginning of a new logical era, or a new concept of logic which is neither Cartesian nor Mediterranean. After centuries of paralysis, Hegel broke the constricting bonds of Aristotle once and for all and grafted his ideas on that latent and ever vital current of Western thought which continued in the works of writers and poets.

Once the new era had begun and fertility been restored, a wealth of fresh ideas based on Hegel came into being. By taking up Hegelian dialectic and putting it back on its feet Marxism merely extended the original flow of ideas. Obviously it is far more daring, and even risky, to claim that Marxism-Leninism is based on Celtic attitudes, but there is no avoiding the facts. By standing against traditional Mediterranean logic, Marxism allows the mind to depart on curious adventures very much in the spirit of Celtic speculation. All Marxism has done, in any case, is to adapt the whims and fancies of a revolutionary movement to the rules of logic. And in the 19th century that movement came to a head with Proudhon and with the great Celt Charles-Louis Fourier, the visionary who created a new universe and brought back to life ideas which had been thought dead.

Hegelianism and Marxism, however, did little to explore the path to the beyond. Nietzsche attempted to take up the thread and extend it towards an ideal which has since been forgotten in "the power of a will". Those shadowy areas which only poets and artists had known still remained to be explored and by offering the means to satisfy that ancestral curiosity, psychoanalysis has filled a large gap. Through their dreaming, their constant denial of an apparent reality, their continual eruptions of the inner self, the Celts had long since discovered a kind of *catharsis*.

After Freud had achieved his revolutionary work in the early 20th century, the way lay open to a scientific exploration of the darker regions of the inner man. This would have been the most natural process possible for a Celt, and whatever else we may say about psychoanalysis, we have to recognise that it excites the self to burst through the narrow confines which have held it for so long. When the hero Cú Chulainn contorts his body so amazingly in the *Tain Bo Cualnge*, it is no gratuitous act, no motiveless gesture, but the expression of his inward being.

The exploration of the unconscious was taken further still in the philosophy of Bergson. Here the emphasis was laid on that intuition which enables us to grasp a specific object, to know it and appreciate it without any previous logical reasoning. Certainly, this intuition was used by the Celts who, in their concern to act, would rather act unthinkingly than think before acting. The spiritualist aspects of Bergsonism also agrees with the ideal aspirations of the Celts, and by opposing the spiritual and the intellectual Bergson concurred with ancient Celtic ideas on the subject. Finally, by allowing man to act by and through himself, Bergson's open morality preserves total liberty for the individual in a far more comprehensive way than the Sartrian doctrine which is too categorical to permit full individual development.

Celtic ideas have come a long way. The Celts have for many years been considered illogical or incapable of logical thinking. But now, when logistics and non-Euclidian geometry are totally changing the classical vision of the universe, when the laws of relativity about time and space are proving many of the Irish and Welsh myths correct, now is surely the time to revise our opinion. Celtic logic may not have been very like the logic of the Roman conquerors, but it is a great deal more like 20th century reasoning.

Literature

As they wrote nothing down, the Gauls have left no works of literature. But this does not mean that Celtic literature as a whole is not especially rich and interesting, Welsh and Irish writing above all.

Ireland has produced an astounding number of prose tales, epics, saints' lives, mythological stories, historical memoirs. One of the oldest is the *Tain Bo Cualnge*, or "Cattle Raid on Cooley" in which the hero Cú Chulainn stands against the combined armies of Ireland. One of the strangest is the *Battle of Mag-Tured*, the tale of a mythical confrontation between the Fomoré and the Tuatha de Danann. One of the most poetic is the *Story of Etaine*, a marvellous dream of a love stronger than death. One of the most puzzling is the *Adventures of Art, son of Conn*, in which the unreal is tantamount to a real institution.

Similar kinds of tales go to form the Welsh *Mabinogion* which tell of the adventures of gods and heroes. And there is the variety of Welsh poetry, the wild beauty of Aneurin, the "savage" romanticism of Llywarch-Hen, the astonishing vision of Taliesin, or those who used his name and the refinement of Dafydd Ap Gwylym.

It is these beacons which lit up the Celtic world with their own peculiar light. Why, one wonders, are they not studied in school, as the Greek and Latin authors are studied. If we owe the Romans much of our language and the Greeks our classical philosophy, we owe the Celts everything which has changed the Mediterranean heritage into something typically Western. We are much closer to the *Raid on Cooley* than we are to the *Iliad*, much closer to Taliesin than to Pindar. This is amply demonstrated in the present day swing of Western literature away from the aims of 17th century classical Europe.

Clearly this does not mean that all European literature is Celtic, but we can discern in it the influence of Celtic civilization. There is no need to describe all Celtic literature in full, we can merely examine the way in which literary currents have evolved from the middle ages to the present day.

Just as the Gallic spirit influenced the Latin language, mellowing it first into Romance and then into French, so the spirit of Celtic civilization made its way into literary works from a very early date. The 12th and 13th century *Chansons de Geste* contain much that has been thought incomprehensible but which can be explained easily enough by a comparative study with Celtic mythology. The Round Table romances are merely reconstructions based on wholly Celtic themes. The Grail myth is Celtic.

In England, Shakespeare, that greatest of all dramatists, used many of the old Celtic themes, transposing them into new settings and recreating the old fairies, witches, wizards and tragic heroes. Hamlet has something of Lancelot in him, Macbeth has the same face as King Ailill of Connaught, Lady Macbeth the face of Queen Mebdh. Merlin and Morgan come to life again in the *Tempest* and *Midsummer Night's Dream*, King Lear is directly descended from Welsh tradition. The Celtic themes lived on in Spenser, whose Fairy-Queen is both airy and subterranean like the ancient Irish world of the Mounds.

After the sterility of the classical period the Celtic emphasis on motion was rediscovered by the Romantics. Pioneers among them were Anne Radcliff and Matthew-Gregory Lewis, the authors of the "Gothic" novel whose apparently confused, wild and disordered works were merely attempts to follow that motion wherever it led. The English Romantics followed along the same road, drawing inspiration from MacPherson's amazing "discovery" of the Ossianic poems. Byron, Shelley and Keats added fuel to the flames and their work led directly to the vision of the American Edgar Allan Poe.

In France it was Chateaubriand who launched a new poetic art upon the world. His work is a bewildering mixture of the dream, of foolish sentimentality, of sickly melancholy, pride, timidity, virtue, honour, stubborness and solitude. But the frenzied activity of his life and the long, majestic sentences of his work in which words and images are taken up and cast down, betray remarkable dynamic energy.

Beside Chateaubriand, the French Romantics pale almost into insignificance, though Balzac's vision of the world is reminiscent of a whirlwind so fast that movement has become indistinguishable and Hugo produced works of epic scale and vision.

Baudelaire took up the theme of the quest as applied to his own destiny. But Rimbaud was the first to declare his descent from the Celtic world: "I inherit from my Gaulish ancestors my whitish-blue eye, my narrow skull, and my lack of skill in fighting . . . The Gauls were the clumsiest flayers of cattle and burners of grass of their epoch. From them I have idolatry and love of sacrilege; – oh! every vice, anger, luxury – above all, mendacity and sloth."

With the beginning of the 20th century it was realised that past achievements were no longer valid, that literature had been corrupted by the aestheticism which sacrificed the inner reality for the outward aspect of the object. This realisation manifested itself in the piercing scream of nihilism that was the Dada movement, a movement which helped to topple the last of the old idols.

The way forward now lay open and Surrealism undertook that total revolution of the mind which was basically Celtic dynamic brought to serve the interests of thought. André Breton, one of the great men of the 20th century and one of the most lucid of its artists and poets, perceptively identified the true goal which is to aim above the real, to transfigure the real that it may live above appearances. This was a revolution indeed, since all previous attempts to discover the real, such as those made by the alchemists and mystics of all kinds, had looked inside the object. By looking inside, the searcher has no choice but to respect forms which are no less tyrannical for being abnormal. What André Breton did was to leave the philosopher's stone, to bring it out of its own form so that it could draw from the outside world and extend into the infinite. The lesson to be learnt from Surrealism, and from Breton in particular, is surely the most recent product of that Celtic dynamic which is characterised by the absolute reign of the image.

Literature has found new means of expression. The Irish Samuel Beckett conveys his thoughts in French, the Welsh Dylan Thomas in English, the Roumanian Ionesco in French.

We can also look to the cinema, for before film became a total art, the art of the 20th century, it was very much an extension of literature. There is no denying the Celtic influence in the *Eternel Retour* by Jean Delannoy and Jean Cocteau, but this influence is manifest not merely in the old myth of Tristan and Yseult but also in the realisation of an unbroken poetic line which runs from pre-history to the present day. For the cinema seems almost unconsciously to have rediscovered the early current of ideas, more readily than written literature. Being relatively new and untouched, it is not confined by the academic form which continues to restrict most writers, however revolutionary. Film also reflects that collective unconscious which somehow preserves all the basic attitudes of the race. However clumsily, everything will resurface in a film. Through the cinema those non-conformist tendencies to explore the dream, to explore a surreal world which is held together solely by the thread of movement, are again being portrayed. Bunuel and Dali's *l'Age d'Or* has been continued into Duras' *Hiroshima Mon Amour*, Godard's *Alphaville* and Bergman's *The Silence* in which the director succeeds in animating immobility itself. Richard Lester's remarkable films, *The Knack* and *Help*, display the triumph of the Celtic spirit with their mixture of fantasy, humour, poetry and apparent incoherence all blended together in a splendid dance of images and rhythms.

The thread of Celtic tradition appears stronger today than ever before. Perhaps it will act as a foundation for a whole new form of thought.

In Conclusion

Celticism is a word that has been much bandied about, but it is not merely a set of human attitudes. It is a whole cultural complex which has conditioned Western civilization in its entirety. Whatever the purists may say, whatever the objections of those who look to Celticism for some kind of initiation, some esoteric doctrine, it forms the basis of our contemporary mechanistic, industrial, progressive civilization.

For by offering an alternative to the static mentality of the Greco-Roman civilization, which discovered nothing in the way of progress for mankind, the Celtic mentality gave the Western world a taste for adventure and risk. All the great endeavours of the Western world can be traced back to the Celtic mind, for behind them there is a dynamic force which seeks always to change, to shatter the narrow confines of arbitrary and unmoving reason. Despite setbacks, this attitude has achieved the most lasting and durable of all revolutions, and it continues today, ever-present even if difficult to see. For the Celts never looked back, they fed on the past solely to build the future. It was a measure of their confidence that myths like that of Avallon or Emain Ablach came into being. The Celts turned their eyes ever outward, above the real, towards the Land of Eternal Youth.

There can be no finer conclusion to this study of the Celtic world than the following extract from the interview André Breton gave on French radio in 1952, which remains the spiritual testament of all those writers and artists claiming kinship with the great Celtic family:

> Speaking of America, I pointed out to the students of Yale University in 1942 that 'Surrealism is born of a limitless faith in the genius of youth'. For my own part I have never abandoned this faith for an instant. Chateaubriand wrote the splendid words, 'Child of Brittany, your moorlands delight me. The flower of indigence is the only one which has not faded in my buttonhole'. I, too, am part of those moorlands, they have often tortured me but I love the will-o'-the-wisp light they keep in my heart. Inasmuch as that light has reached me, I have done what was in my power to pass it on: I am proud to think that it has not yet gone out. As I see it, my chances of proving worthy of the human adventure lay along that path.

Select Bibliography

BENOIT (F¡) *L'Héroisation équestre*, 1954.
  L'Art primitif mediterranéen dans la vallee du Rhone, 1955.
BETRAND (A.) *Archéologie celtique et gauloise*, 1873
  La religion des Gaulois, 1897.
BOULENGER (J.) *Les Romans de la Table-Ronde*, 1941.
BREKILIEN (Y.) *La vie quotidienne des paysans en Bretagne au XIXᵉ siècle*, 1966.
CHAUVIRE (R.) *L'Irlande*, 1925
  Histoire de l'Irlande, 1949.
CAERLEON (R.) *Complots pour une République bretonne*, 1967.
COURSELLE-SENEUIL, *Les Dieux Gaulois d'après les monuments*, 1910.
CURTIS, *History of Ireland*, 1936
CZARNOWSKI, *Le Culte des Héros*, 1919
D'ARBOIS DE JUBAINVILLE (H.) *Le Cycle mythologique irlandais et la mythologie celtique*
  Eléments de grammaire celtique, 1903.
  Cours de littérature celtique, 1883-1902.
DAVIES (E.) *Mythology and rites of the Druids*, 1809.
DÉCHELETTE (J.) *Manuel d'Archéologie*, 1924.
DILLON (M.) *The cycles of the Kings*, 1946.

DOTTIN (G.) *La Religion des Celtes*, 1904.
   Manuel pour servir à l'étude de l'antiquité celtique, 1906.
   La langue gauloise, 1920.
   L'Épopée irlandaise, 1926.
DUMÉZIL (G.) *Mythes et dieux des Germains*, 1939.
   Mithra-Varuna, 1940.
   Les Mythes Romains, 1942, 1943, 1947.
   Loki, 1948.
   Les Dieux des Indo-Européens, 1952.
   Les Dieux des Germains, 1959.
DUPOUY (A.) *Histoire de Bretagne*, 1942.
DURTELLE DE SAINT-SAUVEUR, *Histoire de Bretagne*, 1936.
DUVAL (P. M.) *Les Dieux de la Gaule*, 1957.
ELIADE (M.) *Aspects du mythe*, 1963.
ESPÉRANDIEU, *Recueil général des bas-reliefs, statues et bustes de la Gaule Romaine.*
FALC'HUN (F.) *Histoire de la Langue Bretonne*, 1963.
FARAL (E.) *La légende arthurienne*, 1907.
FERENCZI (S.) *Thalassa, psychanalyse des origines de la vie sexuelle*, 1962.
FRAPPIER (J.) *Chrétien de Troyes*, 1957
FREUD (S.) *Totem and Taboo*
   Three essays on the theory of sexuality.
GOUGAUD (L.) *Les Chrétientés celtiques*, 1911.
GORDON-CHILDE (V.) *L'Aube de la civilisation européenne*, 1949.
GOURVIL (F.) *Langue et littérature bretonnes*, 1952.
   Hersart de la Villemarqué et la Barzaz-Breiz, 1960.
GRENIER (A.) *Les Gaulois*, 1945.
GUEST (C.) *The Mabinogion*, 1849.
HENRY (F.) *La sculpture irlandaise*, 1935.
   Art irlandais, 1954.
HUBERT (H.) *Les Celtes*, 1932.
JACKSON (K.) *Celtic Britain under Roman Rule.*
   Language and History in Early Britain.
JONES (T. G.) *Welsh folklore*, 1930.
JUNG (C. G.) *Introduction to the essence of mythology*, 1968.
LA BORDERIE (A.) *Histoire de Bretagne*, 1896-1914.
LAFFITTE-HOUSSAT (J.) *Troubadours et cours d'amour*, 1960.
LAMBRECHTS (P.) *Contribution á l'étude des divinités celtiques*, 1942.
   L'exaltation de la Tête dans la pensée et l'art des Celtes, 1954.
LENGYEL (L.) *L'Art Gaulois dans les Médailles*, 1954.
   Le secret des Celtes, 1969.
LE ROUX (F.) *Les Druides*, 1961.
LOOMIS (R. S.) *Arthurian Legend in Mediaeval Art*, 1936.
   Wales and Arthurian Legend, 1957.
LOT (F.) *Nennius et l'Historia Britonnum*, 1934.
LOTH (J.) *L'émigration bretonne en Armorique*, 1883.
   Les Mabinogion, 1913.
MACALISTER (R. A. S.) *Leabhar na Gabhala*, 1938, 1943.
MAC CULLOCH, *The Religion of the ancient Celts*, 1911.
   Celtic Mythology, 1918.
MAGEN-THÉVENOT, *Epona déesse gauloise*, 1953.

MALINOWSKI (B.) *Trois essais sur la vie sociale des primitifs*, 1968.

MARKALE (J.) *Les Grands bardes gallois*, 1956.

    Contes et Légendes de Brocéliande, 1962.

    La Sculpture prehistorique, celtique et barbare, 1969.

MARX (J.) *La légende arthurienne et le Graal*, 1951.

    Les littératures celtiques, 1959.

MEYER-NUTT, *The Voyage of Bran*, 1897.

MURPHY (C.) *Duanaire Finn*, 1933.

NEWSTEAD (H.) *Bran the Blessed*, 1939.

O'GRADY (S.) *Silva Gadelica*, 1892.

O'RAHILLY (T. F.) *Ireland and Wales*, 1924.

    Early Irish History and Mythology, 1946.

PARRY, *History of Welsh Literature*, 1957.

PERNOUD (R.) *Les Gaulois*, 1957.

PIGOTT (S.) *British Prehistory*, 1919.

RAFFERTY (J.) *Prehistoric Ireland*, 1951.

RANK (O.) *Le Thraumatisme de la naissance*, 1968.

PEINACH (S.) *Cultes, mythes and religions*, 1905-1912.

RHYS (J.) *Celtic Folklore.*

RIVOALLAND, *Présence des Celtes*, 1957.

SJOESTEDT (M. L.) *Dieux et héros des Celtes*, 1940.

SKENE (W. F.) *The Four Ancient Books of Wales*, 1868.

    Celtic Scotland, 1876-1880.

SQUIRE (C.) *The Mythology of the British Isles.*

THÉVENOT (E.) *Histoire des Gaulois*, 1949.

VARAGNAC (A.) *L'Art Gaulois*, 1956.

VRIES (J. de) *La Religion des Celtes*, 1963.

WAQUET (H.) *Histoire de la Bretagne*, 1963.

WILLIAMS (I.) *Lectures on early Welsh Poetry*, 1944.

ZUMTHOR (P.) *Le prophète Merlin*, 1943.

Notes

NOTES TO INTRODUCTION

1. Written in 1956 and published under the title *Braise au Trépied de Keridwen* as a preface to my book *Les Grands Bardes Gallois* (Falaize, 1956, pp 9–11). Needless to say I entirely agree with André Breton who has been foremost among non-specialist intellectuals in joyfully taking up the Celtic cause.

NOTES TO CHAPTER I

1. There has evidently been some confusion between the name Ahès and the Breton word for key, which is *al c'huez*. The place in question is Pouldavid, near Douarnenez.
2. Triad 126, J. Loth, *Mabinogion* II, 309. See also, J. Loth, *La légende de Maes Gwyddneu*, Revue Celtique, XXIV, 349
3. Black Book, poem 38, in J. Markale, *Anciens Bardes Gallois, Cahiers du Sud*, no. 319, p. 383.
4. Fol. 39a, 41a. Standish O'Grady, *Silva Gadelica*, I, 233–237, II, 255–259.
5. H. Hubert, *Les Celtes*, I, 318–319.
6. J. M. p. 93. Book of Taliesin, poem XV. Adaptation. The poem is a lament for Aeddon, probably, from the evidence of other sources, an abridged form of the name Amaethon.
7. J. M. p. 108.

8. J. M. p. 8.
9. J. M. p. 66.
10. *Aided Conroi*, in Eriu, III.
11. A common occurrence in Ireland. Most of the prose epics were written at a comparatively late date from much older poems which were frequently misunderstood by the
men who compiled the legends, many of them monks. It is for this reason that some
epics still contain a number of verse passages which remain totally incomprehensible,
either because they are themselves ambiguous or because they were altered by the
writers of the legend. The Welsh *Story of Taliesin* was edited in this way in the 13th
century by Thomas ab Einiawn, who based his work on poems previously attributed to
the bard.
12. J. M. p. 90.
13. J. M. p. 53.

NOTES TO CHAPTER II

1. Cicero, *De Orationibus*, II, 66. Sallust, *Jugurtha*, 114. Appian, *Celtica*, I, 2.
2. Strabo, VII, 2; Pomponius Mela, III, 32; Pliny, *Hist. Nat.* II, 167; Tacitus, *Germania*,
XXXVII, Ptolemeus, II.
3. Mela, II, 32 and 54; Pliny *Hist. Nat.* IV, 99.
4. J. de Morgan, *l'Humanité Préhistorique*, Paris, 1937, p. 288.
5. I myself wore one, to which my grandmother attached considerable significance.
6. J. Markale, *Ancienne Poésie d'Irlande*, in *Cahiers du Sud*, no. 335, p. 27.
7. *Ibid*, p. 25.
8. *Ibid*. p. 26.

NOTES TO CHAPTER III

1. This chapter first appeared in *Cahiers du Sud*, no. 355 (1960).
2. A Gallic shield exactly like the one described by Silius is said to have been found in
Brittany, and a drawing of it added to an early edition of the works of Florus. Having
been unable to find either the shield or the edition of Florus' works in question, I am
forced to assume that this information is suspect.
3. J. Markale, *Les Grands Bardes Gallois*, p. 54.
4. J. Loth, *Les Mabinogion*, I. p. 192.
5. See G. Dumezil, *Le Festin d'Immortalité*, pp. 162–3. See also *Revue Celtique*, XLI, pp. 478–9
and W. Nitze, *Le Château du Graal et le Bruiden Celtique* in Romania, LXXV.
6. J. Markale, *Ancienne poésie d'Irlande*, in Cahiers du Sud, no. 335, p. 17.
7. Criticism of Livy in Riemann and Benoist: *Tite-Live*, p. xx.
8. The Gallic coins of the Curiosolitae, the Redones, the Venetii, the Osismii and the
Baiocasses show divine horses with birds' heads or birds as charioteers. See L. Lengyel,
L'Art Gaulois dans les médailles, pl. 7, 22, 24 and 26.
9. D'Arbois de Jubainville, *Tain Bo Cualnge*, p. 90. The same theme occurs on a coin of the
Corispites with a bird, a horse and a bull. See L. Lengyel, *op. cit.* pl. 22.
10. J. Loth, *Mabinogion*. I. p. 256.
11. An Etruscan vase in the Florence Museum includes the episode of Valerius Corvinus
among scenes of the Trojan War, although it has nothing to do with the Homeric
tradition. See Milani, *Studi et materiali di archeologia e numismatica*, t. II.
12. See A Varagnac, *L'Art Gaulois*, Métal et Céramique, pl. 3–10.
13. See the excellent work on this subject, *L'Art primitif méditerranéen dans la vallée du Rhône*,
by Fernand Benoit.
14. L. Lengyel, *L'Art Gaulois dans les médailles*, pl. 22.
15. J. Markale, *Les Grands Bards Gallois*, p. 42.
16. The three last quotations in this paragraph are taken from D'Arbois de Jubainville,
L'Epopée Celtique en Irlande, pp. 352, 353 and 368.

17. Litana or Litava, where the consul is supposed to have been killed, became Llydaw in Welsh, a word used to denote both Brittany and the land of the Dead. Litana may come from the same root as *lituus*, the latin augural rod which is similar in shape to the crosses found carved on many Breton dolmens.
18. J. M. 67. See also the chapter on Taliesin and druidism.
19. J. Markale, *Les Grands Bardes Gallois*, p. 22.
20. *Ibid.* p. 84.

NOTES TO CHAPTER IV

1. This chapter first appeared in *Cahiers du Sud*, no 370 (1962).
2. Strabo (IV, 1, 13) claims that this migration took place following domestic conflict.
3. Theopompus, fragment 41, Atheneus, X, 60.
4. See Lancelot Lengyel, *L'Art Gaulois dans les Médailles*. This work is all the more interesting in that it offers photographs of great sharpness which enable the reader to form his own opinions. Lengyel is also the first authority to have made a systematic connexion between coins and Celtic writings, thereby incurring criticism from official historians of the Celts who dislike what they see as outside interference and confine themselves to non-controversial cataloguing.
5. Justinus, XXIV, 5. Diodorus, fragment XXII.
6. While Brennus can be compared to Brannos, the crow, Kichorios can be compared to the Welsh *ki-cawr*, giant dog.
7. Diodorus, fragment XXII. This episode is important, since it illustrates the Celts' dislike of human representations of divinities. This dislike may even explain some facets of proto-historic archeology, especially as regards early Iron Age art. It is also possible that some megalithic monuments were actually carved, if not, built, by the first Celtic invaders of Western Europe, since they contain representations of abstract designs, like the wheel, the concentric circle, the spiral, and so on, of Indo-European origin, which contrast with the anthromorphic or zoomorphic figures of the neolithic period and clearly indicate some solar cult which may be compared with the Delphic cult of Hyperborean Apollo.
8. *De devinatione*, I. 37.
9. Pliny, *Hist. Nat.* IV, 26. Pomponius Mela, III, 5. Herodotus, IV, 32.
10. In the Triads and in the Welsh mabinogi of *Culhwch and Olwen*. See J. Loth, *Les Mabinogion*. Mabon is associated with the character of Evrain, son of Modron and Uryen, under the name Mabonagrain in the 13th century *le Bel Inconnu* by Renaud de Beaujeu.
11. For the adventures of Bran, see J. Markale, *Ancienne Poésie d'Irlande*, Cahiers du Sud no 335, pp. 21–28 and Caillois-Lambert, *Trésor de la Poésie universelle*, pp. 346–9.
12. J. Loth, *Les Mabinogion*, II, 230.
13. See G. Dottin, *L'Epopée Irlandaise*, pp. 9–10.
14. Although some linguists would dispute this identification, it seems to be beyond question. In the Welsh version of the *Historia Regum Britanniae* Belinus and Brennius become Beli and Bran, respectively.
15. According to the *Dindshenchas*; See Revue Celtique, XVI, p. 142.
16. J. Marchand, *L'Autre-Monde au Moyen Age*, pp. 1–77.
17. See also Elaine Newstead, *Bran the Blessed in Arthurian romance*.
18. Triads 124, 76 and 10 in J. Loth, *Les Mabinogion*, II.
19. Polybius, II, 29. Livy, VII, 10. Aulus Gellius, IX, 13.
20. J. Markale, *Ancienne Poésie d'Irlande*, Cahiers du Sud, no. 335, p. 16 and the chapter on the *Quest in Ireland*.
21. In particular the ban on anthropomorphic representations of the gods, worship in a circle etc. See also Plutarch, *Numa*, XI–XIX. It has been generally supposed that Numa's ideas came from Pythagoras, though this is denied by Livy (I, 18). The relationship between Pythagoras and druidism has yet to be explored.

22. Tacitus, *Annals*, XIV, 35, Agricola, XVI. Dio Cassius, LXIII, 7.
23. J. Markale *Les Grands Bardes Gallois*, pp. 67–71.
24. Bas-relief of the Hotel-Dieu at the Carnavalet Museum, altars at Reims, Langres Soissons, Trèves, etc.
25. The most typical example is that of the three heroes of the Grail story, Lancelot, Perceval and Bohort who were originally one single Perceval.
26. Von Bernus, *Alchimie et Médecine*, pp. 33.
27. See also Herodotus, IV, 32. Pausanias, I, 4, 18, 31; III, 13; V, 7; X, 5. Apollonios, Argonautica, IV, 611. Plutarch, *De Mus.* 14.

NOTES TO CHAPTER V

1. "The rich men drink wine from Italy or Marseilles, and they drink it neat" (Atheneus, IV, 9). "Laden with meat and wine on which they greedily gorge themselves" (Livy, V, 44). See also Diodorus and Strabo.
2. Corbilo has often been identified as Nantes, though that city must surely be Condevincum. Suggestions that Corbilo might be St-Nazaire are equally unconvincing.
3. According to Louis Le Cunff, Hoedic, generally translated as "little duck" from *houat*, duck, is actually a corruption of (*insula*) *Venetica*. This interpretation would certainly fit in with what we know about the way the Gauls accented their speech. See the later chapter on British immigration into Armorica.
4. See *Etudes Celtiques*, 1961, pp. 579–80.
5. J. M. p. 45.
6. J. M. p. 22.
7. Frontinus, *Stratagemata*, II, 12.

NOTES TO CHAPTER VI

1. *Scel Tuain maic Cairill*, from Rawlinson B.512, and the Leabhar na hUidre, edited by Kuno Meyer in the *Voyage of Bran*.
2. Quoted by F. Le Roux in *Les Druides*, p. 41.
3. *Thesaurus Paleohibernicus*, II, 322, quoted by F. Le Roux, *op. cit.* p. 31.
4. Edited by W. Stokes, *Revue Celtique*, XXIII, p. 396.
5. Doubts have been cast on the existence of this bull, as it has never been found. However, both English and Irish tradition refer to it and the archives do contain three letters sent by pope Alexander III in 1172 approving Henry's usurpation of the Irish throne. The papacy was obviously trusting in the power of the Anglo-Angevin dynasty to bring the Irish church back under the Roman whip after the years of conflict between the two, and to restore the payment of taxes to Rome. It is therefore quite justifiable to claim that the papacy sold Ireland to the English, though ironically it was the Irish who defended the church of Rome four centuries later when the English took up the cudgels against Roman Catholicism. Obviously the Irish bore the pope no grudge.

NOTES TO CHAPTER VII

1. Cf. J. Loth, *Contributions à l'étude des Romans de la Table-Ronde*, and *Bulletin bibliographique de la Société Arthurienne Internationale*, no. 4, 1954.
2. St-Gall MS, 1395. Goibniu (Welsh Govannon) is a kind of heroic smith. The feast of Gobniu is a banquet of immortality, a fact which has led Georges Dumezil to interpret this incantation as a recipe for preserving butter on the assumption that Gobniu is a god of cooking!

NOTES TO CHAPTER VIII

1. Dom Louis Gougaud, *Les Chrétientés celtiques*, Gabalda, Paris, 1911, p. 34. This remarkable work is required reading for any study of Celtic Christianity.
2. O'Rahilly, *Early Irish History and Mythology*, Dublin, 1946. James Carney, *Studies in Irish literature and history*, Dublin, 1955.
3. J. M. *Les Grands Bardes*, p. 109. There is a similar story in one of the poems of the Barzaz-Breiz, though this does not necessarily mean that the tradition had made its way to Armorica, as La Villemarqué is quite capable of having built his verse on the Welsh model.
4. *Tirechan*, edited by W. Stokes, p. 367.

NOTES TO CHAPTER IX

1. A similar confusion altered the name of William of Orange, one of the heroes of the chansons de geste from *au curb nes* (hooked nose) to *au Court Nez* (short nose).
2. Pliny, *Hist. Nat.* XXX, I. Suetonius, *Claudius*, XXV.
3. J. de Vries, *La Religion des Celtes*, 228.
4. *Mab.* I, 219. Nennius, XXIII, H.R.B.V.
5. G.R.A. I, 4–8. E. Faral, *La Légende Arthurienne*, I, 247–7.
6. J. Boulenger, *Les romans de la Table-Ronde*, 9–10.
7. So J. Loth thought. Cf. Ifor Williams, *Lectures on early Welsh poetry*, Dublin, 1944, and *Canu Aneirin*, Cardiff, 1938.
8. Cf. Ferdinand Loth, *Nennius et l'Historia Britonum*, Paris, 1934.
9. Cf. Chambers, *Arthur of Britain*, chapter 1.
10. Cf. De Calan, *Chansons de Geste Bretonnes*, in *Bulletin Archéologique de l'Association bretonne*, Vannes, 1898, p. 26.
11. As a matter of interest, the Breton *Kerneo*, Cornish *Kernow* and Welsh *Kernyw* are all derived from the British *Cornovia*, from *Cornovii*. *Cornwall*, on the other hand, comes from an Anglo-Saxon *Cornwealas*, and *Cornouaille* from the Latin *Cornu Galliae*.
12. Edited by Aneurin Owen under the title *Ancient Laws*.
13. Williams, *Eminent Welshmen*.
14. Cf. Stephens, *Essay on the alleged discovery of America by Madoc ab Owain Gwynedd*.

NOTES TO CHAPTER X

1. *Cahiers du Sud*, no. 335, p. 28.
2. There are also names of particular men like Goulven or Meriadek and names denoting something special about the place, e.g. le Faouet, a place planted with beech-trees. But these names cannot be proved to be older than any others, as the process may have been applied later. Similarly, place names starting with *ker*, which originally denoted a stronghold, continued to be formed at a much later date.
3. R. Largillière, *Les Saints et l'organisation primitive dans l'Armorique bretonne*, Rennes, 1955, pp. 219–20.
4. Cf. *L'influence de Carhaix*, in Falc'hun, 99.
5. *Revue internationale d'onomastique*, March 1955, pp. 2–10.
6. When it was decided to commemorate the union of Brittany and France in 1932, an autonomist group called *Gwen ha Du* (Black and White) blew up the monument facing the Town Hall in Rennes which represented Brittany in the shape of a kneeling woman putting her hands into the hands of the seated king of France. Obviously this monument bore no relation to the historical event and apart from showing singularly bad taste was a permanent insult to Breton pride. As it was, there were no attempts to seek out the perpetrators of the crime and there has never been any mention of replacing the monument.

7. In fact Breton has unfortunately not been spoken in this area for a long time. The truth of the matter is that the Breton speaking parts of the peninsula have always been far more forward thinking than the conservative French speaking parts. This difference is still observable today.

NOTES TO CHAPTER XI

1. Not that this has prevented attempts to syncretise druidism and hinduism. R. Ambelain who describes himself as an esoterist and a disciple of the alchemist Fulcanelli, has written a bewildering book entitled *Au pied des Menhirs* in which he seeks to fill the gaps in his knowledge of druidism with the Thibetan *Bardo-Thodol*, with extraordinary results.
2. There is no proof that the Celts believed in reincarnation, although Celtic myths do contain examples of it even if they are confined to a few characters.
3. From Eerny, *Voyage au Pays de Galles*, quoted by E. David, *Etudes historiques sur la poésie, et la musique en Cambrie*, pp. 32–33.
4. H. Martin, *Histoire de France*, I. 55.
5. Manuscript of William Harris ô Môn, 1758, now kept in the Library of the Welsh school in London, published in the *Myvyrian Archaeology of Wales*. The author of the *History of Taliesin* is supposed to have been Thomas ab Einiawn a 13th century poet. The extracts which follow have been translated from the version in the *M.A.W.*
6. Zwicker, *Fontes religionis celticae*, I, 51, 18.
7. Cf J. Gricourt, *Sur une plaque du Vase de Gundestrup*, Latomus, XIII, pp. 376–83.
8. J. Markale, *L'Autre Monde Celtique*, Cahiers d'Histoire et de folklore, VI, 67.
9. Cf. the Entremont heads at the museum of Aix-en-Provence, the skull hooks of Glanum and Roquepertuse at the Borély museum in Marseilles, man-eating monsters like the Tarasque de Noves at the Calvet museum in Avignon.
10. The *Incantations of Mael-Derw* are among the earliest poems in the Book of Aneurin belonging to the Gododin cycle. Although the poem is attributed to Taliesin, the whole tone of it is quite dissimilar from anything else he is accredited with.
11. Math, the greatest of the British magicians, and uncle of Gwyddyon, is also known as Fath or Wath, names which can be compared with Wotan and consequently with the word for wood.
12. Eurwys is unknown. Euron might be Euryn or Gwri Gwallt Euryn, the first name of Prdyeri son of Pwyll. Modron is the ancient mother goddess Matrona.
13. This boar might conceivable be the mythical Twrch Trwyth which Arthur and his knights hunt in *Culhwch and Olwen* or possibly Yskithyrwynn Pennbeidd (Defense of the Chief of Boars), also mentioned in *Culhwch and Olwen*, which is killed by Arthur's dog Cavall.

NOTES TO CHAPTER XII

1. *Jupiter-Mars-Quirinus*, N.R.F., 1941. *Mitra-Varuna*, N.R.F., 1948, *Les Mythes Romains*, N.R.F., 1942-43-47, *Le Troisième Souverain*, Maisonneuve, 1949, *Les Dieux des Indo-Européens*, P.U.F., 1952, *Les Dieux des Germains*, P.U.F., 1959.
2. La Stèle no. 88, *Revue Celtique* XXV, pp, 47-50 and De Vries, *La Religion gauloise*, pp. 88 and 117. In 1904 an inscription was also found in Rome mentioning a Toutati Medurini.
3. In Chrétien's version the base of the fountain is made of emerald, the basin and the chain are gold. When it comes to the actual fountain the tree is an oak and the base a block of granite (a stone unknown in those parts) called *"Perron de Merlin."*
4. It is the nitrogen in the water which gives this impression. The water is actually at a constant temperature of 4°. The fountain itself was the object of processions in the 17th century when local people went there to ask for rain.

Index